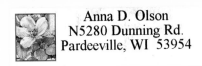
Anna D. Olson
N5280 Dunning Rd.
Pardeeville, WI 53954

W9-CYB-177

The Journey West
Love is a Gentle Stranger

The Journey West
Love is a Gentle Stranger

THREE BESTSELLING NOVELS IN ONE VOLUME

Love is a Gentle Stranger
Love's Silent Song
Diary of a Loving Heart

JUNE MASTERS BACHER

INSPIRATIONAL PRESS

NEW YORK

First Inspirational Press edition published in 1996.

Inspirational Press
A division of Budget Book Service, Inc.
386 Park Avenue South
New York, NY 10016

Inspirational Press is a registered trademark of Budget Book Service, Inc.
Published by arrangement with Harvest House Publishers.

Library of Congress Catalog Card Number: 96-77056
ISBN: 0-88486-154-6
Text designed by Hannah Lerner.

Printed in the United States of America.

Contents

Cast of Characters

Chris Beth (Christen Elizabeth Kelly Craig, wife of minister)

Joe ("Brother Joseph," Joseph Craig, minister)

Vangie (Mary Evangeline Stein North, wife of doctor, Chris Beth's half sister)

Wilson ("Uncle Wil" North, doctor)

Young Wil (Wilson's nephew)

Little Mart, Marty (Martin, adopted son of the Craigs)

"True" North (Trumary North, daughter of Norths—Wilson's stepdaughter)

"Miss Mollie" (Mrs. Malone, wife of the Irish O'Higgin)

O'Higgin (second husband of "Miss Mollie," stepfather of the six children belonging to her late husband)

Nate Goldsmith (self-appointed school board president and chairman of the board of deacons)

Abe and Bertie Solomon (proprietors of the general store)

Maggie Solomon (their daughter)

"Boston Buck" (Indian chief)

Alexander Oberon (new teacher from the East hired to "help" Chris Beth)

"Doc Dullus" (retiring doctor)

PART I

Love is a
Gentle Stranger

Dedicated
to
those valiant pioneers
who
unknowingly
helped to write this book!

With special appreciation to Dr. Horace Robinson (director of *UMPQUA CAVALCADE*), Dr. Gordon Howard (assistant director), Henry Barneck (who did the secondary research), Hallie Ford and the late Charles Brand (historical and scenario committee).

Relentless as the restless tides
That cast their burdens on the sand,
They come by ones, by twos, by hundreds,
Their keys of courage opening portals
Of the river's mountain lock,
Tilling, toiling, forcing nature
To bring forth fruit from stubborn acres,
Building homes and clearing land,
Moulding birthrights for their children. . . .

—From *Umpqua Cavalcade*

Contents

4 CONTENTS

Preface

IN 1952 DOUGLAS COUNTY, Oregon, celebrated its hundredth anniversary. It was my privilege to write the narrative for a four-hour-long pageant, "The Umpqua Cavalcade," to commemorate the spirit of those early pioneers, who brought a wild and untamed country through its infant years, nourished it, and then passed it on. While I found historical facts in state history books, I needed a more personal contact in order to get the feel of the past—a contact with the men and women themselves whose dauntless courage, unity, and faith went largely unsung.

That need took me to the very cradle of the past. I sought out those pioneer people, walked with them, talked with them, and lived with them—however briefly—and in that encounter I saw the beautiful Oregon Country through their eyes and loved it as they loved it. More importantly, I saw its people, whom God had created to have dominion over the paradise it was. "Things were simpler then," they told me; "more gentle."

Can we capture that simplicity? I wondered as I sat on their doorsteps and listened to stories of anguish, tragedy, humor, and irony that they shared. That was the key—*shared!* "We needed each other," they told me, "and we needed to know that God cared."

As the pioneers walked out of my life one by one, having fulfilled their early mission with such admirable spirit, the characters in LOVE IS A GENTLE STRANGER walked in—shadowy at first, with no substance. Perhaps I was too caught up with the spirit of all they told me to recognize the characters as mortals with human needs. But as time passed they fleshed out and became so real that they begged to share their story as their real-life forebears had done.

5

Perhaps you can recapture some of that simplicity in this book. Or perhaps you will find that you have never lost it, in which case the story will serve as a gentle reminder that love is the one force which remains constant. God took care of that through His Son!

As you come to know Chris Beth, who must learn the "New Commandment," Vangie, her "wronged sister," the compelling Wilson North, his patient and compassionate friend, Joseph Craig ("Holy Joe" to Chris Beth!), and the less visible (but nonetheless important) characters, may they bless your life anew. May love in its purest form—though it be a stranger—knock gently and then come into your life.

June Masters Bacher

1
Jilted!

~

THE MID-SEPTEMBER SUN was without mercy. Dust eddied and swirled beneath the horses' hooves, settling on their sweat-lathered bodies as the team strained to pull the stagecoach up the steep mountainside. At times the horses missed their footing on the narrow trail. At those times the coach tilted crazily between the rock face of the mountain and the bottomless canyon below, throwing the six weary-faced passengers rudely against each other. "This heat takes all the energy a body can muster," the capable, prolific-looking woman who introduced herself as "Missus Malone" had said some miles back. It was probably to discourage the red-whiskered, gruff-voiced man beside her, Chris Beth supposed. He had been talking since the group had gathered, some four days earlier, to wait for the Northwest-bound stage—not that Chris Beth heard anything he or any of the others said. Their words were stifled by the turn of the wheels . . . *Jilt-ed, jilt-ed*, they jeered.

Jilted! Could there be an uglier word in the dictionary she had brought along? Had sickness or accident claimed Jon, I'd have lived through it, the girl thought. But this—this she

7

could not survive. Not that she cared, as long as there were no
knowing friends or relatives around to witness her humility
and shame.

"Be ye comin' West to be married?" The Irishman broke the
silence. He seemed to be asking the question of her.

Chris Beth shook her head. "To teach," she said, and turned
her eyes back to the dusty trail.

"Oh, so it's a teacher ye be!" the Irishman exclaimed. "But
how be it a pretty thing like you's travelin' alone?"

How be it? Still gazing vacantly at the timber outside the
small window somebody had forgotten to curtain properly,
Chris Beth tried to put the reason together in her mind. . . .

Jonathan Blake had walked out of her life the way he had
walked into it—airily but with determination. Although it
had seemed a lifetime, there had been only three months
between Jon's passionate whispers against her hair as the
lilacs pouted with spring rain, "We have to set the date—I
can't wait!" and his equally impassioned plea for release in
the magnolia-scented dark of a summer night. How could it
be? Jon loved her. He had told her so soon after they met in
Boston, his home, where she was finishing teacher training.
They were going to be married . . . invitations were ready . . .
Chris Beth had tried to reach out and touch him, but Jon had
moved away. Didn't she hear what he said?

Yes, she had heard. But she didn't believe.

Jon was given to absurd, sudden laughter. That's it—he was
teasing! Wasn't he? She had asked.

No. And she was—please—to make it no more painful than
it was.

Painful? For which of them? A new and sudden fear had
gripped her heart then. *Was there another woman?*

Yes.

The wild pounding within her had stopped then. Chris Beth
felt her pulse slow to normal—and then stop. Her body might
go on living, but her heart had died.

In the white, colorless days that followed, Chris Beth was
sure that her body would die too. If I were a praying woman I'd

ask for death, she thought as she told her mother there was to be no wedding, and set to work on the grim task of returning the gifts. I'd pray for tears, too; they're supposed to heal. But the hurt was too deep for tears.

Dry-eyed, she carried on. There was no purpose left—just one immediate goal: that of convincing friends that she herself had broken the engagement. After that, she would have to get away. Where, she didn't know—just far, far away.

Her mother was no help, Chris Beth remembered bitterly. She simply paced the long length of the carpeted parlor, wringing her hands and murmuring, "What will people say?" Soothing Mama and rewrapping the presents took a long time. Maybe if Vangie were here to help . . . but her sister was now in Boston herself, registering for her first year in nursing school. Anyway, Vangie was like Mama—a delightfully pretty lady who swooned at the sight of a mouse. So what was there to do but face this crisis the way she had faced all the others— alone? *Alone.* Then why not be completely alone, away from them all? That's when the idea of coming West came.

Remembering, Chris Beth sucked her hand to choke back hysterical laughter. How ironic that it was Jon himself who gave her the idea! She had listened with a smile to stories he had gathered from wagon masters who were taking immigrants to some place called the Oregon Country. She knew she would never risk her scalp in such untamed wilderness! "Fiddle-dee-dee," she would say when Jon got dangerously carried away with talk of gold, trees big enough to drive a team of horses through, grass belly-deep to the oxen they were driving, and rivers teeming with fish. "Why would civilized, educated people like ourselves choose such a life?" Still, there was a certain gleam in her husband-to-be's eyes that was contagious. Deep inside, Chris Beth recognized an undeveloped sense of adventure in the "self" she believed she had inherited from the father who had died before she was born. The one photograph Mama had kept when she remarried showed Chris Beth that father and daughter resembled each other in a dark, straight-browed way. Undoubtedly she was like him in other ways, too—a little withdrawn, and certainly with stronger backbone than her mother.

The thought made Chris Beth square her shoulders. "Why not?" she said aloud. "Yes, why not go West? Pioneer children will have to have teachers." There was no sense of excitement in the decision, no feeling of dedication, no feeling at all. Oregon simply sounded like the farthest place away. Dangers of frontier life no longer mattered. In her numb state, she would welcome death. . . .

Lost in her reverie, Chris Beth had no idea of time. It was a surprise when Mrs. Malone announced, "Suppertime!" Without interest, she watched Mrs. Malone open the giant wicker hamper that had bumped over the dusty trails with them for however many days it had been since the stage had met the train two states back. Food! The idea of eating turned her stomach, but it would be easier to accept a cookie and some fruit than to argue with the well-meaning woman who had tried to mother them all. All I want is a warm bath, a clean bed, and the private world of sleep, she thought. Let the others talk about the beauty of the sunset, the increasing number of fir trees, and the fact that they would cross into Oregon tomorrow. Chris Beth was aware only of a merciful breeze that pushed back her heavy hair and the grind of the wheels that taunted, "Jilted, jilted!"

Covering her ears, Chris Beth dozed fitfully. Her untasted cookie and fruit dropped into crumpled folds of the dark skirt she wore and rolled to the feet of Mrs. Malone.

The older woman shook her head. "I do declare! The child's not eaten a morsel."

In her dreams, Jon returned. The rest of the world slept, and in that hushed and timeless silence the two of them were alone. "My darling!" Jon's arms reached out to embrace her, but she was unable to touch him. Some evil force was pulling him away. "Come back—" Chris Beth tried to call, but Jon was gone, taking the silence with him. Mocking voices beat against her eardrums, indistinct at first, then loud and cruel: "Jilt-ed, Jilt-ed!" Then Jon was back. "My darling!" This time Chris cried out the words of endearment. But Jon was laughing—laughing and mocking her along with the other voices. She tried to run away, but her legs refused to support her. She was falling, only to have a bruising grip imprison her. "No! No!" She must fight against him. But struggling was no good. She was being lifted as if she were a feather, and the arms that held her were gentle—gentle in a way she had never known Jon's arms to be. She tried to look into his eyes, but her weary eyelids drooped. The face was no longer familiar. . . .

2
Forgotten Brooch

⤴

CHRIS BETH AWOKE as if from a stupor. Someone was shaking her shoulder gently and calling her name, "Christen Elizabeth—Miss Kelly!" Struggling to put the fragments of two worlds together, she tried to remember the voice of the woman who called. Had there been a woman in her dreams? No. And the face she saw as her mind cleared was that of Mrs. Malone. "That's better! Now eat this like a good girl." There was no recourse but to gulp down the warm broth the woman was spooning into her mouth.

"We aren't moving!" Alarmed, Chris Beth tried to sit up. What was she doing lying down in the first place? And where—?

"Whoa, now, take it easy. Broth ain't that potent!"

Chris Beth, who was used to doing things for herself, sank gratefully against the clean, white pillow. She had slept, Mrs. Malone told her, then "just crumpled like." One of the men picked her up from the floor and carried her when they stopped atop the mountain at Half-Way Station.

Half-Way Station? Chris Beth wondered weakly.

It was where the stage changed horses for the rest of the trip.

12

How long had they been there?

Several hours. "And that's why I woke you. Not enough flesh on them bones to see you through whatever lies ahead."

Chris Beth felt her body grow rigid with fear. The "Injuns and wild bar" the men talked about yesterday she could cope with. But having her secret discovered was another matter. "Did I talk—in my sleep, I mean?"

" 'Twas a mite more than sleeping—more like delirium. And folks always talk when there's fever. Feel like spongin' off a bit? You missed the tub the keepers fixed last night."

A first emotion stirred within Chris Beth. One had to admire a certain spirit this woman possessed. She did what needed doing and expected nothing in return. Whatever secret she may have revealed was safe with Mrs. Malone.

It was still dark outside, but busy sounds from below came through the upstairs window into the bedroom that she and Mrs. Malone must have shared. "Move over, Colonel . . . this away, Joe . . . and you, Bill, thataway!"

"Hitchin' up. Best you hurry now. The others will want to know the fever's broke. They've been asking."

That the other passengers cared whether she lived or died surprised Chris Beth. What was she to them? She shrugged and poured water from an earthen pitcher into the washbowl. The water's chill surprised her. "Lots of that from here on," Mrs. Malone said. "Fresh off the melted snow." With that, she went to join the others.

Alone in the room, Chris Beth looked at her reflection in the mirror above the washstand and gasped. She was accustomed to kerosene lamps instead of candles. It had to be the difference in light that paled her skin like she had seen the ghost of *Hamlet*. But the light could hardly account for the matted mass of her dark braids or the way her usually ripe-olive eyes had given up their luster.

Maybe a change of clothes—but there was no time. "All aboard!" the driver called. Chris Beth poked hopelessly at her hair and wondered wryly what Indian in his right mind would want it. She snuffed out the candle and hurried down the stairs.

The others were too absorbed by their surroundings to notice she had joined them. All eyes focused on the eastern sky, where rose-tipped fingers of dawn tinted the snowy-capped peaks, pausing where the deep green of the timberline began its gradual slope into the valleys below. One peak in particular seemed to brush the very sky, casting a shadow across what appeared to be a lean-to building. "Lumber camp," someone said, but Chris Beth did not turn around. She was watching waterfalls in their cascade from unbelievable heights as if in a hurry to get their journey over and join the river curving around the foot of the mountain range. "That's it! Sure and it is. That be the hill o' home!" The Irishman was near dancing with excitement.

Chris Beth inhaled a lungful of crisp, clean air, a move not to be missed by the red-bearded man. "Ever you see such purity or water so clear?"

She shook her head.

"Flows right by the throne o' God, it does."

Chris Beth moved away. She had no desire to engage herself in an early-morning conversation with the talkative man—let alone about some Supreme Being who had thrown a ball of mud into space and forgotten about the people who inhabited it.

But in spite of herself, Chris Beth felt a strange pull from those majestic mountains. It was as if the whole area and its people were under some kind of magic spell. She shivered. It would be wiser to get aboard then stand there indulging in some silly fantasy.

The driver was bringing a heavy-looking object from Half-Way Station. He looked at her for a moment, then asked, "Feel like journeyin' on? Weather's more to our likin'. Still and all, other things can be tryin'."

"I'll be fine," Chris Beth told him.

Still the driver hesitated, pulling at a leather string on his jacket, stroking his month's growth of beard, and spitting intermittently. "That pin," he said finally. "Don't you want I should put it in the strong box?"

Automatically, Chris Beth's hand felt for the brooch where Jon had pinned it—so lovingly, she had thought—the night he proposed. How could she have forgotten to return it when she had remembered all else down to the least detail? And how could she have failed to notice it when she had dressed for the first lap of the journey by train? She had chosen the suit-dress hurriedly, thinking it was the best garment she had for traveling. Most of her wardrobe was for the city.

"Miss?"

"Oh, thank you, yes." Chris Beth tugged at the hateful reminder, forgetting the safety catch, tearing the lace of her stand-up collar, and pricking her finger. "Ouch!" Stronger words of pain rose to her lips—words her all-forbidding stepfather reminded her often enough placed her in danger of "the fires of hell" in his thou-shalt-not form of religion. Not that he had taught her restraint, but something about these simple people told Chris Beth the words were better left unsaid. Anyway, it was consoling to know she could bleed. Maybe hearts weren't all that important, after all.

Handing the pearl and sapphire brooch to the driver, Chris Beth turned toward the open door of the stage. Yes, she would want to guard the expensive piece of jewelry. Nothing must happen to it before they reached the community or town nearest the school where she was to teach. "Then my number one job will be to mail it back to Jonathan Blake!" Chris Beth whispered fiercely.

3
Getting Acquainted

⌒

THE STEP INTO the stagecoach was higher than Chris Beth remembered. She tripped over her long skirt and would have fallen had a familiar masculine hand not steadied her. Familiar? How could it be? But before she could turn to thank the man, others were coming aboard. Try as she would, Chris Beth found herself unable to associate the touch with any of the four men inside, and she and Mrs. Malone were the only women. It was strange, like everything else that was happening to her.

The driver secured the door with one hand, fumbling awkwardly. "Is that a gun?" Chris asked Mrs. Malone, who had rearranged the seating to put Chris Beth beside her.

Mrs. Malone nodded.

"Then there really *are* Indians dodging behind the stumps?"

One of the men laughed. He was younger, she noticed—at least younger than the driver and the other passengers inside. Cleaner, too, she thought, in his red plaid shirt and high boots.

"They're friendly around here for the most part. More curious than anything else about the 'Bostons.'"

"The Bostons?"

"No offense, Miss, if that's where you're from. Out here, we're all 'Bostons' to them—anybody with a pale face."

"Why did the driver take my brooch?" Chris Beth turned to Mrs. Malone. But it was the young man who answered again. "If we should meet a group of Indians, most likely they will ask for trinkets."

"That was no trinket!"

The young man smiled once more. "Again, no offense, Miss. Their way of putting it."

Chris Beth felt a stir of uneasiness. Mrs. Malone seemed to read her mind. "The gun's not for red men. It's for bandits. This is Black Bart territory."

Chris Beth leaned back and inhaled deeply, trying to take it all in. So this was Oregon Country. Although her unfeeling heart refused to appreciate her surroundings, even then she realized that it was a land of strange contrasts—one that was bound to bring out the best or the worst in its inhabitants.

"I expect you'll be wanting to know more about the settlement where we're going." Mrs. Malone's words were a statement more than a question.

"I suppose I'll need to know."

The older woman removed her yarn and knitting needles from a paisley bag, counted to herself until the needles seemed to move under their own power, and began a monologue. "We're few in number, but close-knit like. Neighbors all pitch in and do what's to get itself done in good times and bad. Lots of women can't adjust—just kind of pale up and die like, or else go back to wherever home is. Me, I never give it much thought. Home's here, but then I been here most of my life. Ma and Pa's buried in the little plot down by Graveyard Creek right near the school. That's where you'll be teachin'."

It occurred suddenly to Chris Beth that this woman knew a lot about her—her name and where she would teach (if she got the contract, and she dared not think of what would happen if she didn't). But why was Mrs. Malone speaking of "we"? Was it possible she would be a neighbor? Oh, she hoped so! She hoped so very much. There would be need of such a warm, friendly person in this strange, new life.

Mrs. Malone must have read her thoughts. "You'll be wonderin' how I got my facts. I'm not given to meddlin'."

"Oh, I never thought that!" Chris Beth protested.

"Well, you had just cause. But when you taken sick like, somebody had to take over and me being the only other woman—"

Chris Beth felt a flow of shame. She had forgotten to thank Mrs. Malone.

"I appreciated that." Chris Beth reached to touch the busy, work-reddened hands whose rhythm never stopped.

"Not necessary in the settlement. Neighborliness is our way of survivin'. But there's need to explain the intrusion. I asked of the driver concernin' you. And anyway I'd guessed a'ready. News travels amongst us, you know. We'd heard about the southern-born schoolma'm, even your name, so when I saw the initials on your handbag—" Mrs. Malone paused to pull out a new ball of red yarn.

"Do you live near the school somewhere?" Chris Beth asked hopefully.

"Clost as neighbors get, just several homesteads away. A married man was entitled to a square mile of land when Pa staked his claim. Bachelors could hold half as much, and most of 'em never got developed without a missus, so there's a heap of timber between."

The Irishman who had been patting his foot to some remembered tune suddenly burst out:

> Me hates all women, and yet it be plain,
> Me must marry soon, or lose half me claim!

Mrs. Malone silenced him with a look. "Men outnumber women folks nine to one," she said meaningfully, " 'specially since the gold rush. Even so, we manage. Boys've learned to do a man's work, and that's good in my circumstances. Ned and

Jed took over when my husband took to his death. And now with Jed gone—"

Her voice broke slightly. "But you've troubles enough. Why'm I bothering you with mine?"

"Until now, it's been the other way around—and it's no bother," Chris Beth said, meaning it. It was a relief to get her mind off herself, even temporarily. "When will Jed be coming home?"

"He's home a'ready." Mrs. Malone's voice was barely audible over the bump of the wheels. "Mine caved in. I been away—burying him."

The simplicity of the statement caught Chris Beth off guard. It would be easier to cry for this acceptant, stout-hearted woman than for herself if her dry eyes could produce tears.

"I'm so sorry," she said softly. "I didn't know."

"Course you didn't." Mrs. Malone drew out a handkerchief with a tattered edge, blew her nose, then folded it away. "Life's like that—rain and sun all mingled, with a whole passel of rainbows in between. Sometimes I think it's the smiles and tears all stirred up together that makes 'em so brilliant."

I want to remember that, Chris Beth thought. It would be something worth sharing with the students if it rained as much in Oregon as people said.

That thought led to another. Clearing her throat, Chris Beth confided as steadily as she could that there was no guarantee she would be teaching—no contract, anyway, but just a letter from a trustee saying, in response to her inquiry, that there was need for a teacher. She might have added that she was barely able to read even that much of a pencil-scribbled message on the back of a supply list which Mr. Goldsmith had sent.

"Well, don't go borrowin' trouble. Nate Goldsmith's as good as his name. And once he sees you, there can't be any questioning. He'll make a grab for you."

"Right!"

Chris Beth felt herself blush under the younger man's single word of appreciation, but she supposed she should not be offended.

"My, my!" Mrs. Malone looked from one of the young people to the other. "We've been under the same roof a spell now and it appears to me we ought to introduce ourselves proper like. Never occurred to me we'd all be headin' so far together."

"Wilson, you do the honor while I unpack us some lunch."

He glanced at Mrs. Malone. "Yessum!" he said in mock obedience, then spoke to the others. "As you see, the two of us know each other. I'm Wilson North and the young lady—"

"Seems they all know Miss Kelly," Mrs. Malone broke in. "Tell them about your book, Wilson, and that you're studyin' to be a—"

A lurch of the stage tilted the hamper dangerously in Mrs. Malone's lap, interrupting her sentence.

"I'm a botanist, studying plant life."

Chris Beth acknowledged with a nod, wondering how he and Mrs. Malone knew each other.

Wilson North turned to the Irishman. "O'Higgin?"

"Sure and that be my name, Irish and Scotch, but a man of mild habits."

"'Tis true," Mrs. Malone agreed as she laid out the fried chicken, fresh bread, pickles, and coconut layer cake from the basket she had replenished at Half-Way Station.

Chris Beth missed the mumbled names of the other men, gathering only that they were fur trappers. She was puzzling over Mrs. Malone's obvious acquaintance with the man who called himself simply O'Higgin. Maybe there were even fewer settlers in the Northwest than she had supposed.

Mrs. Malone packed away the remnants of lunch. Wilson North and O'Higgin talked about the tall stand of Douglas fir mingled with giants of the forest (redwood trees, she overheard them say), and they identified mountain ash (now bright with crimson berries), manzanita, and laurel. Occasionally

Chris Beth looked to where the two men pointed and wondered how the noonday sun was able to penetrate the foliage enough to cast a shadow. The same sense of awe and mystery she had sensed at Half-Way Station returned—something she was unable to identify. Tired as she was, in an irrational sort of way she wished they could stay in the cramped quarters of the stagecoach and just ride.

Mrs. Malone interrupted any question she might have asked. "Now then," she said as she resumed her knitting, "we'd best be thinkin' of where you'll stay. Would you like to come home with me till you settle in?"

Settle in? But where? Chris Beth realized that she had taken care of the little things but had neglected the ones that mattered.

"I—I thought—surely there's a place to board?"

Her words must have sounded ridiculous, for the others looked at her in surprise. Mrs. Malone simply shook her head. "Nothin'. And the nearest town—store, really—is a day's wagon ride."

All the bravado that Chris Beth had felt back in the city was gone. Here she was in the wilderness alone and frightened out of her wits. She had nobody to lean on, even if she had been a leaner! But going back was out of the question.

" 'Twill all turn out according to the Lord's will. You got no cause to worry. Just be glad you know Him!"

This woman spoke as if she and her God were personally acquainted. Well, she found no comfort in such thinking. Maybe she should correct whatever wrong impression she had given, but she felt last night's weakness seeping into her bones, squeezing her heart, and dragging her dry eyelids closed. Wearily, she leaned back and waited for the wheels of the stagecoach to resume their hateful rhythm.

But the disturbing words did not come. Instead, she dreamed a beautiful dream. In it, a man she had never met was reaching out to her. She took his hand. The touch was gentle and they were strangers no longer. . . .

4
End of the
World

❧

CHRIS BETH AWOKE. The stagecoach had stopped in the middle of the green maze she had seen from a distance at Half-Way Station. She shuddered as she remembered the myths and half-truths she had heard about Black Bart's gang of "polite robbers." But the freckled boy (about 11, she judged) looked innocent enough. He stood awkwardly beside a wagon and waved.

Passengers began picking up their belongings. Everybody talked at once. Chris Beth was hurdled through the open door, where the driver waited. He reached a gloved hand to help her from the stage.

"Trail ends here," he told her. Then, turning to a man climbing down from the driver's seat, he said, "Good havin' you, Joe. Better turn back to Redding with me."

"Another time, Hank."

Mrs. Malone, who had moved up beside Chris Beth, followed her gaze. "That's Joseph Craig. Remember?" No, she didn't remember him nor would she remember him the next time. All she saw was a faded trademark where overall suspenders crossed his back. Chris Beth was aware only of the man's immense height.

"He rode atop—'Shotgun Messenger,' you know, protectin' the treasure box and mail." A responsible position, Chris supposed, but her concern was for herself and where she was going.

"This way, Miss Mollie!" the boy called from the wagon. Mrs. Malone waved to him.

"That's Ned. Come on, folks! Room for us all."

O'Higgin picked up one of the bags the driver had taken from under the canvas cover in back of the stage and had placed at Mrs. Malone's feet. "This be yours?" At the woman's nod, the Irishman headed for the wagon.

Chris Beth felt a sense of embarrassment when she saw Wilson North pick up her two bags and hand one to Ned Malone—no, not Malone. The boy had said "Miss Mollie". . . . "Anything more, Miss?" Wilson North asked. Chris Beth felt her face flush.

"No!" she answered with an edge to her voice. So they all thought her helpless because she was new to this part of the world—some Southern belle or china doll unable to do anything for herself. Well, she'd show them.

But the resolve was short-lived. "M-Miss Kelly, I—I believe this is yours?" Chris Beth did not recognize the slight stammer, but she turned and found herself looking into the eyes of the "man from uptop." Joseph Craig pointed toward the driver's seat as if to introduce himself, then reddened when he seemed to realize he had gestured with the object he was handing her. *The brooch! How could I have forgotten—again?* But before she could thank the shy young man, he had placed the pin in her hand and picked up her satchel. Chris Beth realized furiously that Wilson North was watching with a little smile of amusement. She dropped the pin in her bag and snapped it shut.

"Miss Kelly will ride with you, Ned," Mrs. Malone said. "Mind your manners, son, and help her now. I'll ride—no, come to think on it, Miss Kelly had best ride in the spring seat behind us. There's a heap of talkin' you and I need to do."

Chris Beth noted with relief that Wilson North had positioned himself beside O'Higgin at the back of the wagon bed.

Apparently, the two men would ride backward, dangling their feet. The trappers had disappeared into the woods. That left Joseph Craig, and, although she didn't know him, Chris Beth felt that anybody was to be preferred to the man who seemed to delight in her helplessness. How much did he know of her past?

But there was no time to dwell on the past or even on the future. Chris Beth was too busy viewing the strange new world around her. As the team left the main road, they entered an even denser forest, the wagon wheels moving soundlessly over the dry needles that covered the narrow road. Once her eyes adjusted to the underwater green of the light, the country was even more beautiful than the wagon masters had described it. Fir trees brushed the sky in their reach for light, and head-high ferns huddled around their trunks, providing refuge for squirrels that flitted everywhere. Rabbits, unafraid, went on with their play, and once a skunk strolled dangerously near. Nobody seemed to notice, not even when the antlered deer stood watching curiously as the wagon passed.

Chris Beth watched in fascination as the timber crowded in, then widened out a bit to let the wagon through. How lovely!

The man beside her had the good sense not to talk. While she was grateful for her seatmate's silence, it seemed unnatural somehow. Now and then Chris Beth stole a look at him. His expression told her nothing. It was an interesting face, she decided—even handsome, she supposed, in a craggy sort of way. Once, sensing her gaze, Joseph Craig turned. Then he glanced away shyly. But for a brief moment their gazes held. He reminds me of somebody, she thought. But try as she would, she could remember no man with such kind, blue eyes. Something in that brief glance told Chris Beth this man would understand her need to share appreciation for this mysterious, ruggedly beautiful land—without talking it to death.

"It's so unspoiled, so unused," she ventured.

Joseph Craig did not disappoint her. "Ex-actly," he said, and fell silent again.

The fir boughs sighed above them, and somewhere below water rippled in a sort of lullaby. *Restful.* That would have been more like it. The feeling that Chris Beth had in the stagecoach returned. She wished that if life had to go on, it could continue like this. Her tired eyes rested on the eternal green canopy. Her ears listened gratefully to its whisper. Yes, it would be nice, just going on forever. But somewhere beyond all this was a real world to deal with. Already light appeared ahead.

"Will we reach the settlement soon?"

"An hour at most," Joseph Craig promised. "We—we've been travelling about two hours."

Two hours! With another to go? *Three hours from civilization—if one could call the stagecoach civilization!* The forest had soothed her, maybe soothed her dangerously. It would be easy to be mesmerized in this mysterious country where hours flew.

"Look!" Joseph Craig pointed below to where the canyon dipped dangerously. Near-toppled trees, twining their roots in the rocks along the steep walls, somehow managed to hold on. At the bottom of the canyon, a raging river twisted and writhed, as if trying to straighten out its powerful body in its tortuous journey to the sea. *Such force!* Chris Beth shivered.

"Awesome, but one of our lifelines," he volunteered in the quiet voice she had come to appreciate. "Trout, even salmon on their way to spawn early in the year. Lots of our water comes from here too—sometimes too much as you can see," he nodded at the bare roots hanging above the river. "Water table's close to the surface, so most have wells. My place has a spring. Oh! there it is—" and there was excitement in Joseph's voice.

Following his gaze, Chris Beth gasped with pleasure. Far below, the road dipped sharply into a sudden, sunlit clearing. The grass-carpeted valley, hugged by mountains—purple in the distance—divided, like a nine-patch quilt with threads of blue water. The "patches" must be individual homesteads, she supposed. The whole scene looked more like a painting on Mama's wall than a settlement. One proud frame house stood apart, and here and there she was able to pick out a log cabin. Flowers filled the yards. Vines—grapes, she was to learn later—curved along the eaves. The only signs of life were tendrils of smoke rising from fat, rock chimneys of the little houses.

"Most likely smoking jerky," Joseph said to her unasked question.

Jerky? There is so much I'll need to learn—but she had missed something Joseph Craig said.

"—alone since then. See the one that's mine?"

A small cabin stood where he pointed. But as to why he was alone she had missed.

"Oh, it's beautiful—beautiful," Chris Beth said of the valley and wished desperately for Jon—or the person she had thought him to be—to share it with her. But she would never be able to share anything again—not really—especially her heart.

Chris Beth felt the eyes of Joseph Craig fixed on her. It was unsettling. Had she spoken aloud? Surely not—but why was he staring? From the corner of her eye Chris Beth saw concern in the man's face. Well, she didn't want his pity—.

"Whoa!" Ned tightened his hold on the reins, and the wagon stopped.

They were in front of the big frame house, and suddenly it looked lonely. To Chris Beth's dismay, the cabins, which had appeared huddled together, were swallowed up by the forest. *End of the trail*, the driver had called it. More like the end of the world! She shivered again, then squared her shoulders in what she hoped covered all misgivings. She stood up quickly and jumped lightly to the ground before any of the men could help her.

"M-Miss Kelly," Joseph spoke with a little uncertainty; "you left your handbag."

The words, though soft, were not lost to Wilson North. Stopping in midstretch after the long ride in back of the wagon bed, he acknowledged her presence with a little nod, his half-smile mocking and his eyes, though twinkling, mentally calculating her telltale signs of inadequacy.

Chris Beth grabbed the bag angrily and stalked away. *The man was impossible!*

5
An Empty Chair

❧

A N UNMISTAKABLE AROMA of coffee filled the air, plus something else that Chris Beth was unable to identify. The yeasty smell reminded her of Mama's "light bread," or was it the delivery wagon from which she used to purchase raised rolls? For the first time in weeks, she felt hungry.

"The welcoming committee!" Mrs. Malone warned. Suddenly the travelers were surrounded by several children and a wolflike dog. The children tripped over one another in their rush to reach Mrs. Malone first, and the dog alternated between barking and checking out the newcomers and scents on the wagon wheels.

After she had embraced each child in turn, Mrs. Malone blew her nose, wiped her eyes, and became her efficient self again. "Now, Lola Ann, step up front," she said to the tallest of the girls, "and bring Jimmy John." Suddenly aware of an audience, the children stopped their chatter. Awkwardly, Lola Ann came forward, leading a dumpling-shaped boy who tried to hide behind her calico skirt.

"Lola Ann's the oldest and Jimmy John's the baby. This is

Amelia, and—Harmony, where are you hidin'?" She's our shyest. After her, there's Andrew—he's helpin' unhitch the team. And then, there are—was—the twins. Now there's Ned."

The children greeted the men but their eyes, fastened on Chris Beth, were round with fright. "Scamper now." At Mrs. Malone's command they hurried gratefully away. "Set up places for Wilson and Joe. One for Miss Kelly, too," she called behind them. Turning to her guests, she invited, "Come into the front room. And, Wolf, stop that silly barkin'!" But Chris Beth saw Mrs. Malone pat the dog on the head affectionately.

Chris Beth wondered as they filed into the big room how Mrs. Malone kept all the names straight. *And how*, she thought, *does she manage to handle grief so matter-of-factly?* It was as if the routine of a meal were of more consequence than a death in the family. *We're cut off a different bolt*, she thought, then desperately, *I'll never be able to make it here!*

There was no time to look around the "front room," as Mrs. Malone called the parlor, except to note that curtains were drawn against the noon sun. Lola Ann appeared at the door, wiping her damp hands on her apron, to announce that dinner was ready.

"Miss Kelly—" Mrs. Malone began.

"Chris Beth, please, Mrs. Malone."

"Chris Beth," her hostess said without hesitation, "you can wash in the basin. You men wash at the outside pump."

That's the way things are out here, Chris Beth thought, splashing her face gratefully with water. *A friendship offered is a friendship accepted without reservation.* She remembered that in her upbringing strangers were outsiders until established families checked "background and breeding." Well, Western ways were to her advantage. No fear here of people's finding out what she chose to keep to herself. But even with her mixed-up emotions, which kept volleying back and forth, Chris Beth felt a certain sense of warmth that she had missed in her childhood.

Wilson North pulled a chair from the long table, and Chris Beth found herself seated without so much as a "by your leave" right beside him. Mrs. Malone took her place at the foot of the table and motioned for Joseph Craig to sit at her right side. O'Higgin appeared to seat himself at her left. Strange that Mrs. Malone had made no mention of his being a guest. He must be a frequent visitor.

"Amelia, have all you children had your meal?"

The girl nodded. " 'cept Ned—."

Ned was hesitating at the dining room door. Was he uncomfortable before company or was there something else? Chris Beth watched the boy move toward the head of the table and pause.

Mrs. Malone shook her head. "You're the oldest boy now, 'tis true. Still and all, you're not the one to take your papa's place."

The boy looked relieved, Chris Beth thought, as he left the empty chair. He sat down and bowed his head. She looked around the table and saw that all the others had bowed their heads, too. Quickly, she lowered her eyes.

"O'Higgin?" The way Mrs. Malone spoke was a request.

"Lord, we be thankin' Ye for this food," the Irishman responded. "And we be askin' Ye to bless all the people within the walls of this hoose."

"House!" Mrs. Malone corrected. "Amen."

Chris Beth glanced up to see if there was a smile anywhere. Catching her eye, Wilson North lifted an eyebrow in shared amusement. Well, I'll not respond to that, she thought hotly, and busied herself trying to scoop a helping of mashed potatoes from the mountain set before her without tearing it down and giving him cause for a belly laugh!

As the girls brought bowl after bowl of garden-fresh vegetables, venison, and hot coffee, her appetite increased. Then came the enormous plate of biscuits! She knew immediately that they were the source of the yeasty aroma that had welcomed her arrival. "If I take one, I'll split at the seams," she smiled at Amelia. "But if I don't, I'll die of curiosity."

"So might as well enjoy your demise," Wilson North said,

laying one of the fluffy, golden-crowned biscuits on her plate. "I'll give you a starter."

"Starter of what?"

"Sourdough. You'll need it for biscuits like these. It's what the prospectors use in place of milk. You *can* cook?"

Chris Beth buttered her biscuit. Whether she could cook was none of this man's business!

To hide her irritation, Chris Beth turned her eyes to the head of the table and the hauntingly empty chair. The emptiness seemed to symbolize something to her, but she was unable to attach to it anything she remembered. She wondered about it. She wondered, too, which of the children belonged to Mrs. Malone and about a lot of other things. Why had the older woman forgotten to tell the children she might be their teacher? Or maybe they knew. Everybody else seemed to. Then, for the first time, she wondered how O'Higgin, Wilson North, and Joseph—she had come to think of him as Joe—happened to be on the same stagecoach that brought the neighboring Mrs. Malone to the settlement.

The girls began to clear the table, and Chris Beth saw that the two younger men were preparing to leave. "How far away are they from you?" she asked Mrs. Malone as they picked up their gear.

"Four miles across the creek," she replied. "The horses will meet them somewhere in the woods, I expect, and sort of save their legs."

The two men must live close together, thought Chris Beth.

Joe swung his pack easily over his shoulder. "Miss Kelly, if you wish, I—I'll take you to see Nate tomorrow."

"Oh, would you?" Chris Beth answered quickly. She could plan nothing at all until she met the trustee and found out for sure if she had a teaching job.

"Of course," he said. "It will do the buggy good to get s-some exercise." She noticed that Joe had returned to his slight stammer. Back in the forest, it had disappeared.

Wilson broke into her thoughts. "Shucks! I was planning

you and *I* would go calling on Nate. Or don't you like horseback riding—double, that is?"

At that moment, Chris Beth found nothing about this man particularly to her liking and she hoped her cold glance said as much!

Mrs. Malone saved the moment. "The Lord will bless you both—you, too, O'Higgin—for what you did for me," she said.

Joe placed his arm around her shoulders. "It was nothing at all," he said.

Then, as Wilson brushed the woman's cheek lightly with his lips, Chris Beth noticed a change of expression. She could have sworn there were tears in his eyes.

She shook her head in wonderment, suddenly very tired. It had been a strange day.

6
Secret Desires

❧

EARLY-MORNING SUN was tinting the front-room windows (where Mrs. Malone had made down a temporary bed for Chris Beth) when Joe came for her. Fortunately, she had awakened early, brushed and braided her hair, and put on a fresh white blouse. The rumpled suit would have to do until she found a place to unpack and sort her other clothing. The blouse needed an ornament at the neck, but there was no time to rummage through her grip, and certainly she wouldn't be wearing the brooch! Thought of the brooch was a reminder that she would have to check on the mail service. The sooner it was on its way to Jon, the better. Let the "other woman" have it, she thought bitterly.

As Chris Beth wound her braids into a crown and secured them with combs, she had time to look about the great room which had served as a bedroom. The ceilings were high and beamed with mellow rafters. The fireplace looked large enough for the entire family to gather around, and Chris Beth wondered what purpose the big black pot suspended in its mouth served. On the east side of the room, just beyond the dining room door, a wide staircase with polished banisters led upstairs.

The upstairs rooms were unfinished, Mrs. Malone had said last night, "with beds wedged in amongst the packin' crates."

Did they plan to finish the room? Chris Beth wondered.

"Yes—in time—busy workin' out details when the children's papa died."

Chris Beth realized later that the older woman must have sensed her questions. She was such a perceptive person.

Mr. Malone had been a widower when Mollie met him, she explained of her late husband. A man with six children "a'growin'" needed a mate, and she, a spinster, needed somebody to love after "layin' away" both parents. And, besides, there was Turn-Around Inn to take care of.

Turn-Around Inn?

Mrs. Malone's eyes misted with tears as she recalled, "This very house. It was his dream, and maybe it'll come true yet, if the railroad comes on through. Only the good Lord knows. Time was when folks talked of bringin' steamboats up the river. Passengers could've linked up with the stage. But," she sighed, "roads and rails stopped 'bout the same time."

Mrs. Malone had straightened her shoulders then. "Good years, but past." Chris Beth marveled again at the woman's ability to put life in its proper perspective. "Meantime, I've got me a mighty wholesome family! And Turn-Around Inn's name turned out to be just the right name for Papa's house." Mrs. Malone bit her lip in concentration. "Wasn't for that I could put you up proper-like right here. But," she continued determinedly, "the Lord's work comes first."

"I guess I don't understand," Chris Beth said slowly.

"'Course you don't. 'Twould take another Solomon to unriddle some of my sayin's sometimes. You see, folks here in the settlement have no place to worship when the rains come. Till then we use a brush arbor down by Graveyard Creek. Later it floods like the river. So we use the front room here."

Mrs. Malone had told more about her neighbors, but Chris Beth's weary mind absorbed little of it—at least, little that she could recall this morning. Wilson North and Joseph Craig were close friends, both "bound over by profession"—wasn't that the phrase she had used? Both had "suffered deeply" with pox epidemic, and O'Higgin was like "kinfolks" to the Malones. Chris Beth had dozed off while her hostess was explaining how he and the two younger men refused to let her face Jed's burial alone, "even with them tryin' to finish school and all."

All this Chris Beth was mulling over as she readied herself for the trip to see Nate Goldsmith. The rich smell of brewing coffee told her that Mrs. Malone's keen ears had heard her movements and that she was downstairs starting breakfast. Hurriedly, Chris Beth tried to roll up the feather bed the way it had been the night before. She was still struggling with it when she heard Mrs. Malone answer Joe's knock at the front hall door.

"Couldn't have slept much," she heard Mrs. Malone confide. "But she's an independent one—refusin' to take one of the girls' beds."

"Here, let me help." Joe appeared at the front-room door. He looked different wearing a white shirt and tie, and again Chris Beth was aware of his enormous height. She noticed, too, the strength of his hands as with an effortless flip he dispensed with the feather bed. Yet he didn't make her feel helpless.

After the biggest breakfast of her life—who could resist feather-light sourdough pancakes, all crispy-brown around the edges, surrounded by homemade sausages?—and a final cup of coffee, the two of them climbed into the buggy. At Joe's "Go, Dobbin Girl!" the gray mare trotted toward the wooded area that Chris Beth had seen the two men enter the evening before.

Suddenly it was as if they were beneath a multicolored umbrella. Autumn had come early to the area, surprising Chris Beth with its brilliance. Every tree seemed to lean toward the buggy, linking limbs as if to form a gold-and-crimson canopy above the passengers. The beauty of it all made Chris Beth's heart ache. She remembered the rides that she and Jon had taken together on Sunday afternoons, with the horse cantering along the avenue while, heads together, they had talked of their lives together. . . .

Well, she wasn't going to think of him—not about him or the uncertainties that lay ahead. Today was enough. On impulse, she touched Joe's sleeve. "Oh, can't we stop a minute—I mean, can't we? I just want to walk in the leaves!"

"Whoa, Dobbin!" The gray mare stopped on the trail. "I can understand." And Joe smiled.

Together they walked without talking beneath the bright arch, dry leaves crunching and disintegrating under their shoes. They gathered armloads of brilliant branches and filled the box on the buggy. Maybe it *was* good she had come here. Maybe—

"Oh, we must go," Chris Beth interrupted her own thinking with genuine regret.

Joe nodded. "I'm glad we stopped, though." He paused, and she knew he wanted to say more. *Oh, now don't spoil it,* her heart begged. She needn't have worried. What Joe Craig said was, "I wouldn't want you hugging a secret desire like mine. Take a look at the staircase back at Mrs. Malone's."

"It's lovely."

"Every single time I go there I have a feeling I'd like to slide down the banister!"

Chris Beth heard the echo of their laughter even after they had climbed back into the buggy and continued toward the Goldsmith place. Strange, she was to think later, that there would have been no feeling of premonition of what was to destroy her beginning sense of belonging.

7

*Bound by Contract—
And Mountains*

❧

A COVERED BRIDGE spanned Graveyard Creek. Nate Goldsmith heard Dobbin clopping over the loose boards and came to the edge of the clearing to meet Chris Beth and Joe. Chris Beth could see that the man was expecting them. His sparse hair looked like he had dipped his head in the rain barrel, but he had overlooked a thin brown coffee trail that parted his beard like a fork. His one suspender looked ready to pop its button as he leaned against the rail fence.

"Shet up, Coon Dog!" he ordered a barking hound. The animal slunk toward the small cabin, causing the chickens to squawk and take to the air. "You, too!" he called after them. Then, turning to his guests, the school trustee motioned them inside.

"Company fer dinner, Ole Lady!" he called before introducing himself to Chris Beth. But, for all his bluster, she sensed in this man the same kindness she had appreciated among her other new acquaintances. Their acceptance humbled her.

Nate shook hands with Joe, addressing him as "Brother Joseph," and told Chris Beth she was "mighty purty." "I'd ask

36

that we sit a spell, 'cept dinner's most ready and I don't take a shine to talkin' bizness on a empty stomach."

Nate Goldsmith's wife, a small, birdlike woman, made a quick appearance and acknowledged the introduction briefly, her words sounding like a mixture of German and French, and then darted away. She returned only to serve the simple meal.

"Ask the blessin', Brother Joseph, and let's eat," Nate said.

To Chris Beth's surprise, Joe bowed his head. "Lord, we thank You for this day and all its blessings in this land of plenty. We especially thank You for bringing the teacher we needed so much. Give her strength for the job ahead. In the name of Your Son. Amen."

Chris Beth was touched by the simple prayer, even though it disturbed her to be mentioned by name. It was as if Joe were asking his Lord to test her, instead of leaving the matter to the board of trustees! She had noticed, too, that there was no hesitancy in Joe's speech as he prayed. Maybe it was because he was at ease instead of having to weigh words. Well, why should it matter that he and God were on good terms? It shouldn't—but it did.

Nate Goldsmith finished an apple dumpling and pushed his chair back from the table. Looking sharply at Chris Beth, he asked, "Do you reckon as how you can lick 'em an' larn 'em?"

Startled, she nodded. Somewhere in the background there were stifled giggles. So there were children? Better trained than the hound and the chickens, apparently!

Chris Beth realized that the self-appointed "President of the Board" was talking—and that he had little but bad news. As a teacher, she would be entitled to 50 dollars a month "less'n crops fail and folks can't meet taxes." The school term would last about six months, "dependin' on crops," but he wondered aloud if she could last the year out. There had been those, he observed darkly, who hadn't. All this was providing Chris Beth could pass the teachers' exam. "We're a state now," he said with pride, then paused for an answer to something. The exam?

Yes, she thought she could pass.

And was she willing to abide by other stipulations?

Well, yes—

"They bein'," Nate told her, "thet you conduct yourself at all times like a lady, partake in church and gen'ral bizness of the settlement, pull yer share of the work on the grounds and gen'ral upkeep—oh, somethin' else, contract's null and void iffen you marry."

Chris Beth felt Joe's eyes on her and blushed. "I have no intention of marrying," she said stiffly. *Now or ever!*

"Well, then, I'm right pleased to welcome you among'st us. No need fer signin' a paper. Figger yer word's good as mine. Anyway, havin' witnesses like we did," Nate looked at Joe, then jerked his head toward the kitchen, where his "Ole Lady" was washing dishes quietly, "binds us legal enough."

Did she have any questions?

Well, there was a matter of a place to stay.

Cabin on the school grounds. Needed some fixing up, but—

"Could we stop by?" Chris Beth asked Joe.

He looked at the lowering sun. "Better make it another time," he said.

"Oh, the exam," Chris Beth remembered as they prepared to leave.

"I'll tend to thet come next Tuesday. The ole lady will be needin' some supplies and I kin pick up a copy at Jed's Gen'ral Store. You folks need somethin'?"

The trip was a day's wagon ride from the settlement, Chris Beth remembered Mrs. Malone had said. The brooch simply *had* to be on its way to Jon.

"Would it be possible for you to mail a package for me?"

Nate weighed the question, then shook his head doubtfully. "Be glad to 'commodate, Miss Kelly. But there's no tellin' when 'twould go. Like as not mail's delivered by horseback over the hump. Reminds me, though, I'd best be checkin' to see what mail's come fer the settlement since last month."

Month! Had she heard right? Slowly, amazement gave way to disappointment, and then despair. Returning the brooch was the most important thing in her life!

Gone was the mellow mood of the day. The mysterious hills were no longer friendly. They were sentinels, holding her captive.

Chris Beth felt a peculiar sensation of lost hope. But hope of *what*? Escape? No, the stagecoach, irregular and slow as it was, offered a means of departure. It had to be something else. Then, with a flood of shame, she realized the awful truth. Sending Jon's gift back would have done more than finish up the love affair. The package would have given him her whereabouts—offered an opportunity for him to get in touch, beg her forgiveness, and ask for a chance for them to begin a new life in the land he had dreamed of.

"Can I do anything for you, Miss Kelly?" Joe's blue eyes were full of compassion as they waved goodbye to Nate.

Yes, ask your God to hurry along with that strength you asked Him for! she thought wildly. Aloud she said, "I'm fine. Really, I am."

But her smile was too bright—like the autumn leaves which even now were twisting on their fragile stems and dropping one by one to wither and die.

"Oh, Joe—" A little sob caught in her throat.

He placed a gentle hand on her shoulder. Automatically, she touched it with her own hand.

8
A Strange Tranquility

❧

THE WEEK THAT FOLLOWED was busy, and for
that Chris Beth was grateful. She had settled, she found, into
the unfeeling pattern established when she went through the
motions of canceling wedding plans. She was here, bound by
contract, and there was no money to go back home even if she
could face the situation she had run away from.

As for returning the brooch—yes, of course the painful
reminder of false love had to go. It would be too late, but in her
heart she knew its return would be of no consequence
anyway. How she could get it back to Jon was another matter,
but it was too valuable to leave lying in some store whose
owner she had never met with no idea as to when it would be
mailed.

Maybe someday, I'll feel it's better this way, she told
herself. But for now she had no feeling at all, except for the
familiar cold emptiness. *I should never have allowed a notion
that life would be better here.* She bit her lip but was aware of
no pain—just the salty taste of blood.

"Somethin' troublin' you?" Chris Beth had failed to hear

Mrs. Malone come into the front room, where she was sorting through her clothes.

Certain that her confusion showed, Chris Beth mumbled that her dresses were in bad shape and wondered vaguely if what she had brought would be suitable.

"Well, *that's* no cause for worry. I'm finished churnin' and have the irons heatin' on the stove. I'll help," she said, picking up a blue woolen dress and smoothing it with her hands.

I must show more feeling, even if I have to fake it. "Thank you, Mrs. Malone," she said warmly. "Is this lace collar too dressy for school?"

"I've a piece of natural linen in the chest. Think I'll whip up collar and cuffs. It'll take less than a jiffy."

"I'm grateful. Sewing is not among my skills. I *can* cook, though," she added, wondering why she felt it necessary to defend herself. "I pestered Cook until she let me help in the kitchen. Mostly, a seamstress made our clothes at first. And all the fancywork was done by Mama and Vangie. You should have seen my *trousseau*—" Chris Beth sucked in her breath, aghast at what she had said.

Mrs. Malone bit off a thread and mercifully backed the conversation up. "Vangie?"

Chris Beth exhaled gratefully. "My younger sister—half sister—Evangeline. Mama remarried after my father was killed."

Mrs. Malone, squinting to thread her needle, nodded. "Probably wise."

"Not really!" Chris Beth felt the familiar bitterness beg for release. "Mama hadn't recovered from her loss. My father was an engineer—gone a lot, and finally killed in an explosion. She married on the rebound. He—*Father* Stein, the name to his liking—represented safety." Chris Belt felt her pulse quicken hatefully. No wonder Mama complained of palpitations.

Mrs. Malone leaned forward. "Was it so awful you can't forgive?" she asked softly.

"Forgive!" Something exploded inside Chris Beth's chest,

and release came. "It was obedience he wanted. He was a bigot and a hypocrite." She stopped briefly, forcing herself to lower her voice: "conscientious and devout, but *cruel*!"

Memories, too long suppressed, flooded back with tidal-wave force—the self-righteous pseudorector who considered all others his parish to bend to his will, shaking a warning finger at Chris Beth and Vangie, his voice raised in final judgment at the slightest childish provocation. "Everlasting torment is just a breath away. Now pray, both of you, *pray*!" Vangie's fragile face would pale. Her thin, little figure would crouch pitifully at her father's feet—like a tiny, fallen angel. And always her almost-inaudible words sought forgiveness of that condemning man—not his God. On those frequent occasions, Chris Beth refused to yield. It came as natural as breathing to try to protect the younger girl in the only way she knew. "Let her alone!" she would sob, beating at his bulky middle with her small fists. Mama, who was "delicate since the children's birth," would come down with one of her headaches. Vangie was dragged away, and Chris Beth—an "instrument of the devil"—was locked in the attic to "meditate on the Scriptures." She shuddered as she remembered the old Bible prophecies that Father Stein (whom she refused to call by that doubtful title) chose for her to read. And, oh, the awful nightmares that followed. . . .

A merry whistle announced that O'Higgin, his woodcutting done for the day, was "home" for supper. "Sakes alive! How time does fly when we women get sewin' and talkin'!" Mrs. Malone brought Chris Beth back to the warm present and the tantalizing smell of rising sourdough biscuits.

Gratefully she looked around the friendly room, where her ready-for-school dresses lined the walls. She had half-expected to see the menacing face of her mother's husband looming above. Her lip tasted salty again, and her hands were clenched into white-knuckled fists, but something rarefying and sweet had happened inside—something clean, pure, and good. The terrible nightmare was over.

"Oh, Mrs. Malone! How can I thank you?"

"No need. The past is an all-right place to visit on occasion, but we don't want it to nest in our hair." Mrs. Malone patted her shoulder and moved capably toward the dining room, where Lucy Ann was coaxing the last of summer's zinnias into a vase. "Real pretty—" then, raising her voice, "O'Higgin, take off your shoes and don't go trackin' the scrubbed floor!"

Chris Beth leaned back and inhaled deeply. Once, while trying to soothe Vangie in later years, she had said bitterly of Hugo Stein in her growing skepticism, "He's no better, but maybe no worse, than the rest of humanity."

Well, she was wrong. That was before she had met such people as these who surrounded her now. No need to fake gratitude any longer! It welled up inside and there came an unfamiliar urge to express it in a way that went back farther than she could remember with any degree of clarity. But to *whom*? This beautiful Oregon Country? No, *for* it. It's inhabitants? No, for them, too.

The "thank you" Chris Beth sent out through the purpling dusk was directed at nobody in particular—or so she thought. But its utterance brought a strange tranquility to her heart.

9
Graveyard Shack

ॐ

JOE CAME ON TUESDAY to say that Nate Gold-
smith had postponed his trip to the store for two weeks. "As
well as the opening of school," he concluded. "Corn and
pumpkins are still in the field. Apples to pick and potatoes to
harvest."

"But the exam?" Inwardly Chris Beth was thinking about
mailing the brooch. Also, she *must* get a letter off to Mama.
There had been no communication since she had posted a
letter home at Redding. In it she had given a glowing account
of the trip. Mama never liked bad news. Years of shielding her
had created a pattern. Anyway, friends would be asking, *and
I'll give their tongues no chance to wag.* Better a girl in her
position be called fickle over the broken engagement than
jilted! And better yet if she could carry off this "great
adventure" aura she had woven so cleverly before coming
West.

Joe smiled and responded to her question. "Nate will pick
up papers and proctor the test in due time. But you passed *his*
examination last week. He's a stickler on this commitment
business. Which reminds me—he made mention of church."

Chris Beth nodded, wondering what was expected of her.

"Would you like me to pick you up S-Sunday? Any day could be our last for using the arbor before the rains s-set in."

"That would be nice," Chris Beth murmured. Actually, she felt a need to sort things out. Church hadn't been a part of her plans here. Of course, she *had* "committed" herself. But something else troubled her, too. Remembering the harmless little incident coming back from the Goldsmith house warned that she was less immune to love than she had thought. Memory of Joe's hand, warm through her thin blouse, brought a blush. And his slight stammer said he was self-conscious in her presence again.

Abruptly, Joe changed the subject. "Will you be needing supplies for school?"

Chris Beth had given the matter no thought. "Am I to furnish them?" she asked.

"Oh, the youngsters bring their own. I meant personal things—boots and other rainwear. You know, umbrella and a slicker."

She glanced at Joe's face. No, he wasn't teasing. "Are they essential?" Both of them looked at her pearl-button shoes.

This time he laughed. "'Fraid so. Sometimes the general store stocks them. Mostly, people order from the catalogue, or else hope the backpack peddler happens to have a pair that fits!"

"Is there *nowhere* to shop?" This was incredulous.

"Well, there's Portland—a two-day trip. Each way."

Talk of isolation! Well, Mama had said it was a wilderness. Little did she know what it was like to live in one, though!

As it turned out, the arrangement never materialized. On the following Saturday Joe dropped by Turn-Around Inn to say he would be in town several days.

Town?

Well, the general store. Upstairs had some business offices . . . Doc Dullus. Blacksmith shop in shed next door. Smithy sometimes pulled teeth.

Mercy! Did Joe have a toothache?

"Nothing like that," Joe smiled. "The examining board—"

Mrs. Malone called, "Refreshments!" before Chris Beth could decide if it were proper to ask what the board was or what it had to do with Joe.

Over cinnamon rolls and coffee, Mrs. Malone asked about Joe's "tests" as she added to a list of staples she wanted him to pick up at the general store.

"I'm prepared," he said slowly, "except f-for—" he stopped in embarrassment. Chris Beth made a mental note to ask Mrs. Malone what tests Joe was taking and why he was embarrassed.

"Is there something I can do for you, Miss Kelly?"

I must tell him to use my first name, except in front of the children, she thought. He's Joe to me and—

"Miss Kelly?"

"Sorry," Chris Beth mumbled. "Yes, yes, there is, please. I'd like you to mail something." Excusing herself, she went for the overdue letter to her mother.

"Anything more?" he asked when she handed it to him.

Chris Beth hesitated. "No, I think not." She was still undecided how to handle the return of the brooch to Jonathan Blake.

On the front porch Joe paused. "Wilson offered to come for you Sunday."

Chris Beth's lips pursed for a "No!" But before it came, she remembered that the Malones needed no additional passengers. Seven of them, plus O'Higgin (she was sure), made a wagonload. Oh, not to forget the dog. "Wolf always goes," Andy had said, "just in case." She hadn't cared to know of what!

"Miss Kelly," Joe prompted again.

"That would be nice," she murmured, careful to use the same words and exact tone as when she had accepted his own invitation. Then, as an afterthought, she added, "Call me Chris Beth. Aren't we friends?"

"Indeed we are that!" Joe mounted Dobbin and waved goodbye.

Well, out of the frying pan and into the fire. Chris Beth almost laughed aloud when she caught Mrs. Malone's unique speech entering into her own thinking. Anyway, the analogy best described the trip to the brush arbor. She would not be alone with Joe, after all. But she would be alone with that unnerving Wilson North. . . .

Nothing about Wilson should have surprised her, but the wide-tired, two-wheeled cart in which he called for her on Sunday did! The single seat was upholstered in carmine stripes. So was the enormous umbrella which he had opened above it. How vulgar!

And what on earth occupied most of the seat? Wilson's command answered the question. "Wait here, Esau!"

"Esau," whose canine coat put Wolf's to shame, showed no intention of leaving his throne. Back home they would be the laughingstock!

Chris Beth jabbed a hatpin through the wire frame of her plumed hat. Maybe the monstrous animal would "tree" the feather, thinking it was a bird. Remembering Wolf's antics last night, which had sent the 'possum scurrying up the backyard cedar, made her laugh again. Or maybe it was Wilson North, his outlandish vehicle, or the creature he called "Esau"!

Traces of laughter lingered when Wilson knocked, called "Open-Sesame!" and entered.

"Well, now, *that's* a pretty sight, *you* laughing!" But his sweeping glance from the velvet hat to the high-button shoes said Wilson North appreciated more than her smile. She straightened her face primly. Then, in strange contradiction, she felt unexpectedly glad that she had left the lace bertha on the blue wool for the Sunday service.

"Charlie Horse" (Chris Beth giggled at that name, too) was impatient to be off. Once she was wedged between the right rail and Esau, who refused to budge, the black pony shot forward.

The dog, thank goodness, looked straight ahead. To Chris

Beth's surprise, the cart balanced perfectly for easy riding. She found herself almost lighthearted as they entered the stretch of woods leading past the Goldsmith place.

"Easy, Boy!" Wilson reined in as the trail narrowed. Chris Beth again drank in the beauty of the brilliant leaves. She remembered then that the man beside her was a botanist.

"What kind of trees?"

"Vine maple."

"Aren't you writing a book about trees?"

Wilson nodded but changed the subject. "Colorful, aren't they? Sort of the garden variety. See, there's cantaloupe orange." He pointed to a near-gold leaf.

The game caught her imagination. "Beet red," she suggested of a scarlet leaf, realizing that her comparison was trite.

"Watermelon, then?" They both burst into laughter. Strange, she thought, how she had laughed with both men in this same enchanted place. Only there was a difference she would have been unable to explain.

Abruptly Wilson consulted his pocket watch. "Time to drop by for a squint at the Graveyard shack before the singing begins if we step along."

"The what?"

"Place you're considering as a home, so they tell me."

"Oh, the cabin. Is it really called *that*?"

"*That's* what it is."

Chris Beth stole a look at the clean-shaven face above the starched collar—handsome, she had to admit, but not smiling. And something about that made her apprehensive.

"Let's go, Charlie Horse!" At Wilson's words, the pony backed his ears and picked up speed. *It's like a colored kaleidoscope*, Chris Beth thought, *and we're inside. Alone!*

10
Strange Visitor

~∂~

THE STRETCH OF bright woods ended abruptly. A large, two-story house, fashioned much like the southern mansions of Chris Beth's youth, sprang out of nowhere. There was something both inviting and forbidding about the small-paned windows that peered like a thousand eyes from the white exterior. Smoke climbed lazily from what appeared to be an upstairs fireplace. Sun touched the shake roof, but the rest of the house blended into the shady vale of the background. Somewhere a pheasant crowed.

"I call it home," Wilson North said with mock humility.

"It's beautiful," Chris Beth breathed. "But do you live here all alone?"

At his curt "No," she regretted asking. *He always makes me feel in the wrong,* she thought. *I'll keep my curiosity to myself.*

As if to forestall any further questions, Wilson pointed. "Over there's Joe's place."

Straining against the shadows, Chris Beth's eyes picked out the outline of the cabin that Joseph Craig had pointed out on

49

their way to the Malones that first day. Was that only three weeks ago? It seemed a lifetime.

The cabin was close, as settlers measured distance, but a wide stream lay between the two houses.

"Graveyard Creek," Wilson explained. "Looks innocent now, but it can play havoc when Chinook winds melt the snowpack."

"How do you cross these creeks? And," she remembered, "doesn't the river run almost all the way around Turn-Around Inn?"

Wilson nodded. "Joe and I just fell a fir and drop it across the creek. Floods wash them away every year, which is just as well. The foot-logs get mossy and slippery anyway. Once," he laughed remembering, "the parson and his fine lady fell in the creek here!"

Chris Beth laughed with him. He continued, "My mother insisted that a board be nailed atop after that and a wire stretched for a handhold."

The slim, stout log spanning Graveyard Creek was arrow-straight. It looked like it would last forever. The floods must pack a wallop. No wonder settlers dreaded the winter.

Wilson had slowed the horse to a walk. "As to crossing the river, mostly people ford when the water's high."

Ford?

He explained about wading horses across and floating the wagon bed. *Well!* It was becoming clear why Joe thought she would be needing boots!

For some time Chris Beth had been conscious of a distant roar. As the cart moved into the woods again, the noise was closer.

"Graveyard Falls," Wilson raised his voice as the roar became near-deafening. "About half a mile upstream! Furnishes power for the grist mill—mine and Joe's. We supply settlers—and more."

How many more surprises did these two enterprising young men have in store, for goodness' sake?

"Grist—like for flour and meal?" Chris Beth supposed the

question sounded silly and citified. And, sure enough, it was just the "grist" Wilson North needed for his humor to feed upon.

"Ah, yes." He faked a sigh. "Notice how our feet turn inward? That's from tramping flour into barrels for export. And the meal—"

Charlie Horse interrupted his sentence by stopping at a pole gate. They had reached a rail fence which surrounded a building of sorts. At least, a rusty tin roof showed above it.

"Good boy! Well," Wilson alighted and offered his hand. "Welcome to Graveyard Shack." She accepted his hand and stepped down.

He opened the gate and Chris Beth stepped through—then stopped dead in her tracks, aghast at what she saw. Surely this crude lean-to could not be the "cabin" that Nate Goldsmith had mentioned. Why, it offered less protection than the temporary quarters occupied by miners she had seen in California. And they were men! Small wonder Joe hadn't been in a hurry to bring her to such a place.

Aware that Wilson North was watching, Chris Beth mustered as much dignity as possible, picked up her wool skirt, and stepped through the dried thistles. The one-room shanty slanted crazily as if to meet her. Involuntarily she stepped back.

"There's no window," was all she could gasp.

"'No window,' she says," Wilson mused, then—as if inspired—"but oh, what a view! Creek from the front and the graveyard from the back—if it had a back door."

Chris Beth jumped at a strange flapping noise coming from the shack.

"Not to worry!" Wilson soothed. "Not in daylight hours, that is. It's night when the strange visitor comes. He—"

"He who?" Chris Beth realized that her eyes must be round with fear. She was past caring about Wilson's silly banter aimed at her.

"Nobody knows for sure—not even if he's white or Indian. Both, they say, are buried here. He comes to claim them."

He's poking fun at me, she reasoned, *like always.* The noise *is coming from the piece of canvas serving as a door.* Of course, it had been his wild tales . . . and her imagination . . . like Brom Bones and Ichabod Crane.

But it was no use. She was unable to regain her composure. A wild laugh rose in her throat. Escape was all that mattered.

"Miss Kelly." There was sudden concern in Wilson North's voice. "Chris Beth—"

"Please—*please,*" she pled through stiff lips, "take me away."

He touched her elbow, but she tore away and climbed frantically into the cart.

Even Charlie Horse seemed strangely subdued. Like "Gun Powder," she thought, remembering the one-eyed nag in *The Legend of Sleepy Hollow.*

"Chris Beth, listen to me. Please do."

When Wilson spoke, Chris Beth was sure he spoke softly, but his voice had a ghostly ring in the silence of the woods. Charlie Horse picked up speed, and it was comforting to note that the cart rolled swiftly toward another clearing once his riders were aboard. The hammering of her heart was easing, but Chris Beth dared not risk her voice.

"I'm sorry. I truly am." Wilson's voice said that he was unaccustomed to apologizing. *That light touch is a cover-up,* she thought. *He's been hurt—like me.* Fear gave way to surprise.

"I understand," Chris Beth spoke slowly. Yes, she understood more than the graveyard incident—or thought she did. For she was beginning to understand the man, and maybe herself.

But she did not understand his next words. "Joe and me, and the others, had to show you it's impossible for a fine lady like you to live there. I personally will see to that!"

He would see to it! What property did Wilson North have?

But for the first time Chris Beth did not meet his challenge. Maybe *she* was the strange visitor in this new land.

11
Raisin' Praise

❧

IT WAS A RELIEF to feel warm sunshine in her face. This is the *real* world, she said to herself, once they reached the clearing. The other was a dream. But, deep inside, Chris Beth knew that both worlds were part of this Western frontier. And here one must live in them both, or perish.

"Feeling better?"

Chris Beth answered Wilson with a nod. It was good to feast her eyes on the now-golden meadows, dotted with livestock, like "the cattle on a thousand hills." Now *that* was familiar.

Before she could think more about the source, Wilson pointed ahead. "Mount Hood," he said.

And there to the east loomed the magnificent mountain she had seen in geography books. The snow-capped peak seemed to finger into the very sky, but the base of the mountain looked deceptively near. Vision on this kind of day reached into infinity.

"It's unbelievable," she breathed deeply. As usual, the beauty of this land tricked her into forgetting the problems at hand. "Mr. North—"

"Wilson."

53

"Wilson—do you realize I didn't even see the school."

"I realize."

The school . . . a place to live . . . returning the brooch . . . the state board exam . . . even, she thought wryly, a pair of boots! But somehow it didn't matter right now. Those were tomorrow's problems.

Charlie Horse's ears stood suddenly alert. Somewhere he had heard a whinny from another of his kind. And, sure enough, just over the horizon Chris Beth caught sight of the beautiful black taffeta bonnet belonging to Mollie Malone. She had worked until the lamps were out of oil last night trying to get the last of the pink rosettes embroidered around the ruffle. In her lap sat little Jimmy John. And close beside them, Chris Beth recognized the red pompon on top of O'Higgin's Scottish-plaid tam o'shanter.

"Top o' the mornin'!" O'Higgin called when Chris Beth and Wilson were within hearing distance. His cheeks were as bright as his woolen cap. *He's harboring some sort of exciting secret*, Chris Beth decided, and wondered what it was that set the man aglow.

There was a happy babble of children's voices at the intersection. Wolf and Esau eyed each other suspiciously but kept their seats. Greetings over, Wilson let Charlie Horse have free rein, and the cart wheeled away from the loaded wagon.

The road wound in and out of heavily wooded areas and past occasional clearings made for erecting cabins and cultivating. The ground must be very fertile to yield such gardens. Lush pumpkin vines trailed through corn rows, pausing only long enough to dump their golden fruits in any lap they could find.

"It looks so rich."

"Rich enough to mine," Wilson told her. "All virgin soil, you know, sometimes as much as three or four feet down. It's a land with a future, all right."

She could see that. Someday the railroads would come on through. The waterways would be developed. More and more settlers would come and towns would spring up.

Wilson broke into her dream to point out the young orchards. "Prunes, peaches—and see the apples?"

No store back home ever saw the like, she was sure. Huge, rosy, and polished, they glistened in the sun. And the ground beneath the trees was carpeted with fallen, wine-scented fruit! Her mouth watered. Wilson saw and laughed. "There'll be no breaking of the commandments," he cautioned, "until after church!"

Yes, the Oregon Country was a land of promise—for some. Chris Beth wondered what it held for her. But for right now this day was one of Mrs. Malone's "rainbows in between" life's dark days and its bright.

Chris Beth heard the sound of laughter mingled with excited voices of children before she saw the arbor. Up a little hill, a sudden dip in the road, and there it was! Where on earth had all the wagons and buggies come from? From miles around, Wilson told her. "And just wait till you see the picnic baskets and the appetites! Be lucky if we get a chicken neck!"

By the time the men watered the horses and tethered them to trees, Mrs. Malone had her flock "presentable" with Lola Ann's help. Amelia's sash was retied. Harmony's hair ribbon was straightened. "And, Chris Beth—Miss Kelly—will you unsnarl Andy's shoelaces?" Chris Beth was both amused and touched by the matter-of-fact way this woman filled the shoes of the children's dead mother. And the children obviously adored their stepmother. Even now little Jimmy John was reaching dimpled hands to show her that his cowlick was standing up again. Mrs. Malone grabbed an embroidered handkerchief, spit on it, and pushed back the unruly lock. *She's all women rolled into one*, Chris Beth thought, and was surprised to realize that she envied the other woman a bit.

As Chris Beth brushed her skirt free of possible dust and made sure the plume on her hat was still intact, she noticed a sudden hush about her. "Hurry, they're about to begin," O'Higgin whispered.

The group moved quickly to join the assembled worshipers. There was total silence as they stepped beneath the split-rail frame roofed with fir boughs, dry and brittle but sweet-smelling in the near-noon sun. Their footsteps made no sound on the dirt floors. All heads were bowed.

Chris Beth ventured a look around. A crude pulpit stood in front of the congregation (who were seated on split logs), and beside the pulpit was a tin bucket. It contained water, she supposed, since there was a dipper inside. Primitive though it was, there was a certain warmth—something missing in the straight, hard pews back home.

Involuntarily, her mind went back to the stiffly ritualistic services that her "God-fearing" stepfather had forced her mother, Vangie, and herself to sit through. Certainly the speakers had been eloquent, if selective, in their long, solemn sermons, which always gave Mama a headache and left Chris Beth and Vangie scared and depressed. The men were well-educated scholars who literally "scared hell *out* of the parishioners," she had dared tell her "Father Stein" once. She winced at the memory of quinine he had forced under her tongue . . . but these people, uneducated though they were, were more enlightened. They seemed to be freed of the restraints of fear and superstition. It should have been the other way around!

Chris Beth came out of her reverie. A man—why, it was Nate Goldsmith!—rose to stand behind the pulpit. Though almost obscured from view, Nate's voice rose powerfully. "The Lord bless you, one and all," he began. "Now, folks, I am sorry to be tellin' you that there's no big preach today. The circuit rider cain't come till maybe Thanksgiving, at which time we be meetin' at Turn-Around Inn."

His eyes consulted Mrs. Malone. She nodded and he continued: "But there's a heap of food, judgin' by the way my old woman's been cookin'." He paused, and little snickers of appreciation rippled through the crowd. "And meantime, we'll be raisin' praise!"

At his signal, O'Higgin stepped forward, lifted his hand, lowered it ceremoniously, and the group burst into song. "Praise God from whom all blessings flow!"

After that, with O'Higgin's booming Irish voice in the lead, the group sang hymn after hymn. "Who has a selection?" he would ask.

"Bringin' in the Sheaves!" . . . "Ole Rugged Cross" . . . "Amazin' Grace" . . . "Rescue the Perishin'" . . . "When We All Git to Heaven!" One member after another requested.

The crowd seemed lost in emotion as their words tumbled out in song without the aid of a piano or organ to accompany their singing. Chris Beth had never heard "pure song" before. So many of the lyrics had been drowned out by robed choruses and heavy-footed organists.

She listened with sad-sweet appreciation to the velvety bass melting gently into tenor—the plaintive minor keys rising to melodious major key. The very arbor seemed to tremble with praise raised to a God whom her stepfather had never met.

When a small lad suggested "Blessed Assurance," Chris Beth listened carefully to the words, which she was unsure she had heard before:

> Blessed assurance, Jesus is mine!
> O what a foretaste of glory divine!
> Heir of salvation, purchase of God,
> Born of His Spirit, washed in His blood. . . .

O'Higgin lifted his hand. The singing stopped. "'I will sing praises unto my God while I have any being,'" he declared. "Psalm 146:2."

As others quoted favorite passages of Scripture, Chris Beth listened, carefully taking note that all the verses spoke of joy, love, and praise.

And the final quotation struck home: "'Lord, I believe; help thou mine unbelief.' Mark 9:24."

Something stirred within her—something sweet and good, that went beyond her stepfather's coming into her life. She was sorry when the crowd rose to sing "Till We Meet Again."

12
A Family of Friends

PEOPLE CAME FORWARD eagerly to meet "the new teacher," but Nate Goldsmith pushed his way ahead of the group to pump her hand. "Picked 'er myself, I did," he said proudly. "Now, men, she's single and bound to stay thataway. But you women are to welcome 'er, hear?"

One by one, Nate presented Chris Beth to the Smiths (old-timers, he said), Martins ("kinda new, but learnin'"), Beltrans ("Basque folks, who raise wooly critters"—sheep, she supposed), and then Chris Beth lost track of the names. She noticed, however, that the board member paused significantly when he introduced the Solomons. "Him and the missus operate the gen'ral store."

Abe Solomon, short of stature and breath, acknowledged the introduction and bumped into his wife, immediately behind him, in his hurry to get away. Mrs. Solomon, on the other hand, took her own good time in assessing Chris Beth. "I suppose you know about the perils of being alone out here—no place to live and all?"

Chris Beth knew, only too well!

"Rainy weather and need of proper apparel?"

58

That, too—as well as Indians, wild animals, and no mail service.

"Though men outnumber women, finding a man whose intentions are pure is like hoping a peddler will come along with a good supply of darning needles?"

Well, of all the nerve! Chris Beth was tempted to walk away, but Mrs. Solomon seemed to sense that. "This is my daughter, Maggie."

With a rustle of taffeta, Maggie, who appeared to be about Chris Beth's own age, stepped from behind her mother. Maggie's lips, which looked suspiciously like she had rouged them, smiled. But her green-grape eyes did not. "So you've met Wilson North."

Chris Beth ignored the impertinent remark and forced herself to smile. "I hope we'll be friends, Maggie."

Maggie did not return her smile. "Warning—he's not the marryin' kind!"

So that's what put the burr under her mother's saddle! Something of the old spirit flared up: "Then I shall make it a point to see a lot of him," she said pertly. "I'm not the marrying kind either!"

When Chris Beth felt a hand at her elbow, she turned to face Wilson North. She flushed, wondering how much he had heard.

Later, Mrs. Malone asked how she had fared with the Solomons.

"I don't think they appreciate my presence in the settlement," Chris Beth told her. "Not the ladies, anyway."

Mrs. Malone laughed heartily. "Of course not! You're too pretty. Bertie Solomon's been tryin' to marry Maggie off to Wilson or Joe since her bornin' day."

Chris Beth wondered whether to reveal her little set-to with Maggie and decided against it. She wanted to give nobody the false impression that men entered into her planning—now or ever.

"They mean well, though." Mrs. Malone went on to explain the Solomons. "Bertie's just ambitious for that girl. Come an emergency here in the settlement and they put aside such trifles."

Her impression of the others?

Oh, very favorable, Chris Beth assured Mrs. Malone truthfully.

"Good folks—all of 'em. We're *family* here, a family of friends. But," Mrs. Malone sighed, "just like any other family, we're sometimes happy and peaceful and sometimes jealous like."

Well put, Chris Beth thought. She herself had been able to handle a baby sister—be overjoyed by her presence, in fact. But she remembered the all-too-frequent jealousies on Vangie's part.

"So I'd just forget Bertie's petty ways. Today she looked like she'd been samplin' my sauerkraut. Next time it's apt to be my quince honey." Mrs. Malone paused. "Somethin' else wrong?"

Chris Beth related the Graveyard Shack incident.

Mrs. Malone nodded understandingly but said nothing. Chris Beth volunteered, "I just wish I knew what to do about a place to stay. It seems so hopeless."

"Put your hope in the Lord!" Mrs. Malone replied. "Didn't I say you're among a family of friends?"

13
Inventory

❧

OCTOBER'S BLUSH DEEPENED. Soon it would
be November and time for school to open. The Malones, aided
by O'Higgin, had been busily preparing for winter. Fortunately, the rains had held their distance, so corn was in
shocks, pumpkins were piled up ready for storing in the hay,
and potatoes were in the root cellar. Chris Beth had insisted
on helping and, although she stained her hands and broke her
nails to the quick, she found something decidedly healing
about touching the rich, raw earth.

Mrs. Malone, busy with putting up green tomato mince-
meat, pickling, and canning the last of the late pears, welcomed her help in the kitchen. The children, delighted with
her ability to make gingerbread custard pies, redoubled their
efforts to help "Miss Mollie" when promised seconds on
dessert.

But helping was not enough on Chris Beth's part. She knew
that her being at Turn-Around Inn was an added burden.
When the old house sighed and settled down comfortably for
the night, she tried to do the same thing. But sometimes sleep
was slow in coming. She thought about Mama and Vangie and

wondered how they were. She thought about Indian summer back home and a sort of regional homesickness enveloped her. She thought about the heartbreak of her broken engagement. . . .

But somehow through it all she felt the pain lessening to the point that she was able to go about the business of taking and passing her exam when Nate brought it to her, unpacking the necessary school supplies she had brought along, and making arrangements to accept Joe's invitation to see the school next Wednesday. School would start the following Monday. Now if only she could find a place to stay!

It seemed incredibly dark when Chris Beth awakened on Wednesday morning. True, the days were shortening in preparation for the deep sleep of winter. But the darkness seemed too sudden. Before rolling up the feather bed, she opened the brocade drape and checked the sky from the front-room window. The sky was banked with dark clouds, and there was an eerie stillness that portends a storm no matter where one lives. Would Joe be coming when the skies looked like this?

Mrs. Malone's coffee was bracing, but Chris Beth was unable to shake off a sense of depression in keeping with the weather. Mrs. Malone was packing ham sandwiches made with leftovers from "salting down the pork" into a small picnic basket. She paused to note that the "needed moisture to green up the meadows" was overdue.

"But should we go to the school on a rainy day?"

"If you failed to show up on rainy days hereabouts, my child, our little ones would never learn to read!"

Joe, too, took the change of weather in stride. She noticed that he had thrown slickers in the back of the buggy, but he seemed almost unaware that a fine mist—typical of the area, she was to learn—had begun to fall. He seemed cheerful, almost exuberant, as he moved a container of garden-spearmint tea from underfoot. She climbed quickly into the buggy, before he could assist her. She wondered about his tests. Maybe passing explained his mood. But a certain reserve kept her from asking what might be construed as a personal question.

Chris Beth was relieved to see that, although the school was only a stone's throw from Graveyard Creek and the cemetery itself, the hateful shack was down-creek just enough to be out of view. The school building, made of split logs, looked a little more inviting than the "cabin."

"An acre of donated ground for students to romp on," Joe pointed out. And then they went inside.

To Chris Beth's amazement, there was no floor! Suddenly she wished she had failed the teacher's exam after all. "Does the roof leak?" she asked weakly.

"Some," Joe admitted, "but the men plan to reshake it this winter when there's less field work, and maybe even floor the room."

And chink up the cracks, too, she thought. Or was that the settlers' idea of natural ventilation?

"Oh, and Nate told me to give you this," Joe said, reaching into the pocket of his jacket. "Inventory."

Bravely accepting the scribbled list, Chris Beth read with increasing disbelief: "One broom (most new), one box chalk (part used last year), gallon water bucket (no leaks), one dipper (new!), and ten chords of green wood (bought by school board to keep within said budget)." *This was the year's equipment?*

A quick survey of the four walls showed a four-year-old calendar, a faded flag, and a book-lined shelf. She hurriedly examined the titles, laying them aside one by one in despair. "Oh, Joe, have you seen these?"

Joe hadn't, but as he looked, he too laid them aside after reading aloud, *Medical Science, Veterinary Practices, Navigation, Common Works on Engineering. . . ."*

"For my chart class? Why, the eighth-graders can't handle them!"

Joe agreed. And without warning they both burst into laughter. When finally Joe was in control of himself he explained, "Belonged to some professor who came over the

Applegate Trail, as I recall. The children bring some things, I understand."

"And I brought some—" She jumped. "What was that?"

A loud yell had pierced the silence around them. And out of the shrouds of mist the figure of a boy about 12 emerged.

"It's Elmer, one of the Goldsmith boys," Joe decided.

Elmer reached the door too winded to speak. Mutely, he handed a letter to Chris Beth.

And mutely she read the devastating contents.

14
Impossible Request

❧

THE FIVE OR SO MILES BACK to Turn-Around
seemed an eternity. At last the old inn's welcome outline
loomed ahead. The glory of the woods faded without the
sunshine. Shawls of fog wrapped the trees, causing Chris Beth
to wonder if ambush awaited her and Joe somewhere in the
damp quiet. She needed to be home to think.

If Joseph Craig noticed that she too was silent like the trees,
he gave no indication. She had been careful since their first
ride through the secluded stretch of woods that the small
intimate touching of the two of them not be misleading. She
found herself desperately anxious that his hand on her shoulder and her responsiveness had not promised anything further.
She wouldn't have thought herself capable of responding at
all. Well, it wouldn't happen again. It was dreadful to remember that she had forgotten herself . . . but most likely Joe had
forgotten it. He seemed almost formal in his politeness. She
could stop worrying.

But silence today had nothing to do with the incident. Chris
Beth reached into her satchel, hoping that the fateful letter
had been a bad dream like some of the others she had had. But

the letter crackled to her touch, unrolling slightly as if to free itself from the tight wad she had made and to force her to read in full what she had read only in part. *I'll never read it*, she told herself fiercely. *If I do, I'll die again and that's not possible!*

The awful truth, of course, was that what she *had* read stamped itself indelibly in her memory. Nothing would erase it. Trying would only smear it and make it spread, smudging the new page of life she had turned over in the settlement.

Oh, Mama, couldn't you just once have thought of something—anything—instead of putting it on my shoulders? In an effort to stave off making a decision concerning the impossible request, Chris Beth turned her thoughts to the mother-daughter relationship she wished her mother and she could have had. How nice it would have been to feel protected as a child, and then take her broken heart to Mama when Jon broke the engagement. But Mama remained forever the child. The truth was that Vangie was the favorite one—until now! Now Mama wouldn't even assume responsibility for helping Vangie. Poor Vangie. . . .

Thinking of her sister brought fragments of the letter back, dimly at first and then with startling clarity.

My dear Christen Elizabeth:
 By now you are settled, and that's good, for there are terrible problems at home. Your father is most distraught— poor man—and I have been not at all well. This is much more than a mother should be called upon to bear—one daughter leaving me alone to face friends with our recent embarrassment and running away to chase a dream. But now you must put aside all selfishness and come to the aid of the family.

As she stood in the one-room school building, desperately wishing she need read no further, Chris Beth was aware of Joe's eyes on her face. She turned away, afraid of what her eyes might reveal. Whatever had to be handled was her problem.

Mama would see to that! With dread, she returned to the letter but could not avoid skipping some lines.

Your sister has fallen into disgrace! Jonathan . . . Her father has disowned her . . . nobody to turn to . . . my only comfort being that Evangeline will find a place with you . . . families have to rally in such circumstances . . . nobody here need know . . . she'll be able to hide her shame. . . .

Oh, Mama, it's not just her father who disowned your daughter. You did, too! That's when Chris Beth wadded the letter into a ball, consumed by her emotions. What was it she felt? *Hatred,* of course, for the zealot, "Father Stein"! *Disgust* with her helpless mother—and guilt for feeling that way. *Shock,* yes, that Vangie, little Vangie, was somehow caught in such an unbelievable circumstance. In their circle, no "nice girl" gave birth out of wedlock. Illegitimacy occurred only among "trash." "Brier-patch babies," they were called, and Chris Beth remembered with shame that she and her friends had giggled behind their fans about such goings-on. She felt a growing distrust, too. This only confirmed what she had learned from Jon—a man was not to be trusted.

But, above all else, Chris Beth felt a gnawing fear—fear such as she had never known before. It was a writhing, living thing that clutched her heart and squeezed it dry. It had taken all the small legacy her own father had left for her to complete her teacher training and buy the train and stagecoach tickets to the Oregon Country. Vangie would have no money if the devilish man had kicked her out of their mother's home. She fought down a new fury at the thought. That house belonged to her own father. Her stepfather had no right . . . but she must not dwell on that.

If only she could get word to Vangie not to come. On second thought, where would her younger sister go if she rejected her?

Chris Beth was unaware that she had groaned until Joe said softly, "Let me help. I'm your friend, you know."

She realized then that Dobbin had stopped in front of Turn-Around Inn. "You can't help," she whispered through achingly-tight lips. "Nobody can." And sobbing she ran past Mrs. Malone and the wide-eyed Malone children who had waited for her return on the wide porch, eager to hear all about the new school year.

Inside, the first fire of the season crackled cheerfully in the fireplace. Fiercely, Chris Beth threw the wadded letter into it. Tongues of flame leaped up the chimney, taking with them the unread news that her sister already was on her way West.

15
Spreading the News

⌐

EMPTILY, as if in a sleep-induced dream, Chris Beth moved through the remainder of the week. Once again, she realized that the unthinkable is possible. One *could* die more than once—and then go on living. Maybe she had been "reborn" as in the Scriptures, as some of the settlers had quoted at the brush-arbor service. She wondered vaguely if one could be reborn a little each day. All this she was thinking in some distant corner of her mind as she counted with dismay the small sum of cash she had and wondered if it would cover the bare essentials for herself. If she had the nine lives the Malone children claimed for "Ambrose," the roving yellow tomcat, who would hand her crumbs like his? And for Vangie, too? But each time such terrifying thoughts invaded her sleepwalking, Chris Beth pushed them from her conscious mind. They would only bring panic, depression . . . bad dreams . . . hysteria. . . .

"Get a list ready. We're goin' school-shoppin' come Thursday!" Mrs. Malone's announcement dispensed with a need for roll-calling. *All* were going. And no questions. So life went on.

The general store was better-equipped than Chris Beth

would have supposed. The walls were lined with ropes, harness, pitchforks, twine, fly paper, and snakebite cures. Granite pots and pans were heaped on a long counter, and beside them picks and shovels. There were giant bins of sugar and coffee beans ready for grinding. Laces, buttons, garter-webbing, and corset stays on the notion counter were reassuring. She looked further.

Crudely-printed signs (lettered from tar, judging from their odor) boasted of supplies for MINERS, PROSPECTORS, FARMERS, LUMBERJACKS, and MILADAY'S SECRET NEEDS. Nothing secret about the display!

There was no fire in the pot-bellied stove, but men gathered around it anyway. As they whittled or played checkers, they talked of "harvestin'" and "'lection year."

Over all, there was an overpowering smell of camphor, sassafras, and something Chris Beth could describe only as a "new-merchandise scent," even though most of it looked "old enough to vote," Mrs. Malone had warned on their trip in from the settlement. The store should have looked dismal, but instead there was a warm, friendly atmosphere.

O'Higgin hurried to the "Blasting Counter," with the boys at his heels. Mrs. Malone propelled the girls to the dry goods department, where Mrs. Solomon presided.

Maggie stepped from behind shipping boxes without greeting.

"I need boots—" Chris Beth began.

"This way."

As Chris Beth struggled into and out of boots in an effort to find a pair remotely close to her size, Maggie said abruptly, "Did Elmer Goldsmith deliver your letter in proper shape?"

Why, yes, thank you.

Hoped it wasn't bad news.

Well-no!

She would be able to *stay* here then?

Oh, yes indeed! As a matter of fact her sister would be joining her soon.

Chris Beth could have bitten off her tongue. At the same

time she secretly took satisfaction in the look of undisguised shock in the other girl's eyes. *Another Southern belle in the settlement*, it plainly said, *when one's too many!*

Mrs. Malone joined them. "And we'll all be welcomin' her, won't we, Maggie?"

The girl nodded sullenly as she accepted money for the boots and Chris Beth's few other purchases.

How much does Mrs. Malone know? Chris Beth wondered. It didn't matter. Neither did she care how Mrs. Malone had come to know at all. What mattered was to have the news out in the open. She and the older woman exchanged a look of understanding. How better to spread the news than through the spiteful Maggie? Now that it was told, Chris Beth felt as if a boulder had been removed from her chest. She could breathe. And didn't that mean living?

On the way out, Mrs. Malone paused to look at an enormous heart-shaped box. Just below the red velvet rose that decorated the lid, assorted chocolates showed invitingly through the cellophane window—round and plump, topped with nuts and dried fruits.

Unaware that anybody watched, Mrs. Malone reached out and touched the bow, then jerked her hand away guiltily. But Chris Beth had seen a sense of longing in the woman's eyes. O'Higgin had seen it too, apparently.

"Mighty pretty, eh, Miss Mollie?" he said, moving to her side.

"Mighty frivolous, if you ask me!"

Somehow Chris Beth knew that Mrs. Malone had never eaten a chocolate candy. And something in that knowledge made her sad.

The trip back to Turn-Around Inn was festive. The children were exuberant over the bolts of calico that Mrs. Malone had bought. Chris Beth felt relieved to have spoken out. And O'Higgin made it complete; "Horehound for all of ye— though mighty frivolous it be!" His mischievous blue eyes rolled toward Mrs. Malone with the announcement.

Chris Beth saw Andy count the three candies which were

his portion as a king would count his treasures. Then, swallowing hard, he handed one to Wolf. She suddenly wished with all her heart that the whole world knew of the sharing and caring that went on here in this so-called "wilderness." It seemed only natural that she should quietly slip one of her own pieces of horehound into the little boy's pocket.

16
Blessed Assurance

꘡

ON SATURDAY, after helping Mrs. Malone with the baking, Chris Beth asked Ned to take her to the school. The skies had cleared and the building looked, if not brighter, at least less dismal. Ned swept the bare floor, straightened the lines of double desks (logs, really, with rough board tables as desk tops), and wiped away the summer's dust. Chris Beth suggested that the boy lay a fire in the big wood stove while she "decorated."

"Never saw it look so purty," Ned said after she had made bouquets of colored leaves and Oregon grapes. "Can I help more?"

"Yes—if you have a pocket knife, cut out the letters for 'WELCOME BACK.'" She handed him scraps of wrapping paper.

Ned did a fine job with making the letters, but when it came to arranging them, he was lost. Spelling was a problem with the boy, undoubtedly. *I'll have to find a way to help*, she thought.

On the way home, the two of them stopped to pick hazel

nuts. "They're fun for roastin' over the fire," Ned promised for the evening ahead.

Sunday was clear and cold. A crisp wind blew in overnight, bringing what O'Higgin called "butcherin' weather." The beef he spoke of would be put up in jars. "First, we be eatin' all we can. Then what we can't eat, we can!"

Chris Beth smiled at his wit ("natural as his breathin'," Mrs. Malone said of it), but something within her recoiled a little at his words. Winter was near, no doubt about it. She pressed her cheek against the pane of the front-room window and found it cold. A playful breeze was teasing speckled leaves from the oak in the yard and, although clouds were swept behind the mountains, a thin wisp of fog trailed warningly below the peaks. Something whispered frost.

"All aboard!" O'Higgin called from the wagon. Since Mrs. Malone had discovered that there was room for them all in the wagon if they "sorta scrooched up," she no longer felt in the way. Mrs. Malone laid a quilt over the children's feet. They promptly pulled it over their heads—with Wolf in the middle—and huddled together happily.

On the way to church, Chris Beth heard strange cries overhead. And then a familiar voice called out, "Canadian honkers!" Joe had joined the Malone wagon at the intersection. It was good to see him, she thought fleetingly, then returned her eyes to the sky. For a moment she envied the honkers—free creatures heading for the Southern climes. But their cries reminded her that they weren't so free after all. They too were escaping.

"Wilson," Joe interrupted her thoughts, "is giving Doc Dullus a hand over the weekend." He made no further explanation.

Would Joe ask her to ride with him? He did not.

The circuit rider, to the pleasure of the congregation appeared unexpectedly for the worship service. He would be around for a few days, if "somebody can sort of board and keep me." Hands went up everywhere. This meant that they could be marrying off the young folks who had been waiting, have the man say the proper words for those who had suffered losses in their families, and enjoy news of what was going on in churches of the widely scattered communities.

Joe made a special effort to introduce Jonas Brown to Chris Beth, saying, "He's been a great help to me."

She wished she had been able to concentrate on the man's sermon. There should be a word of appreciation probably, but a polite curtsy was all she could manage. The look of surprise on the preacher's face told her that such acknowledgment of an introduction labeled her as a newcomer—maybe a foreigner! It was a little embarrassing and she regretted the formality that her own church had demanded back home.

Of course she had been expected to listen then, too, knowing that there would be a test on the sermon before her stepfather would allow her and Vangie to eat. Well, at least nobody was going to test her here, she hoped. Her mind had been on all the problems that lay ahead—problems which a demanding schedule had allowed her no time to think about until the quiet of today. The dreaded first day of school . . . where she could find lodging . . . what she and Vangie were to do.

When all the Malones were loaded into the wagon, O'Higgin offered a hand to the two women. "Trouble is when there be preachin', there be too little song."

The children heard and came from beneath the quilt. "Let's sing!" they all shouted at once.

The Irishman needed no coaxing. "Bringin' in the Sheaves," he announced, glancing at the burnished heads of late-ripening grain still in the fields.

As the group sang, Chris Beth joined in tentatively. It felt good to sing. It had been a long time, she realized suddenly, since she had sung. Mama had said she had a good voice—one of the few things she praised about her older daughter.

On and on they sang, the wagon wheels and horses' hooves seeming to keep time to their voices. Without realizing it, Chris Beth's own voice rose above the others. Her contralto seemed to drift up the mountain slopes and come back like an echo-chorus.

The others had stopped singing—even O'Higgin—as she sang, "Blessed assurance, Jesus is mine!—" and stopped. The group, apparently thinking she had forgotten the words, picked up the refrain.

Actually, she needed to think. *Blessed assurance!* The phrase echoed again and again—this time against the slopes of her heart. And then she remembered one phrase of Scripture quoted at last Sunday's service: "Help thou my unbelief."

Gripping the arm rest of the spring seat, Chris Beth tasted the words and found them sweet.

Maybe—just maybe—the answers would come. This, after all, was a land of miracles.

17
First Day—
Its "Awful Glory"

⤜

*N*OVEMBER CERTAINLY PUT ON *its most somber garments for the first day,* Chris Beth thought as she prepared herself to greet students of assorted sizes and colors who romped around the schoolyard. Earlier, dark clouds had bumped against the mountains, dumping scattered showers in the valley. Even now, fog was caught along the summit as if in silent watch. At least there would be no need to caution the children to wipe their shoes—not with a dirt floor! It would be damp, though. She bent stiffly to light the fire Ned had laid. She would probably be unable to walk tomorrow, she supposed, after her first ride astride a horse! O'Higgin had saddled the speckled pony for her.

A check of the hard-enameled watch pinned onto the lapel of her jacket said it was time to call the children inside. Chris Beth smoothed her dark hair and on impulse tucked a bronze chrysanthemum behind a heavy braid. Mrs. Malone had picked an enormous armload in preparation for what she called the "awful glory" of the first day!

"Just move in gentle like, knowin' water finds its own

level," she had said with her usual insight. "Things'll right up before you know it. Nothing's ever so horrible—or so wonderful, as the case may be—as the first time around."

Chris Beth remembered and smiled as she pulled at the rope suspended to the giant outside "dinner bell."

Thirty-one children, eyeing her suspiciously, lined up and marched in wordlessly.

"Good morning, children!" she said brightly, hoping that her nervousness did not show. "I am your teacher."

Immediately a hand shot up. The little girl in a faded pinafore (one of the Goldsmith children, Chris believed) spoke in a voice as wee as herself. "Whatta we call you?"

"I am Miss Kelly."

The child nodded. "But whatta we *call* you?"

Confused, Chris Beth was about to repeat her surname when Ned Malone came to the rescue. Politely, lifting his hand for recognition, the boy said, "She means last year we called Miz Andrews Miss Lizzie."

First names then? But Miss Chris Beth was too cumbersome, let alone Miss Christen Elizabeth! Well, if that other Elizabeth could be Miss Lizzie, she could be.

"Call me Miss Chrissy," she smiled, liking the sound of it.

One year's teaching in a city school was little help in a situation like this. Would they like to share a little of what they had done over the summer? The children stared at her blankly. Why, when we all did the same? their looks asked her. Well, then, they could introduce themselves and she would enter their names and grade level in the roll book.

The Malones, she knew, of course—one of them in seven of the eight grades. Ditto for the Goldsmiths, except that she would need to know their first names. Chris Beth recognized some of the other children from having met their parents at Sunday services, but there were strangers, too. She especially noticed a little almond-eyed boy who sat, with folded hands, apart from the others.

"Your name, please?" She made a point of smiling.

There was no reply.

"He can't talk," one of the children said.

A *mute*? But no! "He can too talk!" Another contradicted. "He just talks Chinaman!"

"*Chinese*," she corrected, and smiled again at the frightened child.

"I'll help," an especially bright-eyed child told Chris Beth. "I can speak it a little."

"Good." Chris Beth decided that the boy was probably as bright as his eyes. "I'll need his name—and yours."

"He's Wong—Wong Chu. They live in Railroad Camp way off somewhere. The others don't come to school." He inhaled importantly, "And me, I'm Wil, with one *l*. 'Young Wil' I'm called, or 'Willie.' Just write it down Willie Ames."

My! This one was a talker. Chris Beth smiled in amusement.

The job finished, Chris Beth felt a bit more at ease. But there was the matter of curriculum! With a sudden burst of inspiration, she announced that they would just start in where they had left off last year.

The children seemed satisfied. They rifled through sacks and satchels, bringing out papers—most of them dog-eared and dirty—and a few thin books, too old for titles to be readable. *These* were the supplies the board chairman had promised the children would bring?"

But there were more surprises to come, none of them reassuring, "Oh, I brung a ball," one child announced, and promptly bounced it on the dirt floor. Six others, inspired by the boy's bravery, followed suit.

Startled, Chris Beth confiscated the balls and announced that they would become "school property." The children were awed to silence, and she knew she had won. Now to use the discipline constructively!

"We'll *all* enjoy ball games, if assignments are completed, *if* the floor is swept, *if* the wood is brought in, and *if*," she stressed, "we all behave ourselves!" (*Base hit!* she congratulated herself.)

"Now," she said matter-of-factly, "let's get down to business."

There would be a "division of labor."

A *what*?

Older students will help the younger ones.

Two recesses plus 45 minutes at noon.

But, Teacher, some has to go—

Well, yes, in emergencies.

"And there's a barrel stave outside for wiping their shoes on before coming back, if it's raining." That was young Wil again.

Most of the children had slates—a few of them new, but mostly broken pieces. One child drew out a shingle that someone had worked very hard to smooth with a jackknife. On it the little girl was laboriously lettering her ABC's with a chunk of soft red rock. Chris Beth's throat ached with compassion. What she couldn't do with a little of the money she had always taken for granted!

At recess time an eighth-grade boy (he claimed) sauntered up. "Miss Chrissy, this is my baby sister," he said.

Yes, she remembered the frail, frightened little girl.

"Ma wanted I should tell you she ain't had no time, so she ain't learnt her nothin'."

Chris Beth supposed the gawkish boy's explanation would have been amusing at one time. Even now, it would make a "cute little story" for some afternoon tea back home. But to her, these children's teacher, it was heartbreaking.

There's an awful gap between us, she thought. But somehow that was no threat anymore. *Neither they nor I can push through it. But I understand boys and girls. And they understand me. I'll do what everybody else does in this new land. I'll simply build a stile across that gap and we'll all climb over!*

And there was an "awful glory" in the thought, or was it a revelation?

18
Holy Joe

❧

EVEN WITH THE few books she had brought along, Chris knew there were not enough to go around. And none of them were alike. She wondered aloud just how to manage. These pioneer children, she had seen right away, were good decision-makers.

"I bet everybody's got one of these," one of the older boys suggested. He raised a rumpled sheet of fine-print paper—too fine to see from where Chris Beth stood at the front of the classroom.

A ripple of excitement told her that what the boy said was true. All but the beginners (who would be in a "chart class") pulled out a similar sheet of paper.

A single sheet! They were supposed to learn from that? And what on earth could it be, anyway?"

"Can I read?" the boy asked eagerly.

Before she could say, "*May* I read?" the others had chimed in, each begging to read.

Chris Beth resisted the temptation to rap sharply on the box she called a desk. After all, she certainly did not want to dampen any enthusiasm that these students had for reading.

"I asked her first!" the older boy told the others.

"So he did," Chris Beth agreed. "You'll all get a turn, I promise. And then I'll read you a story."

As the boy stood, she checked the register to find his name. Beltran. Beltran? Oh, yes, he was one of the "Basque" children that Nate had introduced. Sheep-raisers, weren't they? She checked the name again.

"Go ahead, Burton."

Burton, pleased that Miss Chrissy had remembered his name, grinned and said, "Mine's page 500." Then, haltingly, he began to read as Chris Beth digested the news that no pages matched.

"The . . . Lord . . . is . . . my . . . *shepherd!*" The last word came out triumphantly. Then the strange, surprising singsong continued, "I . . . shall . . . not . . . *want!*"

Later Chris Beth realized that she had allowed Burton to read too long. The other children were moving restlessly. But she had been so torn between pity for the children who wanted so desperately to learn and shock that they had nothing to read but a page from the Bible (though they liked reading it) that time meant nothing to her. Was this where they had left off last year?

Still trying to work her way through the maze of emotions, Chris Beth allowed the children to read one by one. But she did remember to call time so that each would get a turn. When the last reader finished, she announced that they would take an early recess.

But the children were having no part of it! "Story, story!" they all cried. "You promised!"

Well, so she had. Chris Beth reached for a copy of *Grimm's Fairy Tales.*

But again the children changed her plans. "Wait till we're ready to go home for that one! We want to hear 'Noah Zark' . . . No, 'Dan'el and the Lion's Den' . . . Ump-uh, 'David 'n Goldilocks'!"

It was impossible for Chris Beth to keep a straight face at the titles. Taking her smile as consent, they leaned forward on the rough-board tables. "She's gonna!" whispered the "Baby Sister" Ma hadn't "learnt." There was pin-drop quiet.

Chris Beth fumbled through her literature books. Somewhere there were some Bible stories in one of them, she remembered. She had fallen into this trap somehow, but what was the harm, she supposed, just this once? Finally she came upon the story of the baby Moses' rescue by Pharoah's daughter.

"But before I read," she said to the waiting children, "will one of you tell me where the pages you're reading came from?"

"The Holy Bible!"

Well, she had asked for that one!

"I mean," she rephrased, "how did you each come to have a page?"

"Teacher let us use 'em," the older Smith boy defended. "A Holy Joe come by givin' 'em away, page at a time."

The rest of the children nodded.

A Holy Joe?

Their name for a preacher, young Wil told her. And the way he said *their* names set himself quite apart.

"Thank you for telling me," Chris Beth said quietly. "But we will not be using that title for a preacher—or anybody else. It's improper and it's—" she struggled for a word, "wrong," she concluded.

As she read the story, Chris Beth noted that every eye was upon her. Did they enjoy stories this much, or was there something about this particular one? Or was it the Bible in general? Nobody had prepared her for this.

Nobody had prepared her for the children's begging—*pleading*—with her to read another and another.

"It's past recess time—"

"We don't care!" they cried in unison.

Chris Beth closed the book. "But I've run out of stories."

"Then read this," and before she could stop him, Burton Beltran was handing her the Twenty-Third Psalm.

Never had children touched her so much. The lump in her

chest moved up into her throat, threatening to bring uncontrolled tears. In that emotional state, she began:

"The Lord is my shepherd; I shall not want."

As she read, the memory came back that she used to read this passage over and over. She knew *how* it should read, to her surprise. The words flowed softly and sweetly—she knew this was so—until she finished: "And I will dwell in the house of the Lord *forever!*"

To her surprise, she had emphasized the final word as had Burton when he read. *Why?* She wondered as she dismissed the children with a wave of her hand.

As Chris Beth reached beneath her desk for the balls to be distributed to the children, she was aware suddenly of a shadow in the doorway. And there stood Joe.

"I've come to ask for your help," he said quietly. "I—I heard you read and—I—could I be one of your students?"

"You mean—here—I don't understand."

I'm fumbling for words as much as he is, she thought.

"Anywhere. The place doesn't matter." He had regained his composure and seemed to try to put her at ease.

"But why—on what? I mean in what area do you need help?"

"Reading," he smiled. "You see, I'm studying to be what you might call a Holy Joe."

19
Born-Again Teacher!

❧

A WEEK PASSED. Chris Beth hurried to school an hour before the children in an effort to be well-prepared for the trying day ahead. She stayed until darkness spread over the valley. She overheard Mrs. Malone express concern to O'Higgin, who had taken to practically living at Turn-Around Inn since the weather had grown damp. "Colder'n north side of an igloo, it is, down 'longside the branch." It was a surprise to learn that his quarters were only a tent to sleep in. It must be miserable.

"Should build a cabin like normal folks," Mrs. Malone sniffed when he complained.

"Should live me in a hoose."

"*House!*" she said sharply, then reddened when the Irishman grinned in agreement.

Both women knew that O'Higgin's services were nearly indispensable. Ned could never carry on alone with the milking, caring for the cattle and stock, cultivating, and harvesting—not to mention constant sawing down trees and blasting out stumps in the preparation of new cultivating ground.

But O'Higgin's presence about the place offered more than two helpful hands. There was a real need for a man in the household—with the children, yes, but Chris Beth suspected that Mrs. Malone secretly welcomed his male companionship in spite of her constant claims of "bein' no leaner." They discussed everything, including Chris Beth herself.

"She's workin' past time for the cows to come home, and it can be downright dangerous."

"I'll speak with the lassie," and for once O'Higgin was serious.

Chris Beth knew they were right. She was working hard. Once she would have felt driven to succeed, and for the wrong reasons. There would have been a need to save face, both with friends and family back home and *herself*. But now the reasons were different. There was born within her a new commitment, a burning desire to help these children learn in whatever way they learned best. If they liked to hear her sing, she would sing! And if they liked to read from the Bible, they would do that, too! Under different circumstances she could have laughed at herself, the "born-again" teacher.

Somewhere in back of her busy mind, Chris Beth knew that there were problems to be resolved, some of them pressing, but they would have to wait their turn. The brooch . . . a place to live . . . Vangie's future . . . a letter to Mama as to why her half-sister's coming West was out of the question . . . some alternate plan that Mama would never be able to come up with in her own helplessness.

And then suddenly would come the realization that the problems were simply on a treadmill, going nowhere toward solution. She was just too busy, too tired.

Then something else would try to push itself from below the surface of her subconscious mind. Joe—Joseph Craig—a *preacher*? Why should she be concerned? She shouldn't be, but she was. *Angry*? No—not now. *Glad*? She didn't know.

"All right," she would say aloud at those times. "So I do have problems. So do these children!"

And the new Chris Beth would reenter her private world of

cutting out letters of the alphabet, preparing sums to write on the battered blackboard, and underlining passages she wished to read from the New Testament. Maybe a discussion would be helpful after reading? She had chewed her cedar pencil in concentration on that one. Of course it would be helpful! And maybe some chart stories, too, for the beginners. The older children could do the artwork.

Chris Beth was unaware that as she worked her face had taken on a new glow. But Mrs. Malone noticed—not that she could mention it to anybody. There was only O'Higgin to talk to. And that silly gander was wearing the same shine! The difference was that she didn't know Chris Beth's secret.

20
Lesson in Waiting

❦

CHRIS BETH WAS WEARING her new glow, enhanced by the rose wool shawl Mrs. Malone had knitted for the chilly evenings, when Joe came for his first lesson. Lesson in what she wasn't exactly sure; she only knew that he had mentioned help in reading.

"You look lovely," he told her as she took his hat at the door of Turn-Around Inn.

Now why should that simple compliment embarrass her? Chris Beth knew that color stained her face and hated herself for the schoolgirl silliness. *When young men paid me compliments back home, I thanked them. When Wilson North says the same words, I'm offended. And what's the matter with me anyway that I keep comparing these two men!* Then, for the first time, came the awareness that Jonathan Blake had not entered her mind at all.

The realization was so startling that her words were more abrupt than she intended in the curt "Thank you" to Joe. Then softening, she asked, "How may I be of help, Joe?"

"Wh-what was your reaction to my being a—a preacher?"

"I'll answer your question with one of my own: 'What has my reaction to do with it?'"

"A lot—everything."

We're talking around the subject, not about it, Chris Beth knew. The fact was that they were talking about their feelings without bringing them out in the open. That was unlike her—probably unlike Joe, too—but was there really anything to discuss?"

Joe broke the silence. "Would you rather have known sooner?"

Chris Beth shook her head. "I couldn't have accepted it sooner," she said truthfully.

"Then I was right in waiting?" He reached for her hand.

Chris drew back, and to her surprise, Joe laughed. "And I'm prepared to wait some more."

"The reading—" she began faintly and was surprised to find her heart was running away foolishly.

Later, reviewing the events of the evening, Chris Beth felt a deep admiration for Joe's acceptance of her little rebuff and his willingness to delve into the business at hand unselfconsciously. The fact was, she admired everything about this quiet man. But there were to be no romantic involvements. . . .

"It's the stuttering. I'm going to need this voice in a pulpit, heaven knows—no irreverence! I only stammer badly when I'm embarrassed or when I read—" He paused.

"We'll work on it," she promised.

And without further ado, the lesson began. So did Joe's waiting, she knew.

21
A Clash of "Wils"

❧

CHRIS BETH TURNED from the chalkboard where she was writing "Articulation Words" from *McGuffey's Fourth Reader* that she had brought from the school in the South. The children had come so far so fast, she thought with pride. It was good that she herself had taken all those speech-improvement courses in Boston, where they teased her about her slurred vowels. This way she could pronounce distinctly and have the children repeat after her.

Of course, young Wil had been a help. He was an excellent student, had a grasp on the reading skills, and was willing to help others. But he was a bit of a problem, too. There were times when he daydreamed—looking wistfully out the window when he should have been doing his sums. Generally he chose arithmetic time to go into his little dream world, and, if coaxed out of it, spent his time pulling Sadie Goldsmith's braids or tickling the bottom of anybody seated in front of him with a feather poked through the crack of a log-seat. And he knew every crack!

In spite of his mischief-making, Chris Beth thought as she looked at the entire student body, *I love every hair on each*

90

head, but there's something so special about this one. Yes, no doubt about it, he was her favorite if she allowed herself to have one. But she refused to let it show. And something about this little spirit let her know that he wouldn't appreciate being "teacher's pet."

"Wil," she spoke from the front of the class. "Will you come up and recite now?"

Chris Beth listened to his reading and checked his arithmetic paper. Finding it less than half-finished, she asked him why. "I don't like it—didn't like it in Portland either! Teacher was a grouch."

Portland? She ignored the *grouch*.

Went to school there till end of school last year. Visited this summer.

Did he like it here?

Shrug.

What part did he like best?

Baseball. Until she took his ball.

The conversation had been quiet, and the nine-year-old had been polite. Still, Chris Beth felt that she had failed to communicate the importance of mastering addition and subtraction. Here was a fine mind that she was not going to see wasted.

She checked the register to find the name of his parents. Several names were still missing, and Wil's parents were among them.

Their little talk had apparently done no good. Wil sat gazing out the window instead of completing the arithmetic paper. Chris Beth went back and whispered that he should finish, as literature time was coming in a few minutes. He enjoyed that, she knew. The boy nodded, took up his pencil, and began what appeared to be the picture of a musket, the best she could tell from the corner of her eye. Well, it had to stop. A note at the end of the week. Today, if this kept up.

The climax came in literature class. "How many memorized a part of 'Hiawatha'?" she asked, and was pleased to see several hands go up. She had read them the poem yesterday, explained its meaning, and assigned as extra credit any favorite lines they wished to commit to memory.

"Volunteers?" she asked.

Most of the children were shy, looking at each other instead of her. Not Wil! As usual, he called out, "Let me be first, Miss Chrissy."

Maybe the recognition would do him good. "Fine, Wil."

Young Wil stepped forward. His face had the look of an angel, but there was a gleam in his eye that she had come to recognize.

Loudly and clearly—and, yes, beautifully, she had to admit— he recited, then stopped as if to make sure he had the attention of the entire class. Or did he need prompting? She glanced at her book. ". . . And the *naked* old Nakomis . . ." as the others burst into smothered giggles, then uncontrolled laughter.

There was no need in going on with the class. Wisely, Chris Beth announced recess 15 minutes early.

"Wil!" she called above the din of voices. "Remain in a minute, please."

When he was beside her, Chris Beth said, "I tried to talk earlier and we didn't get as far as I had hoped. Then you upset the class."

"I know," he surprised her by saying.

"I think we should have a little talk with your parents, and I'd like to have you sit in on it."

Wil sat silent.

"Would you like that?"

He shook his head but said nothing.

"I'm going to invite your mother—"

"She's not here!" The words were spoken fiercely.

"Then I will write to your father. He would be your legal guardian."

"But he—I can't—I don't want—" Tears were about to overflow.

"Please don't argue," she said firmly. "It's for your own good."

She wrote a little "To whom it may concern" note, explaining that she would like to have the guardian of Wil Ames come for a conference Monday after school.

Young Wil looked at her reproachfully for a moment, then squared his young shoulders and shot her the roguish smile she had come to associate with trouble. "A clash of wills," he grinned.

22
When Tongues
Are Loosed

❧

ON SUNDAY THE settlers gathered at Turn-Around Inn as planned. The circuit-riding Jonas Brown was "pourin' out the glory" elsewhere, Mr. Goldsmith told the worshipers, but he was with them "in spirit." Chris Beth wondered what good he could do either group in that disembodied state and carefully avoided Wilson's eyes lest they smile at the quaint phrase.

She looked at the congregation instead. Their number surprised her. The front room was large indeed, but it was totally inadequate for the men, women, and children who had flocked there on this dreary November day. It was probably an illusion, but the very walls of the sturdy house seemed to be bowed out as if it were letting its ribs expand in an effort to accommodate the usual group and the obvious newcomers.

After the singing, O'Higgin laid down his tuning fork and "opened the doors of the church" in an invitation to all who "felt the spirit increased inside" to give testimonials. Chris Beth watched and listened intently as one by one the men rose to speak of the blessings in their everyday lives. "Applies for all who come a'callin' . . . grain for the motley cattle . . .

'nuf eggs to oversupply the gen'ral store . . . and all the love You drop from the windows of heaven." One or two read haltingly (less well than their children) from "the Good Book," and some only held the Bible up in silent reverence. *They are unable to read at all,* she thought. The realization touched her heart. *All the more reason I must redouble my efforts, not slow down.*

Suddenly a familiar voice broke into her reverie. Joseph Craig was reading, "The Lord is my shepherd; I shall not want."

The words of the beautiful psalm were familiar to Chris Beth. What touched her so deeply was Joe's deep, throaty voice, his perfect articulation—and the drama of it all. Tears stung behind her eyelids. Her heart drummed heavily in her chest, and there was a throbbing in her throat. *I'm trembling like a leaf,* she thought. Yet there was such an unexplainable joy within that she wanted to shout "Amen!" when he finished.

As all heads bowed for the benediction, Chris Beth allowed the tears to roll unashamedly down her face. Let Maggie look. Let the whole world see—see that she felt pride in this humble man and the private little miracle that someway, somehow, she had helped loose his tongue. And, yes, let them all see what she knew now—that some invisible hand had moved their callings closer together. The two of them had a job to do in this settlement. So let *all* tongues be loosed!

23
Boston Buck

~❧~

SUNDAY'S STARTLING REVELATION brought with it a reminder that great visions are no more than that unless the one to whom they're given puts them to work. There was a need to be practical. The valley was destined to boom—Chris Beth felt that. As more settlers came, the school would need enlarging, and there would be need for a church. Money would be a real problem, so Mrs. Malone certainly needed space as she offered temporary quarters for worship services to the increasing congregation.

So, Chris Beth decided, *with every conference, beginning with Monday's, I'll inquire about lodging.* Maybe young Wil's father would know of somebody who would take in a temporary boarder. Then if Vangie did come—oh, dear, she must get a note to Mama.

She had written note after note saying that her half-sister, in that "delicate condition" (for Mama's sake she couldn't call it "pregnancy") just must not travel. Always at that point she would pause, wonder what to say next, and then discard the letter. Maybe she should write to Vangie instead—only

96

Vangie wasn't living there. She had better talk to Mrs. Malone. No, she had her share of problems. Joe?

Waiting after school on Monday for Wil's father, Chris Beth pondered further what to do. At least it was good to be able to think clearly. Maybe answers would come.

Suddenly she was aware that a shadow had fallen across the door. Rising from behind her desk, she stepped forward. "Mr.—"

But the figure she saw was the half-nude body of the first Indian she had ever seen. Her first impulse was to cry out, but something about the eyes which pierced hers silenced her. As he stealthily moved closer, she saw strange markings on the muscular body, crude shapes painted with what looked to be berry juices. A beaded band held back the straight, black hair that fell below his shoulders.

And then he reached as if to touch her. She drew back in panic. What did a lone woman do to defend herself? There was no escape—no back door—and where was Wil's father?

He took another step forward, still reaching, but his hand closed around her paisley satchel before it reached her. With sucked-in breath, Chris Beth watched in terror as the man opened the bag and emptied its contents on the floor. In horror she saw that the pearl-and-sapphire brooch lay at the Indian's bare feet. With a grunt of satisfaction, he stooped, picked it up, and pinned it in his heavy hair. Then, wordlessly, he turned toward the door.

A movement at the window caused Chris Beth to look up. What appeared to be a whole tribe was trying to crawl into the classroom. In paralyzed awe, she waited.

What happened next startled Chris Beth as much as the Indians. There was a loud "Boom!" Fire seemed to fly in all directions and the room filled immediately with sulfurous black smoke. The Indians let out cries of fear and fled into the forest, except for the Indian who had taken the pin. He lay prostrate on the dirt floor, writhing and moaning. Surely he must be mortally wounded.

Before she could decide what to do, a familiar voice issued a command, "Give the lady her bag!"

Wilson—Wilson was here! But how? Why? And then she saw him put a warning finger to his lips. She waited, unsure for what.

The Indian rose, but stood in sullen silence, making no move in her direction.

"More fire?"

"No!" There was panic in the Indian's eyes. Still, he was unwilling to do as Wilson had commanded. "Boston name," he said.

Wilson appeared to be considering the exchange. "You win," he conceded. "You are brave, but sometimes unwise. If I give you a Boston name, will you leave the lady alone? She lives here now."

"Boston—Boston." She could see that he agreed to the pact.

"From now on you shall bear proudly the name of Buck—*Boston* Buck! Now return the bag *and* the pin."

Boston Buck did as told and ran away happily chanting, "Name Boston Buck, name Boston Buck!"

And what happened next startled her even more. Chris Beth remembered later that the room grew fuzzy. She swayed on her feet and would have fallen except that Wilson's arms were around her.

Everything that had happened was an incredible dream. But the arms around her were very real—undeniably reassuring. It seemed very natural that he should be there as she broke into uncontrollable sobs.

Wilson smoothed the strands of hair that had eased from her prim hairdo, winding it around his fingers as he did so. "Go ahead, cry," he soothed as one would soothe a child.

"It's just that I get one thing resolved—or think I do—and then something worse happens—and I get in deeper, till I can't handle anything—" Chris Beth knew she was blubbering but she had no power to stop. "And you laugh at me."

"Not anymore." He was right, she realized, but she felt too weary to answer.

He continued softly, "Why must you go on fighting life so hard? Why can't you be like the rest of us and just lean a little?"

"I've been hurt that way." The fatigue was closing in.

"Mostly your pride, I'd say. And we've all been hurt, my dear."

For no good reason, she felt the tears again. Wilson brushed them away gently. "Let's not fight anymore. You're among friends—not in enemy territory. And there's so much we need to talk about."

He had spoken the truth, of course. She drew back. "You first," she said. And together they sat down on one of the split logs, with his arms still around her. And there, in the comforting circle, Chris Beth listened to Wilson North's story, less surprised by it then by her unquestioning acceptance.

24
What Will People Say?

‒⊘‒

THE SUN HAD SHONE BRIEFLY as she and Wilson talked, but as they left the schoolhouse, clouds gathered again. In the sudden downpour that followed, the two of them were drenched. Chris Beth had grown accustomed to the Oregon Country's sudden moods—its sun and rain, with rainbows between. She didn't mind. As they rode in the rain, visions of Mama and Vangie's rushing to close the shutters came to mind. In a storm, Mama would get a headache and little Vangie would wrap her head in the duck-down pillow.

I'm glad I told Wilson about Vangie's coming, but guarded the details, she thought. *When?* She didn't know. And, of course, Wilson had too much style to ask *why*. In fact, *why's* seemed of no importance to the wonderful people of the settlement.

It was growing dark and Wilson would ride with her to Turn-Around Inn, he told her. Having said so much already, there seemed to be no further need for words. Chris Beth was glad. It gave her an opportunity at least to review some of what Wilson had told her. Sorting it all out and putting it into some kind of perspective would take a long time. That made no difference. They had covered enough ground to make her

heart sing like the meadowlark who seemingly was un-
daunted by neither rain nor approaching twilight.

It was good to know about the Indians. Most of them were
on the reservation. "Boston Buck" had refused to go, prefer-
ring the ways of the "Bostons." He was given to wandering
around—even in and out of houses on occasion—but he
meant no harm, Wilson explained. Nuisance though he sometimes was, he more than made up for it by showing the
settlers the best fishing waters, where the wild raspberries and
strawberries grew, and how to trap game and dig clams. "The
grasshoppers we can do without," Wilson had chuckled.

Chances were slim that the Indian would return, and, if he
did, it would be as her friend. As to the others, they were
strangers—probably wandered in from the reservation. They
probably came out of curiosity. Still, Wilson had deemed it
wise to use his usual "magic" just in case. The explosive
concoction was a little trick he used when tramping around in
a strange patch of woods looking for certain botanical species
for his book. "They can't quite figure whether I'm a madman
or a god! Just as well keep 'em guessing."

Indians disposed of, Chris Beth had asked how on earth
Wilson just happened to be there when she needed him. He
didn't "just happen" to be on hand, of course.

"You sent for me, remember?"

The only person she had sent for was Wil's father.

"Guardian," he corrected. "I'm the to-whom-it-may-con-
cern!"

As Chris Beth's overtaxed mind tried to absorb still another
shock, Wilson explained. His sister had made an unfortunate
marriage to an irreputable drummer who divided his time
between liquor and dance-hall women. Eventually, he left her
with a small child, a fact she had been unable to accept.
Wilson had paused there, biting his lip to control his emotions, and Chris Beth guessed that a broken heart had caused
the young mother to take her own life.

"My father was killed shortly afterward in an accident at
the grist mill. It was more than my mother's weak heart could

stand." The three of them were buried in a little family plot behind the big house where he and young Wil lived now. *How sad for them all.*

"But I have the boy," he said proudly. "I tried sending him away to school for his own good, summers too, but he got homesick. He's a bright youngster—isn't he?" He hesitated.

"Oh, very!" Chris Beth assured him. "Fact is, he's outsmarting me. We'll talk about his interests. I can help him better now that I know." Suddenly she laughed. "I understand now what our little wizard meant when he said there would be a 'clash of wills'!"

Wilson nodded. "*Wils*, he meant. My namesake." And again she noted the pride in Wilson's voice.

They had talked some more about Wil's study habits and agreed upon a program to follow. Then they had talked about Chris Beth's predicament.

"There are some things I don't feel like discussing," she said slowly.

"No need to." But somehow Chris Beth had the feeling that he knew some of them already.

"Joe and I have talked about a place for you to stay and come to the conclusion that there is a very simple solution. Promise to go along with it?"

"Oh, yes!" she cried impulsively. "Anything, *anything!*"

Immediately he was the old Wilson. "Lady, you got yourself a deal! I'm helping Joe move in with young Wil and me tomorrow. The big house's far more than we two need. So Joe's cabin is yours."

Chris Beth felt her eyes widen. *Try to act calm*, she told herself. Maybe she pulled it off, but inside her stomach churned.

"That would be—uh, unwise." *I sound like Mama*, she thought.

"Afraid of living just whistling distance from us?"

She stiffened. "Of course not! But what would people say?"

Wilson North hooted. "That's the old Christen Elizabeth, the Southern belle with the Boston accent, speaking."

"Let me think," she whispered, but deep inside she knew what the answer had to be.

25
Anticipation

~♂~

IN A WARM FLANNEL ROBE and with her hair loosed and drying by a crackling fire, Chris Beth shared the events of the day with her close friend. Mrs. Malone hung onto every word, nodding between mouthfuls of huckleberry cobbler and hot coffee. "Don't have your knack for rollin' out pastry," Mrs. Malone explained.

"It couldn't be better this way," Chris Beth said, savoring every bite after the strange, emotional day.

After seconds, there was a lull. Mrs. Malone then asked, "Did Wilson tell you he's studyin' to be a doctor?"

"Doctor?" Chris Beth was stunned.

"The same," the older woman said, picking up the dishes.

"But he's a botanist and is writing a book—besides the grist mill—"

"And studyin' to be a doctor," Mrs. Malone repeated. "Some special big name—*path*-o-something, havin' to do with diseases."

"Pathology."

"Could be. Course, we hope he takes to doctorin'. Doc's getting past house-callin', you know, and Wilson'll be needed."

Very true. *How nice it would be for the settlement*, Chris Beth thought. And the vision returned. The valley would grow . . . there would be a teacher . . . a preacher . . . and now a doctor. And she was a part of the trio! Strange, she thought drowsily, how she would have been annoyed that Wilson failed to tell her this just a short while ago. But there were matters she hadn't revealed either. And it seemed to make no difference.

Chris Beth patted a yawn and tried to listen to Mrs. Malone. It seemed that she too had some news. "Guess what!" She sounded very excited. "The President is coming through—the President and his First Lady! They will stop over at the Pass, folks say, and the Presidential Coach itself will be turnin' right up here at our corner. Oh—" she dreamed, "if only we had Turn-Around Inn ready—who knows?"

"You will, someday," Chris said with conviction.

Mrs. Malone nodded and then went on excitedly. "O'Higgin has promised to take me to the turnoff. I've been studyin' the catalogue for latest fashions and all."

It was good to see her so excited. But there was more.

"Folks say this is the coach that has the 'gallant white steeds' we read about and that the coach is trimmed in real gold. Don't you think you oughta see Nate and ask that the children meet the party?"

Well, of course! That was a wonderful idea. Then she gave way to languor and anticipation. . . .

26
Going to
Meet the President

⤳

ON MONDAY OF THE "BIG WEEK," young Wil asked Chris Beth if he could erase the chalkboard. The request was a peace offering, she knew, and she accepted it as a truce. "What's more, as soon as you've finished back assignments, I'll have you help Wong with language."

"Then, can—may I have my ball back?"

She nodded. "And work on your leaf collection."

It was always good to establish a warm student-teacher relationship, but this one was imperative. Chris Beth, with the aid of the Malone children, had moved her few possessions into Joseph Craig's cabin while Wilson helped him move to the North house. Young Wil's attitude could make or break the success of what in her mind was a questionable arrangement at best.

But she loved the cabin! The inside logs were hewed smooth, the cracks were chinked against the wind, and the floors, though fir, were polished to a hardwood shine. The fireplace was small but surrounded by bright, hand-braided rugs big enough, Chris Beth thought, to stretch out and dream upon when time allowed.

Joe left the furniture—rare walnut bureau, high-poster bed, and round oak dining room table and chairs—which, though beautiful, made the cabin look like a doll house. The heirloom pieces had belonged to his parents, Joe told her, as they worked to complete the moving. The Craigs and Norths had come West over the Applegate Trail and, though forced to abandon most of their Eastern furniture in the steep descent, had salvaged these few, making them doubly precious. Then, the awful fire! It had destroyed the big house up by the waterfall, leaving little but this furniture and the few dishes (which she was welcome to use).

Chris Beth saw that the fire was a painful subject so had decided not to pursue it, when Joe volunteered the reason for his pain. "I lost them both that night—my father and mother. We tried to fight our way through to Dad, but the roof caved. Mother lived only a few hours after we pulled her from the flames. I guess that's one reason Wil decided to go into medicine." He inhaled deeply. "I pray that there'll never be another forest fire here."

"I'm so sorry," Chris Beth had said, reaching for Joe's hand. His large, capable hand had closed over her small, taut fist momentarily. Then, gently he eased her fingers open and straightened them into a relaxed position. His touch was a near-caress.

The tragedies that these people of the settlement had lived through left Chris Beth humbled. Compared to their problems, her own looked as off-scale in size as the antique furniture in the little cabin. But that was not why she clung to Joe's warm hand longer than necessary. It felt so reassuring, so powerful, and so—something else for which she could find no name. . . .

So, with the move made, the larder stocked with enough of Mrs. Malone's chili sauce, apple butter, and succotash to feed the cavalry, the bed piled high with quilts, and a load of backlogs hauled over by O'Higgin, Chris Beth had gone back to school with a singing heart. Not only was she settled (temporarily, at least), but she had a carrot to dangle in front of her young charges' noses. Who *wouldn't* work hard with the promise that maybe—just maybe—the school board would let them meet the stage and see the nation's President! That was, *if* the weather permitted, *if* parents would help with transportation, *if*—

But why go on? The children were so excited they would hear not another word! *And I'm no better*, she thought.

Friday dawned bright and clear. A light frost melted away with the sun's rays, but patches clung to sweetbrier vines that wound around the fence rows. It was a "mitten mornin' for shure," O'Higgin had declared, and Chris Beth cautioned all the children to button up snugly as they piled excitedly into the waiting wagons. She herself rode with Wilson, whose silly cart looked a little more respectable with the gaudy umbrella put away for the winter. Thoughtfully, he tucked a lap robe over her knees but paused before climbing in beside her. "Forgot something," he apologized.

"Oh, no! Not Esau." But Wilson was out of hearing distance.

To her relief, it was not the dog he brought back. It was the black bag, a telltale tool of his profession.

Briefly, Chris Beth wondered why the doctor's kit should make her apprehensive. That was silly. So thinking, she put it out of her mind, concentrating instead on the stark beauty of the woods.

27
The Unexpected!

❧

How DIFFERENT THIS ride was from the first one through the forest! Chris Beth had difficulty identifying with the person she had been then. It was as if she had been given a new body before her time!

That reminded her of Wilson's bag in back of the hack. He wasn't a doctor yet, so why the kit?

He smiled at her question. "Well, the truth is that I *am* ready for practice, but I've been trying to decide exactly how much of my life I want to give over to research or general practice—" His voice trailed off. "As to the supplies, I always take them along. A doctor has to expect the unexpected, you know."

She supposed so, little realizing just how right he was.

The sun was noon-high and Chris Beth was sure the children would be hungry. "Maybe we should stop at the next clearing for lunch."

Wilson nodded. "Plenty of time. Stage is due at two."

Lunch completed, the wagons moved on toward the fateful place, where the driver had announced "End of the trail!" in words that carried a doomsday ring. *Well, things were differ-*

ent now, she thought happily, as she helped parents unload children for a romp before the arrival of the President of the United States! Joe, she remembered, would be "riding shot-gun" on the stage again. Somehow that gave her a feeling of pride—similar to the feeling she had when she saw Wilson check his medical supplies before joining in the children's play. Someday she must analyze these feelings.

The rumble of the carriage wheels was audible long before the line of stagecoaches appeared. How many? Chris Beth gasped as she counted six gleaming coaches, one of them drawn by white horses—undoubtedly the President's! Her excitement grew as quiet spread over the children. Mrs. Malone's eyes, she saw, were as big as theirs.

As the party neared, she tried to make out the names newly painted on the outside of the vehicles: SHASTA EXPRESS, OVERLAND, and CALIFORNIA STAGE. The latter must house the President, she was sure. It was a study in color, with wheels, tongue, and running gear painted bright canary-yellow and outlined with black stripes through which were spaced single red roses. The body was olive green with large hand-painted landscape scenes on the panels. Around the neck of each horse was a chain of ivory rings. The driver, not to be outdone, wore fine buckskin gloves, fancy-stitched jacket and pants, and silver-buckled boots. The finery tattled of the "back East" shops familiar to Chris Beth but foreign to the settlers. The pretentiousness of it all looked a little disgusting to her after her months here with open, unpretending people. Still, she welcomed the experience for the children and suspected that the adults were equally awed.

Mrs. Malone proved that. "Well, I never in my born days!" she exclaimed in appreciation of all the pomp.

"Have ye a look at the whiplash!" whispered O'Higgin. "Big enough it be fer towin' another coach, it is!"

"Precisely," Wilson whispered back. "And strong enough to serve as a noose for a highwayman."

"Be ye sober?" Wilson's grim nod said that he was.

As the caravan drew to a stop, all eyes focused on the

Presidential Coach. But something drew Chris Beth's attention to the last vehicle, which creaked along in front of a heavily loaded supply wagon, drawn by mules and manned by rugged drivers. Sometimes they all traveled together like this for safety, she remembered hearing. This would be especially true with such a dignitary aboard.

As cheers went up, she knew that the President must have made an appearance, but she continued to stare at a face she had seen through the window of the back coach. "Oh, it can't be—" she whispered. And, without realizing she had done so, she grabbed Wilson's arm for support. He followed her gaze to where a fragile girl was being helped from aboard the coach where Joe rode as "Shotgun Messenger."

"Vangie," she whispered. And, even as she spoke, she saw her lovely sister crumple to the ground.

28
Appalling Emotions

~⦿~

WHATEVER EMOTIONS SHE had expected of the reunion vanished at the sight of her sister. The shock of seeing her emerge from the stagecoach, the simultaneous fear that clutched her own heart as Vangie fainted, and the actual wonder of her being here in such an unexpected fashion were too much to absorb without recoil. Like a windup toy, whose action might stop at any moment, she rushed forward with Wilson to where the willow-thin girl lay on the ground. Thank heavens, the others had crowded around the Presidential party, giving the two of them room to get through.

A shaft of sun broke through the trees, highlighting Vangie's pale blond hair with shades of new copper. The beautiful blue eyes were closed, but Chris Beth noted with alarm that the deep circles around them were almost as deep a violet. And the tiny figure, although slender, was now wafer-thin. *She looks like a priceless Dresden doll*, she thought as always about her younger sister. And, as always, she wanted to gather Vangie in her arms and comfort her until her hurts went away. But there was no time. Wilson had scooped up the fragile figure with practiced skill and rushed to wrap her in the woolen lap robe. "Fainted," was all he said.

Wilson North had moved quickly, but not quickly enough for Chris Beth could see the raw emotions on his taut face. There she read a tenderness she had never seen before. She recognized the look. It went beyond professional concern and into the heart.

When Vangie's eyelids fluttered, Chris Beth would have moved forward, but a Wilson she had never seen before restrained her. "Go back with the Malones!" he ordered. "I'm taking her with me!"

Mechanically, she stepped back, waiting for the hurt to come. "Chris—Chrissy—" Vangie tried to whisper. "I'm sorry—"

"Don't talk," Wilson whispered softly. "I'll take care of you." He dismissed Chris Beth with a jerk of his head and drove back toward his homestead. Why shouldn't *she* be with Vangie?

Joe spoke from behind her, and she turned in surprise and near-annoyance to see him leaning against a giant fir. She wondered if he had witnessed her humiliation at being pushed aside—even though, the reasonable side of her said for good cause. But when he spoke, his voice was normal. "Harmony and Amelia are riding back with friends. Miss Mollie has room for you and me."

O'Higgin helped her into the spring seat that she and Joe would occupy before climbing up beside Mrs. Malone in the driver's seat. Chris Beth wished that she and Joe—or she alone—could have ridden in back. *I'd like to dangle my feet and think.*

Instead, there was to be less privacy than she had imagined. Little Jimmy John, exhausted from the long day, fussed, refused his milk and tea cakes, and insisted on riding with Chris Beth.

"Child misses you powerful like," Mrs. Malone said. "I don't get time to read the Bible stories like you did. Funny thing—this one takes to the Old Testament tales. Remember

the picture you showed 'im of the Promised Land and that big
bunch o' grapes?"

Chris Beth remembered. It was from a favorite picture book
of her childhood. The cluster of grapes, she remembered, was
so enormous that two men had to run a stick through the
fruits and share the load. What she couldn't recall was where
the book came from. Someone had shared it with her. But
who?

Jimmy John was squirming sleepily in her lap in need of
attention. Not that she minded the interruption. She had tried
to recall that missing chapter before, but always at this point
her memory dissolved. The baby yawned, stuck a fat fist into
his mouth, and fell asleep immediately. She pressed her lips
against the soft hair on top of his head. She had missed him
too, she realized.

Chris Beth was only aware that the others talked. Most of
their conversation was lost. Try as she would, it was impossible to concentrate. Too much had happened. There were too
many questions.

Most of the talk was about the "greatest thing that ever
happened hereabouts," and Chris Beth realized with a start
that she hadn't even seen the celebrated First Couple! Better
listen, as she would need to be informed for classroom
discussions. But she had lost interest in President Rutherford
B. Hayes and his First Lady.

Joe had remained quiet. Chris Beth was surprised when he
spoke quietly to her. "Glad I could be with Vangie while she
waited."

Waited?

No room on stages for three days. Vangie had had to lay over
in Redding, and hadn't seemed well. "She's exquisite," he
added.

Chris Beth nodded yes to both his statements. Vangie was
far from "well"—and apparently Wilson thought her "exquisite" too!

Then, realizing that she had not thanked him, she laid a
hand on his sleeve. "Joe, I appreciate you."

"You'd better!" He grinned. And somehow she felt comfortable again. *Strange*, she thought, *how he always makes me feel this way.*

Typically, Joe fell silent as they rode farther into the woods. It was good to be allowed to think, or try to. It had been a strange, mixed-up day—a day that brought appalling emotions, some of which she had thought dead. When better than here with Joe to sort them out?

Naturally, it would be a surprise to see Vangie. And just as naturally her arrival brought its own set of problems, compounded by her obvious fragility. Chris Beth once again felt fury at her stepfather's treatment of his daughter, disappointment at her mother's helplessness, and resentment of the new burden when she was just making her own adjustment. *And I thought I'd put those feelings behind me*, she thought in confusion. Instead, another baffling emotion had sprung up to join them.

Yes, Chris Beth had to admit, Vangie's presence here had brought another kind of unhappiness. Maybe it was injured pride. Where there's no love, there could be no jealousy— could there? And she certainly was not in love with Wilson North—was she? Or was she as fickle as she had always thought Mama and Vangie to be? It was a disturbing thought—one she would do away with in short order. She was the strong one. No, it most certainly was *not* jealousy. She had no love to give. But pride—that was another matter. . . .

So engrossed was Chris Beth in her thoughts that she hardly realized that the winter's early darkness had closed in and they were in front of Turn-Around Inn.

Wolf barked happily. The children raced into the house and Chris Beth surrendered little Jimmy John to O'Higgin with a sigh of relief. She hadn't realized how heavy a two-year-old could be. Her arms were stiff and unfeeling as Joe helped her down from the seat of the wagon.

"You'll never know how right you looked holding the baby," he said.

"You'll never know how right I felt," she answered, regretting it immediately. What a ridiculous thing for an unmarried lady to say to a man! Particularly one who, as Mrs. Malone would have said, had "no prospects"! How very embarrassing.

To her added embarrassment, she felt Joe's eyes on her. It was a welcome help when Mrs. Malone called, "Now inside, *everybody!*"

"I have to check on Vangie—"

"Not on an empty stomach! She's with Wilson."

Yes, how well she knew . . .

29
A Tearful Forgiveness

⌦

CHRIS BETH LINGERED, looking inside the window as Joe hitched Dobbin outside the North home. He had insisted on going for his buggy while she helped Mrs. Malone with dishes.

"She may need me," was all he said to O'Higgin's offered ride.

Through the window, Chris Beth saw a scene which both warmed and frightened her. Firelight cast shadows about the large living room and reflected on the mellow beams above. Vangie sat bundled beside the hearth while Wilson peeled apples. She had put aside any feeling of jealousy—if that's what her initial emotion was—but her sister must not fall into another trap. And, she thought in strange contradiction, neither must Wilson. And, then, with a sudden surge of overpowering emotion, Vangie's presence here became a reality too good to be true no matter what the circumstances.

She rushed into the room, and Vangie, tripping over the blanket, rushed into her arms with a little moan. "Oh, Chrissy, Chrissy, don't ever leave me again—ever—ever—"

"Sh-h-h-h," Chris Beth smoothed damp curls from the

feverish brow. Vangie, little Vangie, was again her baby sister, to be loved and protected against the world's evils. "I never will!"

The two men tiptoed unnoticed into the great kitchen.

For a long time both of them were silent, and then they both began talking at once, just as they always had. "One at a time," Chris Beth advised, "but slowly. Don't tire yourself now."

"Oh, Chrissy, it was awful, awful, his sending me away— calling me a 'woman of the night' and saying God would punish the *baby*—" That would mean the pious "Father Stein"!

"I can imagine," Chris Beth said bitterly. "Try not to think about it. You're here now—with me—with us. You're safe!" And, as she spoke, she knew that it was true.

"But," Vangie drew back uncertainly. Chris Beth was surprised to see fear in the younger girl's face. "How can you welcome me?"

"Why shouldn't I?"

"Didn't Mama tell you—I mean—?" Her voice trailed off faintly.

"About the baby? Of course." There was no need to tell Vangie that she had been so astonished and frightened herself at the time that she had burned the letter without reading it all.

Vangie was so still that Chris Beth wondered if she was all right. And then she spoke. "And you can forgive me? Knowing who fathered the child?" Her words were spoken in whispers.

But she *didn't* know, she was about to say. And then the cold, iron hand of fear gripped her heart. It wasn't true. It *couldn't* be! Vangie's blue eyes were looking at her piteously and she was cringing as she used to cringe at the feet of her father. "She *didn't* tell you." A sob caught in her throat. "It was," she whispered, "Jonathan Blake."

Although the words stung like an adder, later Chris Beth knew even then that hearing them spoken was more shocking than the impact of Vangie's confession. Somewhere, in a dream or in some far corner of her wounded heart, she had suspected—maybe even known. Vangie in Boston . . . her letters home saying she had seen Jonathan . . . his sudden cooling ardor. And always Vangie had wanted whatever Chris Beth possessed—first her strength, later her clothes, and finally her suitors—a woman in a child's body. *Odd*, she thought numbly, *I always thought of Mama exactly the opposite.*

"Don't hate me, Chrissy. Please—"

"I don't hate you, Vangie," Chris Beth said slowly and was surprised to know it was true. "It's all a tragic mistake, but not altogether your fault."

Vangie stiffened in her arms. "Oh, but it was! I envied you."

Chris Beth waited until the rigid body relaxed before answering. "I know," she said. "But you were a child, only 16."

"I'm 17 now!" Chris Beth almost smiled at her sister's defensiveness when she was so totally defenseless. But there was no trace of a smile in her heart. Vangie's mention of age reminded her that, although there wasn't that much difference in their ages, it was Chris Beth who must make some provision for the future. She hated herself for the vital question she had to ask.

"Vangie?" She inhaled deeply. "Vangie, did he offer to marry you?"

The girl's eyes, almost purple in the firelight, widened in shock, then closed in despair. "He's dead," she whispered. "Killed in a hunting accident."

Chris felt her own eyes dilate in shock. Jonathan alive was one thing. Jonathan dead was another. "One can't go on hating a dead person," she said more to herself than to Vangie.

Vangie's grip tightened around her. "Forgive me—" she begged again. And her sobbing told Chris Beth that Vangie had not forgiven herself.

"Vangie—" Whatever she was about to say was lost forever because at that point she burst into tears herself.

It seemed like hours later that Vangie whispered, "I've cried myself dry," the words of their childhood.

Chris Beth responded in like manner. "So it's time to pray."

She was forever the "older sister," and it was up to her to take the lead. But how to begin? She was out of practice. But, as she remembered, the God of her childhood didn't demand eloquent prayers.

"Hello, Lord," she whispered. "It's been a long time. . . ."

30
Secrets Revealed

❧

IT SEEMED TO CHRIS BETH that she was sending up more than her fair share of prayers in the days that followed her sister's arrival in the settlement. But she guessed not, since the Lord was taking time to answer them all! Oh, it was good to be back—she smiled at the word—admittedly *leaning!* Everything was going to "right up," just as Mrs. Malone had promised. She could hardly wait until Thanksgiving to tell her friend about her countless blessings. She, Vangie, Wilson, and Joe had been so busy with "living," that, as Joe put it, it left no time for "visiting."

Of course, what the four of them shared was hardly visiting. She struggled for hours for a more fitting word. It was more like—well, she was back to that word again, *living.* And what on earth would the valley folk think she meant by that! She hardly knew herself what to make of the new relationship, let alone explain it to another. She had better do some thinking before they joined the crowd that Mrs. Malone and O'Higgin had invited to Turn-Around Inn for a holiday feast. She and Vangie *had* to move into the cabin. But details?

Well, there would be some details she would keep to

herself. They belonged to her and Vangie. That wasn't quite true either, she was forced to admit. To her surprise, the two men of the new foursome knew the details she had hoped to keep secret. Even now, she wasn't sure, after the initial shock, if she was angry, embarrassed, or pleased. At least she was relieved to know that anything the four of them shared would go no further. *There would have been no way to hold some of it back anyway.*

Chris Beth pushed away from her desk and laid aside the papers she was grading to glance about the classroom. The children had filled the four corners with piles of cornstalks and fat pumpkins. The cornucopia (a real goat's horn, brought in by Nate Goldsmith, instead of the wicker one she had back home!) overflowed with pine cones, mellow fruit, and golden ears of grain. Truly, there was "abundant life" here—just another of the many things she would be praising the Creator for again come the day after tomorrow. Scoring the papers could wait. The boys and girls were doing so very well, some of them excelling, and over the four-day recess the men of the settlement were planning to floor the building. Oh! How wonderful! But for now she needed to think.

Thinking time was hard to find either at the cabin or at the big North house. Not that she minded. Maybe that was the problem. She didn't mind at all! Where was it all leading? How could she stop it? *Or*, she bit her lip in concentration, *did she want to?*

She supposed that it was she who, unwittingly, laid the foundation for the friendships which might be going beyond the usual definition of the word. Both men had befriended her in a grave time of need. And, though they were different from each other, she was attracted to them both. The perplexing part of it was that her feelings toward Joe and Wilson were as different as the two men were from each other. How could a woman possibly be thinking like this when she wasn't a candidate for love anyway!

With a burning face, Chris Beth returned to her work. The papers suddenly seemed important after all. The trouble was that she was unable to concentrate. Scraps of conversations kept coming back.

"Wilson figures the baby will be here toward the end of April," Vangie had said as matter-of-factly as if announcing the arrival of spring.

"He *knows*?"

"You mean the exact date? Of course he knows there's going to be a baby!" Something of the old lighthearted Vangie came back. "He knew the first day."

But of course he would have! Chris Beth felt foolish.

"Does he know—?" She let the question hang, hardly knowing how to phrase it.

"Who the father is?" Vangie shook her head. "It doesn't matter. But he knows that I'm not married, yes."

Another time when the two of them had talked, Chris Beth asked what *she* should tell people. *I sound like Mama*, she thought, and was disturbed at the likeness. Still, she did have to know what course of action to follow. The situation wasn't exactly ideal!

Vangie had laughed. "They'll *know* before too long!" she promised. Then, sobering, she added, "About the name, I'll just use my own. I guess it's good we're half-sisters, though I often wish we had had the same father."

Chris Beth had wished the same many times. But now was not one of them! The different surnames did offer a measure of protection for the unborn child. Then she began to realize that the baby's arrival would extend their family. Why, she would be an aunt! At one time the thought would have been unsavory, but now it was more than bearable. It was as sweet as honeycomb! She wondered what color eyes the baby would have—and hair. Would it be a boy or a girl? Waiting must be hard for Vangie. She could hardly wait herself.

Chris Beth again laid down her pencil. She was remembering something else. It was even more disturbing because it involved a secret all her own.

"Does Wilson intend telling Joe—I mean, the details?"

Vangie looked surprised and, in her usual candid—*naive*,

really—manner, responded, "Oh, I told him myself when we had to wait in Redding."

"Vangie, you didn't—"

"Tell him about you? He knew already—except that it was the same man." The first part should have come as no surprise. She had been feverish on the stagecoach and he had been kind. But Jon's betrayal! Oh, the shame. . . .

Chris Beth's reflections were interrupted by a faint rustling in the hazelnut bushes. Almost simultaneously, the door opened soundlessly. Boston Buck stepped inside.

Several times Chris Beth had thought she caught sight of the young Indian's head bobbing in and out of the thickets surrounding the school building. Hoping it was her imagination, she had tried to dismiss any worry that his presence might have caused.

Automatically her eyes went to her bag. The brooch was still there. Each day she had planned to wrap it here in privacy, and now (even as she faced possible danger, a part of her was thinking ahead) there would be nobody to whom she could return it.

The Indian approached cautiously. Then, as she wondered what to do, he pulled from behind him an enormous, beautifully feathered wild turkey!

Such a flood of surprise and relief flowed over her that for a moment Chris Beth was sure she would burst into tears. But that was the last thing she wanted to do. The gift deserved some dignity.

"Thank you, Boston Buck," she said bowing humbly. Then, taking a shimmering feather from the tail of the bird, she tucked it into her hair.

Whoever said Indians never smiled certainly had never met this one! A smile creased the dark face, revealing a set of perfect teeth. He moved forward, took a brilliant feather from the turkey's tail, and stuck it in his headband.

"Name Boston Buck," he said.

And then he was gone.

31
Surprise Marriage

⌒

THE TWO MEN LEFT before daylight on Thanksgiving morning in order to get the turkey into Mrs. Malone's oven before her hams. They would take Wilson's cart, they told Chris Beth and Vangie, leaving the buggy and Dobbin, the more dependable horse, for them. Young Wil went with the men, and the girls were to bring Esau. It was silly to take the dog, Chris Beth argued. But she was voted down.

Dogs are thankful too! That was Wilson.

Then let them have their "dog days"!

A measure of protection. That was Joe.

But they weren't afraid—

Who isn't? And, besides, he's a dear. Vangie.

Chris Beth gave in grudgingly, but inside she was amused. It was always like this, with their good-natured (and sometimes heated) dialogue, after many a detour, ending up on "easy street." But in this instance, Vangie, though speaking lightly, seemed concerned about something.

"It's the dress—and young Wil," she admitted to Chris Beth. "I mean, I'll be among strangers, and I'm supposed to be widowed. What would be right, Chrissy?"

Yes, that did present a problem. Bright colors would be inappropriate. Chris Beth had misgivings about the implied deception. But there was the baby to think about.

They decided on a simple dark cotton dress with white linen collar and cuffs that made Vangie look like a little-girl Pilgrim wearing her mother's clothes. But, "I look tacky," she said.

Would it make her happier if Chris Beth wore her black skirt and pleated-bosom blouse? It would.

"But what about young Wil?" she asked Vangie.

The younger girl stopped brushing her hair. "He doesn't like me." And that seemed important.

"Young Wil's an introspective child," Chris Beth told her. "He's had more than his share of hurts, and it takes awhile for him to trust others."

"He likes *you*."

"I'm his teacher, Vangie, often the object of a child's first love. Give him time."

It was midmorning when the two of them reached Turn-Around Inn. The men stood around an outside fire where a whole pig was roasting. Smoke billowed from every chimney of the big house, and it was easy to imagine the happy bustle of aproned ladies inside. Mrs. Malone would be issuing orders faster than O'Higgins could carry them out and greeting guests at the same time.

But surprisingly to all, neither of them was in sight. They were greeted only by Wolf at the gate and Ambrose at the door.

Chris Beth noted with pleasure that the settlers gathered to greet the two of them immediately, as she had promised Vangie they would. Undoubtedly Maggie had spread the news, but the girl herself made no move toward them. The others welcomed Vangie warmly, so she wore a flush of happiness by the time Wilson elbowed his way to her.

"Where are our hosts?" Chris Beth asked Joe, who was close behind Wilson.

"Everybody's wondering," he replied, as he took her basket of food. She had worked late the night before preparing Boston baked beans and Southern spoon bread. "Might as well put a bit of all the cultures together," she had conspired with Vangie, who watched with more than her usual interest in cooking.

Chris Beth looked about the front room with appreciation as she hung her and Vangie's hooded capes in the closet. The Malone children had swung festoons of evergreen mingled with bright sprigs of bittersweet and sweet-smelling rose hips from the sweetbriers. She wondered what they would wash dishes in for the big crowd when every granite pot and pan available was filled with the last of the purple-and-bronze chysanthemums. Was Thanksgiving always so festive? And so mysterious? An air of expectancy seemed to hang in the air to mingle with the smell of rising yeast bread and pumpkin pies.

Chris Beth felt the sense of security she had felt when this wonderful family had taken her in. The children gathered around her eagerly, all talking at once. Little Jimmy John tugged at her skirt until she scooped him up in her arms.

The day was all she had promised Vangie it would be, with two exceptions. The large crowd, exciting as it was, would probably make it impossible to get in a private word with Mrs. Malone. The other exception was a certain glint she read in Maggie Solomon's green eyes whenever they met her own. Each time the girl spoke with another of the guests, open hand to her mouth as if to guard some secret, her gaze returned to where Chris Beth, Vangie, Wilson, and Joe were visiting with neighbors. It was plain to see that she was discussing the four of them—and unfavorably.

"I'd better offer a hand in the kitchen," Chris Beth told Vangie. Probably best to break up the foursome for Maggie's benefit.

Wilson answered for her sister. "I want Vangie to meet someone anyway. Young Mrs. Martin's here and expecting her first. She and you," he turned to Vangie, "will want to talk."

Chris Beth nodded. The Martins were the "new but lear- nin'" couple that Nate had introduced to her that Sunday at the brush arbor.

By the time Chris Beth was able to push through the crowd, a loud ring of the dinner bell outside drew everybody's attention.

"Brother Jonas," someone said. "Seems he's about to make an announcement."

The circuit rider stepped inside the back door, followed by men and children from out-of-doors. With a great deal of pomp, he brushed an imaginary bit of lint from his frock coat, stepped onto a rawhide-bottomed chair, cleared his throat importantly, and sang out: "Ladie-e-e-s and gentlemen! By power vested in me, I give you now—the *bride and groom!*"

The guests went so wild with cheers, stomping, and hat-waving that Chris Beth found herself unable to see the honored couple.

"Speech! Speech!" the crowd roared.

"Aye, gunnies! And a speech ye'll be gettin'!"

O'Higgin? Impossible—but it was true. O'Higgin and Mrs. Malone. How could she have known? No, how could she *not* have known?

The Irishman, looking for all the world like the cat who had swallowed the canary, raised his hand for silence. "Aye, gunnies! Miss Mollie said yes, she did—and this marriage doubled me claim!"

Mrs. Malone, her usually pale gray eyes shining, took his words in stride. She extended her hand to show a wide, gold wedding band and responded. "This shows 'im to be my wedded husband and father of these children," she motioned them up front. "But," she paused dramatically, "*one* claim he'll be missin'. I'll be bearin' the name of the little ones."

Jonas, still on his perch, called out, "Rightly so! Vows last night united O'Higgin to one Mollienisia Malone, with name-rights reserved!"

"Shure and cider's a-mellowin' in the cellar—"

"O'Higgin!" His wife's eyes were stern. "Just how mellow is it?"

"Now, ye be knowin' I'm a man of moderation—not given to strong drink, Miss Mollie."

"Right, so it's coffee we'll be servin'." But there was a twinkle in her eye.

They would make a fine pair, Chris Beth knew. There was understanding born of endurance through good times and bad. There was humor and openness. . . . She glanced up to see Joe's eyes studying her face. It seemed only natural that the two of them should smile in understanding.

The bell rang again. The signal for dinner. More, so much more than a dinner, of course. It was Thanksgiving. And it was a wedding feast. Chris Beth felt a great surge of joy as they moved into the dining room, where the tables groaned with food.

Ordinarily the hostess would have seen that all the guests were served, but today she was the honored guest in her own house. She was to be served first, then O'Higgin, and then, wonder of wonders, the Malone children, who always had to wait for a "second table." Her friends would have it no other way.

It was all very touching to Chris Beth, and she felt a rush of tears when she saw O'Higgin hesitate at the head of the table until his beloved "Miss Mollie" nodded consent. *Praise the Lord!* There was no longer an empty chair. . . .

32
Around the Hearth

⁓

SEATED AROUND a crackling fire in the North living room, Wilson, Joe, and the girls went over the events of the day. Nobody was hungry after the enormous dinner, so they popped corn over the open flames and drank cold cider that Wilson had stored below the waterfall by the mill. "Not too mellow for a preacher?" Joe had asked with a smile.

"Or a schoolteacher?" Chris Beth had joined in.

"Feel like I could use a lifter myself," Vangie said, stifling a little yawn. "Or don't mothers-to-be indulge?"

"Come on, you three!" Wilson objected. "That leaves just me, and you know total abstinence is my cup. Doctors are always subject to call."

"I'm going to bed!" From the way young Wil spoke up from the door, Chris Beth knew that the words were more than an announcement to his uncle. "You're leaving me out," they plainly said.

Wilson looked at the small figure, whose sullen face was half-hidden in the shadows. "Stay with us, why don't you? You know it's only cider."

The boy shook his head sullenly. "Good night, Miss Chrissy," he said and fled. Obviously, she was the only one here who counted!

Vangie was right. Young Wil resented her presence, but for a deeper reason than Chris Beth had known for sure until now. *I must talk to him*, she thought. But how did one ease the pangs of first love without breaking a young heart?

The others gave no sign of noticing. And, deep in the usual warm conversation that followed, she too forgot the incident.

Hadn't the day gone well? It had, and what a crowd!

Everybody was there, even a lot of newcomers. And certainly all the old-timers. Just *everybody*!

"No," Chris Beth said slowly. "Not everybody. What about the Chu family, Wong's parents?"

"Nobody knows much about them," Wilson said, stirring the fire. "I guess nobody ever bothered to find out, actually—expected them to move on when laying of the rails stopped." He paused to lay on another backlog. Might as well. These talks always went on and on. "There was resentment among the white workers that they were here."

"They worked for a quarter a day, you know—even used baskets and wheelbarrows. Shame. They had so much to contribute, too. They were the first to come up with black blasting powder," Joe added. "Wilson's 'magic potion.'" The two men smiled over the secret.

"Young Wil knows a few Chinese words. Maybe I—we—"

"Should call on them?" Joe finished for Chris Beth. "Yes."

"And what about the Indians?" Chris Beth paused. Maybe she was on thin ice. "Do any of them have books or Bibles?"

"Very few can speak English, let alone read," Wilson said. "Hey, I thought you Southern ladies avoided the Red Man!"

Chris Beth supposed she had stepped out of character, but an idea came to her about the upcoming Christmas program.

The crackle of the fire died down to a whisper. The four of them talked on around the embers until the room grew chilly.

Mention of the Chinese family brought up the subject of railroads. They were bound to come through, Wilson was sure. Joe was equally certain that waterways would open as planned too, allowing for steamboat trade to resume. And stagecoaches? Chris Beth had wondered, thinking of Turn-Around Inn. They would have need of a post office, and wasn't a telegrapher a nice thought, not to mention a newspaper.

The dreams spun out like cotton candy, with the four of them in the center of it all. The mill was "pulling its own weight" already (paying for itself, Chris Beth supposed), but both men wanted to get on with their studies. "We'll all be needed as growth continues," they assured the girls.

Yes, the settlement would be in need of a young doctor. Talk was that "Old Doc" was to retire as soon as Wilson could take over his practice. "Me and Gretchen's hanging up the pill bag," the aging German had said of himself and his equally-aging mare. Chris Beth wondered if Wilson had decided in favor of general practice and guessed that he had, judging by the rapt look on his face as he talked.

"And you, Joe?" Chris Beth asked when there was a lull.

"I'm glad to report that all exams are passed—written and oral," he said quietly. "I—I've waited to tell you," his eyes sought hers, "that I'll be ordained in the spring."

"Oh, that's wonderful, Joe!" Chris Beth felt a great surge of pride. "We'll all help in every way—" Her voice faltered. Maybe she was promising more than he was asking.

Wilson picked up the conversation. "Congratulations, pal! Folks need their hearts doctored as well as their bodies, I guess."

"And you ladies will be busier than ever," Joe said. "Maybe we can get a new school—" This time it was his voice that faltered. Chris Beth wondered why. Then, "and church," he added.

"And me?" Vangie spoke from beneath the pink blanket that Wilson had spread over her lap when he caught her dozing.

"*You* are going to bed, my love!" Wilson spoke the words of endearment, Chris Beth was sure, without being aware that she and Joe were in the room. But she felt no emotion, maybe because of fatigue.

The evening ended as the evenings before it had ended, as well as the many to follow—beautifully for the four of them.

The hearth of the big house seemed to be the setting for settling problems as well as for dreaming. It was there that Chris Beth finally had an opportunity for the coveted visit with Mrs. Malone (who staunchly clung to the name) and with young Wil. The men insisted that she and Vangie spend most of their time in the North living room, where (they claimed) it was warmer. And maybe it was, as they could lift bigger backlogs than she could handle alone, and she refused to let Vangie do any lifting.

Mrs. Malone rode over just before Christmas, when O'Higgin brought corn to the gristmill. O'Higgin was "fit as a fiddle," as his wife claimed. "Spoutin' off about the grizzly we saw on the way." Chris Beth could hear his brogue through the closed door as he told Wilson and Joe about the encounter. Good, that would give them a brief chat that Saturday morning.

No need to ask if things were going well. Mrs. Malone was radiant. And she knew about the children from school. Likewise, Mrs. Malone knew that the school had a floor, a new roof, and a near-wagonload of used books brought in by "educated newcomers" through the children. They had told her about the plans for the Christmas program on Christmas Eve, too. And would the four of them be coming to Turn-Around Inn for Christmas Day?

"Somethin' bothering you?" Mrs. Malone asked when Chris Beth hesitated.

"Well, yes and no. I'm concerned about what people may be thinking," she admitted.

The older woman snorted. "Who knows what they're thinkin'? It's what they're *knowin'* that counts. They know the men are upright. And given time—"

"You mean there *has* been talk? I need to know, Mrs. Malone."

"Would you look at this? Isn't it pretty like?" Mrs. Malone

held out a tiny, crocheted sweater of white wool. It looked like a fairy cobweb and it was undoubtedly for Vangie. But she was not to be deterred.

Well, there were tongues that wagged anywhere, Mrs. Malone admitted. Still and all, if one went to the source—

And what was the source? Maggie, as she had suspected.

"But not to worry. She's been at Nate, but I know how to handle him. He used to come courtin' me, you know. I'll see 'im Monday. Though let's speak of you now, not others or school. You and your feelings."

"I'm fine—just—"

Mrs. Malone believed in coming right to the point. "Exceptin' in here." She patted her heart and Chris Beth nodded.

The room was silent except for the ticking of the grandfather clock. Mrs. Malone leaned forward just as O'Higgin called.

"What color are Wilson's eyes?" she asked.

"Why, I don't know," she answered, stunned.

The older woman nodded. "And Joe's?"

"Hazel," she answered without hesitation. Hazel, she remembered, with little flecks of gold that showed when the light was right.

Mrs. Malone put the sweater in her bag and pulled her shawl about her. "By the way, that boy to which you was betrothed—what color eyes did he have? . . . Thought not," she answered her own question. Later Chris Beth realized that her blank look must have admitted that she didn't remember. She hardly remembered him at all.

Sleep refused to come that night. "Vangie?" She whispered to her sister's still figure beside her. "What color are Wilson's eyes?"

"Brown," Vangie answered. And her voice trailed away in sleep.

33

The Upper Room

❧

CHRIS BETH WAS PLEASED that Joe offered to do her holiday shopping, just as he had mailed that box of holly, snowdrops, and wild grasses back home, when he hauled excess flour and meal to the general store. There was no time to do such errands with so many demands on her time in preparation for the Christmas program. She considered including some of the cinnamon squares and sugar cookies she had baked for decorating the little tree at school when Joe mailed the package, but decided they would become stale. Besides, Mama loved winter bouquets, and the grasses and berries would be fine for that even if they were dried. She hoped her stepfather let Mama receive the package and wondered if she would understand why she and Vangie were unable to do more. She had not written to the girls.

The program was coming along. Chris Beth's main concern was where to put the spectators in case of rain. Joe suggested stretching a tarp outside and setting up the Nativity scene there, an idea she welcomed. The children were busy learning lines they had created for reenacting the first Christmas. "Why couldn't we call it that?" young Wil asked. Chris Beth

134

was glad the other children liked the title of the play. Indeed, it was a First Christmas in so many ways. It was her and Vangie's first Christmas in the settlement, a first Christmas (if all went as she hoped) for truly "everybody" in the settlement to be together, a first to be expecting a real baby in her very own family, a first—well, in so many ways.

Mrs. Malone sent word by the children that she would be unable to come and "loan a hand" as planned, as she and O'Higgin were trying to finish one of the upstairs rooms for their very own. But if Chris Beth would send a list of costumes needed, she had "a-plenty old drapes for Mary, the angels, and probably the wise men." The shepherds, she said, she could outfit from O'Higgin's long woolen underwear if she didn't think they would spoil things "a-scratchin'."

"I can draw pictures of camels," young Wil said. The others volunteered for paper chains, stars, and snowflakes. Then Bertie Beltran announced that he would bring the hay. Yes, all was coming along.

As Chris Beth and young Wil worked by the hearth on the background scenery, they talked about Wong's progress. "He's reading words, Miss Chrissy, but I don't think he wants to speak pieces for the program."

Chris Beth was sure of that. "Will he come?" She wondered. She had had young Wil ask if Wong would like to have her visit his mother, and the question scared him half to death, he reported. "But they are coming on Christmas. Sort of a miracle, isn't it?" She agreed.

She had had no opportunity to speak with Boston Buck, but she had seen his one-feathered headband dart in and out of the brush and knew he was watching the preparations. Her chance would come.

Young Wil suddenly laid aside his watercolors. "Miss Chrissy," he said hesitantly, "would you like to see my tree house?"

Chris Beth was about to say yes, at some other time, but changed her mind. She needed to have a word alone with him, and it was better that he name the time and place.

The tree house was simply three boards nailed in the fork of the oak in the backyard. Over the boards the boy had stretched two burlap bags ("gunnysacks," the settlers said) for a roof. But to him it was a place of magic. "So," Chris Beth smiled, "what do you call it?"

Without hesitating, young Wil answered, "It's my Upper Room. I come here to think."

And then it all came back. Chris Beth in her playhouse. Daddy at her side. Daddy telling her stories. Chris Beth singing the little songs she had learned in Sunday school. Daddy telling her about God, "Who was so big He could love the whole world, and so small He could curl right up in each person's heart." Daddy telling her the playhouse should have a name—one fitting a need to come and be alone so she could talk things over with God. And, finally, the aching loneliness when Daddy wasn't coming home anymore . . . Mama's shutting herself away . . . and the awfulness of Daddy's empty chair . . . then longing for the Promised Land in her playhouse Upper Room. . . .

Young Wil rushed to put his small arms around her. "Don't cry, Miss Chrissy—though sometimes I do here, too. I cry when I think that Uncle Wilson may marry and leave me alone again."

"Oh, darling, he'd never leave you alone. He loves you."

"But he may marry?" Young Wil paused. "May marry your sister?"

"I don't know," she said truthfully. "But if he does—"

"I'll come live with you! I want *you* to marry Uncle Wilson—or to marry both of us. I love you!"

"And I love you, too," she whispered. "But there are so many kinds of love." The child nodded and she hoped he understood. . . .

34
A New
Kind of Love

❧

THE DAY BEFORE CHRISTMAS dawned crystal clear. Three successive days of rain had soaked more than the earth. They had saturated Chris Beth's spirits in spite of her efforts to believe along with the children that the weather would change for the program. Then, suddenly, the clouds bumped against each other, dumped their moisture, and scurried back over the mountains for another load. Christmas Eve promised to be bright and starry-eyed.

"Then why can't we have the program outside?" Ned Malone asked. The boy was taller than she was, Chris Beth noted. The children had grown in so many ways. The others were ecstatic when Teacher said they could put it to a vote, and the "outsides" won! Actually, "Teacher" was pleased too. Beautiful night. Lantern-light reflecting shadows of the forest. Plenty of room for all. And who knew what unexpected guests might come from behind the tall fir trees?

Young Wil finished the background-mountains. Bertie scattered the hay. Up went the manger. Down went homework assignments, making room for the Christmas tree inside. Streamers. Stars. Bells. The children laughed, sang, and clapped—then stood in near-reverence. Truly, the school looked like a proper place for the Holy Birth.

Rehearsal went well, except for the giggles of "Mary" and "Joseph," a little scratching by the shepherds, and a little shoving by the "heavenly host." After a few admonitions, Chris Beth dismissed them early to go home, where the boys, she suspected, would scrub off the outer layer of skin and the girls would busy their mothers rolling their hair up on rags to create coveted curls.

"I can't believe th' crowd!" Mrs. Solomon said to Chris Beth, who was hurrying in and out just minutes before the Great Performance. "And the—uh, stage—is right nice," Nate said. He cleared his throat as if wanting to say more, but a commotion had broken out among the "cast," and she had to beg his leave and hurry inside.

"Look!" Amelia was pointing, wide-eyed, out the window. "It's Ole Tobe, and look what he brung—brought!"

By the glow of the lantern-light, Chris Beth was able to make out the dark face of "Ole Tobe," whoever he was. Who was the man and what on earth was he coaxing along?

Harmony answered both questions. His wife worked for some of the "rich folks" of the settlement, "scrubbin' and things." And Ole Tobe just "kinda laid around like."

Used to be slaves, somebody thought. Long time ago— maybe a year. Never been anywhere before.

And what he led was a donkey. A real, live donkey.

Mercy! What couldn't happen on stage with "real, live" animals. Chris Beth shuddered. Then, to her relief, she saw Joe come forward, help Ole Tobe shove the balking animal near to the manger, and turn to help Wilson with a *sheep!*

Dumbfounded, she stood there even as the "littlest angel" tugged at her skirt and said, "I couldn't hep it, Miss Chrissy."

Actually, what was there for her to do anyway that she hadn't done in the afternoon? she wondered later. What she would have supposed to be a finished job was in reality only the groundwork for what was taking place. Men and women

were rushing about everywhere inside and outside. The Christmas tree, which recently held only her own cookies, was now
looped with popcorn strands, doughnuts, and what appeared
to be fortune cookies. But who ever heard of *feathers* on a
Christmas tree? That could mean only one thing.

"Missy Chrissy, Missy Chrissy!" *Wong!* Why, he had never
spoken to her before. But, of course, that was no greater than
any of the other miracles of the evening. Wait! What on earth
was he doing taking the rag doll from the manger? She must
stop him. But before she could so much as move a muscle, an
Oriental man, wearing a kimono-like robe, with his dark hair
twisted into a *queue*, leaned over and placed a flannel-
wrapped baby carefully on the straw.

"What do you know!" Mrs. Malone, who had moved
noiselessly behind her, whispered, "a livin' China baby."

Never had there been such a program in the settlement, the
valley folk murmured as they helped themselves generously
to the great baskets of goodies the ladies provided and drank
the rich black coffee that Wilson went home to make while
"Brother Joseph" read Luke's account of Christ's birth. There
just never could be one like it!

Later, lying in bed far too happy to sleep, Chris Beth knew
that they were right. The program had been a miracle from
start to finish. Somewhere between sleep and reality, she
recalled Ole Tobe's getting into the act without intending to,
and the crowd's obvious delight.

"We all dun goin' to have us a Crismas program, iffen we
can get this dum' sheep in the corncrib," he announced to the
audience. Then, turning to the boys and girls, he continued,
"Then, *ooooh*, little child'urn, you's goin' to hear the sweetest
story this side o' heben. . . ."

Well, it had been, she thought drowsily. Never had she
heard the glorious Christmas message read so beautifully.
How could Joe ever have doubted himself? Why, he had had
the audience in his hand. Her too, when he finished with,
"The birth of Jesus was more than a pretty story for children

or an event to record in a history book. It gave us a whole new meaning of love." *A whole new meaning of love.*

As she drifted into a deep sleep, Chris Beth realized that it was so in her life. Here she had met people whose hearts brimmed over with Christian love. Here she had met Joe . . . and Wilson . . . and Mrs. Malone . . . but, most of all, she had met their God. No, not *their* God. And, no, she hadn't met Him for the first time. She had just become reacquainted with the God of her father, who loved the world . . . and could curl right up inside each heart . . . in a personal kind of way. She wanted to tell the world.

Somewhere the chimes were ringing out. It was Christmas Day. But Chris Beth slept soundly, little knowing that she had begun to tell the world already.

35
Exchange of Gifts

~∂~

THE GOOD WEATHER held—one of God's gifts for
the holidays, Mrs. Malone said of Christmas Day. The air was
as crisp as new cider, and the five guests (six, counting Esau)
were in high spirits as they rode to Turn-Around Inn. They
sang carols, trying to harmonize when their vehicles were
close enough to each other. But Dobbin and Charlie Horse
seemed to have sensed the mood of the riders and tried to race
along the still-slippery road. Soon the road would become
impassable, Joe told Chris Beth, but for now she refused to let
anything mar her happiness.

Everything was perfect, or nearly so. She still wondered if
Maggie would make trouble. It would have been a comfort to
see her among last night's happy faces. She wondered, too, if
young Wil would ever soften his stand about Wilson's obvious
love for Vangie. Maybe if her sister hadn't volunteered to take
the dog, he would have ridden with them today instead of
with her and Joe. Well, something would turn up. So thinking,
she had helped load the pile of brightly wrapped gifts which all
the people had said they were *not* going to give. But wasn't
that a part of the wonder of Christmas?

The atmosphere was equally festive at Turn-Around Inn. The children were wild with anticipation, and even Esau and Wolf wagged their tails at each other. After Joe read the Love chapter in Paul's letter to the Corinthians, and there were a few moments for "silent meditatin'," O'Higgin announced, "That be meditatin' long enough!" and everybody crowded around the table, Mrs. Malone making an exception and not insisting that "company go first."

Dishes done, O'Higgin took all of them upstairs to inspect the progress on the building project. "Do you have a name for it?" young Wil asked of Mrs. Malone.

"Hadn't thought on it," she admitted.

To Chris Beth's surprise, Vangie spoke up. "Why don't you come up with a name, Wil?"

The boy looked at her suspiciously a moment, then raised an eyebrow in question. "Well?" the older woman prompted.

Please, Lord, Chris Beth's heart whispered.

Wil allowed himself to think, of course. And then he said, "Why not call it the Upper Room?"

"Oh, *do!*" Vangie broke in. Mrs. Malone agreed. And Chris Beth let out a wee prayer of thanksgiving. Vangie had won the heart of young Wil.

In exchange of gifts that followed, it seemed to Chris Beth that each one, for its own special reason, outdid the one preceding. There was Vangie's gift of "Cozy," the white kitten she had found near the mill, to young Wil (which explained why she had insisted that Esau ride with her and Wilson, the little animal having ridden quietly in a basket without a mew!). Then there was young Wil's obvious delight (a gift in itself). Colored-yarn strings came off packages so fast that it was impossible to remember who gave what to whom.

But some of the gifts stood out. There was Wilson's little book of pressed leaves to Chris Beth, with the leaves apparently saved from their first trip through the autumn woods. *Now, don't cry*, Chris Beth warned herself. But why not? Everybody else seemed to be spilling tears all over the front-room carpet—enough to water the Christmas tree! Mrs.

Malone was crying over a big, red, heart-shaped box from O'Higgin. No wonder! It was the box she had handled so longingly at the general store. The Malone girls were not crying exactly, but their eyes looked suspiciously bright as one by one they unfolded their spanking-new dresses of bright calico. The way Joe opened the small copy of the New Testament that Chris Beth had ordered from the catalog made her wonder if he too would cry. Instead, he squeezed her hand. She felt the color rise to her cheeks. Maybe she should remove her hand. But she didn't.

Emotions reached their peak when, after a scramble of mittens, mufflers, and "pound cakes all around," Vangie presented an intricate piece of needlepoint to Mrs. Malone, saying it was for the Upper Room. Mrs. Malone, trying to get "my silly self under control," brought an entire layette for the new baby! It was Vangie's turn to cry—and O'Higgin's when he opened the package from Mrs. Malone. "Begory!" whooped the big Irishman at sight of the braided whip. "Not that he'll use it and not like I could afford it either, but it's not right his covetin' it since seein' the like when Mr. President passed through."

The timing was just right. Chris Beth handed a plain envelope to Mrs. Malone. "For the two of you," she said. And there inside were probably more dollar bills than they had ever seen at a single viewing.

"I will not take this," Mrs. Malone said stoutly. "You was my guest, not my boarder!"

"And this is my gift, not my payment."

Instead of further objecting, Mrs. Malone blew her nose, and led Chris Beth to the corner where sat a hand-finished chest. "Made it in his spare time." She nodded to a beaming O'Higgin.

"Oh, Mrs. Malone, its *beautiful*!"

"Open it, then."

Chris Beth stared in astonishment at the stacks of bleached flour sacks, all snowy-white and embroidered with everything from wild flowers to teapots—each bearing the initials C.E.K.

"Now there will be no more foolish tears," Mrs. Malone said matter-of-factly. "It's time for mince pie and coffee before the sun sets. Oh," she called over her shoulder, "them's for your chest!" No crying, Mrs. Malone had said, but how about blushing?

One couldn't gild a lily, Chris Beth had always heard. Well, Joe and Wilson could! As the five of them sat toasting their toes by the fire back at the North house, Joe spoke to Wilson, "Me first?"

At Wilson's nod, Joe removed a velvet box from his pocket, opened it unceremoniously, and removed a dainty gold lavaliere. "My mother's," he said simply. "Will you wear it, Chris Beth?"

"With pride," she said with equal simplicity.

Young Wil left his new books, notebook for leaf collections, and tool chest to watch as Joe fastened the chain around Chris Beth's throat. Did he intend to say something? Apparently not. The boy went back to his gifts and Wilson, ill-at-ease for the first time Chris Beth remembered, tried to untie the ribbon on a small box—obviously a gift for Vangie.

"Here, let me do it," young Wil said with the special impatience that children reserve for adults. His uncle handed him the box.

Vangie gasped, "Oh, Wilson!" when she saw the ring with a pearl mounted in the quaint style of his mother's generation. Without another word, she extended her left hand and he slipped the ring on it carefully. The lavaliere had been a surprise. The ring was not, it was plain to see.

Suddenly everybody seemed to be embracing everybody else on this wonderful day which had held so many surprises and emotions. This was so right for Vangie, Chris Beth realized. She herself had long since put away any feelings she might have had to the contrary. As she had told young Wil, where was he? To her relief, he was still with his gifts, though it was plain to see that he was not concentrating.

"Yoo-hoo! Congratulations are in order," she called to him.

"Want to be first to kiss the bride-to-be?" Wilson smiled.
Young Wil studied his shoes. "Kissing's silly."

"Often is," Vangie surprised Chris Beth by agreeing, "but
how about a handshake?" She watched as young Wil com-
plied—proud of them both, and a lot in love with everybody
in the room!

36
Flood!

꘎

THE WEEKS WENT TUMBLING end on end, and
suddenly it was February. Although the mountains were
robed in snow, the valley put on its green girdle of spring. The
meadows, kept growing all winter by the rain, were embroidered here and there with sleepy buttercups. O'Higgin pointed
to the heavy catkin-wigs that the walnut trees wore and
predicted the best crop ever. Chris Beth filled the classroom
with fat pussy willows. Mrs. Malone let the early baby chicks
out for occasional days when sun and showers played tag, but
kept a "weather eye" out. "It's a false spring we're gettin',"
she said darkly. Chris Beth and Vangie smiled indulgently,
ignoring the older woman's warning that "nobody predicts
Oregon weather but fools and newcomers." The worst was
over.

The roads had been so bad at times that the wagon wheels
mired to the hubs. The valley folk had almost everything they
needed, having looked ahead, and what they lacked some
friendly neighbor supplied. But there was a need for Brother
Jonas to make one of his seldom visits. Nobody felt the need
more keenly than Wilson and Vangie. Vangie, Chris Beth

146

noted, had blossomed. Approaching motherhood became her. Under Wilson's watchful eye, things had gone well in spite of her fragility. But it was easy to understand her decision to yield to Wilson's insistence that they be married before the baby's arrival. Not that neighbors doubted her widowhood (Maggie's attempt at gossip had been more about the living arrangement the four of them had settled upon). The real reason for wanting the wedding before April was that Wilson wanted to make the baby a "true North."

As Vangie sewed the doll-like garments which the new arrival would need and Chris Beth worked long hours on lesson plans that she hoped would meet the needs of her at-all-levels students, the sisters laughed a lot as they wondered which would arrive first—the stork or the circuit rider. "Wouldn't we shock Mama right off her daybed?" Vangie giggled. "First we're wayward, then we're liberal!"

Mama's package (slipped out by her one remaining servant, she had said) came after the holidays. It had silk (for making a long christening gown, she said). Instead, Vangie used it to line a padded "receiving box" which she could transport in the buggy. She and the baby would be making house calls with Wilson, she said proudly. Mama had sent velvet for drapes, too. It was totally inappropriate for a log cabin, the girls admitted, but one of these days, who knew?

Some of the work slacked off at the mill, which gave both Joe and Wilson time for further preparation for their professions. Wilson was to take over Doc's practice in late spring, having put in more time than internship required when the bad epidemic of measles broke out. "Someday," he said, "there will be no need for losing children with complications resulting from childhood diseases." That hope, Chris Beth knew, was his reason for pursuing pathology as time allowed.

Joe was looking a little tired. Mrs. Malone said it was "his liver," and Chris Beth wondered if he ate right when she wasn't around. Wilson assured them both that it was neither. He was studying too hard. "Not afraid he won't make it, but to him it makes a difference how *well*." Yes, Chris Beth knew,

Joe was like that—a totally dedicated man. Occasionally she let her mind wonder foolishly just what being a minister's wife would be like. Surely nobody in her right mind would consider the role! Once, talking about "somebody else," of course, she had said that most women would feel unworthy.

Joe's smile looked a little crooked somehow. "Most ministers feel so, too. I—I'm not exactly preparing for my final exam for the sainthood myself."

But don't let the little doubts keep you from the pulpit, her heart pleaded. Still, she felt she had no right to speak out. Inwardly she hoped that something would prove to this wonderful man just how right he was for the ministry.

There was to be a taffy-pull at the general store the night the flood came. *Would people really travel that far?* Chris Beth wondered. They would. *In spite of the rain?* Yes, unless the creeks were rising—and certainly the February break had helped dry out the roads. Well, it made little difference to the four of them. They had said polite "No's" to pie socials, quilting bees, and even the "Big Stomp," when (for good luck) it was customary for the entire population to turn out. The purpose was to smooth the newly laid floor as children played and adults square-danced away the night. It was unwise for Vangie, Wilson said. Yes, and all of them were busy. As a matter of fact, Chris Beth made certain that O'Higgin and Mrs. Malone were along when the four appeared anywhere together. Maybe Maggie would have less of a case if they were properly chaperoned. One day they would have to reckon with what they were doing, she supposed. Vangie and Wilson would "make things right," but—she always stopped her thinking at that point. She would just have to find a place when Joe moved back into the cabin. . . .

Clouds began building up early in the day of the taffy-pull. They were innocent-looking enough at first but later built into white towers edged in darkness. "Back home I'd think we were to have a real blow," she told the children. Looking again, she felt an uneasiness growing inside. "Since it's the night of the party at the Solomons, why don't we dismiss early?"

The youngsters romped through the door and disappeared their separate directions, whooping with the joy of school-let-out. Then there was an eerie silence. Maybe she should go home too. Even as she reached the decision, she was aware of great puffs of wind. Thinking it would be cold outside, she secured her cape about herself.

Outside, however, it was warm—too warm. Why, the wind was almost hot! Even so, its force was terrible. Bracing herself against it, she rushed toward the footbridge. A heavy tattoo of great raindrops nearly swept her off her feet. The sky was black now, and it was hard to see. Her cape was wrenched from her hands as the rain came down in torrents. Her hair fell in wet, tangled disarray and her long skirt—drenched through and through—clung to her boots, threatening to trip her every step. "Joe! Joe!" she screamed wildly against the roar of the storm. Behind her there was a splintering crash. The school? No, the graveyard shack! Then she knew she had become disoriented and had traveled in the wrong direction. She was near the cemetery, on flat ground, near the creek on the opposite side. Water was roaring through the creek, but how could it all happen so fast? She had no way of knowing, of course, that the Chinook winds—fear of the settlers—had come too early, melting the snowpack and causing streams and rivers to rise, breaking the feeble dam the men had built in hopes of staving off such disasters. She only knew that the earth trembled.

Somewhere back of her a light flashed. Lightning? Where *was* everybody? Vangie would be scared . . . water was rising around her boots . . . she couldn't move . . . the light of a lantern exploded in her face, blinding her, and she was lifted in a pair of gentle arms. . . .

When Chris Beth became aware of what was going on about her, she realized that she was in a strange room. But the face above her was dearly familiar. "Joe, *Joe*—" she whispered. Then his had been the arms!

"Thank God," he whispered against her wet hair, which had fallen hopelessly around her shoulders. But before there was time for further conversation, a familiar voice said from the doorway, "Joe!" She recognized it as belonging to Mrs. Malone. She looked around her. Of course! She was in the Upper Room of the Turn-Around Inn. But where was all the noise coming from? What had happened?

As she began to recall the events, Chris Beth knew that by some miracle Joe had come for her. But now others were in need. She could hear sobbing and screams from below. Hurriedly, stumbling at first, then more sure of herself, she wrapped her head in a towel from the washstand and hurried to the top of the stairs. Joe would be needing her, as would Wilson, Vangie, and all the others! For, to her great joy, she had spotted them all below—even young Wil, who was helping his uncle lay the writhing body of a young woman on a stretcher improvised from a quilt. And *Vangie!* Vangie was standing on the other side, rubbing the woman's wrists and speaking in the professional tones of a much-concerned nurse.

The group moved into a downstairs room, but not before Chris Beth recognized the young Mrs. Martin, who was about to give birth to her child. She sent up a little prayer and motioned for Joe to help some of the people upstairs, who appeared uninjured but were sobbing in the way that told her they had suffered losses too great to bear. She met him halfway, offering words of encouragement.

After that she lost all track of time. In one sense it seemed to drag through eternity while in another it was all over in the twinkling of an eye. How many times, she wondered later, did she and Joe travel wordlessly downstairs and up again? How many people did they comfort? She only heard enough to know that homes were gone, people were missing, livestock was swept downstream before there was time to get them to higher ground, and that young Mrs. Martin wasn't going to make it. Her husband had been drowned in trying to get to Doc Dagan, but the baby boy, maybe, would live. . . .

It was unreal. It was a bad dream. It would go away. Nothing would come into focus except Joe's dear face as his great eyes met hers over the huddled forms of those bereaved.

The long gray fingers of an ugly dawn were poking at the windows. The world outside was sodden. But inside all was quiet—temporarily. Sometime during the "awful glory" of the night, Joe had leaned over one of the sleeping guests and whispered, "Will you marry me?" And she, too weary to speak, had nodded, "Yes." Then, with hands clasped across the bed, they had fallen into an exhausted slumber.

There Mrs. Malone found them when she took a head count and brought in great mugs of steaming coffee. It was still raining, she told them. In spite of that, the water was receding because the snowpack had melted. "It was like the end of the world," Mrs. Malone said of the storm. "An awful boom, then without warning the big wall of water. Lots of folks on their way to the gen'ral store got stranded, as you see—just God's blessing they was near." She paused just as her husband brought still-hot sourdough biscuits with butter oozing tantalizingly down their sides. "Eat up, both o'ye. 'Twas like the demons o' hell, that wind! Took down our peach trees and blew away the chicken coops."

Between the two of them they told of the death and destruction which the now-receding river and the big blow had left behind. "But the good Lord always brings good from adversity," Mrs. Malone summed up the tragedy. "Land that was swept away's replaced, I wager, with rich silt from the riverbed. Things'll green up for sure now. And here in the settlement, miracles are goin' on." Her knowing eyes told Chris Beth that she and Joe were one of them, and then she went on, "Dare say one took place in the downstairs side room where poor little Miz Martin died—givin' us a chance to rally round—"

"*Died!*" Joe sprang up, but O'Higgin restrained him. "Your job not be finished here—or Wilson's—that be why we have ye sleepin'. Jonas showed, he did, and he took care of the needs."

"Put her away real nice," Mrs. Malone added. "Poor little

thing died never knowin' her husband's body's now on its way to the ocean to be buried at sea, or that their cabin in the lowlands went with him. But," she brightened, "she rallied long enough for Wilson and Vangie to let 'er know the baby's alive—very much so. Lustiest lungs I've known for a spell. Well, best we get downstairs, O'Higgin. Others need feedin'."

"I'll go with you," Chris Beth said quickly. "I need to wash up." She needed time to think, too. Had Joe really proposed?

As she washed in the basin by the pump, Chris Beth wondered if some of what happened in the Upper Room could have been a dream. Would Joe—quiet, unassuming, and shy though he was—take so great a step in such circumstances? Wouldn't he choose a more appropriate time and place? The cold water on her face and the bracing coffee did their job. She was wide awake—and wildly exhilarated. Of course he would! What better setting than as the two of them did the job the Lord had chosen them for in the first place?

She tiptoed back upstairs. There were things they needed to talk about. The circuit rider would be here a while, as was his habit, to stay "bindin' up wounds." There was the matter of the contract, of course. Well, she would let Joe come up with some solutions.

But he had no opportunity. Mrs. Malone, having witnessed so many miracles during the last 24 hours, seemed in need of one more. Soundlessly she tiptoed up behind Chris Beth with the newborn Baby Martin in her arms. "Well, which of you wants him?" Chris Beth and Joe both reached out, joining hands as they did so. It was all too wonderfully incredible to be believed, even by the settlers who had gathered below. Prayer was a powerful instrument, but this time the Lord's answer left them astounded. *Brother Joseph was sliding down the banister!*

37
Double Wedding—
Triple Joy

❧

IT WAS A BEAUTIFUL WEDDING. Valley folks talked about it for years. Like the Christmas program, they said, there had never been anything like it in the settlement, and most likely they would never see another one so grand.

Of course, it was a "mite peculiar," what with one bride ready "to deliver" and the other with a week-old baby! All understandable, though, since the one ready for "her confinement" was widowed and the other had taken in the orphan child. Nice that he'd be "wearin' the family name of the other parents—probably call him 'Mart.'" A little unusual that a woman Mollie Malone's age would be a bridesmaid—well, matron-of-honor—but circumstances warranted it, considering that somebody had to hold the Martin baby and everybody knew that young teacher refused to let him out of her sight. Lucky child, they all agreed.

Didn't young Wil look handsome standing up there like a little man, handing out rings all around? First double-bestman they'd ever seen. Maybe that's the way folks did things down South or back East, " 'specially when it's double kin," what with Miss Chrissy marrying Brother Joseph and her younger sister marrying young Dr. North. Why, the boys were like brothers!

O'Higgin looked like he had just licked the cream off Mollie's churning! Likely the only reason he got to do the honors of giving Miss Evangeline away was to keep him from those croupy things he called bagpipes! But one thing there was simply no explaining. How in the world did Nate Goldsmith get hog-tied into giving their beloved teacher away? He had vowed all over the neighborhood that contracts were binding come "you-know-what and high water." Of course, some said the president of the board got himself a bit of both! Seems Mollie and Olga descended on him at the same time. *Olga*? His "ole woman"!

Wilson North would be a fine doctor. He was bound to prosper with all he had going on, and folks were sure to get sick even with home remedies. But Brother Joseph? He was a "called preacher" all right, but wouldn't a church be out of the question after all the damages of the flood? Well, they'd all pitch in and help. It was customary to "pound the preacher," and they sure had everything to do it with—all the dried fruit, smoked hams, and canned goods. And Bertie Solomon had talked about their need for staples. Depend on Bertie to come through in time of trouble!

Chris Beth and Vangie waited beside the fireplace-setting of the improvised altar. How good of Mrs. Malone to have thought of it, but, then, how good of her to have taken over the entire wedding completely as she did! It would have been unwise for Vangie to try to descend the stairs, lovely though it might have been. Chris Beth tucked in the corners of her mouth lest she smile when the grooms came down instead. Mrs. Malone had declared herself "bound and determined" that somebody was coming out of the Upper Room. What would these wonderful people think if Joe decided to *slide* down to meet her?

What the audience saw as Miss Chrissy, "a vision in white wearing Miss Mollie's wedding dress," as she looked demurely at her bouquet. Little did they know (Chris Beth hoped!) that it was hard to erase the memory of Joe's wild trip down those banisters when she had said "Yes" to his proposal and to their taking the baby just as readily. One look at her lovely bouquet—lilies of the valley and early daffodils from Mrs. Malone's "protected side of the house," plus the leaves Joe had so thoughtfully preserved—eased the urge to smile and brought the urge to weep with tenderness. Never would she forget the beauty of their first day in the autumn woods. That was the day the two of them had expressed their "hidden desires"—hers to tramp through the autumn leaves and his to slide down the banisters at Turn-Around Inn. Surely God had fulfilled each desire, hidden or unknown to them.

Vangie's nosegay of violets (to match Mrs. Malone's blue crepe "second-day dress" she had so thoughtfully altered for her) trembled, but Vangie's smile was reassuring as their eyes met across their bouquets.

I guess I'll always feel a need to protect her, Chris Beth thought. But, mixed with the tenderness and concern, she felt a growing admiration for her sister. Why, the two of them were true "pioneer women" now—maybe possessing, if the truth were known, more courage than most. After all, other women their ages who had braved the challenges of the frontier had men at their sides—husbands or fathers. They—two frightened, gently bred girls—had come alone. And made it!

Somewhere there were the faint but unmistakable strains of *Lohengrin*. The Goldsmiths had brought the old organ to Turn-Around Inn at the height of last week's storm, when it looked as if the floodwaters might take their cabin. "Might as well leave it for services. Planned on donatin' it to the new church anyway," Nate had decided. "Old woman plays fer funerals and weddin's—glad it's the latter this day!" It could have been the other way, his voice implied, as he apparently recalled the battle over the broken terms of his sacred contract.

Somebody in the audience began to hum the wedding march along with the organ. And then the crowd joined in.

Yes! It was a beautiful wedding, but Chris Beth was unaware. She only knew that Joe, wonderful Joe, was coming down the stairs and that his eyes, never leaving her face, sparkled with tiny flecks of gold. . . .

38
Bless This House!

~&

LATER, AS THE ladies of the settlement opened their
bulging baskets to lay out the wedding feast, Chris Beth
placed the sleeping baby in his father's arms. "Joe, try and
understand. I need just a minute with Vangie." Of course he
understood, Joe's eyes said as proudly their gaze met over the
tiny form of their first son. The baby inhaled deeply, then
settled back into the fleecy, pink-cloud blanket shared from
Vangie's layette.

"Joe—" She wanted to tell her husband that everything was
going to be all right. One day they would have their church.
God had brought them together for His purpose, and He would
see to it that His purpose was served.

And there was so much else she wanted to say about this
love they shared, for it was very special. Beginning in friendship, love was the gentle stranger that moved in silently—and
then caught fire. It understood and shared and forgave through
good times and bad. It did not, as the Bible said, "seek its own
way," but allowed for human frailties. And when a woman
had the love of a good man, a family, and a circle of loyal
friends, she was rich! Without it, though she gain the whole

world, it would never be enough. Money could not purchase liberty, life—or love!

"Chris Beth—Chrissy darling, what is it?" Joe looked at her with concern.

The eloquent words would not come, of course. Love such as she offered could only spell itself out in the heart-to-heart living from this day forward—hoping all things for the future and forgetting all things that were past. No longer did she wish time to stand still. Love must blaze new trails, riding over petty irritations and big problems, the little heartbreaks and the great sorrows, into the bright new tomorrow— together.

Instead, she said, "Nothing. It's just—just that I love you so much!" then, as tears streamed down her face, she shooed him away as he would take her into his arms and motioned Vangie into the side room where she and Wilson had brought little Mart into the world.

Vangie, still clutching her violets, walked in. As the two couples went their separate ways later, they just had to toss out their bouquets together, Mrs. Malone insisted. They owed her that.

"Are you all right, Chrissy?" Vangie asked. Thoughtfulness was new to her, and Chris Beth's heart warmed even more at how it became her.

She nodded and reached into the bag she had packed for little Mart's use while she and Joe had a few days alone at the cabin. "Come closer," she said, pulling a small satin box from among the receiving blankets and hand-hemmed dresses. From it she lifted the exquisite pearl-and-sapphire brooch that Vangie had never seen.

Vangie gasped. "What—where?" She begged an explanation.

" 'Something blue,' " she said. "I couldn't bring myself to look at it again until after your wedding." She held up a restraining hand when Vangie would have spoken. "Someday maybe, but not now, Vangie. Just wear it for me. Please do. Turn it into a beautiful memory instead of the nightmare it has been."

Vangie, still puzzled, obliged. She tried very hard to pin the brooch at the high neckline of her blue "second day" dress. "Here, let me," Chris Beth said when Vangie fumbled.

The brooch, once a hateful reminder, nestled among the ruffles of the crepe gown as if it had always belonged there. If pearls were for tears, as Mama always said, they had been shed quite enough, Chris Beth knew. The blue of the sparkling sapphire matched the Oregon sky outside, where a few soft cumulous clouds promised fair weather ahead. Not a trace of gloom remained in her heart.

The two sisters embraced wordlessly. No words could express their emotions. And sometimes, both of them knew, silence was better.

PART II

Love's
Silent Song

Dedicated
to
Arlene Cook,
my inspired and inspiring friend!

From the Calapooias to the Siskiyous,
The Cascades to the sea,
Comes the history of the Umpqua—
This mighty land!
To say a century—a hundred years—
How long is that
To battle hardship, hunger, death,
And wash newborn babes in iron tears?
How long is that
To free a country, plow it, and hand it down?
Let us review those mystic moments
To portray with heartfelt reverence
Those immortal pioneers—
Those faithful to the Lord Almighty,
Those led in truth by unseen hand,
And salute our flag of freedom,
Symbol of this mighty land.

—From *Umpqua Cavalcade*
Copyright © 1952 by June Masters Bacher

Contents

162 CONTENTS

Preface

THERE WAS A SAYING among the early Oregon settlers which may well hold true today: "Them that wanted to find gold went to California, but them that came to Oregon wanted to find a home." And there are a lot of Northwesterners who would make the same claim today. There's a majestic spell about the region—a something indefinable that makes it *home*.

The Oregon Country is beautiful whether seen as autumn wraps a misty shawl over sun-ripened harvests, winter adds a fresh blanket of snow to the lofty peaks, or summer puts on the green girdle—laced with silver streams—that shapes the state into a nature-lover's paradise. But Oregon is best understood in the spring. It is then that azaleas and rhododendrons try to upstage one another and a million meadowlarks burst into song along some of the best of our nation's highways. Yet for a real glimpse of what the land was once like, the setting in which this book was written and a remnant of which remains, seek the back country. There you will find the near-extinct trillium and lady-slipper orchids, the fern-green glades where moss is made, and the gnarled apple trees which descendants of the pioneers declare were planted by the legendary Johnny Appleseed.

Listening to the residents, you will believe, as I came to believe. Inclining an ear to nature, you will find renewed faith. And faith is what *Love's Silent Song* is all about.

But this is not a history book, nor is it a travel folder. It is a gentle, romantic novel, a sequel to *Love is a Gentle Stranger*, written as it could only be written by one who has lived in the beautiful green corner of God's footstool—one who has seen it through the eyes of the pioneers and has come to love it as they did.

June Masters Bacher

163

1
Spell
of the Brooch

⌖

DOBBINS' LOUD NEIGH from behind the cabin
broke the tranquility of the afternoon. Another horse must be
approaching. A first caller? Careful not to awaken little Mart,
Chris Beth tiptoed to the front window.

How ridiculous to be apprehensive! Mama had seen to it
that her daughters grew up receiving guests, making small
talk, and serving tea—a practiced skill that became an art
when they left Atlanta to attend school in Boston. Ridiculous
or not, the sense of nervous excitement persisted. Maybe
because the role as lady-of-the-house was so new? No, it was
something more. She was sure of that even before spotting the
lone rider in the ancient buggy.

Chris Beth, bride of two weeks, turned to look at herself in
the bureau mirror for reassurance. She saw the same dark
brown hair, braided and wound into a smooth halo, and the
same blue eyes—brighter now, aglow. And her cheeks were
flushed with what her minister-husband called "that married
look." The blush deepened at the intimate phrase, but she felt
a little more in control. With cheeks still warm, she moved
quickly from the mirror to answer the knock at the door.

165

"Mrs. Malone!" A flood of relief swept over Chris Beth at sight of her dear friend. "How nice of you to call."

"Wanted to check in on you like." The older woman spoke in her usual warm, no-nonsense manner. "Thought you'd be needin' leaven for sourdough biscuits."

"Indeed!" Chris Beth smiled as she ushered Mrs. Malone inside and pulled Joe's "study chair" forward. "Please sit down and let's have a long chat."

"Not too long. Best I be on hand when O'Higgin and the young'uns bring in the milk. Lots of commotion 'bout then."

Chris smiled again, remembering the general bedlam of Mrs. Malone, her husband O'Higgin, and their six step-children trying to get past Ambrose, the cat, to strain the milk and set it to cool. With O'Higgin's Irish wit, *commotion* was a mild word! Such a warm, loving, hospitable family . . . Chris Beth wondered when Mrs. Malone would elect to make use of her new husband's name. Their marriage, like her own—and, yes, her sister Vangie's too—was one of the many miracles of this wild and beautiful country. She loved Oregon's every whimsical mood. *Even the flood brought us an orphaned baby to love*, her thoughts raced on.

"Returned this, too." Mrs. Malone fished in her knitting bag.

"This?" Chris Beth repeated, puzzled, as she accepted the small package. "I'm sorry. My mind was wool-gathering—"

The words died on her lips as the wrapping fell to the braided rug. For there inside lay the pearl and sapphire brooch, its gems, like evil eyes, mocking . . . taunting . . . threatening. . . .

"Are you all right, child? Why, you're pale like you'd seen a ghost?"

I have, her heart answered, *I have*. Unable to answer, Chris Beth nodded mutely. Fumbling with the wrappings, she managed to get the piece of jewelry out of sight. "I'll put the sourdough in the cooler and make coffee," she murmured, and was grateful that Mrs. Malone took out her knitting instead of offering to help.

In the sanctum of the small kitchen, she went about the

comforting routine of setting up the old tea cart as the coffee
perked contentedly. But her thoughts went back to the symbol
of the brooch . . . the excitement of first love, the whirlwind
courtship with Jonathan Blake . . . the thrill of engagement
parties, wedding plans, and "forever after" dreams . . . then
the heartbreak and humiliation of Jon's broken promises, his
plea for freedom, and her emotional death when he confessed
that, yes, there *was* another woman. The sun slipped out of
the sky at the memories. Long shadows grew and stretched,
blotting out the new life she had built here. But, cruelly, the
memories persisted, bringing back her escape to the Oregon
Country . . . her stagecoach meeting with Mollie Malone,
O'Higgin, and the men she and Vangie would eventually
marry. There was Wilson, an aspiring doctor . . . and her half
sister's arrival . . . and their tearful reunion . . . and then
the awful news that Vangie, her own sister, was to bear
Jonathan's child! Oh, the shame of it all!

"Ouch!" Chris Beth almost welcomed the pain she felt
when boiling hot coffee splashed onto her hand as she tried to
pour it. Almost fiercely she wiped up the spill, unaware that
she had used one of her embroidered tea towels.

"But then there was Joe!" she whispered almost prayerfully
as she reached for a clean cup. Dear, wonderful Joe, with
hands as gentle as his smile and concerned hazel eyes. Joe,
whose boyish bronze cowlick looked out of keeping with his
big tan frame. Her husband's little lisp when he was under
stress endeared him all the more. *And he always smells of
good earth*, she thought with a rush of affection for him . . .
for their adopted baby . . . for Vangie and her new husband
Wilson . . . and all the wonderful friends who had helped her
put down roots here.

Mrs. Malone accepted the china cup and looked at Chris
Beth above its gold rim. "It was a pretty weddin', wasn't it?"

"It was beautiful!"

So beautiful that it hurt. And the brooch she had forgotten
to return to Jonathan, strangely, made it more so! It looked as
if it belonged in the blue ruffles of Vangie's wedding gown.

The younger girl's eyes had glowed like the sapphires themselves when Chris Beth pinned it there just before their double wedding. Little did Vangie know that it was a gift from the man who had betrayed them both. That's what hurt.

Without realizing that tears were close, Chris Beth spoke. "But it hurts to look back—on the ugly part—"

Mrs. Malone drained her cup before answering. "How well I know," she said quietly as she folded her napkin and pressed it neatly with her hands. "Has its value, though. Like as not, we have to return to the troublin' past before we can find the future."

Then, tucking her knitting into her bag, Mrs. Malone turned tactfully to other matters. But Chris Beth heard little more. Jonathan was dead now. The past was dead too. But her memories were not. They would live on to gnaw away at her life as Mrs. Joseph K. Craig until somehow she broke the evil spell of the brooch and its power over her.

"If I could just come to understand the strange hold it has on me," she said aloud as she put the tea cart back in its corner.

2
New Signs of Life
~

CHRIS BETH REMEMBERED the brooch as she pulled the flannel robe closely to her body as a protective shield. The unexpected glimpse of it yesterday had chilled her bones to the marrow. In spite of her resolve to put the brooch out of her mind she had slept little, and this morning the cold crept up from her fingertips and encircled her heart. She wished fervently that Mrs. Malone had waited a while to remove the pin from the second-day dress that Vangie had borrowed from her for the wedding. Of course, the generous lady had no way of knowing that a piece of jewelry could bring back all that was hateful and frightening—even threatening—to the new life that she and Vangie had made for themselves here.

But she had best not dally. Joe would be in for breakfast shortly. Checking for needed supplies for the gristmill he and Wilson owned wouldn't take long. He deserved a square meal, a well-groomed wife, and, she thought sadly, one who was in control of the past, happy with the present, and looking forward to the fulfillment of his dreams as a minister of the gospel. That was his life. He had told her so. But she so wanted to put down roots. Could she be jealous of his dedication? The thought was unsettling. Maybe fresh air would help to rid her of such silly misgivings.

Quietly, lest she awaken her little adopted son, Chris Beth opened the bedroom window. New signs of life rushed in to greet her senses.

"Good morning, Lord," she whispered in wonder. Then, thoughtfully, she added, "Forgive me for any unworthy thoughts."

Then in reverence she turned back to the scene around her. March had turned to April, and suddenly spring was born. Wild plums bloomed out in white abandon, and budding sweetbriar softened the angles of every split-rail fence bordering the homesteads of the settlement. Valley women planted early gardens. Their menfolk cautiously sowed spring grain along the warmer slopes and set to work deadening trees for new ground, then turning the rich, mellow soil up to dry in the sun for later corn-planting. Children's squeals of joy and birds' incessant song became "an absolute nuisance" to at least one of the settlers. "Cain't even hear Bossie's cowbell!" Mrs. Malone had complained to Chris Beth when leaving yesterday.

Higher up, in the grazing lands, the Basque sheepherders rounded up the older animals for shearing. Baby lambs grew round and fleecy, and their frolicking bleats blended with the happy sounds of the busy valley below. All was peaceful, beautiful, and comforting—until the memories came back. Chris Beth shivered again, knowing that the chill had nothing to do with the cool of the dew-wet morning.

"And how is my beloved bride?"

The sudden sound of the deep, dearly familiar masculine voice startled her. Joe always removed his muddy boots at the door—"as trained," he teased. So she hadn't heard him enter the room.

"Fine—oh, Joe—"

He drew her close with a little laugh which changed to concern when he felt her trembling. "Think I was going to ambush you? Hardly!"

The strength of Joe's arms around her and the closeness of his body against hers were warmly reassuring. Why, then, was she unable to stop the tremors of her body?

Stroking her hair gently from her face, Joe let his big, capable hand slide down its long, dark cascade over her shoulders. "I should have been braiding it," she murmured vaguely.

"It's beautiful," he said huskily. His hand moved from her hair to her chin, tilting it slightly so he could look into her face. "Something *is* wrong."

When Chris Beth failed to respond, Joe steered her gently to the antique sofa, sat down, and pulled her onto his lap.

But the timing was wrong. This wasn't the time to talk. There were some things she had never discussed with him in their two weeks of marriage or before that. And he had never asked—until now.

Joe's arms tightened about her.

"Sometime—but not now, please," she whispered.

His arms loosened. "I'm sorry." There was hurt in his voice.

But drawing her close again, Joe tucked her head beneath his chin. "Tell me all about it, Chris Beth."

Settling back into the safe, warm, curled-up position, Chris Beth wondered how she could let the memories or ghosts from the past come between her and this gentle man. One of the things she loved most about him was his *caring*—about her, yes, but about others too. She wanted him to follow the Lord's call. Well, didn't she? Even if it meant taking them away from the roots she had worked so hard to put down here? "Whither thou goest" had been a part of their wedding vows.

She touched his cheek. "It's just that sometimes I think it's all too good to be true—our being here like this—and that maybe it can't last."

"Is *that* all?" Joe hugged her so closely that it was hard to breathe and he could hear his own breath shorten. "I agree with the first but not the second. Just what do you expect to wear out? Not our love, surely?"

"Oh, no!"

"And you don't regret saying 'Yes' to a struggling, country minister's proposal?"

"Oh, Joe, you *know* I don't!"

For one luxurious moment, Chris Beth wound her arms around her husband's neck and snuggled close, wanting to wipe away any hurt she might have caused and longing to share the insecurities she harbored in her heart. But a little whimper from the cradle in the corner reminded her that they were not alone.

Joe grinned. "The look on your face says it would be foolish to ask if you regretted our taking little Mart!"

The very thought brought tears. Joe wiped them away with his thumb. "Then the rest can't matter. Just as long as you don't plan dumping us two and going back to Boston."

"Never, *never!* I'd never leave here—"

There was no further sound from the cradle. The ugly memories were fading more quickly with each return. Maybe the time was right, after all, to mention her concern with their new lives together. *Just mention, that's all I'll do*, she promised herself. *There's such a need for roots. Little Mart deserves that much from us.*

"Joe, you do think we'll be staying—I mean, that there'll be a need for you here?"

Joe looked at her thoughtfully. "I've given it a lot of thought. I know there are needs. And I'm hoping we can hold on till our neighbors can afford us," Joe ended with a smile.

"But if I could teach—"

"Marriage is *verboten* in the school's contract. And it wasn't in our plans. I've been thinking that we should take some steps— maybe talk with church boards in other communities—"

"Oh, Joe, no!" The words came before she could stop them.

"I know. I feel the same way, but the ministry requires sacrifices—"

When his words trailed away, Chris Beth knew that Joe wanted with all his heart to remain here. And here they belonged. But she knew too that his first commitment was to the Lord's work, wherever it might lead. The "where" of serving was secondary. *And, for that matter*, she thought with a stir of the familiar bitterness, *so are we—little Mart and I! He's right. The ministry requires sacrifices, maybe too many.*

Immediately she was ashamed of the thought. Joe, she realized, was waiting for her reaction. "We have my salary," she began.

"Chrissy," Joe chided gently. "That ends at the last of the month. And that's not the way we planned it—living on your income."

The gristmill would hardly support the two of them, let alone Wilson and Vangie and their growing families. Of course, Wilson might sell the botany book he was writing. Or the aging Dr. Dullus might retire on schedule so Wilson could take over his patients. That would help them all indirectly.

Joe interrupted her thoughts. "It's all in the Lord's hands. We are not to worry. It'll all turn out right."

He was right, of course. Hadn't she turned over her worries to the Lord since coming here, and hadn't He done right well with them up till now? Why, counting her blessings would be like trying to count the stars.

Chris Beth was unaware that she smiled until Joe asked, "What's amusing?" and tried to draw her close again.

"A dipper full of stars!" She giggled and pulled away. "Joe! The biscuits will burn."

"I'd settle for that," he smiled, but let her go. "Sunnyside up on the eggs and I'll take care of the baby's needs."

Chris Beth's mind flew busily ahead as she poured fresh honey into the pitcher and set the coffee to heating. She had best prepare herself for the likelihood that one of the churches in the widely scattered neighborhoods would call Joe to deliver a trial sermon. That might mean leaving this beloved cabin, their first home—and how could she part with friends? And what if they called him before school was out? But that was the Lord's business, not hers.

She stopped setting the table when it occurred to her that it was possible they might leave before Vangie gave birth to her baby. She had a doctor for a husband, but a girl needed her mother, or at least an older sister. And in some unreasonable, unexplainable way, she was sure the two of them would need each other more than most sisters. Maybe because the baby was Jonathan Blake's. Somehow that tied them together—bitterly, sadly, but tenderly. Well, the Lord knew about that too.

Joe interrupted her thinking. "We men are hungry! Will you feed us, sweet teacher?"

The baby stirred noisily—another sign of new life around her.

3
Fear of
the Unknown

❧

LATER THAT MORNING Chris Beth decided to pay a call on Vangie. Outwardly she was calm. With little Mart wrapped in a warm blue blanket, she crossed the foot-log spanning the creek which separated her and Joe from Vangie and Wilson. Inwardly, something of the early-morning uneasiness remained even though she had assured Joe she was fine before he and Wilson left to purchase supplies at Solomon's General Store. It was true, really. She would feel better once she and her sister talked.

Vangie was in back of the "Big House," as the four of them distinguished the Wilson place from the Craigs' cabin. She waved and motioned for Chris Beth to join her beneath the peach trees. Chris Beth signaled back that she would wait by the back door, a safe distance from the beehive that her sister had taken on as her private project.

It seemed unsafe to take the baby any closer to the bees than that. And to be honest, she would feel safer to keep her own distance too. Over and over she cautioned Vangie about bee stings. "Bees are like piecrust. They know if you're afraid."

175

And, though singing was more Chris Beth's gift than Vangie's, "I can hum a ring around the bees," she always giggled.

This morning even her humming was off-key. Brahms' *Lullaby* was scarcely recognizable, but the bees didn't seem to mind. Busily they went about the business of gathering pollen from the pink-petaled fruit trees.

"I'm glad you came," Vangie said as she opened the back door and crooked an inviting finger into the big kitchen. "Coffee's still warm, I think."

"And you've baked a coffee cake!"

"Your recipe—but I'm learning!"

Learning lots of things, Chris Beth marveled at her sister's courage and strength. *She's more to be admired than I.* Mama had always overprotected her younger sister, and leaning had become a way of life. Out here where adversity abounded, Vangie had bloomed into a frontier woman almost overnight.

But then Vangie inhaled shakily. "They give me courage—the bees. You know what? This summer I'm going to harvest the honey all by myself—with the baby, of course. I don't want the baby to be plagued by fear like I was. Then," she rambled on, "we can have honey all winter and—"

"Vangie," Chris reprimanded gently when she recognized the sure sign that her sister was avoiding a painful subject.

Vangie stopped, then blurted out, "I—I'm so afraid of childbirth! Oh, I want this baby so much—you understand?"

Oh, Vangie! Her own heart cried out. *Do you really expect me to understand the way you want me to when it's Jonathan's child you are carrying? Can't you see that I'm frightened too?*

Vangie's violet eyes were wide. "You have forgiven me—us—the baby, I mean?"

With that she tumbled into Chris Beth's arms exactly as she used to when it thundered or when her father went into one of his rages. Only Vangie wasn't a little girl anymore. And she was wedging Baby Mart between them.

"There, there," Chris Beth found herself soothing as always. She unpinned little Mart with one hand and tried to support her sister with the other. "Let's talk!" She made her voice purposely brusque. "Now, just what are you afraid of?"

"The unknown. Does that make sense?"

It did. It made more sense than her own fears, which were just the opposite: *known* fears—great green-eyed monsters always standing in the wings, awaiting their cue for reentry, to reenact the tragic moments of her life, to tear down and destroy her new world.

"Chris Beth! What am I going to *do?*" The great, childish china-blue eyes sought her own dark blue ones.

Chris Beth forced a courage she did not feel. "First," she said, hoping to calm her sister, "you are going to hold your nephew. Then you're going to count his pink toes and fingers and enjoy the miracle that God is creating inside *you*. And, while you think on that, I'm going to read our favorite passage. We've been afraid before, you know."

"And you always read the Twenty-third Psalm!"

"Right." Chris Beth reached for the large Bible that she guessed had belonged to Wilson's parents. Somehow it was no surprise that the purple satin ribbon marked the very Scripture that she planned to read.

"The Lord is my shepherd . . ." she read. ". . . He restoreth my soul . . . Yea, though I walk through the valley of the shadow of death, I shall fear no evil. . . ."

At the end of the chapter, Chris Beth stopped. She doubted that Vangie noticed. She was too busy gazing with awe and reverence into the tiny face of the sleeping baby. And softly she hummed the sad-sweet strains of the lullaby she had sung to the bees. Only this time the pitch was perfect.

Life, Chris Beth thought as she crossed the foot-log on her way back to the cabin, *is not a matter of well-executed lesson plans. I can't work out every detail and expect the how, when, and where of it all to unfold on schedule.* Actually, she admitted to herself, she had gone to Vangie to line up forces. Maybe if they both expressed their true feelings about not wanting to leave the settlement . . . But, even as she thought of such a plot, Chris Beth felt a surge of relief that her sister's needs had changed that. Such action would have been leaving out Joe and Wilson's thinking—and God's guidance. She had overlooked the *why* of it all.

The calm she had pretended before came now, settling on her shoulders like a warm shawl. It was strange how helping another person brought strength to handle her own problems! "Just help me learn to handle them one at a time, Lord, and not without consulting You and Joe. . . ."

4
Guide Us, Lord!
❧

YOUNG WIL RAN breathlessly to share the news with Chris Beth instead of going to his own home when he, his Uncle Wilson, and Joe returned from the general store. Although she adored the boy, Chris Beth wished for the sake of the still-new relationship between himself and Vangie that he would not shut her sister out so obviously. He was courteous, Vangie said. Well, that was a start. But Chris Beth knew that more was needed. His first-love crush on her showed signs of developing into the kind of more mature relationship that would leave no permanent scars. As his teacher and wife of his uncle's best friend, and because she and Vangie were sisters, it was essential that there be no jealousies.

"Guess what?" young Wil gasped at the door. Esau's wild barks and the excited honking of the three white geese welcomed him. The boy stopped short, lowering his voice. "Is little Mart asleep?"

Not likely now! Well, then, guess what! Chris Beth couldn't, just as he hoped, so he would have to tell her.

"A *really* big wagon train came just last Thursday and another one this morning. Then . . ." He drew a quick breath and rushed on, ". . . the drivers said a third one's coming over the Applegate Trail—all gonna settle here and—"

Chris Beth was having as much trouble breathing as young Wil. A thrill of excitement filled her. Maybe all their doubts about the future would resolve themselves. Maybe the valley would grow and boom as she, Joe, Wilson, and Vangie had dreamed about around the hearth before the wedding. Waterways opening . . . railroads coming through . . . stagecoaches linking California and Oregon from Redding to Portland. That would mean business and new neighbors. Oh, wouldn't it be *wonderful* if—

"You're not listenin'."

"Stop swallowing your g's," Chris Beth said automatically.

"Had to so you'd listen. So *if* you're listening?"

She was. Then there was more, he said. Cattle drivers coming through with herds and herds! Did he know for sure? Well, he had it on "good authority" about the settlers and cattle for sure, and about the other stuff—well, Uncle Wil and Joe *said* it was bound to happen. Wasn't that good enough? Chris Beth nodded happily.

But wait! "Wil, were there children?"

The boy whooped and somersaulted dangerously near the round oak table where supper was laid out. "Hundreds. *Zillions!* There's bound to be more kids than parents, you know."

That figured. Pioneer families were large. But what on earth would she do with even one more student? The one-room school was already overcrowded, and families had pooled every available resource to floor and roof the building. Of course, her contract had only two weeks to go, and most likely the "zillions" of youngsters would be more valuable to their parents at home until next year. Yet there were little Mart and Vangie's baby to think about sometime . . . but that was a long way ahead. Maybe none of them would be here.

"Miss Chrissy, what about me?" young Wil asked abruptly. "What'll happen to me next year? Will *I* be here, too?"

"I don't know, Wil. I honestly don't know," Chris Beth

answered, avoiding his frightened eyes. It had taken her so
long to coax the bright young mind into constructive chan-
nels. Just remembering brought a set of new concerns.

Outside, the men were unloading grain they had hauled
home for grinding. It was hard to tell in the gathering dusk
whether their faces showed the concerns that she and young
Wil shared.

"We'll just count our pennies in the sugar bowl." She forced
a smile, although the words were closer to the truth than she
wanted him to know. "And ask the Lord to help us, of course."

"Right now? I mean the prayer part?"

The question caught her busy mind off guard, but she
answered as naturally as possible. "What better time?"

Young Wil hesitated. Chris Beth knew he was struggling
with his faith, as well as with his schoolwork and a growing
child's changing emotions. To him she was ever the teacher.
Whatever concerns she had must be set aside for him, as they
had been set aside for Vangie earlier.

"Aw, shucks!" The boy shuffled his worn brogans. Chris
Beth noted with tenderness for the motherless child that both
his shoelaces were untied. "I don't like praying out loud.
Couldn't we just—let's *think* the words. Some I want to keep
secret."

"Me, too," she smiled. And the prayer she prayed was
simple. "Guide us, Lord," she thought wordlessly, "to accept
Your will."

5
Counting Heads–
And Days

❧

THE SUN WAS JUST RISING on the morning of another school day. Counting this Monday, there were only ten more days to go before school would end for the year. Chris Beth dressed hurriedly, put the coffee on to boil, and checked on little Mart. Although Joe always saw to transporting the little fellow to the Big House, where Vangie kept him until the end of the school day, Chris Beth liked the morning time with him. "Love begins in the cradle," she said repeatedly to Joe. Joe was such a wonderful father . . . little Mart was such a wonderful baby . . . and this was such a wonderful country.

All this she thought as she braided her hair and packed a quick lunch. "Truly, Robert Browning was right," she smiled at Joe as he came in from outside. " 'God's in His heaven, all's right with the world. . . .' " And it *was* as her husband hugged her close.

At school, although there were no new heads to count, the children buzzed with excitement. All ran to meet her with the rumor (started by Young Wil, she suspected) that soon the school would be "jam-packed" and would need 14 rooms and maybe an upstairs.

"Will they be gittin—gettin' . . . *getting* here afore school's out?" Harmony Malone wondered.

"Or in time fer the end-o'-school program?" Burtie Beltran asked.

Mercy! She had hardly thought about the program—a "must," the children assured her. But the Basque child had a solution: "I could bring another lamb, like at Christmas."

"Lamb *tongues* ud be better." There was still a high nasal twang to Wong Chu's voice, like a taut bowstring suddenly released. Yet it was amazing how far the Chinese child had come during the school year. But lamb tongues?

"They're flowers, little yellow ones that hide around rocks," young Wil volunteered. "But they grow here, too. Unless maybe we could picnic up at Wong's? I've never been way up there to the railroad camp." He looked at her hopefully.

Chris Beth recalled the shy Oriental father who had won the hearts of the audience by laying his own infant son in the manger in place of the rag doll the night of the Christmas program. She doubted if he would want guests, however. It was best not to push things—just let them happen.

Wong cast his almond-shaped eyes downward. "I'll ask." But before she was able to explain that he need not ask that of his parents, the others were talking.

"We could ride wagons—like when Mr. President come— comed . . . and there's dogwood . . . and shootin' stars . . . and lady's slippers—"

"Orchids," young Wil corrected. Then, turning to Chris Beth, he added, "*Fissipes acaulis*, little purple flowers shaped like a shoe. They're rare."

And so are you, she thought. What a mind!

They were having a wonderful time—children and teacher— when Nate Goldsmith stepped inside the door. There was no reason for the president of the school board to be critical, but Chris Beth doubted if this scene fit his "lick 'em and larn 'em" philosophy. She blushed, hating herself for it.

Her flushed face or the unexpected "company" silenced the children. But, at her signal, they chimed in unison, "Good morning, Mr. Goldsmith!" as she had taught them to greet guests.

Nate Goldsmith answered curtly, adjusted a suspender, and touched his sparse hair nervously. Then he approached Chris Beth.

"Best we speak in private." He motioned to an empty corner.

"Yes, Sir," she answered, wondering what could be so important. "Boys and girls, quietly go about your work," she pleaded more than ordered. Dutifully she tagged along behind her visitor.

"Warned you I'd be comin'," he said, reminding her of his previous promise.

"You're welcome any time." (But I do wish you'd have warned *when!*)

"Wonder sometimes if you teachers realize jest how important education is." He patted some document in his vest pocket.

"I think we do. We've worked hard."

"Then none o' ye'll have trouble passin' my test."

"Your *what?*" There was only a moment to study the deep lines on his face. Gravity had been his worst enemy, some faraway part of her mind thought, as she noted his nose dropping toward the floor like the beak of a great bird.

"Test!" One I conjured up." Mr. Goldsmith pulled a sheet of paper from his pocket—questions for his self-styled "oral examination."

Chris Beth tried to regain her composure. "Wouldn't you like to have me write the questions on the chalkboard?"

"Nope! I'll do it oral. Anyways, you'll be takin' it too." And before she recovered from her surprise, the man was at the front of the room telling the children to prepare for the test "determinin' whether you git promoted or sit here like dummies."

With a roomful of fear-whitened faces looking back at her

for support, Chris Beth nodded encouragement and tore a sheet
of paper from her rough tablet. And the ridiculous test began.

The hand on her enameled watch crept toward recess, but
still Nate Goldsmith's test went on. The first President of the
United States. The *now*-president. Your first name. The last
letter in the alphabet. The square root of the number of feet in
a square mile. How to spell *Constantinople*—by syllables!

"Too bad ye'll not be comin' back," he said to Chris Beth
when finally the exhausted children were outside to play.
"If'n you passed th' test, it might've meant a five-dollar
raise—if crops is good. Need good teachers with all the
newcomers. Hear 'bout that?"

Chris Beth nodded mutely. What she and Joe couldn't do
with the added five dollars! Or with any job at all, for that
matter. But she knew the terms of the contract. "No marryin'." Nate Goldsmith had "warned" her about that, too, she
remembered a little bitterly. Still, it was good that he had
allowed her to violate the sacred terms long enough to finish
the remaining month of the school year.

" 'Marry in haste; repent in leisure,' my old mother used to
say."

Fighting for control, she started to protest. "But I—"

He waved away her interruption. "Wait'll I'm finished." He
cleared his throat loudly. "I overheered the talk, y'know,
while standin' at the door. We cain't have that."

What had he found so offensive? She tried to remember the
talk.

"Talkin' 'bout the business of transportin' children so fur."

"Oh, the end-of-school picnic—"

Again he silenced her with a lifted hand.

"Any picnic'll be hereabouts."

"I hadn't planned—"

"Parents in these parts wouldn't like goin' near them
railroad shanties and—" he fumbled for words, "well, mixin'
with Chinks."

Something inside Chris Beth exploded. "Mr. Goldsmith, I
don't allow the children to speak like that. And, you'll pardon

me, Sir," she drew herself up full height, "I'll not allow it of others!"

Immediately she regretted the hasty words. She had made a mistake. Probably the man would not permit her to finish the remaining weeks now. "Lotsa teachers cain't last the year out," he had warned direly when she signed the contract. But she wasn't going to make an apology when she was right. And suddenly she was bold again.

Wiping away the beginning of a tear, she rang the bell sharply. And, before Nate could make a getaway, he was surrounded by bright-eyed children whose coltish play stopped as they lined up to reenter the room. Sensing that something was wrong, they lowered their voices to whispers.

"Boys and girls!" The children straightened. But the warning in her voice was not for them. "Mr. Goldsmith has an announcement!"

She took a near-wicked satisfaction in the man's obvious discomfort.

"We—you—" he said haltingly, "well, there mayn't be a picnic. Leastwise over yonder!"

Young Wil's hand shot up like his cowlick. "You mean to Wong's, Sir?"

Nate tugged at his beard. "Th' same."

"But we *want* to go there—if his folks'll let us. And Miss Chrissy always lets us help decide—"

"Yeah," the other children interrupted, "we wanna go . . . he's our friend . . . we wanna go!"

Maybe she should reprimand the children. Well, she wasn't going to. Let him demonstrate the educational "know how" he boasted about.

The chants grew louder. Frustrated, Nate Goldsmith yelled above them, "*I* make the decisions." And with that, the president of the board whirled and stalked out.

The nerve of him! She watched him go, wanting to hit him in the back with the nearest schoolbook.

6
Unbelievable Events

⤴

THE EVENTS OF the next two weeks were unbelievable. Chris Beth shared each detail with Vangie, whose "time"
was too close at hand for her to risk leaving home. She was
hungry to hear of the outside world and hung onto every
word.

"It helps me keep my mind occupied and from getting rusty
until the baby comes," Vangie kept saying. And invariably she
would always ask, "Do you think I should go back to my
nursing then—part-time, anyway?"

"You'd be a wonderful help to Wilson. Is he still working on
his botany book?"

"When he has time—and when he's not doctoring me. For
your sake he's trying to coax the littlest North to hang on
until after school closes."

Calling Jonathan's unborn child a "North" touched off the
memories again. Of course, Vangie and Wilson *had* hurried up
the date of their marriage to make the baby a "true North,"
they said—

Vangie interrupted her thoughts. "Tell me about today!"

Grateful to get back to the present, Chris Beth shared. And what she shared set both girls to rolling with laughter.

The two of them had decided not to mention Monday's slurring remarks that Nate Goldsmith made about the Chinese family. Joe and Wilson had enough to think about without human relations entering in.

"Well, this morning guess what I found in my trash can?"

Vangie giggled. "A gun with the initials *N.G.* and a notch on the handle."

"I won't be needing a weapon," Chris Beth laughed in return. "There, wadded into tight balls, were all the answer sheets to that make-believe test he administered!"

On Wednesday, the Goldsmith children gathered around Chris Beth with the news that their pa was coming to school again. And this time he was bringing Ma. It was Ma's first time to visit, they said excitedly. Chris Beth was excited, too, but anxiously so.

The couple arrived in reverse order, with Ma bringing Pa! The little lady looked as defenseless as ever in her dark dress with the white collar and cuffs. But she wore the same determined look that Chris Beth remembered at Turn-Around Inn as she jabbed a prompting elbow into Nate's ribs until he made an "exception to the rule" and allowed Chris Beth to complete the school year—married or not.

"The ole woman has something to say—she wants *me* to say," he said sheepishly.

He hesitated then, but the flash of Olga Goldsmith's eyes warned of a barrage of French-German if he didn't deliver the message in English.

"She thinks—we think—maybe, bein' good Christians and all, we should ought to go to the Chu family's place, after all. Kind of a goodwill gesture, you know. We could surprise 'em."

Above the children's whoops of joy, Chris Beth (trying to keep a straight face) answered, "I think they'd rather know. Wong can help us plan today."

"Us neighbors will arrange some wagons like always—and the dinner and all. Think Brother Joseph can join us?"

Joe? He wouldn't miss this for the world and 10 percent more, she thought. Aloud she said, "I will talk to him."

As it happened, there was no need to plan with Wong. On Thursday he brought his father to school!

Chris Beth was unaware that Mr. Chu waited by the door to be asked inside, until she called the roll and it was sharing time. She began in the usual alphabetical order of names.

But Wong, who was usually very meek, could not wait his turn. "Missie Chrissy, Missie Chrissy!" he burst out. "I 'ave someone!"

It was good to see the boy so eager. Supposing the "some-*one*" to mean "some*thing*," Chris Beth was surprised when Wong ran to the door. "My *fath*-er!" he announced happily.

All the other children clapped. Chris Beth felt tears of pride close to the surface. *They've all come so far, so far,* she thought for the thousandth time. *How can I leave them this year?*

Mr. Chu bowed politely to her and then to the class. " 'Scuse please," he said, and reached for the only piece of chalk remaining for the school year. With it he made a series of signs on the chalkboard, which she supposed to be Chinese language symbols. The children were delighted and clapped again.

The man bowed to his son. Wong bowed back. "My father wants me to say you are to come please to the meadow of our home. There the lamb tongues grow."

"Oh, can we—may we—*please!*" Boys and girls alike chorused.

She nodded and Mr. Chu smiled broadly for the first time. "Ancestors will be pleased," he said. Then, tucking his hands inside his kimona-sleeved coat, he padded softly through the door.

Vangie stitched skillfully in and out on the intricate pattern of her latest piece of needlepoint as Chris Beth shared the week's events. Her hands stopped their almost-musical rhythm only when she paused to bite a thread or to laugh.

Chris Beth loved to watch. How like Mama her sister was—so delicately beautiful, so able to shut the whole world out with colored yarn and a piece of canvas! A feeling of homesickness swept over her as she remembered watching the two women together. Swallowing the lump in her throat, she concentrated on the embroidery.

The work was exquisite as always, a rainbow design of flowers, birds, and leaves, as beautifully intermingled as the seasons in the lovely Oregon Country—or the loving hearts of families and friends here. Symbolic and beautiful.

"I wish I had half your talent," she sighed.

Vangie smiled. "Oh, but you do it with people—sort of embroider their lives with love, you know?"

"Oh, Vangie, I will cherish that thought."

"Wilson embroiders with his hands. Just his touch makes people feel better, wouldn't you say?"

The question startled Chris Beth, but Vangie didn't seem to notice. "And Joe makes the world beautiful with words. Finished!" She laid the tapestry aside. "Well, it's been a week of surprises."

Yes, the week had furnished its share of surprises, all right. As Chris Beth carefully catwalked the foot-log back to the cabin on Friday afternoon, she suspected—no, she *knew*— that the next week would afford more. She "foresaw" it.

Some would say it was fantasy, she supposed. Vangie's father would have said it was a "work of the devil." Chris Beth knew it was neither. But just what it was she didn't know— this certain unique power to foresee the future under certain conditions. Always, as now, she first felt a little breathless before a curtain parted in her mind. Today the dizziness passed quickly. She inhaled to still the rapid beating of her heart as spread before her she saw a wide meadow filled with people, their arms linked around her, their song echoing against the hills. . . .

7
The Picnic
and Its Revelations

"CIRCLE THE WAGONS!"

The children, not understanding Abe Solomon's remembered call along the Applegate Trail bringing him west from Missouri, giggled and ran excited circles around the wagons, dangerously near the horses' hooves.

"Chil-*dren!*" At the single word from their teacher, the boys and girls quieted down and waited for instructions as to who would be riding in which wagon on the way to Wong Chu's home. Most of them clustered near the wagon carrying the bulging picnic baskets. Chris Beth made a mental note that neither they nor their assorted dogs, including the Norths' Esau and Malones' Wolf, should ride in that one!

"You have a way with children," Mr. Solomon said with shy admiration. "They're gonna miss you. All of us will."

Chris Beth thanked the merchant with a smile, wondering if "we" included his wife and daughter. Mrs. Solomon certainly had "come through" during the winter flood, just as Mrs. Malone had said the older woman always did "in time o' trouble." But there was undisguised regret in her eyes on the

day of the double wedding. And her green-eyed daughter
Maggie failed to show up at all.

Both women had either Joe or Wilson picked out for Maggie,
Mrs. Malone had confided, adding that they would get over
the defeat. Well, they'd better. Neither she nor Vangie intended to relinquish her man! But, for all of their sakes, she
hoped they would put aside their petty jealousies instead of
letting them turn into spite.

Excitement resumed as the children scrambled into their
assigned wagons. Chris Beth insisted that O'Higgin and Mrs.
Malone ride in the spring seat of the O'Higgin-Malone wagon.
"Joe and I will ride back here with you to guarantee that we
get there with the food."

Secretly, for sentimental reasons, she wanted to ride with
her feet dangling, as they had ridden to see President Hayes
last autumn. Joe was obviously pleased. "Shows our marriage
hasn't grown stale," he said with a smile.

"In four weeks? Hardly! We're married for as long as we
both shall live. Remember?"

Somehow the words made her uneasy—until Joe took her
hand.

As the wagons pulled away from the school, O'Higgin burst
into song, his rich, Irish voice rising above the rattle of the
wheels over the rutted roads:

> One I loved, two I loved,
> Three I loved, then four—
> Until I met me Mollie-wife,
> And them I loved no more!

"O'Higgin, stop that!" Mrs. Malone said to her husband, but
her satisfaction was poorly disguised when the four crowded
wagonloads of children joined his throaty song.

The wagons left the school far behind, traveled through the
heavy timber, and reached another clearing below which the
valley lay. Chris Beth gave a gasp of delight. "It's like a giant
opalescent jewel!"

"Worn by a lovely lady as lightly as her laugh," Joe answered.

"We're in a poetic mood—reminds me of our ride in the autumn woods. Oh, Joe, it's good to have an all-season kind of love!"

Her husband squeezed her hand as together they listened to the joyous trills of the nesting meadowlarks and sniffed with appreciation the sweet perfume from the fragile blooms adorning countless budding young orchards. It was good to be alive.

The blended white, cream, and pink blossoms of the fruit orchards—outlined with rims of orange poppies and purple larkspur, and edged by the green forest—was a patchwork of color. "Like one of Mrs. Malone's quilts," Chris Beth said.

O'Higgin overheard. "Yep! Shure and the Lord's good to His children in these parts. Oregon wears heaven's undergarments!"

Chris Beth's eyes feasted on the panorama of color until they fastened on a very large and tumbling building. It was too large to be a house or barn, and she had seen no other fences that tall.

Joe followed her gaze. "The old stockade."

At times like this Chris Beth realized that she had forgotten that she really *was* living on a wild frontier. It was so easy to forget in the comfort of their cabin or when surrounded by friends.

"Are the Indians peaceful now? I mean, are they happy on the reservation?"

"Peaceful, yes. Happy? It's hard to say," Joe said slowly. "We'll pass nearby. You can judge for yourself."

"I never realized the Chinese workers lived so near the Indians. Or how far little Wong rides that donkey—and right by the reservation. Are they on good terms, the Indians and Chinese?"

"At a distance, I'd say. They respect each other, living out the only way of life they know and trusting their own gods—Buddha and the Great Spirit."

"But, Joe, doesn't anybody try to enlighten them?"

"Tell them the story of Jesus? Not since the missionaries. They still talk about the visitor who wore a long black robe and carried a book that 'talked'—probably meant he read to them. Wilson speaks a little of their language and has gathered sketchy information from the young brave who paid you a call at the schoolhouse last year!"

Chris Beth smiled, remembering the day of "Boston Buck's" christening. "Hard telling who was more scared that day—me of an Indian in my classroom or the Indian of Wilson's explosive potion!" She recalled the Indian's horrified look when Wilson fired the warning shot at him.

The young Indian still wore the name Wilson had given him with pride, however. And, although he left no signs, she was sure he frequented the school in curiosity. She was no longer afraid of Boston Buck, but she felt a mixture of concern and fear at passing so near the unseen tribes.

"Do they—uh—like us?"

"Unfortunately, they don't trust us," Joe said regretfully. "You know—the wars, the broken treaties, even the semi-restriction of the reservation. And from what Wilson gathers, the man in the black robe did a lot to twist up their thoughts with his pictures."

"Pictures?"

Joe nodded. "From his book. He used the pictures to reward or to punish. Dealt with the tribes severely, from what Boston Buck remembers of his grandfather's stories."

"But the pictures?"

"When they obeyed him, the man showed them pictures of a beautiful land they call *Siah Close Illahee*. Wilson translates that to mean 'Good Land Far Away.' Said they'd go there when they died."

"And when they didn't obey?"

"Scared them half to death with pictures too dreadful to describe, I guess. A place down below where the wicked go for everlasting punishment. Even looking at the pictures, the way he forced them to, made the Indians *hiyiu cultus seek*—very sick."

"And they never learned about love? Is this story true?"

Joe shifted positions in the wagonbed before answering. "About love, no. But, yes, the brave vouches for the story."

"Where did this missionary finally go?"

"Died here, and supposedly he's buried in the cemetery by the school." Joe studied her face momentarily before continuing. "I think that's where the legend of the strange visitor started—you know, the one who's supposed to haunt the grounds in search—"

Chris Beth felt her face blanch. How well she knew! The legendary apparition was supposed to be searching for his ancestors, Wilson had said. Fortunately, he came only at night when she was gone!

"Could that be why Boston Buck keeps coming back?" she asked. "Hoping to see—"

He sandwiched her hands between his big ones, almost upsetting them both as the wagon jolted suddenly.

"The only one he hopes to see is the lovely Boston lady with heavy dark braids." He let go of her hands so she could right herself.

"And I aim to keep them! Seriously, Joe, I'm going to find a way to invite him to the Sunday services at Turn-Around Inn."

He took her left hand again and tenderly touched the plain gold band encircling the third finger. "That's why we joined forces here, Chrissy—you and me, Vangie and Wilson—to further God's cause."

Chris Beth realized with regret that they had missed Joe's promised peek of the reservation. Buried so deeply in conversation, she had no time for sight-seeing, but she was glad to have had Joe fill her in on the Indians' background. After all, although it seemed a lifetime, she had been here only since mid-September. There was still a lot more that she needed to know.

Instinctively, even as she and Joe talked, Chris Beth had

kept an ear tuned to the voices of the children. She knew they had long since abandoned their wagons and, under the watchful eyes of their parents, were romping alongside the caravan with the dogs. She herself felt cramped from the long ride and was glad when O'Higgin brought the wagon to a sudden halt.

Children surrounded the wagon. "We're here! We're here!" Wong elbowed his way to her side. "My mother ees finished with the lundree washing." He pointed with pride to a long, sagging line of wet clothing flapping in the breeze. It was easy to recognize Wong's labored printing on the piece of fir wood nailed to one of the line's supporting poles. The letters disregarded all rules of shape, and some were upside down in the child's attempt to print with tar: CHINEZ LUNDRY— FIVE SENS A TUBB!!

Chris Beth felt a warm surge of compassion. "You've done a wonderful job, Wong. Do you help your mother?"

He nodded proudly. "And Honorable Father help also. No workee seense rails quit."

"Honorable Father" appeared at the door. With a broad smile, he bowed politely and then spoke to his son in his native tongue.

"He show us!" The other children whooped with delight, knowing that Wong meant the wildflowers he had promised.

"Oh, it's good to stretch!" Chris Beth had jumped from the back of the wagon and stood watching as the other adults climbed stiffly from their cramped positions.

"Better put your sun hat on," Joe cautioned. "The April sun can be deceiving, although we'll be lucky if it isn't showering before the day's over."

"Begory! 'Twouldn't be a picnic now, would it, boy, without the rain and the wee ants?" O'Higgin made either sound gleeful.

"We could do without 'em both, but we'll take it in stride," his wife answered as he helped her from the wagon. "Look, Chris Beth," and Mrs. Malone held up a pair of pale blue soakers for her inspection. They were undoubtedly for little

Mart. Before she could comment, the incredible woman held up another pair.

"Yellow," she explained, "since there's no way tellin' which the new one'll decide on bein'—boy or girl."

"You mean you knitted instead of relaxing on the way here?" The woman's energy was astounding.

O'Higgin sidled up to stand at his wife's side. "Miss Mollie'll knit at her funeral, she will! 'Tis her way o' findin' peace."

"And most likely, lest you mend your ways in my presence, you'll not be witnessin' it!" Then, turning to Chris Beth, she asked, "Do you want I should stay and help with lunch while you take care of the thunderin' herd yonder?" She tilted her head toward the children, who were eager to be off.

"But there's a lot of work—"

Mrs. Malone waved away the protest. "Nonsense! Jimmy John's sleepin'; and there's lots of hands amongst the other women. Some of the men'll want to go along, I'd guess?"

Joe nodded and the older woman continued, "Big boys and other menfolk can hay the horses and catch up easylike."

And so they were off on an expedition which was to uncover more than shy wildflowers. For no more had she turned on her heel than a little rush of breathlessness came. The curtain of her mind parted to reveal Joe standing in back of a pulpit, hands upraised. People thronged down the aisle to meet him. She wanted to join them and stand beside her husband, where she belonged. But people kept crowding between them—standing between her and the joy she should be feeling. What did it all mean?

The curtain snapped shut as she heard the children calling her name. Shaken, Chris Beth hurried up the little hill to join them.

8
Muslin City

❧

AT THE TOP of the little rise, Chris looked to where young Wil and the eldest son of Nate Goldsmith pointed. A narrow path zigzagged up the steep mountain beyond— probably a footpath the Indians had blazed, she supposed—and came to a halt at the broad ledge about halfway up. Above the ledge lay another thick belt of timber.

But the object of the boys' fascination was a cluster of peculiar-looking, gauzelike tents, looking like quickly-spun spiderwebs after a storm. Smoke curled from their midst and formed a sort of halo above them in the morning sun.

"Indians?" Chris Beth was unaware she had whispered the word until Nate Goldsmith himself responded at her elbow.

"Settlers," he said, stroking his beard in concentration. "Sure musta had a devilish time gettin' here over them mountains, 'less they treed the wagons."

Young Wil wondered aloud what "treed" meant.

A drag, Nate explained, meaning a tree hung on behind for "gettin' down faster'n a road'd allow."

Chris Beth shuddered and he nodded. "Dangerous. Lotsa

folks claim it'd be more civilized to think 'bout road buildin' instead of school buildin'. Me, I favor education."

The inflection of his voice required a nod. Then Chris Beth turned back to the flimsy tents. "What are they made of?"

"Muslin cloth. Cheap, and so thin that when a body lights up a candle inside, folks can see right through. Keeps insects out, but you'd have t'sleep under a saddle fer privacy!"

"What about fire?" Chris Beth recalled with horror Joe's account of the terrible fire which destroyed the home of his parents, then had snuffed out his mother's life.

Nate turned helpless palms upward. "Not fire season yet, though the rain's stopped early. Them folks'll move or—oh, no, they won't! Wil you look at that? See the fellers 'n mules? Cabins soon'll replace Muslin City!"

She looked where Nate pointed and was barely able to distinguish movement in the heavy timber. Men or animals?

"Snakin' poles means they're stayin'. Whadda you know!"

Somewhere from the dense stand of timber came a triumphant call of "Tim-ber-r-r!" followed by a crash that echoed and reechoed against the ledge. Immediately there were shouts and swarms of people everywhere. Then all was quiet where Chris Beth and Nate stood. Too quiet.

"Oh, dear!" She laughed. "We've lost track of our own group." Even Josh Goldsmith and young Wil had left them. "We'd better organize a searching party."

"Plenty help. The other men are comin'. You catch up with Brother Joseph and the kids. Us men better be talkin' over some plans fer the future here in the settlement. We're growin'."

9
Fit for a Prince—
Or a Pauper!

◆

HEAD STILL GIDDY from the steep climb, arms
laden with wildflowers, and heart left in the haze of the
redbud grove behind them, Chris Beth descended with the
others to join the waiting parents.

"I do believe," she said, catching up with Joe, "that we
found the most beautiful spot yet."

Before Joe could respond, young Wil raced back to join
them. "Look what we found—Joe and me—for Uncle Wil's
book!"

It would have been nice if the boy's timing could have been
better. She so wanted to talk with Joe as they strolled the new
territory. But young Wil chatted away about the flower he
held up. A trillium, and real rare, he said. Did she know that
this flower grew in three parts? She did not.

"It does! Grows in three parts—leaves and petals, too—you
know, like the Trinity." Chris Beth buried her face in the baby
orchids and field lilies, inhaling their fragrance, as young Wil
talked.

When finally he ran on ahead, she asked, "Did you see the
newcomers, Joe?"

"I did. And I was thinking what a beautiful place for a church back there in the redbud grove. Sort of a central location . . ."

Joe's voice trailed off and she reached for his hand. If that meant what she hoped, he wanted to stay here as badly as she did. But it would be comforting if he would come right out and say it.

Mollie Malone began to beat the rim of a wagon wheel with an iron spoon just as Chris Beth and Joe approached. Dinner was laid out on snowy cloths spread on the ground under a large, sheltering oak. The other women stood fanning the great platters of fried chicken, homemade breads, and pots of baked beans as if to drive away imagined flies. Their greatest pests were the children. They darted in and out trying to sneak a doughnut or a wedge of devil's food cake without being noticed.

But Mrs. Malone saw. "Not a morsel until the food's blest, you young'uns! Brother Joseph?"

Joe stepped forward. "Bless this bounty, Lord," he said quietly. "And teach us to be more grateful of heart. Let us be sharing neighbors—sharing with every person who crosses our paths this day and every day. And, Lord," he paused, "m-may our every d-decision glorify Your Name. Amen."

The children responded with the Lord's Prayer as planned, with young Wil's voice in lead. Chris Beth was glad that he remembered his cue. Her own mind was less alert. She was too busy trying to interpret the return of her husband's stammer. It was a sure sign that he was under stress. And the part he stumbled over had to do with decisions.

O'Higgin's invitation boomed out: "Step up, folks! Shure and it's a feast we're 'avin, it is. Done by the bonnie ladies and lasses. Fit for a prince, it is."

"Or a pauper," Mrs. Malone said in a near-inaudible voice. Nate Goldsmith called out, "Dig in, kids! It's yore day!" and the children scrambled to heap their plates. Then Chris Beth's glance caught the older woman's eye and followed it.

There, at the top of the little knoll leading toward the ledge, stood a long line of dirty, ragged children. Even at a distance, their sad, too-large eyes said starvation. With gaping mouths, they stared at the food in a hungry—almost animalish—way.

"Immigrant children. And starvin' to death, poor babies," Mrs. Malone whispered to Chris Beth. "Applegate Trail folks, for sure."

Chris Beth felt her scalp prickle. She had heard the horror-and-sorrow stories of that route into Oregon. Who hadn't? But she had never seen what it did to the children. All her appetite left her.

"What will we do?" She questioned desperately, unaware that she had spoken aloud.

O'Higgin, who spotted the children then, waited for no instructions. "Come here, ye wee ones!" he called lustily and waved a drumstick in invitation.

Frightened, the children turned to leave. Young Wil saw them and held out a ball made of discarded twine. "Catch!" he ordered, tossing the ball in the air. It fell short of where the children stood, but one of them ventured forward and shyly picked it up.

"Throw it back and let's get a game going. But come on down. We've all got to eat first. Teacher's rule!"

Chris Beth could have burst with pride in the boy. She felt a tear trickle down her cheek and was dimly aware that Joe wiped it away with his thumb as the children advanced.

It took some gentle urging from Mrs. Malone for the children to accept food. But once the tallest of the group, a gaunt, redhaired boy, reached for a slice of thickly buttered bread, the others followed. "Eatin' like a bunch o' coon hounds," Nate said in quiet satisfaction.

As the children finished second helpings, Chris Beth saw something that made her heart turn over with pity. The boy who had accepted the bread dropped to his knees, looked around fearfully, and snatched as much of the bread as his two sunburned hands could hold. Warily he stuffed it into the pocket of his ragged pants.

Mrs. Solomon saw, too. "Let's not be frightenin' 'em away

now. The Lord knows their needs and He's found a way to supply 'em."

"You're so right, Bertie," Mrs. Malone agreed. "And we all of us know this food would be spoilin' on us before we reached home."

Yes, they all knew. So who would take the leftovers to the newest neighbors? Men know how to talk to men, the men said. But us women know how to talk to women. And everybody had witnessed that children know best how to talk to children. So best they *all* go. Could just finish the picnic up there.

Back up the little knoll they went. Then, with directions from the now-talkative children, it was on up to the ledge and the muslin tents. Chris Beth wondered, as they trudged upward, what sort of reception they would receive. She saw that the games so carefully planned, the program so carefully rehearsed, and the visiting which the women cherished so much were now forgotten by all. But something infinitely more important was taking place.

"You're wearing the look that's so becoming," Joe said, suddenly catching up with Chris Beth and matching his steps with hers. "Happy?"

"Very!" But there was not time to say more. "Cap'n Jack," as the man introduced himself, extended a callus hand in welcome. "I'm sort of navigator and wagon master here. And this is my recent wife. Lost my other one, rest her soul, on the trail. Never thought any one of us would make it."

The pale, sad-faced young woman, jostling a crying baby on her hip, came forward. Suddenly the men, women, and children divided into their respective groups. "The young'uns have been fed," Mrs. Malone explained to Captain Jack's wife. "Some of the older folks as well—men, mostly. But us womenfolk—well, we like t'talk and eat without bein' interrupted." Without further ado, she set about unpacking the picnic baskets again.

Chris Beth moved among the women, introducing herself. "I'm Mrs. Craig, wife of the handsome minister over there."

Invariably the words coaxed smiles from mouths that looked unaccustomed to smiling. And small wonder, she thought, as she listened to the pitiful accounts of the wagon train's three-month tortuous journey from the Mississippi Valley and their reasons for coming West.

"We all had the ague, just shook with it," the nervous and rapid-talking Mrs. Cliborn explained. "Then there was hot summers and bitter winters. Then them cockleburs was taking over farmground. Me and my man, we figured 'twas as good dyin' on the trail as shakin' to death with ague—or starvin'. 'Course, little did we know!"

Well, they found out, she said. And the others joined in—the shy, sandy-haired Mrs. Emory; Mrs. Westmoreland, the capable lady who reminded Chris Beth of Mrs. Malone; and all the others, none of whom seemed to have much in common except for the agonies suffered along the Applegate Trail and the desire for a better life here in the Oregon Country.

Well, there was one thing more—their concern for their men. Even as the women talked, they kept excusing themselves one by one to reload plates of food for their husbands, who stood apart from the women, often scraping their plates loudly in signal for refills.

Chris Beth was relieved to see that the food was holding out. She wanted so much to help these people. She wanted—and needed, too—to hear their stories as well. It made her realize that her own trip to Oregon by stagecoach had been easy compared to what the Mississippi travelers had suffered. "I remember most the storms, women and children hid under mattresses, men struck down by lightnin', and all our belongin's blowed away . . . Me, I recall most the floods, washin' away our last cow, then the awful mire up to the axles afterward. . . . Not much hurt me like havin' to discard Mama's walnut bureau—throwin' it down the mountain, hearin' it splinter below . . . but nothin'—*nothin'* (the women covered their faces then) compared to the other . . ."

"The other?" Chris Beth asked of the chatty Mrs. Cliborn.

"The scalpin's," she whispered. Chris Beth felt herself choke on the single bite of food she had taken, as the woman went on. "Indians, you know, painted and screamin'—killed whites by the hundreds—had to bury folks we loved in one grave, the few of us," she nodded toward the group around them, "left out of the eight hundred."

"*Eight hundred!*" Why, there were fewer than a hundred here now.

"And lost near that number, countin' the ones born on the way." Chris Beth was thankful when the woman changed to a lighter topic. "And what I *missed* most was soap! We're washrag people where I come from."

Mrs. Emory spoke up shyly. "What I missed was fresh fruit—well, any food at all after a while. But at first it was fruit I craved, expecting the baby."

Mrs. Cliborn interrupted. "And then to cap the climax, you shoulda seen what happened along the river at Fort Vancouver. My pore little Lecretia here was standin' lookin' at a boatload o' sailors unloadin' cargo. One yelled, 'Hey, little lady, have uh apple!' She tried and tried to catch 'em with her skirt, but they was laughing at her petticoat 'n all till she dropped 'em. Just had to stand and see 'em float down the Columbia whilst they laughed. But tell me now, are these apple dumplin's?"

"Ladies, we must be goin'," Abe Solomon said, looking at his pocket watch.

There were hasty good-byes, fervent thank yous, and warm invitations for the callers to return. "And soon!" Chris Beth promised as she squeezed back the tears. The threadbare garments, the pitifully inadequate "tents," the hunger—all of it had wrenched her heart.

"Sure hope they have the stayin' power," Mrs. Malone said as she and Chris Beth hurried back down the knoll to where the men were hitching up the teams. "We've got a powerful job ahead helpin'."

They were down the hill by then, and O'Higgin heard his

wife's last words. "But crops be the best yet. We're able! Where's me plaidie, Mollie Love?"

Mrs. Malone handed her husband his woolen cape and he spread it on the wagon bed for Jimmy John. As the caravan was about to pull away, there came a call of, "Welcome 'gin. Vellee good!" in Mr. Chu's broken English. It was Nate who responded.

"Sure, Brother! See you for Sunday services at the brush arbor, weather permittin'. Just glad us folks thought of comin' here fer the day's outin'!"

Chris Beth sat down gratefully on the back end of the O'Higgin-Malone wagon. It was good to relax beside Joe and dangle her feet after the long, strange day. "Joe," she said, "there were some startling revelations today, weren't there?"

Joe appeared to consider, then said, "Most revealing was hearing you introduce yourself. You could have called yourself the teacher. Instead, you said you were my wife. I liked that."

10
Singin'
Against the Dark

❧

JOE REACHED FOR Chris Beth's hand as O'Higgin turned the wagon toward home. She felt a great rush of love mingled with excitement. "I'm a silly goose," she mused half-aloud. "Being away from little Mart this long seems forever!"

"Sauce for the goose is sauce for the gander," he whispered in her ear, and together they giggled at his use of Mrs. Malone's favorite words of weapon to make her point with O'Higgin.

"Do you know, Joe, that I know so little of the baby's background—I mean, I hardly met his poor parents, the Martins before they died during the flood. What were they like?"

"I didn't know them well either—just who they were. They were very young, and she was well-educated but homesick for Missouri. No sickness like it, you know."

How well she knew!

"Never saw her wear anything but black with white collar and cuffs. Very shy, too. All traces of their background washed away in the flood—but does it matter?"

"No," she answered slowly, "except for little Mart's sake, when the times comes."

He squeezed her hand hard. "We'll manage. And speaking of time, isn't Vangie's baby overdue?"

Chris Beth had been worrying about that, although Wilson had told her repeatedly that it was not unusual for the first baby to be late. But poor little Vangie was miserable—and scared.

Her thoughts were broken suddenly by a distant wail of fiddles. "Swing your partners right and low!" a male voice called, and the clapping of what sounded like a thousand hands picked up the rhythm.

"The newcomers," Mrs. Malone called over her shoulder, "singin' against the dark." The poignant notes faded away.

As the lowering sun turned the snow on the mountain peaks from rose to mauve, Chris Beth was grateful for the long twilights of the Oregon Country. There was a lot she wanted to talk about and sort out in her mind.

"The people back there—will they manage?" she asked Joe.

"With our help," he answered.

"But," she hesitated, "Joe, we have so little—"

"We have everything, everything that c-counts."

Except a job, or an income, or maybe even a future here, Joe's slight stammer said plainly.

Chris Beth longed to share her own insecurities. But how could she explain the phenomena which kept transporting her mind to places and situations yet to be experienced? It was not that Joe would laugh at her, but what was there to tell? Her head said there was a reasonable explanation, but her heart said something else. The Lord was speaking to her—maybe sometimes *through* her—but until she knew *what* He was saying, the visions must be put away in some corner of her heart like she had stored the brooch at the bottom of the camphor-wood chest.

Aloud, she shared only the happy part of the repeated vision. "Everything that counts, indeed! We're surrounded by people we love and who love us in return."

The sky turned navy blue. The unmistakable bass hoots of a night owl said the wagons were nearing the forest. Sensing danger, the gray squirrels scampered up and down the fir boughs so haphazardly that they tumbled against each other in their effort to escape the claws of the forest monarch. Blue jays sounded a raucous alarm from the topmost branches. Then all was silent—until the crickets and katydids tuned up their own fiddles as if they too were singing against the dark. Chris Beth felt the same wonder and awe she had felt on first coming into this wild, new land where neighbors needed one another just as the forest creatures did.

"Did you happen to meet a Mrs. Robbins among the newcomers?"

Chris Beth wondered if Joe had asked her more than once. She had been so lost in thought that words could have gone unnoticed. "No," she responded tentatively. "Not that I remember, anyway."

"You'd remember. Her husband says she knew you, or knew *of* you. Seems your mother had spoken of your being here— you or Vangie. He asked of you both by name."

Chris Beth's blood ran cold. "By *name*?" She whispered the word through tight lips. "First or last?"

"Both. He seemed to know you were half sisters. You'll probably enjoy news from home." His voice was suddenly concerned. "Are you cold?"

Not really. Not in the way Joe meant. But she snuggled close for comfort. *Vangie—poor little Vangie*—who had used her maiden name as a shield against people's knowing her child was illegitimate.

11
True North

⁓

IT WAS LIGHTER as the wagon pulled out of the woods and onto the main road. "We'll walk from here," Joe offered at the crossroads. Young Wil, eager to share his rare trillium find with Wilson, raced toward home before waiting for Chris Beth and Joe.

"Shure and ye'll be spoonin' before the wagon's over the wee hill," O'Higgin said jovially as he drew the team to a stop. "So'll me and me Mollie-love, most likely."

"Behave yourself, O'Higgin!" Mrs. Malone lifted a hand to tuck a stray lock of graying hair into her tight bun, and her Irish husband dodged the pretended blow with a roguish roll of his eyes.

"Been a wonderful day, thanks to Nate," she said in mock sincerity. "Did you ever see the beat of how that man takes credit for every miracle in the settlement?"

The families shared an understanding laugh; then, after sleepy good-byes from the Malone children, the wagon moved toward their home at Turn-Around Inn.

"Let me know when Vangie's confinement comes. I'll be helpin', you know!" Miss Mollie's voice called.

"One I loved; two I loved . . ."

O'Higgin's mellow voice rose, then faded as the wagon topped the hill and disappeared. Hand in hand, Chris Beth and Joe turned home. Yes, it had been a wonderful day, filled with surprises and opening the gates for more, but Chris Beth felt an urgent need to be back with Vangie and little Mart. Maybe Joe noticed, for his step quickened. She matched his long strides, hoping that the feeling of apprehension was only her imagination.

"Vangie," Joe spoke suddenly. "Back there when I mentioned Mrs. Robbins—"

But whatever he had been about to say went unsaid. The air around them split by Esau's excited barking and the frightened screams of young Wil.

"Hurry! Hurry! Vangie—the baby—little Mart—"

Chris Beth's heart hammered so heavily against her ribs that it was hard to run. In her terror she broke away from Joe and cut through a thicket of heavy brush laced with wild blackberry vines. The briars tore at her flesh, but she felt no pain.

At first Chris Beth was sure something had happened to little Mart. He was screaming lustily, which both frightened and comforted her. Then, before she could unfasten the latch of the Big House's front door, she knew it was Vangie. Her agonized moans were coming from the front bedroom. Later she was unable to remember how she managed to get inside or when she became aware that little Mart was lying safely in an ancient cradle alongside the bed where her sister lay writhing in pain. Wilson stood over her.

"Chris Beth! Hot water! Clean sheets in the bureau!"

But Chris Beth could only stand frozen in terror at the sight of Vangie's blanched face, her body doubled grotesquely and her tiny fists clenched against the convulsive contraction.

"Chris Beth!" Wilson's voice carried a command, lost on Chris Beth.

"We'll have to have Mrs. Malone—"

"There isn't time! *You'll* have to help."

"Me?" Her voice sounded far away even in her own ears. "But I don't know—I've never seen—"

Wilson ignored her completely. He was suddenly a man she had never known before. All doctor. And she—not Vangie—was nurse.

Bring water. Mop brow. Hand him the damp cloth. Hold Vangie down until the contraction was over. Move. Hurry. Don't think. Don't feel. Just work. And hurry. And *pray!*

Yes, pray, for things were not going right. Even in her inexperience, Chris Beth knew. Maybe they were losing the battle.

"Wilson," she whispered once, "Wilson, is she going to make it?"

That's when he had said, "You know how to pray, don't you?"

Dimly she was aware that little Mart had quieted down. Young Wil and Joe were talking in subdued tones. And there was the unmistakable aroma of coffee. That should have been bracing. But instead it made her sick. "Wilson," she gasped.

Seeing her white face, Wilson—without change of expression—said brusquely, "Go get rid of it and get back here with me!"

Outside, Chris Beth allowed herself only a minute to be sick before hurrying back to the nightmare. Faint as she was, it never occurred to her leave Vangie's side. At least, although queasy, she felt a certain pride in the fact that she was seeing it through. Vangie needed her—always had, but now as never before.

And even as the thought came to her, Vangie spoke her name.

"Chris Beth—"

Vangie's voice was nearly inaudible. Chris Beth leaned close to hear the faint words.

"If—If I don't make it—you'll love the baby?"

"Don't talk like that!" Tears streamed down her face so fast she was unable to wipe them away with the back of her hand.

"Chris Beth—you'll raise the baby as a true North—"

The question was so startling she was unable to answer. It had never occurred to her that she might have to raise Jonathan's child!

"Promise—" The childish voice was weaker.

"I promise, Darling, I promise—"

Vangie dozed fitfully. "Wouldn't you like coffee, Wilson?" Chris Beth whispered across the sheet shielding Vangie's quivering form. Maybe if she could get away—even a minute—things would come into focus. But Wilson was shaking his head.

"No, don't leave. I don't like the way things are going. The baby's too small. Heartbeat's faint. In a wrong position—" Vangie stirred and he leaned over her, motioning Chris Beth to move closer.

"She's pale, Wilson," she whispered, then said desperately, "Oh, Wilson, is she going to make it?"

Wilson shot her a hard look. Maybe it was meant to silence her, but the look revealed more to Chris Beth. It told her that Wilson was scared too.

"Of *course* she'll make it!" He ground the words out through clenched teeth. Then, as if talking to himself, Wilson continued in a hoarse whisper, "She has to, Lord. She *has* to! But she should have delivered before now—she's weakening and the delay's doing the baby no good—Oh, God!"

There was a cry of anguish from the bed. Vangie, almost wild in her pain, rolled from side to side and would have fallen from the bed had Wilson and Chris Beth not restrained her.

"Hold her down!" Wilson's tone was sharp. "And wipe her face."

Chris obeyed automatically. Wilson watched, biting his lip in concentration. Then, in a somewhat softer voice, he said, "Brace yourself, Chrissy. It's going to take all we have within us to save Vangie and the baby—maybe either of them."

"What are you going to do?" she whispered desperately as again she mopped Vangie's ashen forehead. "Wilson! Her lips are blue! What can we do?" She felt cold sweat form on her own face.

"I have to take the baby. It's a risk and you have to help me or we'll lose them both. Do you hear?"

She heard, but she didn't believe. It couldn't be. If her little sister was going to be taken from her, she couldn't witness it. "I can't, I—"

But her words were drowned by Vangie's scream. The scene took on a feel of unreality. She gathered her sister close and whispered words of comfort. She herself was in the lap of a great pain. Then she felt nothing at all so she handed items to Wilson on command and repeated after him the words he told her, "Push . . . relax . . . once more . . ."

Somewhere a clock chimed midnight, then one o'clock . . . two . . . three . . . "She's too exhausted to help," Chris Beth whispered. "She's not responding to me, Wilson." She wondered then if the still form was moving up and down with breath. In a near-primitive effort to preserve life, Chris Beth urged, "Push . . . relax . . . push, Vangie!"

As the clock struck five, Wilson spoke for the first time in hours. "You'll have to come here. The baby's head is turned wrong. *Hurry!* It's choking!"

Choking. The baby was choking. Vangie's baby! It no longer mattered who the father was. Nothing mattered except saving the little life. And the mother's. *Nothing* else mattered. Not her own feeling. *Nothing at all.*

Through a white haze she saw Vangie's even-whiter face. "Hang on, Chrissy," Wilson whispered. "You're doing fine. Hang on. We need you—"

Vaguely Chris Beth was aware that Vangie's screams had stopped. Through the haze around her, she tried to read Wilson's exhausted face. "What happened?" she gasped. "Did she—did we—?"

But Wilson dropped on his knees beside the still form amid the sweat-soaked sheets. He was whispering little words of endearment. Panic rose to her own throat. And then she saw the tiny bundle that Wilson was laying beside her sleeping sister. Alive! Both of them . . .

Suddenly a wild laugh rose to her lips. "You mean—you mean we made it? We—you and I—we delivered a baby?"

"Come and see," Wilson said without looking up. "Just come and take a peek at your little niece."

Niece! She had a niece. Vangie had delivered her "true North."

With a deep sense of emotion—almost as if she had been God's helper—Chris Beth looked at the tiny piece of humanity. "Did she have a name picked out?" she asked foolishly.

"Trumary," he whispered, getting up from his knees. "True North! And *now* we'll have that coffee! My wife and daughter must rest."

12
Heartbeats of Heaven

～

CHRIS BETH GASPED with delight at the first glimpse of her new niece. She noted with relief that every infant feature was Vangie's. *And Vangie's alone!* The delicate skin . . . the little tuft of golden hair already threatening to curl . . . even the Cupid's-bow mouth that made her look like the china doll Mama used to keep on the mantle. Thinking of Mama made her sad. Mama should know about her granddaughter.

But Vangie's face had blanched at the suggestion. "Oh, no! Chrissy—*promise!*"

"No promise is necessary, Darling," Chris Beth assured her sister. Both of them knew that getting mail to their mother was virtually impossible now that the one remaining servant had been dismissed. "We both know that your father—my stepfather—wouldn't let us be in touch. And certainly not about the baby."

"I hate him. I *hate* him!"

"Vangie, you mustn't. We have to forget." Chris Beth pulled Vangie near in an effort to soothe her.

Vangie drew away. "But to throw me out, isolate me from

216

our mother, all for one mistake—and the *baby* is not a mistake! She's the greatest thing God ever created!"

"Except for little Mart," Chris Beth agreed, and was relieved to see Vangie smile. She knew, however, that all ties with home were severed, barring a different kind of miracle.

"Dear little heartbeats of heaven," Mrs. Malone declared of the sleeping babies when she came calling as quickly as corn planting and setting out the tomato plants would allow. "Livin' proof the Creator intended life in this world should go on!"

And life went on in the settlement, too. O'Higgin's "Bossie" came home with a new calf, so the girls were able to have fresh milk for the little ones. Wild strawberries stained the hills and neighbor children weeded the corn rows fast so they could slip up the ridge, out of the sight of slower-moving adults, and fill pails—after they filled themselves. The pails of wild fruit they brought to Vangie and Chris Beth "fer eatin' with Jersey cream." Birds stopped quarreling and chose mates. No hoped-for rain was in sight, but the water table was high from the heavy rain storms of the winter, keeping the valley lush and green.

Chris Beth took Mrs. Malone's advice and "stored against the winter," making use of her jelly-making skills learned from "Cook" in her childhood and learning how to sun-dry early fruit. Vangie harvested the honey from her well-tended hives and sewed with inspiration. Easter was late, and what better time to show off both new babies?

"Wasn't it sweet of Mrs. Malone to include scraps in the layette she gave me for a wedding gift?" Vangie's eyes held a Christmas-glow. "So right for our 'heartbeats of heaven'!"

13
Easter at the Arbor

❧

ON GOOD FRIDAY Wilson surprised Vangie, Chris
Beth, and Joe by bringing a secondhand carriage home when
he returned from his weekly delivery of ground wheat and
corn. "Abe probably skinned my teeth out," he grinned in
telling how Mr. Solomon had bargained to get the two-
wheeled cart that Wilson had used for transportation.

While Vangie and Chris Beth looked excitedly at the new
vehicle, Wilson and Joe talked of the progress around the
general store. Although excited over the two leather-covered
seats and the fancy fringe around the top, Chris Beth listened
to Vangie with only one ear and was glad when young Wil,
equally excited, came to talk with Vangie. Her other ear had
been tuned in on the men's talk, and she wanted to hear more.

Some of the conversation was good—the part about the
progress. The rest of their talk frightened her.

"The Muslin City people were just a handful of the newcomers," Wilson was saying. "The Solomons say the store's
surrounded with them. And the store was a madhouse.
Miners. Ranchers. Farmers. Few businessmen."

218

Joe listened intently. When he spoke, she was sure he lowered his voice.

"Any talk of a doctor?"

Wilson laughed easily. "Nope! No preachers, either. Or, for that matter, teachers or nurses. They're hard to come by—or keep."

Chris Beth was unable to hear Joe's reply, but Wilson broke in to say, "I wouldn't worry too much. They're going to have to have us eventually, and, like O'Higgin says, crops never looked so good. And, Joe," Wilson said, as he unhitched Dobbin and the one-eyed horse named Battle he had traded some pelts for, "the rails are coming. Half the men in the store have been hired already!"

"That means we can ship our goods and get people in and out instead of waiting for the stage."

"But, wait, I haven't told you what the other half was hired for!"

"You mean—"

"What I'm meaning is that the waterways are going to open for sure. But let's wait and share the rest with the girls."

The two men moved away, but not before other fragments of the conversation reached Chris Beth. Wilson had seen "Doc," and, sure enough, he was going to stop doctoring.

"But that might mean we'd have to move into town—and *town* it'll be all right. Did I tell you that an assayer has up a sign? Oh, the Solomons plan a hotel . . . progress brings the other, too . . . yeah, dance hall . . . reports of dance hall women . . . hard to keep the seamy side of society out."

Joe voiced concern about money, and Wilson gave a characteristic shrug. There'd be need for doctors and preachers with all the new element coming. Joe smiled and Chris Beth did too, until she distinctly heard Wilson mention the name *Robbins*. Then her heart gave an extra beat. Wasn't that the name of the woman who knew Vangie as Mary Evangeline *Stein*? If she let the name drop around the store, it would be all over town. Then everybody would know that Vangie had not been a young widow at all—just a "wayward girl"—and that her child had been on the way, unblessed by marriage, when the frightened 17-year-old girl came to the settlement to hide in disgrace.

How horrible! *I must talk it over with Joe,* Chris Beth thought. *Now is the time—maybe at supper tonight.* Meantime, she mustn't worry.

But, try as she would, it was impossible to dismiss the fears. Memories of "poor little Becky Lee" haunted her memory— the frail little outcast who stood aloof, watching as the other children played. "You can't play with *her*! She's a ———!" They dropped their voices then—dropped them so low that Chris Beth and Vangie were never able to distinguish the word.

"What does it mean, Mama?" Chris Beth, being older, was always the speaker. And Mama would shut out the question with slender, blue-veined hands.

"Poor little Becky Lee," she would moan. Then she would say something mysterious like, "It means her mother's a bad woman. Poor little Becky Lee. But you must not even *talk* about such things or you will be bad, too." Then she and Vangie would pray that never, ever would they be bad. Bad like poor little Becky Lee's mother. . . .

At supper, when they were alone at the cabin, Joe had some news of his own. "I'll be preaching Sunday," he said without preliminaries.

"You'll *what?*"

Joe smiled at her surprise. "I did tell you I was a preacher?"

"Stop teasing, Joe. When—how—why didn't you tell me!"

Joe looked more serious. "I take it you're pleased, but," he cautioned, "don't attach too much of it. I offered at the picnic when I heard Jonas' rheumatism had worsened. No longer able to ride the circuit."

"But doesn't this say the people want you, if they ask you?"

"It does. What it *doesn't* say is that they want me permanently—or that they can pay—"

" 'Less'n crops are good and folks kin meet their taxes' " she mimicked Nate's admonitions when she signed the contract to teach.

"Now *you* be serious." Joe captured her hand and held it as she was about to spoon gravy over his second slice of venison roast. "I just don't want you planning too much. You might as well know I'll be preaching at Willow Grove—just filling in—the next Sunday after Easter."

Willow Grove was miles away. Yes, and they would want to meet his wife. *But little Mart?* No problem—Vangie would take him in. *But what did Joe want to do? Where was his calling?* These questions Chris Beth did not ask. She knew the answers already. Joe would know them Sunday.

But on Sunday he did not know, she thought, as the two families rode toward the brush arbor for outdoor services. At least, the answers hadn't come yet. Joe was even quieter than usual. But who wouldn't be when confronted with preaching a first sermon, even to friends? A little chill ran down her own spine at the very thought. *How silly*, she thought, and concentrated on the beauty of the morning.

"I'd know it was Easter even if nobody told me!" Vangie said above the chuckle of the new buggy wheels.

"True," Chris Beth answered, adjusting the brim of her wide hat to shield little Mart's face. The snow was gone from their side of the mountain, except for the fretted lace along the top, and in its place a million pink and white azaleas in triumphant bloom came down the slopes to meet the valley. Somewhere a robin called, plaintively at first; then, as if joy overcame all doubt, he poured out his song of elation. Something inside Chris Beth responded. It was Easter—the Lord's day of triumph!

Never had there been such a day. And never had there been such a sermon. *Nobody* could've reached 'em all like that, the valley folk said.

'Em all referred to the great number of totally unexpected worshipers who were congregated already when the buggy pulled in from the main road—a crowd which almost doubled before the singing was finished. And small wonder, Chris

Beth thought with a smile. O'Higgin was at his best at leading the singing. His red hair seemed to pause for breath only whenever members of the congregation called out a request. Then, in the midst of "Glory to His Name," the man got himself carried away and went into something akin to an Irish jig. "Oh, the devil's mad and I am glad!" he called out lustily. "Sing on, brothers and sisters—second verse!"

Chris Beth, having forgotten all misgivings, leaned back and joined the group. And, like the robin, she felt her own doubts dissipate and her song turn to pure joy. "Watch it, or you'll be dancing around with O'Higgin," Vangie whispered, then, in astonishment, put a finger to her own lips. Both girls realized it was the first time either of them had whispered in church.

When Joe rose to "take the pulpit," as Nate announced he would do, the demon of misgiving returned to snuff out Chris Beth's earlier exultation. It was as if, suddenly, she and Joe were transported back to last night's supper table.

"Maybe I'm not r-ready," Joe had said haltingly.

"Stop doubting yourself, Darling," she had begged. "You know you'll do a great job."

But Joe had ended their talk with a stammer which made her apprehensive. "I—I *don't* know—that's the problem. And a f-first sermon means so much. To me. And to *them*. D-don't you know it'll leave a lasting i-impression?"

Yes, she did. She knew last night. And she knew now. Doing the job well today was important to Joe because the ministry was his life. And today he was on trial. But Chris Beth could only think of what his success today meant to her—staying. Unconsciously she folded her hands and closed her eyes in unspoken prayer.

She caught her breath when Joe murmured a thank you to Mr. Goldsmith. *If I keep my eyes closed, maybe the problem will go away*, Chris Beth thought foolishly. And then Joe was speaking!

Her eyes flew open and focused anxiously on his face. He looked calm, but his words said he was not. "Th-thank you, too, O'Higgin. The singing was w-wonderful."

Anxiously Chris Beth looked around her. The faces of the audience told her nothing. Apparently their ears had failed to pick up the telltale stammer. Then, when her eyes met her husband's, she realized that he was looking at her for strength. She forced a little smile. Then, miraculously, Joe was in control. She saw it in his eyes. "Thank you, Lord," she whispered reverently. "He made it over the first hurdle. Now *You* take over from here!"

"God bless you all!" Then quietly, almost gently, Joe greeted the audience by name. The transition from the work-out in song that O'Higgin had given the group was perfect. Pleased to be recognized, each family stood when he spoke out: "And good morning to the Smiths—the Beltrans—and the Solomons."

"Did you take notice how long Maggie was in standin'?" Mrs. Malone was to ask later. Yes, she noticed. And she noticed, also, that until the girl stood, her green eyes were fixed on Vangie. She knows, Chris Beth thought in the split-second time that her own eyes intercepted the revealing glance.

But there was not time to give the matter further thought. Joe had asked each "old-timer" (and with a thrill of joy she realized that included her and Vangie) to look about them, center out the face of at least one newcomer, and smile. She felt tears close to the surface as her glance caught sight of the faces of people in the Muslin City settlement they had met on the last day of school. Then the tears were out of control when she saw Wong—and, miracle of miracles—Mr. Chu and behind him the tiny figure of his wife.

Yes sireee! It was a wonderful service, all right. Conducted just right for new folks. Brother Joe was a called preacher, fer sure—not any fancy words or "scary stuff," just "Bible talk."

When the crowds pushed in around Joe to shake his hand, Chris Beth felt such a thrill of joy that she was sure her heart would burst. Surely, *surely* nothing could go wrong now. She wanted to be beside him to tell him what she was thinking, but the crowds were moving ahead . . . and this was their time with him; she would wait.

Waiting gave an opportunity to remember fragments of Joe's beautiful sermon. "Easter is a time of hope and faith," he had said. "The farmer, forgetting last year's small harvest, tills the soil and seeds it again, knowing the harvest will come. And the Christian, forgetting the trails and losses of last year, has the same reassurance. As the seed must die to be born again, so must man's body. But Easter is our hope. Easter is God's promise of life after death through the resurrection. We wilt; we wither; we become a part of the earth. But the Lord is frugal, like the farmer. Nothing in His heavenly kingdom is wasted, especially the soul of mankind. So rejoice and be glad."

With that, the crowd drowned out Joe's words with shouts of joy. During his short benediction, Chris Beth breathed a prayer of her own: "It was a beautiful sermon, Lord, and he didn't even stutter!"

The crowd at last drifted from beneath the arbor. The newcomers would have turned back to the ledge, but the settlers would have no part of such. Why, sakes alive, there was twice more'n was needed—want all them cakes and pies to go beggin'?

"Did you ever see so much growth at Eastertime?" Mrs. Malone marveled. "Babies, new folks, and all the greenin'." Then, raising her voice, "Come see my grandchildren!" she invited.

Vangie smoothed imagined wrinkles from her baby's long white dress and, with a rapturous look, held her out for all to see. "And I'm just as bad," she smiled to herself, "holding little Mart out like an offering." Well, wasn't he an offering—a special offering to the Lord? With that thought a general sense of well-being crept over her.

Why, then, was there a catch in her throat and a peculiar sense of unreality? The crowds she had envisioned had materialized. And while it was true that she had been unable to make her way to stand beside Joe, they were among friends. For today she would rejoice and be glad.

14
Stay . . . Stay . . . Stay!

MAY BROUGHT THE rhododendrons out in a
scarlet blaze of glory. Usually noted for their good sense,
old-timers claimed, the tree-tall evergreens bloomed in a
breathtaking explosion of color instead of testing a few
secluded spots. April showers had been sparse, and these
flowering plants found May's warm breath to their liking.
"Too docile," farmers complained, scratching their heads.
"May weather's not shapin' up proper-like."

Chris Beth understood their concern. First there were
winter's torrential rains, and now a near-drought meant lush
growth. It was good for the gardens and early hay-cuttings, but
bad for the forests in case of fire. But wasn't it too early to
worry? After all, it could rain from almost no cloud at all, she
had learned from Oregon's playful way with sunshine and
flowers. She, for one, was simply going to enjoy the beauty the
month had brought. Never had she seen more splendor than
the rhododendrons in the hills that hugged the valley.

Almost vain in their glory, the 15-foot-tall shrubs virtually
leaned down from the higher elevations, bending with the
gentle winds to form floral arches above the roads. Chris Beth

filled her galvanized washtubs with armloads of branches that passersby found it necessary to hack off in order to see through the maze of flowers. And still the rhododendrons bloomed on.

But for now the exotic beauty of the settlement had a strong magnetic field. Always spring had restored fidelity to old dreams for her. And this year was especially so. As May's near-summer breezes lifted hay-smells from the tall grass and mingled them with honeysuckle, she felt a sense of wanting to charge ahead. Part of her longed to linger in the dreamlike setting, drinking in its loveliness, listening distantly to the soft-vowel quality of the speech that flowered around her, the potpourri from birds, bees, and neighbors. The other part knew that there must be some sacrifice. Drowsily, this Saturday morning in May, she found herself musing that maybe all progress was bittersweet. One had to let go of one set of values to achieve another.

So it was almost with reluctance that she looked forward to tomorrow's trip. She and Joe would be leaving at four *in the morning* for Willow Grove. What would the church be like, especially its people? And how did they expect her to act? Here there was no reason for concern. Valley folks just accepted and loved "Brother Joseph" and his teacher-wife exactly as they were. Would it be the same in Willow Grove?

Chris Beth stopped folding diapers for little Mart and sat down to think. Already she had prepared enough clothes for the baby to last him a week instead of an extended day. And, even if he ran out of something, Vangie had more than enough. "I guess that's just the way we mothers are, Lord," she murmured.

Mothers! Even yet it was hard to realize the wonder of it all. When, in her infrequent letters, Mama spoke of the "hardship and deprivation you foolish girls have chosen," Chris Beth could only feel a certain pity for her. "Chosen" was hardly the right word. And as for hardships—well, how like her mother to lose herself in some minor detail and miss the miracle.

In the kitchen the clock struck 11. Goodness! She had a way

to go . . . irons to heat to press a dress for tomorrow . . .
Joe's suit to check for buttons . . . and the singing kettle
reminded her that she had better make starch for his Sunday
shirt. Better get the coffee going, too. It was almost time for
the noon meal.

The big stove gobbled up the firewood she offered, and Chris
Beth wiped her brow with the back of her hand. The others
were right. It *was* unseasonably hot. It would be nice to let the
fire die down, but there was bathwater to heat.

Chris Beth set the coffee to perking and sliced yesterday's
leftover ham a little thinner than usual. It was the last in the
pork barrel and there was little left of it except the bone for
boiling with beans. Of course, meat was no real problem. The
speckled trout in Graveyard Creek were one source, and all
the neighbors were talking of the salmon run up the river. She
remembered with appreciation the smoky succulence of the
rich, red-fleshed fish after it had been cured in the under-
ground pits. And, of course, wild game abounded.

But these days a shortage of *anything* bothered Chris Beth
more than she admitted to Joe. He had so enjoyed last night's
buttermilk pie, and it *had* been especially translucent in
appearance and refreshing to the tongue, she thought with
pride. Although there was a nice wedge left for today, she
decided her husband would enjoy it better if she made no
mention that the filling had taken the sugar bin down
dangerously low.

It was a blessing that there was no shortage of meal or flour
because of the mill. The meal took care of her husband's yen
for cornbread. The flour took care of his breakfast sourdough
biscuits and the other baking—and, she realized, some other
needs as well! For when she started to make starch, there was
no more than a scant spoonful remaining in the sack. Well,
she would improvise, the way she had seen Mrs. Malone do.
Quickly she made a flour paste by adding the boiling water,
remembering with a laugh O'Higgin's complaint about his
wife's "starchin' me drawers in flour paste, she does, to keep
me upright!"

The sound of men's voices reminded Chris Beth that Joe and Wilson had finished the morning's work. But Joe's words caught her off guard. "Enough for two hungry men, Honey?" he called through the window. "We need to get right back to work—"

Whatever else Joe may have said fell on closed ears. Wilson could hardly be called "company," but even family members had a right to be served a proper meal.

Quickly Chris Beth checked the ham. Not enough for two hungry men. She would have to cut closer to the bone. In her rush not to be detected, she clumsily sliced into the forefinger of her left hand and saw a little spurt of blood run onto her chopping board. Biting her lip to keep from crying out, she sucked at the bleeding finger as she sliced and buttered the salt-rising bread.

"Plenty!" Chris Beth called out cheerfully (mentally adding, "of fried potatoes and buttered carrots, that is!"). Then, making sure the men were not watching as they washed up outside the door, she quickly divided the buttermilk pie in half.

After Joe and Wilson had returned to the mill and she had put little Mart down for a nap, Chris Beth returned to the tasks of preparing for tomorrow's trip to Willow Grove. But she found that her hands were fumbling and her mind was confused. At such times, she knew, it was time to take time out, rest, and pray.

Seated in the quaint old rocker that Joe's mother used to rock him in, Chris Beth raised the window and listened to the laughing of the waterfall. But today it failed to calm her. It seemed to be saying, "Stay . . . Stay . . . Stay."

Chris Beth felt tears dangerously close. She closed her eyes. "I don't know how to pray about this, Lord. I just don't know. I want the people to like Joe tomorrow, but if they do, it might mean we'd have to go—" She burst into tears then. "And I want to stay!"

There was still a lot left to be done. She should be working. But instead she sat reviewing her struggles in the settlement, in trying to make a new life for herself and for the others she loved so much. It had been so hard. So *very* hard.

"But it's all worth it—more than worth it," she mused aloud. "Joe. Little Mart. Warm friendships for myself and Vangie. And love. Most of all, *love!* Without all this I might never have rediscovered God—"

Fear clutched her heart at the thought of what the settlement meant to her. Then more tears rolled off her cheeks, and with them a little moan.

"It's me again, Lord, with another problem—the biggest one yet. Please, *please*, don't let it all be taken away now!"

15
Willow Grove

❧

CHRIS BETH HAD been too preoccupied with her own thoughts to wonder how a team of horses could possibly find a narrow road in the predawn darkness. As she sat close to Joe, thankful for the warmth of the worn lap robe he had thoughtfully tucked around her feet and legs, she asked, "Can they see?"

"A little, but they go more by instinct."

"I could use a little of that myself."

"Scared?" Joe's voice was quiet but concerned.

"Maybe. I've never ridden at night without lights—"

"It will be light soon or I'd have hung the lanterns in front. We're heading east, by the way, in the general direction of Portland. You'll see some new country."

Were there animals there?

Well, yes. Lots of deer and elk—even geese, ducks, quail, Chinese pheasants . . . grouse . . . and did she know what Hungarian partridges were?

She did not. But she was more interested in the possibility of wolves, bears, and cougars.

Could be, Joe admitted. But, he insisted, "Could be doesn't mean *are*."

True, but the feel of a cold steel object lying between the two of them told Chris Beth that the possibility was very real. Why else would Joe have brought the shotgun? She wished for Esau, but Joe was right, of course, in saying it would be too long a day for a dog. He'd have to sit in the buggy so long while they were in the church. She fell into an uneasy silence.

"Doze if you can," he advised, pulling her head gently onto his shoulder. And maybe she would have—she was so weary from the days of preparation—but just as she was on the edge of slumber, the tinkle of a bell—and then dozens, or was it hundreds—broke the eerie silence.

"Joe," she whispered, "sheep?"

Joe stopped the buggy with a jolt. "Sit right where you are."

Without answering her question, Joe jumped out and disappeared into the predawn darkness. She was alone, *alone*.

What could be going on? Why had he left her here when he knew she was afraid? When she whispered Joe's name there was no answer. Maybe Wilson was right in saying she was no match for this country. Maybe she *was* the fragile "Southern belle" he had gently poked fun at when she first came. She stiffened at the thought. That was a long time ago, and just because she longed for the security of the cabin right now didn't mean she couldn't cope! She would show him and Joe—as she had shown Mama—she would show them over and over—

But the sudden rattle of brush near her side of the buggy dissolved her resolution. "Joe!" she cried out before she could stop herself.

"Right here," Joe said softly, and Chris Beth could hear him picking his way through the darkness. Then, to her immense relief, his familiar form loomed through the darkness, which seemed to thicken every second. At least they were together, no matter what the danger.

Joe climbed in beside her. "There's a little pullout just a way ahead. We'll have to hurry. Road's not wide enough for them to get past." Even his whisper seemed to echo in the stillness.

"Them?" The word sounded hollow in her ears.

"Freight wagons—Mariettas, most likely, the kind drawn by six spans of horses. It's the bell teams you're hearing, our signal to make way."

Fear clutched her heart as the team responded to Joe's "Giddyup!" and moved forward—in the direction of the approaching wagons! If only he would break the silence—touch her, even—but he was silent.

Clang! *Clang!* The bells were louder, as were the hoarse voices that sang lustily. Chris Beth scarcely breathed. Then the unmistakable smell of horseflesh and something she could only imagine as carnage told her that the men were within a stone's throw. And then she was overcome with a wave of nausea. The smell, *the awful smell!*

"What—" But before she could finish her whispered question, Joe's hand closed over her mouth.

And then she realized that the revelers were right alongside the buggy. For one horrible moment, the wagons slowed as if to stop. Then, at the crack of a whip, they picked up some speed once they were past the curve of the turnout in the road.

When Joe did not speak, Chris Beth ventured shakily, "Th-the smell?"

Her question seemed anticlimactic, but it was the best she could come up with. Her adrenalin slowed. But she felt totally exhausted.

"Pelts," Joe answered matter-of-factly. It was a relief to hear him speak in a normal voice. "Usually the wagons return to Redding empty after the haul."

"Of what?"

"Supplies. Immigrants. All bound for Portland. Sometimes it's gold. But the skins are about as valuable as gold itself. You'll get used to all this."

She doubted it! "Are they always so noisy and—and frightening?"

Joe reached to pat her hand. She wished he would take her

in his arms, but the stop had slowed their timing, she
supposed. He took the reins in both hands and then answered,
"They're a pretty rough-and-ready bunch—mostly boozed up
on the return trip. Most act civilized if there are womenfolk
along."

Chris Beth shuddered at the thought of travel-weary immigrant women making the long journey westward under such
conditions. And she had thought a stagecoach primitive! Even
this morning's encounter shook her new-found confidence,
and she wished again for the security of the cabin. Ordinarily
they would be getting up about this time. Joe would have a
warm fire going, and together they would watch little Mart,
all rosy with sleep, yawn his infant "Good morning!" She was
homesick. That's what she was. Just a few miles away from
the settlement, and already homesick!

"Giddyup!" Joe clucked his tongue again, then said to Chris
Beth, "We'll have to clip along to make up for lost time. The
trail's going to be rough from here on, too."

"That's all right," she said stoutly—a comment she was to
regret as the trail grew more narrow and dusty. It was a relief
to see a few windows light up here and there, but cabins were
far apart and often far from the rutted road. Finally they
seemed to recede into the shadows of mountains which even
the promise of sunrise did not seem to light up.

The coffee would be bubbling away happily now and the
sourdough biscuits ready to pop into the oven. *Stop it*, she said
fiercely to herself.

"Tell me about Willow Grove," she encouraged Joe, more to
get her mind off home than because of interest in their
destination. But as he talked, Chris Beth found herself keenly
interested.

"First of all, we need to get to know these people and their
ways. Little Mart's parents were among their followers." She
nodded, remembering only that the young Mrs. Martin was
reserved, said to be well-educated, and wore black dresses that
were collared and cuffed in white. She touched her own
dove-gray cotton with its little nosegays of pink roses and

wondered if her apparel would be out of place. Joe had said, "Something cool for this unusual May weather—and your umbrella." She hoped Joe had picked up her pink umbrella by the door—not that she could do much about either matter now. She would rather hear more about Willow Grove anyway.

"Do they worship like we do in the settlement?"

"Services vary, depending on lots of things." Chris Beth had a feeling he was hedging and was reasonably sure of it when he added, "At least they have a building." A real church! That would be nice. If *that* were the only difference—

"I know, too, that they didn't take to the circuit riders. Too emotional, they said, and," he chuckled, "violent."

"Violent? *Jonas?*" She asked of the preacher who had married them.

"No, Noah Somebody—I guess he was quite a character. The congregation, 13 of them, I hear, called themselves 'disciples' and said they only needed a quiet leader who knew how to break bread but not their silence." Joe chuckled as if remembering something funny—or to divert her. But she was not to be diverted.

"You mean he wasn't supposed to *preach?*"

"Something like that, but that was a long time ago. They've probably changed the requirements. D-don't worry about it, Chrissy."

Her husband's stammering told her that he was worrying enough for both of them. She shifted the subject.

"You were laughing at something."

Joe threw his head back and laughed heartily before sharing the anecdote that had made its way from community to community in the new land. "The story goes that Noah was dubbed a 'sundowner' by just about every group he visited. He seemed to reach one of the worshiper's houses right at sundown, then pointed out that it would be cruel for them to refuse him bed and board for the night what with the wolf at the door, so to speak."

It was good to see that Joe had relaxed. As he went on to

describe this Noah fellow, Chris Beth wondered if there wasn't a bit of the man's personality deep inside Joe himself. It wasn't a new thought, really. Gentle though he was, there was a strength to Joe that seemed to need testing and tempering. She hoped he would continue so she could gain more insight. And he did.

"He made quite a name for himself—said to have baptized more than 3000 converts, some kind of record among the circuit riders."

"Well-educated?"

Joe shook his head. "But bright! Knew the entire Bible by heart and quoted it by memory. Miss Mollie heard him preach once and said he couldn't have read the Bible he owned anyway, as he 'beat it to pieces tryin' to pound the Word in!'"

"Sounds like Mrs. Malone," Chris Beth laughed. "Did she say what this man looked like, this supposedly violent preacher?"

"Big and strong, and took no foolishness. Some roughneck came to the meetinghouse one night and started making trouble. Noah supposedly left the pulpit and threw him out bodily. But what I was laughing about was his contribution to politics—" Joe paused to look her direction, "Am I boring you?"

"Oh no! I'm enjoying every minute." (*And I wonder if you know how much*, she thought, for she was seeing not a new man but one who fleshed out more and more each day.)

"Well, if you're sure—just one story more and then we'll take a break." Goodness knows she needed that, but she needed to hear Joe's story even more.

"One of the legislators decided that once Oregon was a state and no longer a territory, there ought to be a chaplain. The only preacher around was old Noah, and they all dreaded him. He was noted for his long-winded sermons. But he surprised them! The men prepared themselves for a long, loud prayer. What they got was one of his favorite passages: "Father, forgive them for they know not what they do!'"

Even as the two of them laughed together, Chris Beth knew that Joe was sharing with her a need, possibly unrecognized by himself, to make use of his inner self—to minister to people the way he felt the Lord intended. Maybe Willow Grove would be right, but what he had told her made her wonder. And they *did* have to be practical, too. Even ministers had to support their families.

"Joe," she hesitated, then—encouraged by his listening nod—continued: "Joe, can these people at Willow Grove afford a resident minister? They must have paid Noah as well as fed him."

"Well, yes and no—about paying Noah, that is. He took in a lot of money from some of the churches," Joe laughed again. "He made friends with the owner of a saloon-keeper up north—even baptized him, and then encouraged the man to bring his 'talent' with him!"

Talent? Yes, Joe explained, that of raking in cash. "He would just lock the doors and refuse 'leavin' rights' until Noah's big black hat was full." *How awful!* Yes, Joe admitted, but the notorious circuit rider built a lot of churches that way. Some even thought that, secretly, some of the funds for the Willow Grove Church may have come from Noah's coffer. Well, today should be very interesting. But her question about a resident minister remained.

Joe reined in at the next turnout. The shade of the fir trees looked inviting, for the sun had grown hot already. "Salmon-berries are ripe!" Joe, pointing excitedly to the giant red-orange berries, failed to see how stiff and lame Chris Beth was from the long ride as he helped her down and offered her a juicy berry.

She scarcely tasted it. She was too buried in putting together a picture of Willow Creek. Already an alien world had opened along the way. But in a sense she dreaded the uncertainty ahead even more. What would the church be like? And what would it do to their lives?

16
Upon This Rock

ↄ

CHRIS BETH WONDERED if she had a muscle anywhere in her that didn't ache from fatigue as she tried to align herself in order to enter the church with a measure of dignity. Joe made no complaint, but he looked tired. He took her arm wordlessly as they neared the door, and wordlessly she smiled in appreciation. Then she inhaled deeply, hoping to ease the tremor inside her being.

At least it was good to see a church building again, one with a spire! It wasn't so tall, but it reached toward the heavens all the same. And it was good to see real panes of glass in the windows. But there ought to be some sign of welcome, some little show of warmth, someone there to greet them. An open door, or even the sound of music or song from inside.

Joe's large hand fumbled with the latch. Chris Beth disengaged her hand from his elbow, and then she saw that he was hesitating.

"Are you ready, Chr-Chrissy?" he asked in a low, uncertain voice.

After the long ride, the gray dress probably looked like it hung from a peg. She tried to smooth the soft folds. As for her

237

hair, earlier she had drawn it smoothly from her forehead, but
by now—

"Do I look a fright?" she asked anxiously.

"You look fine," Joe said without looking. "I meant, are you
r-ready for this—if—?"

Joe didn't finish. There was no need. She knew the question—the same one that lay in her own heart. *Ready for this?
Oh, Joe, I don't know if I'm ready for this church or any other
outside the security of the settlement. Don't you know that?*

"But you're only here to see, aren't you? Then decide?"

"That's part of it. But these people decide, too. And you!"
He turned to face her. "You do—do understand, Chrissy, that
I *have* to preach? That there's no decision about that?"

And the place doesn't matter. But she forced a tight smile.
"Like Noah?"

Joe studied her face, then smiled in gentle conspiracy.

"Like Noah," he whispered. "Only my way."

Then she must try to understand.

There was no time to think further. Joe opened the door
cautiously. It was dark inside the church in spite of the
windows. For a moment she wondered foolishly if there were
a congregation. And it was so quiet that she and Joe might
well have been alone. When her eyes adjusted to the shadowy
darkness, Chris Beth saw that all heads were covered with
black, giving a strange feeling of mourning. None of the
worshipers lifted bowed heads as she and Joe entered. Could
they all have gone to sleep waiting for them to arrive?

What do we do? Her eyes asked Joe. His slight palms-up
gesture signaled back, *I don't know.*

When, in due time, one of the men stood, and—with eyes
closed—began to speak softly, Joe motioned her to be seated
in one of the straight-backed, homemade pews. The speaker's
voice was so muted that it was hard to hear his words. And
when he sat down, another man stood, and then another. *They
must be giving testimonials,* she thought.

Maybe her own head should be bowed, but Chris Beth was
unable to resist looking at her strange surroundings and the

equally strange people in it. The women all looked alike, at least to an outsider, she thought. The similarity went beyond the dark clothing. It was in their faces, so unreadable and expressionless. It was hard to tell whether the immobility of the women's features spelled quiet desperation or serenity.

And the men! Why, they looked like rows and rows of prophets, lined up the way they were, eyes either cast downward or staring upward with a glazed expression. In their unbelievably long beards, they reminded Chris Beth of the mossy oak trees in her southern home.

Chris Beth was suddenly aware of a prolonged silence. She glanced at Joe questioningly. He smiled in response. Then, as if seeking support, he squeezed her hand before he rose and, to her surprise, made his way down the dim aisle to stand before the group.

Seeming to take a cue from the others, Joe spoke softly. "Upon this rock I—I build my church—" he began.

She had heard him use the text before. Even under normal circumstances, it was not one of his better sermons. Today it seemed to convey no message at all. The words sounded empty. And Joe was stuttering badly.

"Th-the church s-spoken of here is—is the human h-heart. And it—it m-must be centered upon Jesus Ch-Christ—"

Oh, Joe, my darling, her heart cried out, *it's not an inspired sermon. They aren't even listening! You can never be a Noah here—*

She squeezed her eyes shut and, without warning, the curtain in her mind parted. The scene around her dissolved. Joe's voice floated away. And she was transported to some future state. Hammers pounded. Saws whined. And, above it all, there was the sound of singing. And then a voice (*O'Higgin's?*) saying, "We'll observe the Lord's Supper by candlelight. Here! *Upon this rock!* Until the buildin' be finished!"

17
Pancakes at Midnight

❧

THE TRIP HOME was long and hard. There were times when Chris Beth longed to cry out, "I can't go any further!" Once, long ago, somebody had told her that she couldn't be hungry and scared at the same time, but that wasn't true! She was starving and she was scared out of her wits.

Surely the fir trees hadn't been this dense just this morning. It had been dark then, too, but in her mind there was a difference between morning-dark and night-dark. This was so *total!* This morning the predators of the night had been finishing their shift. Now they were just beginning. Coyotes were calling hungrily from all directions, their wails of despair sending a chill down her spine. Once she had been sure that the deeper, more throaty howl was that of a wolf. She regretted having asked Joe. Uncertainty would have been better than knowing.

"That was a mating call—nothing to fear," Joe had tried to reassure her. "It's only the *packs* that sometimes are a threat to man." Well, cougars weren't like that. One was all it took.

She squeezed her hands tightly in her lap and tried to think of something else.

But the "Whoo—owwwww! Who, who, who, whooooow!" hoots of the watching owls would allow her no peace. When she felt one of the night creatures glide effortlessly by—she let out a little cry in spite of herself.

"It's only an owl," Joe soothed, pulling her closer to his side.

"'An abomination among fowl,' some say. Who ever called them wise?"

"I, for one! Just look what the fellow did for me—brought you snuggling up close."

"I'd have snuggled anyway. I'm cold."

"Shucks! And here I thought it was my fatal charm."

"That too," she giggled, moving a little closer still.

"I guess the owls are hungry like two others I know of, hmmm?"

Chris Beth laughed. "I wasn't going to complain, but I'm caved in completely. Of course, it's been—what, 18 hours between meals?"

Joe inhaled deeply. "You don't need to tell me that my sermon, if you could call it that, wasn't what the Willow Grove people hoped for." When she made no answer, he continued, "But it ought to please 'em that we're fasting right along with their tradition!"

Well, they might as well treat the matter lightly. It wasn't going to do them in to go without food this long. It was more that it was so unexpected to find the worshipers spending the Lord's Day fasting and meditating instead of singing praise and celebrating at the Lord's Table, either in communion or at an after-church picnic.

"I should have eaten my oatmeal this morning."

Joe leaned to kiss her forehead. "I promise you a real breakfast when we get home."

"At midnight?"

"Does it matter?"

"No." Nothing mattered right now—not ever the disappointments of the day—except that they were together and that Joe wasn't as discouraged as she thought he might be. Actually, she decided, he seemed relieved, almost jubilant.

Since that was his mood, there was no reason why they could not discuss the day openly. She was glad about that.

"Did the men say anything after the meeting?"

"Very little. Mostly they talked about fear that there will be poor crops if the drought continues. They use grain as their medium more than money, I think. Sort of a common storehouse arrangement."

She understood that but wondered what they did for cash. Turned grain in (sort of like the miners did gold), Joe supposed. But for paying a preacher? Joe said he suspected that they took care of their leader with food.

"Did any of the women talk with you?" Joe asked.

"Just nodded. I gather they say nothing in church?"

"Apparently. I don't think they intended to be unkind."

Chris Beth hadn't gathered that either. Just shy, and in keeping with what they thought a woman's place ought to be. She had noticed, however, their unusual pattern of speech when they spoke to the children: "Get thee into the wagon . . . has thou forgotten thy manners?"

"And the men *did* look a little like rows and rows of prophets marching down the aisles, didn't they?" Chris Beth asked, remembering the unbelievably long beards that they all wore.

"Tradition seems important. Different from my own practices. But they are sincere people. I could feel that."

Chris Beth had felt that, too, and found herself thinking that she was sure they would come through in time of crisis.

"Tell you what," Joe said as he helped her from the buggy. "You run in and get into something snuggly and warm. Brush your hair and—would you mind letting it hang loose?"

"Why, Joe—Brother Joseph!"

"Well, it occurs to me that the bride and groom have never had a night alone since that little stint right after the vows."

"But what about that breakfast?" she teased.

"This one's on me! First a fire. Then I feed the horses and my wife."

Strange that all the fears of the day seemed silly now. Outside, darkness cloaked the cabin. But there were no pockets in the night from which highwaymen and wild animals could emerge and then pounce! It was a kind of starstruck darkness that spoke of warmth and peace of mind.

Languidly—and for some reason, happily—Chris Beth unwound her dark braids and brushed her hair until the red glints came back. As she was about to follow the unmistakable aroma of coffee and buttermilk pancakes, she turned and smiled into the darkness.

18
Bearing of Gifts—
And Burdens

~~♂~~

TWO WEEKS AFTER the trip to Willow Grove, two of the "disciples" paid the Craigs an unexpected visit. Chris Beth was pitting cherries for a cobbler when an unfamiliar voice called from the front gate, "Hello, hello! May we enter in?"

Joe, Wilson, and young Wil were setting out tomato plants on the little section of land they called the "island" down by the creek.

"Soil's sandier there and retains the water. Maybe the plants will grow in spite of the heat," Joe had said. She hoped so, for they were going to need all the garden produce possible to tide them over until one or more of the two family members could be back on some kind of payroll. The babies were growing like weeds and seemed to thrive under any conditions (unlike the domestic plants). And young Wil was in need of shoes and a few school supplies come fall. The rest of them could manage, barring some emergency. Of course, emergencies *did* arise when least expected.

Hurriedly Chris Beth looked out the cabin window and, recognizing the men by their dark clothing, opened the door.

244

"Do come in!" she invited, unlatching the door. Then, remembering that she wore a long apron over her floor-length
skirt, Chris Beth pulled it over her head, dried her wet hands
on it, and dropped it into Joe's easy chair in the corner he
reserved for a study.

Silently the two men came up the petunia-bordered walk
side by side. She wondered foolishly if they would try to enter
the doorway in the same fashion. She doubted if it would
accommodate both men, even though they were sparse of
frame. But at the door the gentleman on the right stepped
formally behind his companion and bowed with the words
"Brother Amos." Brother Amos stepped ahead at the signal,
then lifted his hat to his hostess and said politely, "Mrs. Craig,
this is my Christian brother, Brother Benjamin."

Chris Beth nodded to the two men, bade them sit down, and
offered coffee. Brother Amos and Brother Benjamin looked
surprised. "No, thank you. We do not partake," they said in
unison.

Oh, dear, she thought, *I've done something wrong!* What
could she offer? Maybe some cold cider? But before there was
an opportunity to phrase the offer, Brother Amos said, "Water
will be sufficient."

In the kitchen Chris Beth set out glasses and then "yoo-
hooed" to Joe. At her call Joe came running. Shaking her head
to indicate there was no problem, she put a warning finger to
her lips and whispered, "The 'disciples'! Fetch cold water
from the spring."

When she reentered the front room, both men stood. "We
bear gifts," said Brother Amos. "Wouldst thou receive them?"

"I would be honored," she said, wondering if that was the
right response.

By the time Joe had come in and shaken hands with the two
men, Chris Beth had poured them tall glasses of fresh, cold
water. She excused herself and, while Brother Amos spoke in
low tones with Joe, Brother Benjamin made the first of several
trips to the two pack mules they obviously had ridden the

long distance. It was terribly hot. They must be exhausted, Chris Beth thought.

Admittedly they were strange, but something about them touched her deeply. And it warmed her heart to see that her husband was talking openly with Brother Amos.

"Lord," she whispered, "I find something more to love in this wonderful man every day!" Unconsciously she hummed as she popped the cobbler into the oven. She had little more than tidied up the kitchen when Joe told her from the door that their guests had refused his invitation to supper.

"I'm sorry," she said truthfully as she went in to say good-bye. Then, before she could stop herself, she gasped, "What on earth—?"

For there, in the middle of the room, stood sacks of all the whole-grain breads, cookies, and cakes that she could name— and then some. How could they have known that her sugar bin was all but empty? To hide her tears of gratitude, Chris Beth hurried out into the pantry to bring them honey and jars of her favorite wild plum jelly.

"I just wish there were more I could do," she said.

"There is," said Brother Amos. "Thou canst pray for rain. My brother and I have had a vision. The drought is the first of our several plagues. Wouldst thou and thy house help bear our burdens?"

"Indeed, we will!" Joe assured Brother Amos. The two "disciples" raised their hands as if in benediction, having brought all they had to offer.

19
The Second Plague

JOE SHOWED NO DISAPPOINTMENT at there being no monetary offer for him at Willow Grove. Instead, he seemed almost relieved. However, the two of them agreed that the encounter had been a blessing. "And we're to meet again, you know."

"Really? When?" Chris Beth was very surprised.

"Brother Amos said some of the members will be with us Sunday at the brush arbor—praying for rain, you know."

"Joe," she said slowly, "is it really that serious?"

"It will be unless there is rain soon. Everything depends on rain in the Oregon Country. Crops. The mill. Possibility of more waterways opening for shipping . . ." Joe paused as if wanting to say more, then almost to himself he added, ". . . timber."

She had taken this too casually. Here she was worried about summer gardens and little Mart's prickly heat when their entire way of life was at stake. It simply had not occurred to Chris Beth that the beautiful timber needed water. Yes, they must pray. And she must keep Joe's spirits up.

So there was an air of festivity on Sunday when the Craigs

and the Norths boarded the buggy. If Dobbin and Battle felt that four adults, two babies, one growing boy, and the basket of honey and breads was an overload for two horses, they took it in stride. Seeming to sense the attempted lightheartedness of their family, the team clopped along at a pace that belied their years.

"*Oh*, but it's good to be home!" Chris Beth said happily.

The others laughed. "Makes one appreciate home to be gone so long," Wilson teased. "Like one day!"

"It was a *long* day," she defended.

The men began talking in low tones then, and Chris Beth was able to catch little of the conversation. She thought Wilson said something about going to Portland to see a publisher. Maybe that meant he had completed his book . . . but wasn't he saying something about setting up an office? Did that mean so far away, and did Vangie know? Either way, her sister apparently had heard none of the talk this Sunday morning. For, taking advantage of the men's talking, she had whispered, "How do I look? Any different?"

Chris Beth surveyed her with admiration. Vangie always looked beautiful. Her delicate features, almost marblelike in their smoothness, and her silver-blonde hair, which always looked as if each strand were backlighted by sunlight, gave her the look of a visiting angel. But, as usual, she felt a nagging concern for the younger girl. It seemed to Chris Beth that Vangie looked more delicate with each passing day.

"You're lovely. You have a way of making anything you wear look new!" she answered Vangie's question.

Vangie was delighted. "You *did* notice! The reason the dress looks new is," she paused to lower her voice modestly, "I was able to get into my corset today!"

She was unaware that the horses had slowed down for the bend of the road leading to the arbor and that the men had paused in their conversation. "You and who else?" Wilson called over his shoulder. "I see, Joe, why they chose to ride back there!"

"Wilson!" Vangie's cheeks were pink. "Don't you dare—"

Wilson was enjoying himself. And suddenly so was Chris Beth. It was like old times—no matter what lay ahead.

"Found my bride strapped to the bed post, I vow to you, trying to take her own life by strangulation—around the waist!"

"*Wilson!*" Vangie wailed. "This seating promised privacy."

Young Wil was enjoying himself immensely. Then, to Chris Beth's surprise, Joe chimed in, "Isn't there a better way of having our ladies look wasp-waisted? I've meant to ask Chrissy."

Chris Beth put a warning finger to her lips. After all, they were nearing the church. Brother Joseph, his teacher-wife, Doctor Wil, and his wife (wasn't she a nurse?) were expected to maintain a certain air of dignity. But she did whisper, "You find a way, Brother Joseph, and we'll all be rich!"

Usually Chris Beth would have been viewing the scenery. She just never seemed to tire of Oregon's panorama of beauty, no matter what the season. Today there had been so much banter that she had failed to notice that some of the sheen had gone from the leaves of the laurel and manzanita bushes and that the needles of her beloved fir trees looked dusty and tired.

She did notice, though, that the brush on the arbor had curled and twisted in the hot sun. So many of the leaves and needles had dropped from the boughs that the sun had found its way to the dirt floors. Not that the condition of the temporary roof made any difference in attendance. Indeed, it had doubled or more just since Sunday before last.

Neighbors swarmed to meet the buggy, and Chris Beth saw from the corner of her eye that the Muslin City people had gathered beneath the arbor. The Chu family stood just outside as if awaiting an invitation. She must get to them quickly, although she doubted if there would be seating space. And then she saw Mrs. Malone—leave it to her to find a solution—engineering the spreading of quilts and blankets, taken from wagonbeds, for the late-arriving guests. And still they came!

Chris Beth turned to Joe to flash a message of appreciation, but Brother Amos (and what appeared to be a dozen others in the same somber black-and-white attire) had approached. Joe, bless him, was shaking hands and introducing the men to Nate Goldsmith, who took over with a flourish as Joe made his way to the pulpit.

Joe prayed for the presence of the Lord. And surely the Lord answered his prayer. It was evidenced in the singing (the "disciples" took no part, but they gave no indication of offense). It was further evidenced in Joe's inspired sermon (so different, Chris Beth thought, from last Sunday's!). But, most of all, it was evidenced in the general feeling of fellowship. Despite differences of race, creed, color, and forms of worship, there was a common bond of love.

"Am I right, Lord, in thinking Joe is helping You create this bond?" And, deep in her heart, it was as if the Lord said, "Yes."

Chris Beth felt the presence of the Lord in their midst even more when Joe invited all to join in a prayer for rain. Many of the men rose at the invitation and walked up to kneel at the altar. Some of those remaining behind, having given their seats to women and children, knelt just outside the brush arbor. Most of the women remained where they were and, with heads bowed, offered silent prayers. Only the Willow Grove guests rose, raised both hands imploringly, and fixed their gaze upon something seemingly invisible to the eyes of those around them.

The farmers prayed one by one, then waited for Joe to offer the benediction. Chris Beth always loved this part. Joe's words were invariably the same: "The Lord bless you and keep you. The Lord make His face to shine upon you—"

But today he seemed to hesitate, as if waiting for something. And it came. Brother Amos, still standing, began in a soft monotone which at first Chris Beth was unable to hear. Straining to catch the words, she unconsciously opened her eyes and looked into the face of the visiting "disciple." What she saw made it impossible to close her lids again.

The speaker, whose near-transparent skin was etched with soft creases—not the deep ones she would expect from a man who had endured so much sun—wore the look of an ethereal being. His wide-open eyes, a deep blue that only very old people or babies seemed to have, were fixed in a trancelike stare. The lips kept moving . . . moving . . . until finally words were distinguishable.

". . . And where there is one, there will be more, and more, then hordes. Ah, yes, my brothers, we saw it happen in Utah. And we shall see it again. We have brought you the signs."

All heads lifted then as Brother Amos held out his handful of grasshoppers. "The second of the plagues . . ." his voice trailed away.

"Strange they didn't stay for dinner, what with that long ride back to Willow Grove," Mrs. Malone said after the "disciples" had made a hasty departure.

"They fast on Sunday," Chris Beth explained as she helped the other women weight the tablecloths down against a possible wind.

"*Ach!* Tell that to mine *bon* ol' man!" Olga Goldsmith said tartly.

Rachel Beltran moved closer to Chris Beth. "Been thinkin' 'bout them grasshoppers. Know 'bout that, too?"

"No," Chris Beth admitted slowly, aware that the eyes of all the other women were focused on her. "It was news to me too, and I don't know what to make of it. I do know that these are devout men. And somehow I don't take this lightly."

"They don't know any more'n we do!" Bertie Solomon declared, picking up a covered bowl and tugging at the lid.

"Now, now, Bertie, they jest might," Mrs. Malone said. "They jest might."

The bowl slipped from Mrs. Solomon's hand and bounced onto the white cloth below, spilling the shredded cabbage. She stopped to scrape up the contents. "I refuse t' believe it and that's that."

The men came then, and they too were talking about the possibility that there might be "a mite of truth" to what "them peculiar men" said.

"Me, I ain't losin' sleep over it," Nate said in a tone that boasted courage. "Still 'n all, I wonder jest how we'd recognize a real, honest-to-goodness prophet. Any ideas 'fore blessin' this food fer our bodies, Brother Joseph?"

"We'll know it was a real prophecy if it comes to pass, won't we?" Joe asked quietly.

A strange silence fell over the group.

20
Fulfillment of the Prophecy

✦

BOTH CHRIS BETH and Vangie cried when Joe and Wilson left for Portland. "You'll be all right, Darling," Joe hugged Chris Beth. "I wouldn't leave you except that—well, you know why."

Yes, she knew. How well she knew! It was mid-June and the heat hung like a thing alive over the settlement. The gardens had failed miserably. The only hope of canning lay with the peach, pear, and apple orchards. The wheat looked promising because it could survive with less water, but the corn hadn't made it.

What it all amounted to was that Joe must be on the lookout for a church, even if it meant moving far away from the people she loved—far away from the very spot where Joe felt called to do the Lord's work, and far away from the dreams they had promised themselves, each other, and the Lord.

But knowing did not stem the tide of tears. "It's just—just that we—we've never been apart. And the two months seem so short—"

"A lifetime seems too short together," Joe whispered understandingly. "That's why there is eternity."

"But first there's life here!" Chris Beth objected.

When Joe turned to face her, love lighted his eyes so that the gold flecks showed through. But his voice chided gently. "Yes, there's life here. And I never underestimate its value, Darling. Quite the contrary! It's because of the brevity of our little mortal span that we have to work hard at following the will of the Lord."

"You mean the ministry, don't you?"

"In my case, yes. In yours—oh, Chrissy, don't you know how important it is that I have you with me all the way—*here* and *there*? Don't you know how much I love you and need your help to do what I must?"

Chris Beth bit her lip to hold back the tears. Yes, she knew. And she wasn't going to cry. Was she? *Yes, she was!*

How on earth, she wondered, *do women without wonderful Christian husbands survive? Who reassures them? Makes them know that everything here and hereafter will be all right?*

"Young Wil will be with you. He's becoming quite a man, you know."

She nodded through her tears. It wasn't as if she would be alone. There were little Mart . . . Vangie . . . True . . . and Esau. Not alone—no—but *lonely*. Why, she wouldn't even be a whole person without Joe.

Joe touched the back of her neck where the dark tendrils curled with perspiration. "Wilson's waiting," he reminded her gently.

She walked with him to where Wilson stood beside the two saddled horses. Vangie, she knew from experience, would be sobbing her heart out, her face buried in the biggest feather pillow she could find. But Chris Beth felt an urgent need to gain control of herself, to show Joe she *was* developing into the kind of pioneer woman he needed to fulfill his ministry, and to wave until he was out of sight. She squared her shoulders bravely and hoped her voice was steady. "Good luck on the book, Wilson. I'll look after Vangie. And the Lord bless both of you!"

Turning, she was about to run into the house and let go of
a few more tears when she caught sight of young Wil leaning
against one of the twin fir trees just outside the slat fence
around the cabin. His shoulders were convulsing with sobs.

Ashamed of her thoughtlessness, Chris Beth ran to the boy.
Of course he had wanted to go with the men! Why, a trip by
horseback to Portland would have been a lark. She squatted
beside the small figure, wondering what to say. But he spoke
first, "I wanna be a man!"

"Well, now, your being the man of the house this week will
prove you're on your way," she said, trying not to sound
patronizing.

Young Wil made a helpless gesture. "That's not what I
mean."

He had dark eyes, so like Wilson's, but pale hair—like
straw. His usually smooth skin was sprinkled with a few
blemishes now, bearing out what his behavior told: adoles-
cence. It was a boy pleading for help—sullenly.

Patience. Patience. "Just what *do* you mean?" she asked
calmly. When there was no answer, she extended her question. "You mean, I think, that you wish something big would
happen. The kind of thing that makes one into an instant
hero?"

"Yeah!" young Wil said without thinking. Then, looking
sheepish, he added, "Shucks! I didn't mean that—not exactly."

"But *I* have felt that way!"

"You have?" He was all attention.

"Lots of times," she admitted, wishing it were not true.

"Name one," young Wil begged, his liquid eyes no longer
sullen.

"Well, now—" She pretended to think, and they both
laughed. "Today!" Taking advantage of his change of mood,
she hurried on. "Yes, this very day I'd like to be Chicken Little
so I could run and tell the news!"

"That the sky's falling?" Young Wil, a child again, giggled.

"The same. And you know what? I've a feeling that before the week's over, you'll get your chance."

The boy studied his bare feet. "You always understand me," he said, "like you were my own—" To Chris Beth's disappointment, he checked the words. "But, Miss Chrissy—"

"Chrissy to you, Wil."

"Chrissy," he said without hesitation, "the sky *wasn't* falling."

"You're right," she said slowly. "Help me remember that, will you?"

The grasshoppers came the next day. Chris Beth had built a fire beneath the black, three-legged, iron washpot in the backyard of the Big House early in preparation for boiling the white clothing. Young Wil was bringing rinsewater from the spring. And Vangie was tending the bees when the first of the insects came, as if by chance, on silent wings. The hens stopped dusting themselves beneath the shade of the row of sunflowers in the garden and did away with the invaders in short order.

"Good riddance to them, girls," Chris Beth said to the lady fowl.

Later she wondered why she felt no real foreboding at the appearance of the first of the hoppers. She had been more disturbed than she cared to admit when Brother Amos had presented the grasshoppers in such a dramatic way several weeks before. And, even though some of the other settlers tried to light-touch the prophecy, she sensed that they too were upset by the very suggestion that even a few of the creatures were hereabouts.

Wilson had suggested that Boston Buck and the rest of the Indians would have a field day, since one of their confessed loves was for grasshopper cakes! And Nate Goldsmith had teasingly proclaimed it to be the Year of the Grasshopper.

Fiddle! What did he know? Mrs. Malone had wondered.

Got it from Mr. Chu, O'Higgin had chimed in—something to do with the Chinese New Year or *Poor Richard's Almanac.*

The conversation ended when Miss Mollie gave him a withering look and said, "A week ago it was the Week of the Rabbit because you caught one in the remains of the garden. Then 'twas the Year of the Leprechaun 'cause you couldn't find both your socks. Men!"

But deep down Chris Beth sensed that Brother Amos's warning held some credibility.

It was young Wil who first noticed a faint whir in the morning stillness. "Do you hear it?" the boy asked Chris Beth as he finished hauling the rinsewater.

She listened. Yes, she did. "Help yourself to cornbread sticks. Butter's in the cooler. I'll see if Joe and Wilson left something running in the mill."

Everything seemed in order when Chris Beth entered the cool, damp building, shut up tight the way she would have expected. Any sound coming from the mill would have been drowned out by the noise of the waterfall anyway, she realized once she was inside. But what a relief to be in the building with the machinery not grinding away. So quiet. So restful. And so cool to her warm skin. When her eyes adjusted to the dark, she noticed an empty barrel—just begging, it seemed, to be sat upon! The fire would be blazing. The washwater would be boiling. But young Wil was on hand in case the baby woke up. So, for one luxurious moment, she would rest. . . .

She had slept little last night. The bed was so empty without Joe. She had taken little Mart from the cradle and cuddled him close, but, comforting as the round little body was, she had been afraid to doze for fear she would roll on the baby.

"I'm so tired," she said aloud, "maybe ten minutes worth of rest will do no harm—"

Chris Beth awoke with a start. Tired or not, she had not expected to sleep this morning! She struggled to her feet, and, her eyes still glazed with slumber, hurried toward the door.

There she was startled by a buzz and then a roar that pounded against her eardrums as she pushed at the iron latch. When the heavy door yielded to her weight and the door opened a crack, she was even more startled by the absence of light! How could clouds have come so quickly? Still not thinking clearly, Chris Beth hoped for rain.

But before she was able to scan the sky some objects struck her face with a stinging blow, followed by another and another. And, suddenly to her horror, she was attacked from all directions—by what she was unable to tell. She only knew that her face was stinging and burning . . . that she was blinded . . . and then that her entire body was weighted by the driving force. "Oh, no!" she gasped as she stepped outside.

For, although she dared not open her eyes, the awful truth came, and with it revulsion. Fear turned to terror. *Grasshoppers!*

In an effort to breathe, Chris Beth covered her face with the apron she wore, taking a deep breath. Panic was her worst enemy. Stay calm. She strained her numbed senses in an effort to recall how far and in which direction she was from either house. Then she wondered if Vangie had made it back from the beehives. She must check . . . no, it was best to wait inside the mill until the hordes of insects passed. But before reaching the door, it creaked shut and she heard the latch click inside as Joe had often warned it would.

Chris Beth tried to remember Joe and Wilson's wilderness survival instructions. What would work with rain and snowstorms would work under these conditions—if she could just remember. Wind and hills could distort perception, but imagination was the worst offender. Keep calm. And look for protection. Branches would help, Wilson had stressed. Blindly she felt for the trees. But when she tried to reach for limbs, they were elusive. She felt on the ground and was able to find twigs enough to shield her face so that she dared risk opening her eyes to get her bearings.

Then, making the worst mistake of all, Chris Beth staggered forward only to be driven back by a new horde of insects. When she tried to retrace her steps, the mill seemed to have disappeared. Completely disoriented, she pressed against the force of the winged creatures.

How long she wandered or how far, Chris Beth had no idea. Her last coherent thoughts were a series of questions: *How far am I from home? Did I close the windows of the cabin? Where is young Wil? Where's Vangie? Dear God, who is looking after the babies?* It was almost a relief to feel herself sink weakly and senselessly into Graveyard Creek's shallows even though she couldn't remember if she was upstream or downstream from home.

Stifling the urge to scream, she sat down in the water. Curling up, she thought foolishly that she would just wait until the creatures flew away.

It must have been only minutes, but it seemed like days, before her numb body felt a cold, wet nose on her arm. A wolf? Bear? Did it matter? And then, as if in a dream, she heard a familiar voice, "Esau, good boy! You found my mother!"

21
Where Two or Three
Are Gathered

❧

STILL DAZED, Chris Beth looked around her. Gradually her eyes focused and she was able to recognize the familiar settees beside the native-rock fireplace of the Norths' Big House.

"Me and Esau just about dragged you all the way," young Wil said proudly at her side. "I mean, Esau and *I.*"

Chris Beth tried to manage a smile. Bits and pieces of the preceding events flashed before her eyes but refused to stay in place. Just as she was able to arrange them into a pattern they fell apart, like a tilted kaleidoscope, and a whole new design emerged. "I'm so confused," she said weakly.

Young Wil was suddenly in control. "You didn't *act* confused," he defended. "You did everything right. Most folks— 'specially women—would've been screaming and tearing through the forest. But you—you just stayed put, like a fawn hid out."

Waiting was smart, he said. (*But I had no choice. I was lost!*)

And getting in the water was good. Lots of people had

survived "fire and stuff" that way. *(My being there was by accident!)*

"Uncle Wil will be proud of you, M-Miss—I mean, Chrissy."

At the faltering speech, another vague memory-pattern shaped in her mind. Grasshoppers. Near-panic. Being lost. The dog's friendly nose. But something else . . . *Mother!* That was it—young Wil had called her "Mother."

Maybe the child had been disturbed at the men's leaving him. Or maybe their going to Portland reminded him that his mother had lived there. *More likely,* she thought, *he's in need of affection.*

Impulsively she reached out and drew the small figure close. Well, he was *indeed* a man! A "growing boy" would have pulled away to prove his independence to her and to himself. But young Wil gave her a quick embrace instead. It was a warm and wonderful moment for Chris Beth. The look on the small face, so like his Uncle Wil's, said, "I needed that!"

"Am I a mess?" Chris Beth asked as young Wil straightened quickly.

Vangie! Chris Beth forced herself up from the couch. "Is Vangie all right? And the babies?"

"True and little Mart slept through it all while Vangie took care of shutting up the house—that's why it's so dark. Not from the hoppers. They're gone. Some died and the rest flew somewhere else."

Vangie came in. And, even though her eyes were shadowed with fatigue, she set to work on what must have been a thousand cuts, stings, and bruises. Chris Beth allowed herself to be daubed all over with camphor, but refused the peach-tree-leaf poultice. "Nonsense! There's too much that needs doing. I'm almost afraid to ask about the damages. Bad?"

Yes, the damages were bad. Very bad. Vangie and young Wil tried to describe the situation, often interrupting each other, their words tumbling over each other in their excitement. Surely they must be exaggerating just a little. But no! When

Chris Beth looked out the window, she realized that what
they told her had been understated, if anything.

To her horror, she first saw that every clapboard of the
beautiful white house was obscured in a jellylike mass created
by the millions of insects which must have swarmed blindly
against the building. Thank goodness for Vangie's foresight in
closing the windows, or the inside of the house would be in
the same shape!

Fascinated, Chris Beth's eyes fastened on the washpot and
the tubs of rinsewater. All were topped with thick layers of
dead grasshoppers. She could feel no remorse at their demise.
She hoped instead that the creeks and rivers were rising to the
floor stage with the huge, evil-looking skeletons. They could
flood the Pacific Ocean for all she cared!

Then, when she looked at the three-year-old orchard—
which only recently had bloomed like the Promised Land—
Chris Beth felt a kind of panic that was worse than what she
had experienced when caught in the blinding swarms of
grasshoppers—for the beautiful orchard was stripped of all its
fruit before the summer sun could color a single one. It was
stripped of every vestige of bud, leaf, and new-growth limb.
Only bare branches reached out pitifully as if begging the one
small, unpromising cloud to bring rain to drown the ugly
memories. Oh, how awful!

Numbly Chris Beth looked at the ruins about them. Another setback. Another broken dream. Another reason why
they undoubtedly would have to move from here . . . if there
was anywhere left that the demons hadn't attacked . . .

"The older trees?" Chris Beth asked through stiff lips.

"Ask this young man," Vangie said. "He saved some of the
fruit."

"It wasn't much." But there was pride in young Wil's voice.
"I just did what the books say to do when the trees need
protecting from the migrating birds."

"Which is?" Chris Beth encouraged.

"Drape 'em in muslin cloth." She nodded, remembering the
gauzy fabric of the Muslin City people. "We use it for

straining cider sometimes. Uncle Wil had some on the back porch."

Young Wil followed her gaze to the gnarled apple trees, misshapen with age but still bearing, and the peach trees, which were at their prime of life. The boy somehow had managed to wind the thin material around the limbs of several trees. These trees had blossomed heavily, giving promise of what O'Higgin had predicted to be the most bountiful harvest yet. Now they stood like mummies with little to offer the settlers or the bees. It was unbelievable.

Studying her face, young Wil spoke uncertainly. "I told you it wasn't much."

"Anything is *much* at this point," Chris Beth assured him. "What you did was very brave and thoughtful—something Vangie and I wouldn't have known to do."

He brightened. "I didn't have much time. When you didn't come back we had to find you. But I beat the grasshoppers down off some of the branches. Got the leaves for poultices and stripped off some green apples to bake. Not much," he hesitated, then continued, "but the Bible says, 'Where two or three are gathered in His name—'"

Chris Beth forced a tight smile at the interpretation.

"Well, the second plague *was* a real prophecy, wasn't it?" Chris Beth mused.

Vangie moaned in agreement. But young Wil replied, winking at Chris Beth, "Yes—but the sky *didn't* fall!"

22
Homecoming

❦

THE REST OF the week passed quickly. Chris Beth, Vangie, and young Wil worked long hours to clean away as much of the invading grasshoppers' signs as possible. It was indeed a hateful task and a most depressing one. Every day brought new revelations of the damages the insects had done.

"They left nothing in the garden but weeds," Vangie moaned, holding a hand to support her obviously aching back.

"And the stink!" young Wil added, holding his nose. He had been raking and burying the remains for days, but still the stench remained. The chickens, having eaten their fill, had lost interest and wandered around to find shade. They would miss the giant-leafed sunflowers, which had been stripped of their foliage and promising heads by the hungry insects in their migratory flight. Only dying stalks were left.

Chris Beth paused on the upper rung of Wilson's pruning ladder. Her arms ached from scrubbing the higher sections of the Big House's once-white siding.

"I've heard that these creatures follow a narrow path. Do you suppose the rest of the valley escaped?"

The others hoped so. They resumed their respective chores.

And, even though Chris Beth felt that she could not move even one more muscle, she doubled and redoubled her efforts, doggedly determined to somehow make this a nice homecoming for the men.

"I'll soak for hours, then put on the white blouse you like—maybe let my hair hang down, even bite the stem of the rose from my hat! All to please *you*, Joe. *All to show how much I love you . . . miss you . . . and need you!*"

It was true. She had missed Joe more than she had thought possible, she reflected, as she pushed scrub brushes back and forth. Her hands were red and raw, her nails broken to the quick. Maybe, she thought as she paused to remove a long splinter from her left hand, old Jonas was right.

"Oughta pray for adversity," the circuit rider had declared just before pronouncing Joe and Chris Beth man and wife. "Strengthens the innards and sets th' heart in tickin' order."

But that thought was kind of hard to go along with. Yet Joe's absence had given her a chance to "set her heart in ticking order"! Compared to life with Joe, the past was nothing. Nothing at all. Smiling she worked on.

When the pain in her arms and legs became almost unbearable, she whispered her never-changing, simple prayer: "Carry me just a little further, Lord," she implored. Then, strengthened, she worked on.

Why on earth, then, did she simply crumple up like a rag doll when she finally fell into Joe's arms? And why did she cry now that it was all over?

Reckon the Lord carried me as far as He thought He ought to, she thought through a maze of relief and happiness at seeing the men safely home.

"Sh-h-h-h, sh-h-, sh-h," Joe whispered, holding her close to his warm, familiar body while stroking her hair. Chris Beth was glad she had stayed up far too late the night before to bathe and shampoo. Every last detail had to be right. And she could tell from the heavy pounding of her husband's heart that her efforts were not lost upon him.

But he would never know what a struggle it had been. His

next statement proved that: "Let me look at you!" Then, holding her off a short distance, he added, "Well, you look none the worse than when I left you—but maybe the pesky hoppers missed these parts!"

Of all the—then, suddenly, it was funny! She glanced at her sister, whose blue eyes above the circle of Wilson's arms caught her own. Vangie rolled her eyes heavenward, signaling Mrs. Malone's usual comment, *"Men!"*

23
News
from the Big City

❧

"MAYBE I OVER-EGGED the pudding," Chris Beth recounted to Mrs. Malone later. Certainly her feverish binding up of the wounds left by the life-sucking insects had misled the two men. Joe and Wilson were totally unprepared for the devastation, even as she, Chris Beth, and young Wil were unprepared for the news that the entire settlement had suffered equal loss.

"Wheat crop's completely destroyed—all the gardens and fruit. Not a peach, apple, pear, *anything* left."

"There's *some*," young Wil said stoutly. It was hard to tell who was the prouder of the two, the boy himself or his uncle.

"Any reason why we can't celebrate with green apples?" Wilson asked with the characteristic twinkle in his eyes.

"You'll get a bellyache!" young Wil giggled.

"If so, there's a doctor in the house. Bring me the salt."

Chris Beth relaxed for the first time in days. There was a lot to be talked about and settled. But for now she could see that they were heading for one of those family confabulations that drew them even closer together in times of stress. She offered a silent prayer of thanksgiving. All of them needed this moment.

"What're we celebrating?" Young Wil's eyes danced in anticipation of praise.

His uncle pretended to think. "Well, now, it sounds to me like my nephew's reaching the age of accountability."

The boy stood soldierly tall.

"Then—" Wilson scratched his head as if to revive his memory. "What else was it, Joe?"

"Let's see," Joe played along. "Had to do with books. Oh, I know—the Sears catalogue!"

Vangie let out a squeal. "Did you bring one, Wilson? I mean, did you *really*?"

Young Wil did not wait for an answer. He dived into the saddlebags, bringing out the coveted mail-order catalogue and a sack of peppermint sticks—also knocking over a square package in his rush.

"Whoopee! Enough for everybody to have one—or—" he paused, "five for me?" He licked his lips as the scent of peppermint filled the air.

"Both, if you'll take time to count. And you can hand the package to the ladies."

Together Chris Beth and Vangie ripped off the wrappings, with young Wil getting in the way in an effort to see the contents. "K-A-L-S-O-M-I-N-E," he spelled. "What's that?"

"A new kind of paint for the cabinets," Joe told him. "Sort of like whitewash, only there's tint to be mixed in with the water."

" 'Jersey Cream Color,' " Vangie read. "Oh, how wonderful! Just matches the ruffles on my curtains. Too bad, Chrissy."

" 'Too bad,' she says! Why everybody knows the kalsomine will be the exact shade of the yellow 'Gingham Cat' appliques on mine!"

"Ladies, *ladies*!" Wilson implored. "I suggest to you as I suggested to this young man that there's enough for both, if you'll measure. Now, we're hungry. Does anybody care?"

Vangie sliced the coffee cake she had been saving for just

such an occasion. Chris Beth put the coffeepot on to boil. Then both of them ran to sit at the feet of their men and demand that they tell everything—absolutely *everything*—they had seen and heard in the big city. As they listened, Chris Beth determined to savor this time together and put both the past and the future in the Lord's hands, where they belonged.

Portland was big and bustling, the men reported. And awfully dusty. Still rough, though. Rutted by wagon wheels. Lots of potholes from horses' hooves in the winter mud. *Those were city streets?* Chris Beth had pictured their being somewhat like the cobblestone streets of Boston or at least the hard-packed streets and roads of her Southern home. No, she was on the wild frontier now, they reminded her, and went on to tell about the "pinchers."

Pinchers! They didn't go in *there?* She shuddered, remembering the stories whispered behind fans about "women of the night" who pretended to be dancers but—well, behaved unseemly. And the men—

But these pinchers were of a different nature. Businessmen of another sort. Carried pouches and—

Oh, chewed *tobacco*, Vangie guessed.

Wrong again. These were men making purchases by measuring a "pinch" of gold dust from a pouch with the thumb and two fingers. Gold, lots of gold. More women now, too. Men could mail-order wives. And (hurrying past that subject), there were ferries most of the way now—well-worth the charge of 12 cents per unloaded horse.

Churches? Yes, several new ones. Rumor had it that the "fair sex" divided their time between "bustin' up" the spirits barrels and going into the gambling halls for church donations.

Scandalous! Did they *really?* And would the men allow it?

That's how they collected. The men were in such a hurry to be rid of the good women that they handed over the day's take.

But now were they ready for the *real* news? "Tell us," Vangie begged.

"*Now!*" Chris Beth ordered.

Young Wil tried a conspiracy. "Whisper it in my ear," he teased.

"Well, for one thing, the *Eagle* is navigating the Rogue River. And the *Swan*—steamboat, remember?—made it up the Umpqua River." Wilson paused, obviously enjoying himself.

"Yes, yes? *Go on!*" Vangie pleaded. "Are waterways coming closer?"

"The *Lady Oregon* is steaming up and down the Columbia to deliver supplies, pick up mail, and carry passengers."

Excitement mounted as Joe took over to tell of the progress on the railroads. Rails would reach from San Francisco to Portland. "And the first people to be put to work will be our own Chinese families, although talk has it that 4000 more are on the way!"

"Do you mean they beget that fast?" Young Wil's eyes were roguish. His uncle shushed him with a look.

"The newcomers are immigrants," Joe smiled. "A lot will settle here, since tracks are to extend a hundred or so miles south of Portland."

The talk went on for hours. "I'll reheat the coffee," Chris Beth said, although reluctant to miss a word.

"Not until you hear the best!" Joe detained her with a hand. "Wilson has news." She sat down again and waited breathlessly.

But Wilson evaded whatever Joe referred to. "About the stage?"

Chris Beth breathed a prayer. Oh, she hoped for the stagecoach to come through! Most of all, she hoped for that!

"It's coming, all right—" he raised his voice above their squeals of joy, "which means that Turn-Around Inn is in for big business!"

How wonderful, how wonderful! But even in her excitement, Chris Beth found herself thinking, "Now where will we worship come winter and bad weather?" But that too was in the Lord's hands. She returned to her listening . . .

Young Wil, taking advantage of his new role, finally interrupted the conversation. "I'll start the chores." True and little Mart reminded their parents with lusty lungs that somebody had lost track of time. So, guiltily, the adults sprang to their feet.

Later, back home in their cabin, Chris Beth went over the events of the day in her mind as she tucked the baby into his cradle for the night. She and Joe had to talk, she decided, even though she ached with fatigue from the recent nightmare and she knew he must be exhausted from the long trip. Still, she had to know what the men had found out as a result of their journey. Pleasant as the homecoming had been, and interesting though their reports had been, she realized that they had left the main questions unanswered.

24
To Mend a Broken Dream

❧

CHRIS BETH SNUGGLED gratefully against her husband's warm body. She wished with all her heart that all women everywhere knew the warmth and security that the love of a good husband provided. Why, the love of a good man was second only to the love of God! If all marriages were like this, then there would be no quibbling, and maybe, eventually, no wars . . .

She struggled against sleep, but in spite of herself her eyelids drooped. In an effort to stay awake, she tried to elbow herself to a sitting position. Joe immediately eased her back into the circle of his arms and tightened his grip around her protectively. "You rest," she heard whispered drowsily in her hair.

The warm bath she had prepared served to further relax his body—instead of reviving it, the way she had hoped. She drew back just enough to look at the strong, rugged jawline of her husband's face. The light of a near-full moon outlined the high, aristocratic cheekbones. A sculptor's dream, she thought. But the kind, understanding eyes were closed. Maybe what

272

she needed to know could wait . . . No, she must have reassurance from the sensitive mouth.

"Stop studying my face," Joe's words came so suddenly in the stillness that Chris Beth jumped. Both of them laughed, then he continued, "Unless you want to get kissed?"

Joe drew her close again and claimed her lips with a soft, gentle kiss. Her senses reeled a little, as they always did when he kissed her. *Please, Lord, let it always be like this,* she prayed inwardly.

"If you're wondering if I missed you, my love, that should answer your question!"

"I guess I did want to hear you say it," she admitted, "but that isn't what I was wondering about—" Her voice trailed off, for she was reluctant to break this spell or to postpone his need of rest. *Just one question,* she promised herself. All else could wait for a more opportune time.

"About what?"

"Joe," she burst out, "did you find out anything—I mean about the need of a minister up there?"

He inhaled deeply. "Oh, there's a need, a crying need, Chrissy. I'll tell you about the vigilantes and the fear on both sides—I'll explain everything later. It's nothing we can resolve in a single question-and-answer talk."

Neither the fact that Joe had closed his eyes again nor that she had planned just one question could hold back another. "Do you think one of the churches will call you?"

"More than one, I think. And, by the way, Wilson had encouragement on his book—" His voice trailed off.

"That's wonderful! But, oh, Joe, what happens if our dream here gets broken?"

"We mend it," he said in sleep-softened tones, "with prayer."

Joe's last words were no more than spoken when his even breathing told her he had entered the private world of slumber. Without her! She should be glad he could sleep. Should be, but wasn't. A little resentfully she reached for her cotton wrapper and padded barefoot into the kitchen. She decided against lighting a candle—better conserve every match—and the embers had died in the grate. She moved in the darkness, thinking that it fit her mood, and poured herself a glass of milk. Then she sat down at the small table to think.

"If Joe knows more, why doesn't he tell me?" she whispered to the quiet around her. "I'm his wife!"

Did she imagine the voice that said out of the stillness, "But there's a part of him that belongs to God alone"?

Well, she had no quarrel with that, did she? Rinsing the glass quietly, Chris Beth felt the familiar uneasiness churn within her. Maybe all ministers' wives felt this inner conflict—this need for a certain security they never could have . . . loving God . . . wanting their husbands to serve Him . . . but feeling shut out.

"Oh, Lord, forgive me," she murmured. "I know he loves us both. But how can I help when I don't understand?"

No satisfying answer came, but there was a kind of peace as Chris Beth snuggled against Joe's back a few minutes later.

I'll simply have to resign myself to a different life. Different from back home. Different from other women's lives. Joe has to put God first . . . and sometimes bear other people's burdens before mine . . . and I have to understand . . . maybe that's how dreams are mended. . . .

She drifted off to sleep without a clear resolution.

25
The Burial

-ᕯ-

STRAIN SHOWED ON every face at Sunday morning's service. Even O'Higgin's song was less lusty, his voice more subdued. *If I'd walked into a group wearing faces like these, I would have gone right back home,* Chris Beth found herself thinking. Instead she had found loving countenances, smiles, and words of encouragement.

"How do you do it all?" she remembered asking Mollie Malone, thinking of what the older woman had gone through caring for her late husband's seven children, the death of one, and all the other hardships—alone.

"Love strengthens the arms," the unflappable Mrs. Malone had said matter-of-factly, "so we can hold each other up."

Remembering that now, Chris Beth felt her own arms—and her heart as well—grow stronger. These people held her up when her legs were limber. Maybe it was her turn now. She felt a surge of strength and joy such as she had never known. It would help Joe to know.

If she could catch his eyes where he stood talking with a group of somber-faced settlers, she would signal for him to give her a minute before going to the front of the arbor. But there was no opportunity. He was moving forward and the others followed. Strange, wasn't it, that they always seemed separated by persons or things just when she wanted to stand by his side?

But Joe needed no help. He had spent long hours on his sermon for today. Still, she was sure that his notes were untouched. Instead, he had taken his inspiration from the congregation. No, the *needs* of the congregation. The inspiration could have come only from the Lord!

"We're going to have a burial," Joe announced without his usual preliminaries. The announcement brought dead silence. Chris Beth was as surprised as the rest of the crowd. "Buryin'" meant a funeral and death that they didn't need on top of all the rest of the week's losses.

"Beforehand, I'm going to ask that each of you share your concerns and problems, no matter what their nature. Just talking about our burdens lightens the load."

Brother Joseph was admittedly a special breed of preacher. "Horse of a different color," so to speak. "Kind of a maverick," cattle raisers said. "Never knowed 'im to preach a no-account sermon even on a empty stomach," Nate Goldsmith had declared on occasion. *Still and all*, the school board president's look said, *today could be an exception. Could be*, those who caught Nate's eye agreed.

Seeing the telltale looks, Chris Beth felt a quickening of her own pulse. These people needed help. But it was for her husband that she prayed. Her prayers were so fervent that she failed to hear the faint words from the far front of the arbor at first.

When his voice strengthened, Chris Beth recognized the speaker as one of the Muslin City men. "But we don't ask a handout, just a hand in felling logs afore the rains set in on the ledge."

Now there was a real problem, she found herself thinking. Here they had met to pray for rain while the newcomers were praying that the floodgates of heaven remain closed until they could erect their cabins for protecting their families.

Abe Solomon, usually so retiring, stood to say, "We're havin' real trouble at the store. Folks needin' credit. And supplies hard to come by." Mrs. Solomon affirmed every word with a birdlike bob of her head.

One by one the other men stood. Folks need rain, they said, or the valley would be turned into a desert. There was likely to be a real shortage of food, what with the drought and then the plague. No rain could spell fire, like many years before— and maybe diseases too. The people sure needed a doctor, a real "live-in one," they said pointedly. Even two doctors, or at least a helping hand, like a nurse. 'Course, with no crops now, where was money to be had to pay 'em?

"We need more'n doctors and preachers, too. What're all these young'uns gonna do without dedicated teachers?" There was grave concern in Nate Goldsmith's voice. "Education's our best investment—better'n roads and full stomachs."

A murmur of agreement passed through the audience. The crowd was getting worked up. Women fanned themselves with their bonnets. Some of the men unbuttoned their starched collars. And voices rose to a crescendo. There was no panic, just strong emotion. *These people share their worries like they share all else,* Chris Beth thought—*their joys, their sorrows, each glory of a victory won, each agony of defeat.* Even as she suffered with them, her own heart warmed at the thought. *These are my people! Mine and Joe's . . . Wilson's and Vangie's . . .*

Mr. Beltran spoke then. "People are like sheep," he said haltingly, "lost without a shepherd." He paused, then continued more certainly, "We need a shepherd! We Basque folks know how bad we need one—or two—" He looked over the group, "Or more!"

The man's appeal was the first to draw an "Amen!" from what sounded like the entire congregation. Even the cattlemen, who ordinarily treated "woolly raisers" as "trash," added their voices.

When Brother Amos rose, the crowd fell silent. *Not another plague,* their eyes begged. But his words were to reaffirm Mr.

Beltran's plea (so obviously aimed, the crowd knew, at the Craigs and the Norths). "Would that Jehovah speak again to those He has called. And this time a mite louder!"

O'Higgin broke in. "Sure'n ye be right," he said. "We be needin' them that can counteract the demons o' darkness—like them dratted hoppers. Regular devil's helpers, they are. And so're the worries that be plaguin' ye all!"

Silence fell over the group. Chris Beth wondered how her husband would respond. She did not have to wonder long. Sensing that the timing was right, Joe began to speak quietly.

"Thank you, one and all." His words were gentle, with humility. "How good to come to the house of the Lord and share our problems. It must warm the Master's heart that the concerns here today are for the good of us all. Not one has brought a personal problem, though I know that every household represented has its share."

Joe waited until the ripple of agreement made the rounds. "Now," he spoke in a louder voice, "it is time to get on with the burial!"

Beneath the arbor, every eye focused on Brother Joseph. Men stopped fingering their wilting collars. Women laid down their fans. Even the feeble breeze stopped toying with the dry leaves overhead. The worshipers outside, who had raised their umbrellas against the sun's merciless rays, strained forward to hear his words.

"I will ask young Wil—may I call him our junior deacon?—to unleash the canoe by the creek. Then, before the rest of the ceremony, let's examine the Scriptures together, praying for the inspiration of the Holy Spirit. Jesus tells us that no man can serve two masters. I ask you then to consider O'Higgin's words. Are we going to be enslaved by our worries, which are forged in the devil's furnaces? Or freed of them by the only Master who can wash away our sins?"

Fascinated, the settlers waited as Joe opened his Bible. In the moment it took for him to locate his text, the curtain lifted in Chris Beth's mind again without warning. The crowds . . . the longing . . . the reaching . . . and the four of them, God's "called people," standing in the center for one wonderful moment. Then the vision faded, but this time it left no dizziness. This time it left no confusion. For this time she knew with a spiritual kind of knowing that her "Why, Lord?" questions to the significance of the phenomena were about to be revealed!

Raptly she listened, along with the settlers around her, as Joe read from Matthew:

"Therefore I say unto you, Take no thought of your life, what ye shall eat, or what ye shall drink; nor yet for your body, what ye shall put on. Is not the life more than meat, and the body than raiment? Behold the fowls of the air: for they sow not, neither do they reap, nor gather into barns; yet your heavenly Father feedeth them. Are ye not much better than they? Which of you by taking thought can add one cubit unto his stature? And why take ye thought for raiment? Consider the lilies of the field, how they grow; they toil not, neither do they spin; yet I say unto you, that even Solomon in all his glory was not arrayed like one of these."

Joe paused and looked directly into Chris Beth's eyes. She nodded, wondering if her face revealed a certain transfiguration of her heart.

Joe read on, his voice rising with new confidence:

"Wherefore, take no thought, saying, What shall we eat? or, What shall we drink? or, Wherewithal shall we be clothed? . . . For your heavenly Father knoweth that ye have need of all these things. But seek ye first the kingdom of God, and his righteousness; and all these things shall be added unto you."

Joe's voice slowed deliberately. And as he concluded, his eyes sought and held the enraptured gaze of each member of the group.

"Take therefore no thought for the morrow; for the morrow shall take thought for the things of itself. Sufficient unto the day is the evil thereof."

Joe raised both hands in supplication and closed the Bible. The crowd seemed to exhale gently in unison. Still, they waited, as if knowing—as Chris Beth knew—that a very dramatic moment was near at hand.

With hands still uplifted and facing his audience, Joe spoke with a forcefulness that none of them had heard him use before. "And so it is that this day we will rid ourselves of the burdens which are barriers between us and the true glory of God—these worries which are tormenting us, twisting our very souls, and robbing us of our visions and dreams!"

Lowering his hands, Joe looked away from the faces in the crowd, his eyes traveling to the banks of the creek, where young Wil stood at attention. The others followed his gaze.

"The boat is ready," he announced to the expectant crowd. "If you will, follow me in person—or at least in your prayers— to the edge of the water."

A little murmur ran through the crowd. Then the group fell silent as, with a purposeful stride, Joe walked toward the little craft. Abe and Nate were the first to respond by stepping behind Joe. Their wives followed. Chris Beth fell in step with Mrs. Malone, aware that the others were close behind. So far, so good. But what on earth did her husband have in mind? She wondered as they walked silently.

At the water's edge, Joe turned to the mystified crowd: "I'll row out to the parting of the current. And there I will deposit these worries of ours, these demons of darkness! We will send them down the creek to the river—and from there to where the river joins the ocean. There they will be buried at sea!"

Joe picked up an oar. Chris Beth knew a panicky moment as he stepped partway into the rocking boat. She wondered if he knew how to row. They had never talked about it. The current was swift out there, but with surprising expertise, young Wil righted the canoe, gave it a shove with the other oar, and somehow managed to leap in beside Joe.

A shout rose from the worshipers standing on the bank of the creek. Joe's face gave no sign of whether he expected it. Maybe he didn't hear. His eyes were closed against the sun and his lips moved as if in prayer.

"Best we be raisin' praise, it is!" O'Higgin boomed. "What song be your choice?"

"Shall We Gather at the River?" the crowd chorused. Seeming to respond to some inner voice, they linked arms then. Their bodies swayed like the ripples on the water's surface. Their voices joined its song.

Chris Beth was too overcome to join in. She clung tightly to the solid comfort of Mrs. Malone's arm on her right and Vangie's on her left, as if she doubted the laws of gravity. But there was a silent song in her heart.

"So *that's* what You and he had in mind, Lord!" she whispered.

26
United We Stand!

THERE HAD NEVER been such a sermon preached in this valley before. At least, not that the valley folks could recall. It was sort of like the Bible-poundin' Noah stories. Grandma Pritchett claimed to have known the circuit rider well, but she was given to rememberin' some things that never happened, they said. Maybe he wasn't as all-powerful as Grandma made out. Even *he* couldn't have brought such a varied congregation together the way Brother Joseph did.

"I reckon they'll be stayin'," Nate Goldsmith said.

"Surely, surely," everybody nodded, there being no doubt that *they* meant the Craigs and the Norths. Not that they out and out promised. Best nail down a contract. Speaking of which, something better be done about a teacher.

"Hear that?" Mrs. Malone whispered, giving the tablecloth a popping shake to rid it of dinner crumbs.

Chris Beth moved toward the older woman to fold the corners of the cloth together. "I hear!" she whispered.

"Humph! Year of the Grasshopper, indeed! This is the Year of Miracles. Take my word for it—'United we stand!'"

Almost overcome with the joy of all that had happened this day, Chris Beth could only nod. Together, she and Mrs. Malone packed up the remains of the Sunday meal for the Muslin City people to take home.

"Team's rarin' to go!" Wilson called.

"So are we!" Vangie called back from where she was talking with some of the most recent wagon-train settlers. Then, beaming, she ran to Chris Beth to whisper, "This will be another of our fine evenings together. But let's you and I ride in back again. I need to talk first."

Joe overheard and nodded. She was glad to see that his eyes promised the talk both of them needed together later. Then the two families, including a very proud "junior deacon," boarded the buggy and the team turned toward home.

"Did you bury some of your feelings at the 'burial' today, Chrissy?" Vangie asked as soon as the turning of the wheels would guarantee privacy.

Chris Beth caught her breath in surprise. "Yes," she said slowly, "I did—I mean, I *think* I did—"

Vangie was studying her face, and the knowledge made her uncomfortable. "What about you, Vangie?" she asked quickly without meeting the probing blue eyes.

But her younger sister was not one to be deterred. "I mean the hate, Chrissy."

"For your father?"

"Him—and *me*?" The voice was small.

"Oh, Darling, I never hated you!"

"Of course you did. And you had every right. If I hadn't— well—done what I did, everything might have worked—"

"And I'd have married Jonathan and lived happily ever after? You know that isn't true, Vangie. He deceived us both." She turned to face Vangie then. "Tell me, did you hate *me*? I stood in the way."

"Hate?" Vangie considered a minute. "No, that's not the word. I envied you. And I was jealous. But that's all gone— even before today it was. I guess I needed today just to count blessings, though. And, yes, I was hoping you could bury the past—bury it completely."

"You know, Vangie," Chris Beth spoke slowly, wondering why her breath felt so shallow, "I think I did—the bad parts, anyway. What remains will be disposed of, I promise!"

Just as soon as I can find a way, she added mentally. She realized then that it was not a new thought. Over and over she had tried to rid herself of the brooch, only to have her plan foiled. Was it possible that deep in some secret closet of her heart she had clung to it? Not out of love or sentimentality, nor for its worth (although she knew it was valuable), but because it was a link that spelled security?

For no reason she could account for, Chris Beth suddenly wanted to cry—not bitterly or sadly, but just to "have a good cry," as Mrs. Malone would have called it. She fished in her bag for a handkerchief.

"What are you doing?" Vangie asked as a jolt of the buggy threw them closer together.

"Burying my past," she sniffed.

"In *there*?"

Suddenly both of them were laughing and crying at the same time, their arms locked about each other in warm embrace. "We should thank Jonathan, Chrissy."

"We should."

"We have so much here because of his—our—folly."

"We have."

"And we won't worry about the future?"

"We won't!"

Oh, I will try, Lord. I will try. Just stay with us—unite us. . . .

27
The Miracle
of Decisions

❧

"MRS. MALONE SAYS this is to be the Year of Miracles," Chris Beth said as she and Vangie put away the supper dishes.

Vangie extended her lower lip charmingly to blow at a stray curl clinging to her moist forehead. "The first of which would be a breeze."

"No, that would be the second," Chris Beth said as Vangie turned to hang the dishpan in the closet. "Joe's sermon today was the first—Ouch!"

Joe had entered the kitchen noiselessly and had given her a swat from behind. "Joe," she whispered, "the others!"

"Oh, they know about us!" he whispered back. And, instead of backing away as he usually did in public, her husband imprisoned her in his arms. With her back against his broad chest, Chris Beth was defenseless. "Young Wil's outside—just called us to come see the full moon. And Vangie—well, Wilson's retrieving her from the closet. See for yourself."

There was no need to look. Vangie's giggle told the story.

"The moon, you two!" Chris Beth reminded the two men. She pulled herself from Joe's reluctant arms, gave him a teasing kiss, and said she would check on True and little Mart.

The babies were fine. Chris Beth hurried happily to where the rest of the family she loved so much waited in the bright moonlight.

Young Wil stood to motion her to a cane-bottomed chair. Already the men were deep in conversation. In a matter of seconds, she was aware that another miracle was in progress.

"I guess Doc's gift decided me—and, yes, Vangie knew." Wilson's eyes left Joe's long enough to look into Vangie's face. Chris Beth saw the look of adoration that passed between them. "Probably entered it in her diary, but let me break the news. Much as we wanted you and Chrissy with us, we felt it had to be your decision."

"Uncle Wil's talking about all the instruments and stuff that Doc Dullus had," young Wil said in a little aside to Chris Beth. "First, we tried to buy 'em. Office'll be right here for a while."

Chris Beth gave the small hand a squeeze of appreciation, then listened to Joe's words. "I tried—I honestly did—and I prayed, but I just couldn't do it."

She tensed at his words, but only for a moment. "I found I would never be happy anywhere but here," Joe continued. "I guess some are called to serve no matter where. But the Lord called me here."

Surprisingly, Wilson's voice dropped to a confidential, almost confessional tone. "I guess He called us all here," he said slowly.

"I guess decisions are kind of a miracle," Vangie said. "Maybe this is the second one, Chrissy."

28
Miracle
in the Meadows

~∂~

THE FOLLOWING WEEK Chris Beth fluctuated between elation and despair. She, along with the rest of the family and the entire community, was elated over Joe's sermon and its impact—so elated that Joe, noticing how her feet glided so airily and in such perfect harmony, teased her that the cabin floor seemed unnecessary.

That was true. She had put up with the bare ground of the school long enough to know that a person could live without floors. But food was another matter—food and the money to buy it with. And there were days when a certain despair squeezed hard at her heart, trying hard to rob her of the elation. Saturday was such a day.

In an effort to drive away her gloom, Chris Beth decided to try her hand at a green-apple pie. She knew she shouldn't, but young Wil had begged so hard. And, she reasoned, the fruit he had saved from the grasshoppers would be their last of the season. She was in the midst of cutting the lard into the flour for pastry when Mrs. Malone called from the front door.

"News!" she said.

News from the valley's beloved "Miss Mollie" meant *good*

news—so good this time that it would not keep until she could tether the horses. The reins lay on either side of the team as she rushed into the door.

"Go on rollin' out the dough," she said practically. "And me, I'll just be parin' the apples. If," she paused tactfully, "you feel they're gonna take a mite more sugar than's good for a body, try some honey. It'll even mellow the flavor."

Then, wrapping an apron around her ample middle, Mrs. Malone shifted the scene of the news to the Beltran living room. A miracle, she said, had taken place in the Basque family's countryside. . . .

Rachel looked up from her spinning. "Supper's nigh heated," she said as the Beltran men and Watch, the giant shepherd dog, came in from the day's work. "You taken the sheep to the high meadow, Rube?"

But Burton answered for his father, "Yes'm."

The family ate in silence. Then, at the close of the simple meal, Ruben Beltran spoke for the first time. "Been thinkin' a prayer mightn't hurt none."

She nodded. "Been thinkin' the same."

Again the boy spoke out, and there was a note of excitement in his voice. "Let me—let me!"

With no show of emotion, his parents nodded.

"The Lord is my *shepherd*; I shall not *want* . . . He maketh me to lie down beside the still *waters*—and I can't remember the rest, Lord, but I learnt it in school and I kin study it some more. Bless my teacher. *Amen!*"

"Been thinkin' some more." Words came hard for Ruben Beltran. "Caint let minds like them go to waste—Burtie Boy's and hers."

Burtie's eyes sparkled. "Miss Chrissy?"

"The same."

"Hush when your pa speaks." Rachel's words, quietly spoken, carried a note of warning. Her son listened with poorly concealed excitement.

"Think I oughta hep out, Wife?"

Help on the school board or that board of deacons that folks been talkin' about? *Both*, his wife said. Gonna take a lot of thinkin'. *No problem, seein' as how he'd started ahead o' the others*, Rachel assured her husband. Was she feelin' welcome to join up? *'Course!* Not much in the way o' crops, what with the drought and all, but Brother Amos made mention o' usin' God's natural gifts in place of money. *Meanin'?*

"Well, I been thinkin' one such gift's my sheep. 'Nother's my wife."

Bertie's eyes flew open wide. Admonitions forgotten, he burst out, "You not gonna give my mama away! It's right you should sacrifice a sheep, but not my mama! You can't, Pa—"

"Finish your meal."

"My meal's finished."

"So's your talkin'." Ruben turned back to Rachel. "You're good at dyin', cardin', spinnin', and weavin'."

Rachel blushed but surprised her husband by saying, "The best."

In the kitchen of the Big House, Chris Beth stopped criss-crossing pastry over the top of the green apple pie. "You mean? What *do* you mean?"

Mrs. Malone took off her apron. "I mean Joe made 'em all feel a part of us all—woolly raisers or not. I mean Rube's on his way to see Nate. Figure he and Olga can handle the *Cause!* I mean he took Rachel, too. She's never campaigned before, but this time they're stoppin' at every homestead in the Basque parts, gatherin' support."

Chris Beth felt like a slow-reading child who had spent his last dime on an adult-level book. The impression was of viewing an enormous picture—too beautiful and awe-inspiring to believe until she could examine each detail. Only then would she be able to put it together, and believe what she *thought* she was seeing!

"I've talked too much, as usual," Mrs. Malone said. "Least-wise, too fast." She checked on the team with her eye, then continued, "Started a program they're callin' Shearin' and

Sharin' 'mongst the Basque folks. Sheep take less grass and water, you know, to produce fine wool. Rachel's gettin' the women together to teach us all the skills we never should've put aside. All of us can knit, given the yarn she's goin' to donate to the Cause."

The *Cause?* Mrs. Malone capitalized the word with her voice.

Oh, *that!* Should've made that clear the first thing, Mrs. Malone apologized. The Cause was the good Lord. Seemed He spoke to Ruben when Joe conducted the buryin'. And, havin' heard the Word, he was spreadin' it. All the Basque people would "join up" Sunday and be pledgin' their goods towards a salary, sort of. And Mrs. Malone wouldn't be a mite surprised if they put a part in the school coffer.

"Mark my word, you'll be offered a contract."

"Contract! You mean to teach *school?*"

"What else?"

"But—but—I'm married—"

"I should hope so, but Nate's been known t' change his mind, if I recall rightly. This'll be one o' th' times. Mark my word!"

"Oh, Mrs. Malone!" Chris Beth rushed forward to throw her arms around her wonderful friend. "It's too good to be true! It would take care of all our needs. Just when I thought everything was falling apart at the seams!"

"Well, now, the Lord jest always seems to have some surprise up His sleeve. You oughta know that by now." And, with a pat of affection, Mrs. Malone hurried out to where the untethered horses grazed.

Chris Beth watched her friend drive away. Oh, there was so much to tell Joe! Of course, Mrs. Malone could be wrong—no, she wasn't going to let doubts spoil this wonderful day. She would set the table with Joe's mother's best china and light a candle. "Joe," she would say calmly, "how would you like to have a guaranteed income so you could—"

Oh, mercy! The pie had boiled over in the oven. Yesterday that would have been a real irritation. Today it was funny.

Happily, she pulled it from the smoking oven, noting with relief that it was golden brown from the honey oozing through the upper crust.

Let tomorrow take care of its "evils thereof"! Today's joys were "sufficient unto themselves"!

29
Spread of the Miracle

⤲

THE MIRACLE SPREAD quickly throughout the valley. For, as Mrs. Malone said, "Love's mighty powerful—only thing I know that no amount o' reasonin' can't keep home!"

News of the Basque contribution reached Willow Grove. Brother Amos took the matter to Brother Benjamin. Then Brother Amos and Brother Benjamin called the rest of the "disciples" together. After a meditative silence, the concensus was twofold.

"Our granaries are filled with last year's harvest," said Brother Amos, with face uplifted as if in prayer; "wouldst Thou have us share with our Christian Brother Joseph that which we would plant next year?"

When he sat, Brother Benjamin stood. "We, having no leader save Brother Joseph, perchance should confess to him that our treasury doth hold a widow's mite of gold—from unnamed sources. Moreover 'twas designated for temple-building. And, our bodies bein' Thy temple, wouldst Thou have us nourish, maintain, and repair the temple of Thy servant and his chosen wife?"

Mutely, each head bobbed consent. "Then," said Brother Amos, "we two shall depart forthwith to so advise our total church body."

Mrs. Malone speculated to Chris Beth at the Fourth of July picnic that Bertie Solomon could be depended on in time of crisis to come through. And crisis or no, a body could depend on her to spread the news. And so it was that Mrs. Solomon had declared to all "payin' customers" that prices would have to be *upped* a mite to "help out, you understand. And them that we have to carry till crops is in best be prepared to square up on time. Else no bonus gift on payday, right, Abe?" Abe guessed so, although the arrangements were obviously news to him.

"But turned out he had some news for her, too," Mrs. Malone laughed. "Abe showed some starch right in front of everybody—just up and said, 'Any staples the Craigs buy'll be wholesale. And that goes fer the Norths likewise, all bein' kinfolks of the Lord!'"

O'Higgin said, "Amen be to that! The Good Book tells us that spreaders o' the Word needn't be burdened down with packin' needed garments and bread. 'Twill be supplied!"

When the Muslin City people heard, they tuned up their fiddles and played a bit louder. True, they'd hoarded the corn for next year's planting, but wouldn't hominy be more sustaining for empty bellies? Surely the Lord has heard their prayers and given them an opportunity to repay in part the many kindnesses of folks here.

People as far away as Portland heard. Trappers were newsbearers, the settlers agreed. Portlanders would be sending books—passels of 'em—for the bigger school. They would be needin' one, wouldn't they? And just maybe, in case of a fire sale or some such, they'd send a peddler around with reduced goods. The miracle enlarged like the hearts.

30
Sacrifice Sunday

⤙⤐

B Y MID-JULY the heat was unbearable. The settlers stopped talking about the weather. But today was different. This was Sacrifice Sunday!

Two fat little clouds, looking like cumulous kittens, played tag briefly over the mountain, then enlarged with promise.

"Wouldn't it be something if it rained, today being so special?" Young Wil's face was red above the collar of his Sunday shirt, but his eyes sparkled with excitement.

"Very special," Chris Beth agreed, handing him three-month-old Mart as she climbed from the buggy at Turn-Around Inn.

"I can hold True, too," he said stoutly.

He could hold anything this day, Chris Beth knew. The boy had been too excited to eat or sleep since word came that "Sunday next" was the day decided upon to bring "natural gifts" to the altar. Plans were that the "disciples" would show the settlers how to make a common storehouse of their goods. The Craigs and Norths were to be looked after first. The remains would be distributed equally among the others.

Mrs. Malone opened the door. Chris Beth sniffed in appreciation. Coffee. Rising sourdough. "Irish stew?"

"Sure enough. O'Higgin's had the pot boiling out back since daybreak. Give me the babies, Junior Deacon!"

Young Wil's chest swelled with pride, but his eyes were puzzled. "How did you know? Serving's my gift, I mean?"

"Well, I never!" Mrs. Malone pushed the screen door open wider. "Now, what could be a better gift to offer than your young *self!*"

Chris Beth wanted to tell the boy how proud his uncle would be—how proud she was, too—but the O'Higgin-Malone tribe descended upon them all. Six children, an exuberant dog, and an oversized cat, winding in and out between the feet of the guests, made conversation impossible.

"I get little Mart—please, Miss Mollie!" Lola Ann reached to take the sleeping baby from her stepmother's arms.

Amelia and Harmony shoved each other rudely, each wanting to hold the other baby. True took care of the matter. Awakened, she produced the kind of scream that says nobody's arms would do but Vangie's.

"Mind your manners!" Mrs. Malone reprimanded, and then added more gently, "Don't know what I'd have done without these girls this morning. Took a little doin', bein' ready and all."

"I know," Chris Beth said. "It was thoughtful of you to have us over. You're right, it would have been hot at the arbor."

Mrs. Malone pinched the bosom of her best white blouse between her thumb and forefinger and moved it up and down as if to fan her body. "Hot, yes, and fire danger. The arbor's tinderbox dry."

Chris Beth was aware then of Jimmy John, who was holding the family cat up for her inspection. "Him's growed."

"And so have you!" She scooped the youngest of the O'Higgin-Malone clan of stepchildren up in her arms and cuddled him close.

He wiggled free only long enough to show her three fat fingers, then settled back for his share of her attention. *Three years old*, she marveled. One of these days little Mart would be this size. Then he'd be growing like the other boys who had gone to inspect O'Higgin's stew . . . Andy, young Wil, Ned. And then we would be ready for a life of his own. What would that life be like? Would he be more of the spirit than of the flesh? Would he help preserve the human race? She could watch, love, and protect. But what else would he need? Companionship, for one thing. Yes, as soon as possible, little Mart must have a brother or sister.

"We'd best hurry along now." *Mrs. Malone must have let me dream out my fantasy*, Chris Beth realized guiltily. The others would be along any minute, and there was sure to be a crowd.

"I'm sorry. It's just so homey that I like to do my thinking here where I was courted and married. And where little Mart came into the world. Now I'm through dreaming. Put me to work."

Mrs. Malone waved away her offer to help. "Take the baby's things upstairs—oh, here come the Smiths!"

In the upper room, Chris Beth lovingly ran her fingers over the posts of the bed where she had laid her satchel. Here, leaning over sleeping flood victims that she and Joe had comforted, he had proposed. Here she had known that it was God's will that they serve Him in this wild new land—for better or for worse.

As she came down the stairs, Chris Beth saw through the east window of the living room that a large crowd was gathering. Women and children were unloading baskets, as usual, but the men, knotted in a group, paid no attention to their horses. Instead, they pointed at the sky. Some looked hopeful while others shook their heads. Did she imagine it or had a cloud passed over the sun? Oh, she hoped so. Rain would come too late to benefit this year's crops, but there was next year to think about. The river was too low to furnish power for the mill, Wilson had said this morning.

He and Joe had tried to lighten the conversation by saying that at least they could cross without fording in most places.

But the water table was so low that the wells were drying up. People in some parts had to haul water for miles, then use it over and over. She wondered fleetingly what Mama would say to using washwater to scrub the floors—after the family had bathed in it. How good that there was a spring in back of the cabin! But, oh, she wished it would rain.

During the service there was thunder. Even Vangie, terrified of storms as she was, leaned over to whisper "Goody!" in Chris Beth's ear. Most of the others called a loud "Amen!" at each clap.

Chris Beth was overcome with emotion during the service. Caught up in the spirit of the meeting, she tried to hang onto every word that was said. But, with her ears tuned to the sounds of what she hoped would be a rain-storm, she was sure she missed a few words.

"Wife and I wanta join up," Ruben Beltran said simply. "Been thinkin' on it some time—wonderin' what we had to offer. Well, here's my wife. Rachel, show 'em your goods— and the rest o' you come on up like you was supposin' to!"

More command than invitation, Ruben's words brought a rewarding response. What appeared to be a dozen couples (men in overalls and women in faded calico dresses and sun-bonnets) shyly joined the Beltrans. Joe met them at the fireplace, which Mrs. Malone had improvised into an altar by draping it with her best damask cloth.

Extending his hand, Joe greeted the Basque people. "We welcome you," he said warmly. And Chris Beth thought for sure that her heart would burst with joy when a murmur of "Yes, yes" passed through the crowded room and echoed from group to group standing at the doors.

Led by Brother Amos and Brother Benjamin, the "disciples" marched soundlessly forward. "We could share grain from last year's harvest for thy daily bread."

"And serve as their stewards to count the costs," added Brother Benjamin.

Chris could feel rather than see that most of the worshipers seated around her were weeping. But, as Mrs. Malone would

say, " 'Twas a good kind of crying," the kind that cleansed the
heart.

The "disciples" marched back like the line of prophets they
were. The Solomons waited politely until they were seated,
and then went up to face the congregation. "Now, our plan
is . . ." and Abe went on to outline the contributions from
the general store—with many an interruption from his wife.
To avoid Vangie's probable look of amusement (and lest they
both laugh), Chris Beth let her glance slide to her left. And
what she saw cut short any desire to smile. Maggie Solomon's
green-grape eyes, narrowed like a cat's when watching a
helpless fledgling fallen from the nest, were fixed on Vangie.
And an attractive young woman (could it be the Mrs. Robbins
who claimed to have known the family?) was nodding as if she
had made an identification.

Chris Beth forced herself to concentrate. Nothing was going
to spoil this service. It was wrong, if not downright wicked, to
entertain unworthy thoughts. She must bury them "at sea."

"—More corn than we know what to do with," one of the
men from Muslin City was saying, making it sound true.
"Some grape cuttings we brung along the trail takin' root. And
apple seeds. Mankind! You never saw so many. We know how
to graft 'em, you know." He hesitated, then said slowly, "You
been so kind—" His voice broke and he was unable to
continue.

More tears. The "good kind." But there was no emotion on
the face of Mr. Chu when he padded forward, followed by
Wong. Politely the little man bowed. Then, patting his heart,
he said, "Theese Jee-sus ees here. No speekee Eeng-*leessh*
velle well—one son speekee!"

Wong bowed to his father and then to Joe, who bowed back
as if it were his custom. "My fath-er wishes to make gift," the
boy said. "We have rice and we know Oriental secret how
to make grow the rice. My fath-er will make paddy on island
by Missee—Miss—Chrissy's school. 'Twill take not much
water—"

Miss Chrissy's school! Chris Beth's heart missed a beat. What on earth would people say to *that?*

She was soon to know! Nate Goldsmith signaled by clearing his throat. Four other men stood. "My helpers, *Mr.* Solomon," Nate emphasized the title, "*Mr.* Beltran, *Mr.* O'Higgin—and this here's the other member of the board. A newcomer. Name's Orin Robbins."

Robbins? Wasn't that the name of the couple who had known her family? Chris Beth supposed that would be Mrs. Robbins beside Maggie . . .

An earthshaking clap of thunder interrupted her thinking. But the "President" refused to let an act of nature steal his moment of glory. As the thunder rolled on to jolt the surrounding mountain, Nate shouted his announcement. "Your next year's teacher!"

Somebody new—oh, no! The entire audience seemed to inhale sharply along with Chris Beth. Then the rest happened so quickly that Chris Beth was uncertain which happened first—Vangie's hand squeeze, Wilson's pat on her shoulder, Mrs. Malone's embrace, or Nate Goldsmith practically dragging "Miss Chrissy" forward.

That first "Amen!" may have been a response to the thunderbolt. But the rest of them were for their beloved "next year's teacher!" Not that Nate was to be upstaged by an audience, either. "Contract's more liberal—got it right here in my breast pocket. I call on ye all to witness the signin' if'n ye be of a mind."

The crowd would no longer be called to order. Did she know? *Well, not really.* Did "Brother Joseph" know? *Well, maybe—no, not really.* Look at them books! Did she know 'bout them. *Well, sort of.* Was she 'ware that the *legislature* was gonna help? Their questions left Chris Beth no time to think beyond the moment. It was real. The vision was real! She, Joe, Vangie, and Wilson stood in a circle of love.

31
Gathering Storm

~

THERE WAS NO RAIN on Sacrifice Sunday. After blowing themselves up into genielike proportions, the playful thunderheads floated back to sea. Chris Beth's body was filled with vigor in spite of the enervating weather. She cleaned the cabin, pressed and repaired her school clothes, and fussed with her hair. Would bangs be a nice change? Should she do away with the braided crown and maybe do her hair in chignon like she had seen in the mail-order catalogue? Or maybe a pompadour? Maybe Joe would help her decide.

But Joe disappointed her. He was so busy with the new responsibilities of full-time pastor that he seemed unaware of any change in Chris Beth's appearance as she tried the styles one by one. Or was something troubling him? Didn't he want her to teach?

A little piqued at her husband's seeming indifference, Chris Beth had tried to attract his attention several times. "Are you writing your sermons now?" she asked one.

Joe looked startled. "Not exactly. Did you need something?"

Yes, she did! But how does one put it into words?

Then, another time, seeing Joe hitching Dobbin, she said, "If you're calling this afternoon, I'm free. Little Mart and I—"

Joe's answer was too quick and his tone too abrupt. "No! What I mean is, it's business."

Anger, unreasonable though it might be, flared inside her. And, turning away from a probable good-bye kiss, Chris Beth gathered little Mart in her arms and hurried across the foot-log to the Big House. Vangie would understand. Not that she would tell her, of course. But they could talk, stopping just short of what troubled them, and understand. Of course, today might be different. It would feel good to say, "Joe is cutting me out of his life—just when everything should be so perfect!" No, she wouldn't say that—not when her sister had a story-book marriage. Wilson was more open, more expressive, more *ardent.*

With that thought, her face burned. That was a disturbing thought. Chris Beth stopped and, making sure young Wil had not spotted her, stepped behind a tree. What was wrong with her, anyway?

"I'm being unfair to your father," she said to the baby.

Little Mart clutched at the air with both hands. She kissed a fat fist. And, at his coo, she whispered, "I was being disloyal and—maybe *unfaithful*—comparing him to another man."

Back home, Chris Beth took down her pompadour and braided her hair into a crown, then busied herself with Joe's favorite molasses pie. "Maybe," she mused aloud, "something of the old Chris Beth pride sealed my lips." But inside she knew it was more the new-woman love and understanding that changed her course of action.

"Thank you, Lord, for teaching me restraint," she was to pray that evening. For, when Joe came home, he reached out his arms and said, "Ummm, nice—cinnamon! Molasses pie? And I like your hair."

Ashamed, she turned away to hide the tears. Joe didn't notice as he was drawing her to his easy chair. "We must talk," he said.

There, in the circle of his arms, Chris Beth heard a story

which explained Joe's preoccupation and drew them closer together than ever before. It was a story which shocked, frightened, and repelled her, and showed her how trivial by comparison her dark imaginings had been. It was a story which portended a storm far greater than any clouds in the sky could threaten, no matter how ominous.

When Joe finished his report, he waited quietly for Chris Beth to react. There was so much to say, and so little! She marveled, as she had so often before, at his sensitivity—always so silent and so gentle in a time of crisis. And crisis seemed to be her way of life!

"This—this Susanah Robbins told Vangie's whole secret to Maggie?" she asked at last.

"All she knew. Enough for creating an ugly story. Maggie has a way of siphoning information and adding to it. Probably posed as a near and dear friend of yours."

"And Susanah's in need of a friend. But, Joe, what will it do to Vangie if Maggie spreads the story now?"

"She has," he said quietly.

"Did she make Vangie sound like—like a bad woman? How did Maggie know what to ask—I mean, where and who? But, of course," she said slowly, "postmarks, and the name *Stein*—Vangie's use of her maiden name to pass for a recently bereaved widow. But he would have married her—Jonathan would!" She felt herself defending her younger half sister as always, even at her own exposure. "He jilted *me* because of the baby—and True's *not* illegitimate. She's a North!"

Joe held her close. Her storm soon passed. But Vangie's lay ahead. . . .

32
The Plain and Simple Truth

⤫

ONE WEEK PASSED. Then two. Quickly, time fled in the lives of the Craigs and the Norths—too quickly, Chris Beth felt. They were so busy putting their houses in order that there was little opportunity for their cherished talks. By nature an introspective person, she missed her more leisurely days of being able to think things through. Being the wife of a minister demands its pound of flesh, she admitted in her heart. But even that thought was cut short by a familiar voice.

"They came! You know, the instruments and stuff—they came. Doc Dullus brought 'em!" Young Wil, who had come for Joe to help shift some furniture to the upstairs of the Big House, was panting with excitement.

"Really?" Chris Beth and Joe chorused. She laid aside the schoolbooks she was sorting and Joe stopped sacking the remaining cornmeal he had brought in from the mill. These jobs could wait!

Joining hands, with young Wil leading and Joe following Chris Beth with little Mart in his arms, they formed a human chain. Laughing, they almost skipped across the foot-log, and Chris Beth could have vowed that the baby laughed out loud!

Wilson met them at the front door, outwardly composed. But when he spoke, his voice was unsteady. "Joe, old pal, it's happened. I'm a doctor. These instruments say more at this point than my degree!"

Chris Beth smiled with the others, but her eyes rested on a new wooden plaque on the west wall of the large living room: WILSON JEROME NORTH, M.D. Beneath it hung the sacred Hippocratic oath—second only to his Bible, she knew.

Vangie, who was sewing a button on a white garment, followed her gaze. "That says more than either the instruments *or* the degree to him," she whispered to Chris Beth.

"You, too, I can see—but what are you sewing? I thought you'd be holding a board or something?"

"My nurse's uniform," Vangie said simply. "This will be the reception room. Opens into the library, you know. Closet's for supplies. And there what his parents once planned to be a music room will be used for surgery. Upstairs we may make room someday for overnight patients."

Wilson measured a bureau and laid down his yardstick. "Dream on, Florence Nightingale," he said with a smile of appreciation at Vangie's glow. Then, turning to the others, he added, "But we *will* be needing the room as industry spreads and the settlement grows."

"Undoubtedly," Joe agreed. "And meantime you'll be making house calls like Doc?"

"By mandate of my benefactor—not that I mind. Nice, huh, for me and my angel of mercy? The right instruments. And a live-in nurse!"

Chris Beth studied her sister closely. Flushed with happiness, she looked less tired, but the beautiful planes of her face were too thin and a small blue vein that Chris Beth had never noticed before pulsed along the left temple. Something about the look was disturbing.

"Are you tired out from all this, Vangie?"

"No—well, I guess I am, a little. I'll rest later. For now, everything's perfect. *Everything!*"

Please, Lord, let it stay that way, Chris Beth prayed inwardly. *How good that God hears silent prayer!* she thought. Otherwise He would never hear above the bumping and groaning as the men moved the heavy bureau upstairs.

The workday ended with an omelet supper—no real surprise, since young Wil prepared the meal, and omelets were his specialty. But the meal had a surprise ending—spiced apples from one of the limbs the boy had wrapped against the onslaught of the grasshoppers!

"This is a good omen," Vangie declared. "Now, what would you like for a reward?"

Young Wil looked questioningly at Wilson. At his uncle's nod of consent, he refilled the coffee cups, then took a cup from the china cupboard for himself, filled it with milk, and added a single teaspoonful of coffee.

In such a happy-ever-after atmosphere, how could anybody really believe a fellow human being capable of malicious mischief? But Maggie Solomon, Chris Beth was soon to learn, was doing her homework well.

August came. The month itself seemed to be gasping for breath. Little dust devils, a sight seldom seen in the usually verdant, grass-woven valley, danced in hot-breathed glee and sucked at the few leaves which the grasshoppers had missed.

"What I wouldn't give for a great big watermelon!" Mrs. Malone said one Sunday at church. "Usually ripe before now."

"And what *I* wouldn't give fer a rain." Mrs. Solomon's voice carried its usual ring of complaint and then a sound of accusation: "We *prayed* for rain!"

Her husband wiped his face with a red bandanna, measured the distance between himself and Bertie, then wondered, "Did ye set a date?" She flounced away without replying.

That very day, clouds again gathered. Briefly they furnished a relief from the sun. Then, mockingly, they moved over the mountains.

Chris Beth wondered fleetingly if Maggie could be playing the same kind of game—moving in, threatening, and then moving away as if biding her time. Certainly her eyes wore the same mocking expression. She dismissed the thought but decided that she must make a point of introducing herself to Susanah Robbins. She should have done so long ago, but the young woman seemed shy, usually hurrying away as soon as the worship service was over.

Wilson's practice grew rapidly. One of the children on the ledge—no longer Muslin City, as most had cabins now— broke a collarbone. Lucy Smith gave birth to twins, with her labor made more difficult because of her fear of a doctor, Wilson reported. A midwife had delivered her other two children. Vangie had assisted and had come home vowing that the next addition to the North household would be twins.

Chris Beth cared for True on the days that Wilson made house calls. When the buggy was available, Joe called on newcomers and bereaved families, and it was her turn to leave little Mart with Vangie and accompany her husband.

"Truly," she said to Joe on one such day, "it's all a dream come true."

Joe squeezed her hand, but he looked preoccupied. "Is the heat getting to you badly today? I mean . . ." he hesitated, "I thought we'd stop by the Robbins' cabin."

"Oh, let's," she agreed. "And I'm fine, Darling—no problem."

The Robbins family, unfortunately, was not at home. A note on the door said "At General Store."

"Just what I'd like to discourage," Joe murmured as if to himself. "Oh, here's Nate."

Nate Goldsmith reined in alongside the Craigs. "Heat's botherin' my gout. Thought I'd best see Wilson. 'Course, could be I'm bilious. Need to see 'im anyway. We're choosin' up rightful deacons, you know. Still and all, there's a matter needin' discussin'." It was hard to tell if the sigh he gave was one of regret or pleasure, Chris Beth thought with amusement. And then his words struck full force.

"Them chose jest hafta meet standards! Like preachers 'n teachers, ya know? And (ahem!) him—Doc—Brother Wilson— bein' a doctor 'n all—"

"I'm sure Wilson qualifies," Joe said quietly. "What's troubling you—I mean *really* troubling you, Nate?"

Nate shifted his eyes from Joe's steady gaze. "Well, their families—uh—hafta measure up. Can't have no talk—and talk is—" He stopped as if expecting Joe to understand.

"Yes?"

"Well, we'll be discussin' it come Wednesday noon. Maybe you'll wanta be there too. I mean, you kin tell *him*. Meetin's at my house."

Nate would have wheeled away, but Joe raised his voice, "Stay put, Nate. I think it's wise we leave Wilson out of this for the time being. But, yes, *I* will be there. And I expect you to have the accuser there, too. Understood? Come to think of it," Joe went on slowly, "let's switch the meeting place to the general store. That's where all the talk began, isn't it?"

Clearly the question caught Nate off guard. He flinched under Joe's steady gaze and concentrated on the rear of his mule. "Needs his tail curried. Gen'ral store 'tis then," he muttered in his beard. Obviously anxious to be off, Nate rapped the animal sharply with his cowhide crop. "Giddyup, you sluggard!" He all but shouted and disappeared in a swirl of dust. Chris Beth choked back a sob.

It was all too much. The dust. The heat. Plus the ugly situation and what it might mean to the four of them— particularly Vangie. There was no holding back the tears of frustration. "They're making it all up. I mean, they're adding to it—stacking the evidence—"

"And we'll unstack it." Joe's voice was firm. "We'll tear down their little house of dominoes. But you and I have to talk, Chrissy."

Something in his voice unnerved her. "What about? Oh, Joe," she burst out, "just hold me in your arms!"

He bent and kissed her gently. "Later, Darling—and for the rest of your life! No distractions now, though. We have to finish the conversation before we get home."

Mutely, she nodded.

At Joe's signal, Dobbin moved forward. "Whatever information I have has come piecemeal," Joe said.

"Ordinarily it wouldn't. You know that. But now it does. I have some ammunition which has nothing to do with you girls. The other will have to come from you."

"What do you want?"

"I want the plain and simple truth."

The truth—plain and simple. Chris Beth bit at her lower lip until she felt the salty taste of blood. *Oh, Joe Darling, don't you know that the truth is seldom plain, and never is it simple?*

She told him then, haltingly at first, then with gathering strength. There would be no more secrets—even little ones—to stand between them. Any remnants of the glacier once inside her heart melted into warm new seas as she talked of Jonathan Blake's proposal . . . their wedding plans . . . the broken engagement because of "another woman" . . . the bitterness when she found her rival was Vangie . . . and then the heartbreak and humiliation when she found that her half sister was carrying Jonathan's child.

Then, from force of habit, Chris Beth found herself defending Vangie's honor. "She was a child, Joe, a 16-year-old child and very naive. She was overprotected by her mama and disciplined by her father. That's how it all started, you know, with the difference in our names."

"You mean Vangie's having used her maiden name to differ from yours? Yes, I know."

For a short time all was silent except for the sound of the buggy wheels and the rhythmic clop of Dobbin's hooves. At last Joe spoke. "Is there anything else I should know?"

"No—well, do I need tell you that it was Vangie's only mistake? I mean, there had never been anybody else—"

Joe remained silent. What could he be waiting for? Surely he didn't think—oh, no, he *couldn't*! At the thought, Chris Beth felt hot color stain her cheeks.

"Joe—Joe, you don't think—I mean, you know there was nothing irregular between him—Jonathan Blake—and me."

Her voice dropped. "There's never been a man in my life—that way—but you—"

Joe halted the buggy. Then deliberately he folded her in his arms as if keeping his promise. Maybe he would never let go of her again! "And I thank you. What a beautiful gift to a man!"

Chris Beth loved her husband as never before. And that was the truth—*plain and simple!*

33
Wednesday at Noon

❧

IN THE TWO NIGHTS following the encounter with Nate, sleep would not come easily for Chris Beth. She lay wakeful and restless after Joe slept. It was so hot! Even the white rays of the waning moon brought imagined heat through the open windows. But it was not the heat that made her listen to the eerie hooting of the owls in wide-awake fear and fascination. It was dread of the Wednesday noon meeting (*or was it a trial?*).

On Wednesday morning she stole from bed even earlier than usual. The slice of moon had moved behind the western mountains. In the inky blackness she felt her way to the bedroom door and, careful not to latch it, closed it softly behind her. In the kitchen she lighted a lamp and shielded its light from the window lest Joe awaken and advise her to stay at home today. But all precautions failed.

Before she finished braiding her hair, a soft click of the latch told her that Joe had discovered her bare pillow. She felt rather than saw his questioning eyes in the dim lamplight.

"Good morning!" The greeting was bright enough, but her next words sounded insincere even to her own ears.

310

"I—I need a few things. I mean, I'll look more than buy—get ideas, you know, to see if bustles are in or out. In or out of style, that is."

He looked down at her seated figure a long time before answering. "You are welcome to come along, Chrissy. You know that. But do you think it is wise?"

"I do for a million reasons."

"You need not name them," he answered, turning up the wick of the lamp. "Now let's get the coffee brewing."

CENTERVILLE! The sign loomed up as Joe called, "Haw, Dobbins!" and the horse made the ordered left turn for the general store. Before Chris Beth could ask questions, she saw the crowds congregated around the buildings she knew, and the new buildings as well.

"Joe," she gasped, "are they all here for the same purpose—to witness our humiliation?"

"I don't know why they're here, but not that, I'm sure." He hesitated. "Chrissy, are you sure—?"

"Of course I'm sure! I belong by your side no matter what." When his head jerked toward her in surprise, she laughed. "In spirit, I mean. Actually, I will be shopping around."

The few hitching posts were taken. As Joe drove past the buildings in search of a shade tree where Dobbin could rest, Chris Beth had a chance to see just how much development had taken place since her one-time visit . . . IVERSON'S LUMBER . . . LIVERY STABLE . . . FEED & SEED . . . BIG TIME SALOON . . . CENTERVILLE HOTEL, *Cheapest in Town & Only One* . . . CASCADE SHIPPING . . . TOM BURGHER, ASSAYIST . . . Her eyes smarted from the dust and she was unable to read the other signs. She made a mental note to meet this Tom Burgher. Then, forgetting the mission of the day, Chris Beth felt the old frontier excitement. "It's all happening, isn't it, Joe? The growth's really taking place."

"Yes," Joe said, "it is! And let's hope the growth's heading in the right direction."

"I see what you mean." Some of the hastily built structures

housed essential businesses. But with them came the less desirable ones, such as the saloon. And she wondered about the hotel itself, especially the upstairs rooms. She was sure she saw women's faces hidden discreetly behind the soiled muslin curtains. No churches, though. And no doctors, as far as she could tell.

As Joe tethered Dobbin beneath an oak tree near the blacksmith shop, more questions rose in her mind. Loud, angry voices came from the direction of the general store.

Where are them sheep the crooked Yankee promised to deliver? Yeah, *yeah!* Purebreds they wuz, too. Good money paid out 'n lost.

Be here in time. Replacements comin'.

Replacements? Fer what? Well, first herd was drowned. Had to float 'em over the Columbia on a raft. Raft upset in the rapids and stupid critters cain't swim. Second herd, kinda hard to explain, but all uv 'em turned out to be males . . .

Bully fer them! Us cattlemen never wanted them woolies here . . .

Joe took Chris Beth's arm and guided her firmly toward the store. As they entered the door a shot rang out, followed by the sound of horses galloping away. "Nobody hurt, folks! Come on in!" Abe Solomon motioned from the door.

The smells of camphor, new linsey cloth, liniment, and Kennedy's pills were inviting to the nostrils compared to what was going on outside. Mrs. Solomon was nowhere to be seen, but the pretty, voluptuous Maggie was very much visible! Wearing a low-cut, tight-fitting red dress, the girl moved from one male customer to another so obviously that it was embarrassing. *This woman dared bring charges against Vangie!* Anger filled her body. Then, sickened, she turned away.

"Meetin's in the side room, gents." At Mr. Solomon's announcement, there was stomping of boots mingled with squeaking-new shoes and then the soft padding sound that said Mr. Chu. Chris Beth clenched her hands into tight fists and tried to concentrate on an outdated copy of *Godey's*

Lady's Book. "Printed in Boston," she read. How well she knew! Mama used to study the fashions by the hour.

Boston! Where she had met Jonathan . . . where he had led Vangie astray . . . the reason for this terrible meeting. No, she must concentrate on the fashions. She opened the book.

"Oh, here's a beauty. Bell-shaped skirt and probably hooped. Wouldn't it be lovely made of the velvet Mama sent last Christmas. Lots of crinoline petticoats, of course—"

Chris Beth was unaware she had spoken aloud until a soft, familiar hand touched her elbow. "It would indeed! And there's enough for both of us."

Vangie!

34
He That Is
Without Sin

๏

CONFUSION FOLLOWED. Chris Beth and Vangie embraced and clung to each other, too overcome with emotion for words. Somewhere in a part of her mind, too numb to function at the moment, Chris Beth wondered about the babies. But before she could gain control of her thoughts, she and Vangie were surrounded by a pair of motherly arms.

"Mrs. Malone! Where—how—?"

But her words were drowned out as another pair of arms circled the group from the other side. And then another! Faces she knew and loved—all of them drenched with tears—appeared one by one until all the women in the settlement knotted together in the center of the store. Through her own tears, Chris Beth tried to force her eyes to focus and her mind to think clearly.

"How did you all know? Who told you—and why—?"

"Now, does it matter a-tall? Folks always rally 'round in time o' trouble. And if you're wonderin' where the babies are, young Wil's carin' for 'em both. Now, for goodness sake, let's get from under this flypaper. Dollars to doughnuts it's stuck in my hair a'ready!"

After speaking, Mrs. Malone touched her hair experimentally and, finding it free of glue, blew her nose and tried to back away. The others were not to be rushed. Each in turn, with unaccustomed show of emotion, kissed the two girls before joining the outer circle of women, most of whom Chris Beth knew only by sight.

"Now!" Mrs. Malone was her usual practical self. "I suggest we ladies jest kneel right here for a word of silent prayer."

And that is how the men saw them when the door opened quietly to let Mrs. Solomon out of the side room. "Musta felt right ashamed," Mrs. Malone was to comment later. *Mrs. Solomon?* "No," she said to Chris Beth, "the men, no less! Bertie come through like I told you she does in time o' trouble—downright told th' men she didn't have much evidence, at that."

But Wednesday noon Chris Beth saw only the woman's whitefaced fury as, with a rustle of starched skirts, she passed the kneeling group without a nod. "You!" Mrs. Solomon hissed from the back of the room, "you go next."

"*Me!*" The voice was unmistakably Maggie's. "I'm not the one who gave birth to a—"

"Mind yer mouth. Yer the one who brung it up. And yer gonna prove it or hold yer tongue ferever. Now *git!*"

Guiltily, Chris Beth realized she was kneeling for prayer and eavesdropping at the same time. "Forgive me, Lord," she whispered, and rose to her feet.

Vangie rose with her. "Watch for Wilson," she whispered. "He's treating the Smith baby's colic. He may try to stop me."

"From what? You don't mean—"

"I mean," Vangie interrupted in a firm voice, "that I'm going in there."

And with that she was gone. As if in a terrible dream, Chris Beth heard the gasp of protest from the men as Vangie followed Maggie into the meeting. At the door, her beautiful baby-sister-grown-tall turned, sent a small and uncertain smile her way, and quietly closed the door.

Some of the women rose. Others, aware of a new crisis,

remained on their knees. For how long Chris Beth was unable to determine. She lost all track of time as her surroundings seemed to shimmer and swirl in warning. Again the crowds. The happiness followed by anger. The reaching out to Joe but being unable to reach him. Then someone dragging her— toward Joe? Backward? Or into the future?

"No!" Had she actually cried aloud? Did she imagine the viselike grip on her arms? There could be no doubt as to the reality of the voice.

"Vangie! Where's Vangie?" Wilson demanded, shaking her.

Wordlessly she pointed to the closed door. Immediately Wilson spun on his heel and turned. But when he would have left her, Chris Beth reached out and caught his arm, gripping it as he had gripped her own arms just moments ago.

"Wait! We're all in this together. I'm going with you."

Wilson did not object.

At the sight of them there was a long hiss of intaken breath, followed by strained silence. In fear and humiliation, Chris Beth faced the group. Back home, "ladies" did not make such unladylike entrances. And here in the settlement, "women-folk" did not "meddle in men's affairs." *So what!* She was her father's daughter. She was Joe's wife. And she was a child of God. As such, she claimed rights none of them better dare dispute!

Maybe something in her eyes said as much. The men seemed to exhale as Joe moved to the front of the room where Nate stood. "May I take over?" Actually, the question was more a command. "We are *all* here now. And the rest of you have had your say."

Faces showed no expression. It was hard to tell what had gone on before. Chris Beth observed only that one of the men had given Vangie his chair and that Maggie, white-faced but defiant, stood pressed against the wall near the back of the room.

"Wilson and I have served you all our lives," Joe said quietly. "We intend to go on serving—but we can only serve those who are willing to be served. If, for whatever reason, you find us unworthy, we need to know. But as for this—this tempest in a teapot—I am ashamed, yes, *ashamed* that those responsible would stoop so low!" His voice rose powerfully. "Who is Vangie's accuser?"

When the men turned to look at Maggie, she had the grace to blush. But her eyes were cold and merciless. She looked incapable of remorse. Then, to Chris Beth's horror, she took a step forward.

About midway the girl seemed to hesitate, but defiantly she said, "I am! I'm not afraid of her kind—"

"*Her* kind!" Wilson would have sprung forward except for Chris Beth's restraining hand.

"Don't," she whispered. "Please—you'll only make it harder for Vangie!"

Then, mercifully, Joe was speaking in crisp tones. "Let's get on with this at once! You may come on up, Miss Solomon. And you men may feel free to interrogate the witness. But I would remind all of you, and that goes for you, Maggie, to use discretion! In the words of Jesus, let he that is without sin cast the first stone."

Maggie's hips swayed as she walked toward Joe.

Nate stood. "You got any proof, girl? Proof that Doc's missus is less'n she's supposed to be?"

Maggie's laugh was harsh. "What better proof than that b-b—that *child* of hers!" Chris Beth flushed. Why, *child* sounded bad!

Wilson pulled away from Chris Beth's grasp. Joe, seeing the struggle, left the front of the room and hurried to Wilson's side. The men spoke in low tones above the sudden commotion in the room.

"Should be tarred 'n feathered . . . cheap, no-good woman startin' such commotion from hearsay . . . and all fer what purpose . . . now, lest you get more proof than this . . . say, what's *your* occupation anyways? Be ye without sin?"

Fear clutched Chris Beth's heart. What was all this leading to? What were they accomplishing? *And where was Vangie?*

In her preoccupation with making her way through the

group to find her sister, Chris Beth bumped into Maggie Solomon, who was attempting an unexpected getaway. "You haven't heard the last of this," Maggie hissed. "You and your sweet-faced little sister!"

Before Chris Beth could recover from the unprovoked attack, Joe pounded on the table with his gavel. "Let her pass!" His voice carried a command. "Then please remain standing for the benediction: *Father, forgive them, for they know not what they do!*"

35
The Third Plague

❧

THE CENTERVILLE INCIDENT was history. Only on occasion was it a topic of conversation in the Big House or between Chris Beth and Mrs. Malone.

"Is it all behind you now, Darling?" Chris Beth asked Vangie once as they made soap in the coolest part of the morning.

Vangie's violet eyes widened. "Oh, I put it all behind ages ago," she said innocently. "I just pray the others have. Poor Maggie—"

Chris Beth suspected that Joe and Wilson discussed the matter. Wilson, given more to quick anger than Joe, seemingly held no grudge once matters were settled. And Joe was good at calming him. Their main concern was only that the girls not be humiliated or left with blemishes on their names. Chris Beth and Vangie knew that Wilson had put the incident in its proper perspective when he accepted the deaconship with humble pride and made plans for his and young Wil's ordination.

Mrs. Malone caught Chris Beth up on other outcomes. "Poor Nate—maybe one day he'll learn," she said, shaking

319

her head. "He's a good man—just self-important like. Couldn't a' married a more fittin' wife. You wasn't in the store when Bertie made Maggie apologize?"

"To *Vangie*?"

"No, to the august body of men who'd been beguiled into havin' that silly investigation! They ordered her to stay away from Vangie—said Mag wasn't fit to keep her company."

"That seems harsh, doesn't it? Maggie must feel terrible."

"Maggie never felt terrible in her life—less'n she's ignored by a man. And you know what place has no fury like a woman scorned! Gettin' back t' Nate Goldsmith. His wife said mor'n Maggie was to blame. Marched 'im right in and talked a streak. He'll be apologizin' to the rest—Vangie, you, Joe, and Wilson."

"Oh, but—" Chris Beth started to protest.

"Olga's verdict, not mine. And, child, Nate *did* put you through a heap."

Yes, he did, at that. He and Maggie. But it was past. The Lord had seen them through it. And the hard part now was to pray for a girl like Maggie. But she had learned that enemies are no longer enemies in a true sense when she prayed for them. And certainly the girl needed prayer. She had all but taken up residence at the Big Time Saloon ("*Bed* 'n Board," Mrs. Malone phrased it, emphasizing the *bed* part just enough to convey the message).

But for Vangie and those who loved her so much the nightmare was over.

In the days that followed, Chris noted gratefully that it was business as usual with the valley folk. There were no curious stares and no overeffusiveness. They simply folded the matter away and forgot it as quickly as possible in the same manner they disposed of long underwear after a long, hard winter.

Anyway, there were some pressing matters at hand. Lots of unfinished business. Then the new business, which caught the already weary, emotionally drained settlers completely by surprise.

"Best we git all things settled," said Nate Goldsmith (acting as president of the board instead of as judge or chairman of the nomination committee for deacons) when he called on Chris Beth the first week in September.

In his hand was the "revised contract" for the coming school year. "Terms bein' much the same as last year— exception bein' this allows fer teacher's bein' married. This meetin' with your approval?"

"I'm sure it's all right—" Chris began, but when she reached for the folded paper, Nate drew it back.

"Wanted t' say it's too bad 'bout the misunderstandin' 'n all. But let bygones be bygones, I allus say?"

Chris Beth nodded soberly at his implied question, smiling inwardly. That was as close to an apology as Nate could come, although his obvious face-saving tactics were amusing. His words *sought* no forgiveness. They gave it!

"Jest sign on the dotted line!" he said, obviously relieved that she did not pursue the "bygones."

Unfolding the paper, she saw that Nate had handed her the old contract. He had simply crossed out her signature and penciled in a line of dots above it. "Make sure you sign your married name!"

"Making sure," she said.

In mid-September, the new board of deacons met to decide how to proceed with erecting some sort of storehouse. The "disciples" met with them, and Brother Amos brought a plan he had sketched. "Art thou willing to consider a silo constructed of split rails?"

Wilson and young Wil brought the sketch home and excitedly shared it with Joe, Chris Beth, and Vangie. "Looks practical," Joe decided. "Did hands volunteer to help?"

"All present," Wilson said. "And word will spread."

"How much money's involved?" Joe's brows knitted in concern.

Young Wil could keep silent no longer. "None! That's the

good part. Abe—I mean Mr. Solomon—is furnishin' nails an' stuff."

A week later the school board met to decide which the community should devote its energies to first—the storehouse or enlarging the school. Unanimously they decided to tackle both! "Been thinkin'. They's nuf uv us now t' do the Lord's labor," said Ruben Beltran.

Then the following Sunday O'Higgin announced that the deacons thought a choir might be nice. "Be ye of th' same mind?"

The congregation responded with loud hand clapping. "Then I be th' leader and Miss Chrissy there, will ye be soloist, me bonnie lass?"

Again, the clapping. "I will be happy to!" Chris Beth answered, feeling tears of joy near the surface. Finding time to do all the responsibilities she was assuming would be a problem. But, like Mrs. Malone said, "A body always ends up doin' what he calculated bein' important!" Well, singing again—and this time for the Lord—was important. And it would be so wonderful to sing publicly again, wonderful indeed! Vangie had Mama's fragile beauty and nimbleness of fingers with embroidery hoops and needles, but Chris Beth had Mama's voice.

Farmers, cattlemen, and sheepherders alike continued to scan the sky for signs of rain—each in his own way. Abe Solomon claimed that sight of a seagull wheeling this far inland would be a good omen. His wife snorted, "Nonsense! No single way o' tellin' without consultin' the almanac, an' it says the whole year'll be dryer than a bone." Mrs. Malone quoted, "Red sails at night, sailors' delight." To this Brother Amos nodded an agreement: "Yea, ye brethren can discern the face of the sky. 'When it is evening,' quoting from the Good Book, 'it will be fair weather,' ye say, 'for the sky is red.'"

O'Higgin listened with respect, then with merry eyes dancing, announced, " 'Tis a cloud I look for, I be tellin' ye—a wee cloud, sized fer patchin' a Dutchman's pants!"

Equinox came on Sunday. Surely the shifting of the seasons

would bring the usual temperamental weather. But house-
wives turned their calendars from summer to fall and skies
remained cloudless.

Joe finished his sermon a little early. It was hot and it was
easy to see that the children were restless. Chris Beth found
herself wishing again that there were some way to build a
church house. Then there could be Sunday school classes for
the young people. She secretly had the site chosen. The
building just had to nestle among the redbud trees above the
ledge and—

Her thinking was cut short by the sudden silence in the
group. She realized that Brother Amos was standing, face
uplifted and hands raised heavenward. "Hast thou observed
what the dust and lack of pure water means? We must prepare
for the third plague—sickness and death!"

Dire predictions the settlers did not need. Sickness, Brother
Amos had said—and *death!* Some of them believed in "signs."
Others did not. "Folklore," they shrugged. But nobody dared
dispute the prophesies of the Willow Grove "disciple." Just
how he knew was a mystery, but he knew all right. Chris
Beth, watching a late September sky—which should have
been beautiful but wasn't—wished fervently that she doubted
Brother Amos' prophecy of disease. Last September, she
remembered, had been glorious. The lowering sun had sent
shafts of light through thinning colored boughs of oak and
dogwood, which, seen through the thick-needled fir trees,
reminded her of stained-glass windows in a great cathedral.

Idly she picked up an eighth-grade reader. She must get at
some lesson plans. The addition to the school was progressing
nicely and, if she didn't work up a bit of energy, she would be
the only person unprepared for opening day.

Something poetic would be nice for the bulletin board—
something autumnish. "October is a month of flame—" Oh,
dear! She closed the textbook. The only flame was the
relentless sun. And it had done more than golden-glow the

leaves. The entire countryside was scorched to an ugly brown
from its fiery rays. No moisture remained in the air.

Maybe it would be cooler out-of-doors. But no sooner had
she settled little Mart on a quilt in the backyard than Vangie's
familiar "Yoo-hoo!" signaled a need for her presence in the Big
House. Interrupting the baby's game with his fat toes, she
scooped him up and hurried across the foot-log.

Vangie's greeting was in breathless, incoherent phrases,
characteristic of her speech when she was disturbed. "Scarlet
fever's all over the settlement. Doc can't help—has it. And
Wilson's packing medicine—what little cure there is. Everything's there—for taking care of True, I mean." She pointed to
the bureau and then to the cedar chest. "My uniform—where
is it? We may be gone over night. Longer maybe—some have
died already and—"

Chris Beth felt herself staring at her sister in horror. "What
can you do? I mean should you go?"

"I should. What's more, I *must*. I'm a nurse. You would,
too—teach, I mean. Why, you'd go into the reservation if they
called you. Is my uniform buttoned in back? Anyway, I belong
at Wilson's side in sickness and in health and—"

"Stop it, Vangie! You know what I mean. This is dangerous,
life-threatening. It *is* infectious?"

"Of course. We'll wear masks—do the best we can. Wilson
will take care of me—you know that. You didn't button it. I
feel a draft!"

Chris Beth knew a moment's bitterness. Wilson had no
right to ask this of Vangie—or even allow it. Vangie was frail
herself and prone to contract any disease with which she came
in contact. But, yes, she *would* do the same thing—with her
teaching or with Joe's ministry.

"Chrissy!" Vangie, looking far too young to wear the
professional white uniform, turned to face her. Although her
cheeks flushed with excitement, her eyes looked troubled.

"What is it, Vangie? Are you all right?"

"You would take care of True, wouldn't you? If anything—

nothing's going to—but if anything *did* happen? You'd tell her—you know—what you feel is best and—promise me?"

"Don't talk like that!" Chris Beth felt the words torn from her lips. Even as she spoke, the men's voices cut through the stale and sultry afternoon air.

"Everything's ready except my Florence Nightingale!" Wilson called from the front yard.

"Promise!" Vangie whispered.

"Oh, Vangie, I promise," Chris Beth whispered in reply and choked back the tears as the four of them embraced. The epidemic had come just as Brother Amos had said.

Young Wil came onto the porch to wave. Thoughtfully he pulled a dried bud which had never had a chance to bloom from the scarlet runner vine. "Will folks die?"

Chris Beth would have tried to shift the conversation, but Joe spoke man-to-man. "I expect so," he said quietly.

"Things would never be the same, would they?"

Young Wil turned tortured eyes to Chris Beth. She longed to comfort this half-man/half-child—to tell him the bad dream would pass. Instead, she answered gently, "No, they never would."

36
Death's Angel

❧

IN THE DAYS that followed, every home in the settlement was touched by the epidemic. Death's angel seemed to hover overhead, as if undecided which family to visit next. The first one taken was Doc Dullus himself.

When Elmer Goldsmith, who was "runner" for the neighborhood, brought the sad news, Chris Beth's first thought was for Wilson. The old doctor had been like a father.

"Can Wilson manage without him?" She asked Joe through her tears.

"Wilson isn't without him, Chrissy," Joe assured her. "Old Doc left a far greater legacy than instruments and medical books."

That was true, she knew. Wilson had little more than driven away when Joe pointed out the careful list of precautions he had left: "Boil water, bring cow's milk to scalding for babies, soft diet for all (poached eggs, milk toast, custard, rice, broth) . . . light garments (to be boiled after wear or burned in case of contact with infected patient . . .)." The list went on and on.

"We'll have to go break the news to O'Higgin and Mrs. Malone," Chris Beth told Joe.

He nodded. Young Wil would look after the babies.

As they approached Turn-Around Inn, the sound of O'Higgin's mellow voice floated across the dry meadows. With a little catch in her throat, Chris Beth remembered Mrs. Malone's words when the Muslin City folk were tuning their fiddles at twilight.

The singing stopped in midmeasure when horse and riders drew near. O'Higgin's usually merry eyes were grave as he summoned his wife.

"It's Doc—" Joe began.

Mrs. Malone's face blanched, but she raised a hand to stop Joe's words. "Coffee's brewin'," she said briskly, turning toward the door.

Then, over coffee and aged pound cake, the four of them recalled the memories of the lovable doctor—white-whiskered, short and plump, baggy pants tucked into knee-high boots, his cultured voice with its broken English—but, most of all, his medical skill and loving service.

"Best we be preparin' a place. Ye ladies be stayin' here." O'Higgin said.

Joe nodded. "I've put in a lot of time reading up on scarlet fever. The medical journals say to isolate the sick from the well. We *have* to stay on our feet. It's up to us to keep panic down."

"Chrissy—" Joe opened his arms and held her for one sweet moment. O'Higgin attempted a wink, but tears got in the way. Wordlessly he climbed onto Dobbin's back behind Joe.

Quietly the two men buried their beloved friend in a little glade near his house. "Someday," Joe told Chris Beth later, "we'll put up a granite marker. For now there's just a little wooden cross."

Young Elmer's next message was directly from Vangie and Wilson.

"They cain't come home—" the gawkish lad panted, "Cause uv this awful sickness. It took ten more—they was Willis

Long, his wife and kids, Otis Flannary—they bein' new—and, oh, yeah, the China-baby—"

"Wong's little sister!" Chris Beth felt as if her heart were in a vise squeezed tighter and tighter. "But—but—"

"Easy, Chrissy, easy," Joe, who was bracing her from behind, whispered against her hair. "Be brave for Elmer and young Wil's sakes."

Chris Beth didn't want to be brave. She wanted to be a little girl cradled in her father's arms, a helpless Southern lady swooning at her husband's feet. She wanted to cry and cry . . .

Instead, she lifted her shoulders and looked steadily at the obviously distraught Elmer. "You are a great help, Elmer. Now, can you tell us about the doctor and Miss Vangie?"

"Yessum. That's why I come. They wantin' you should let young Wil come home with me. Then they wantin' you should take the little babies to Miss Mollie—'n you should meet with 'em to help."

Involuntarily Chris Beth's hands went to her face. What if something should happen to the four of them? What would happen to True and little Mart *then?* Surely this was the greatest crisis yet.

In her state of shock and fear, it was not until later she realized that Elmer had said, "They're makin' headquarters at the gen'ral store!"

Chris Beth closed the door softly behind her, careful not to disturb her sister, and walked to the window of the upstairs room to look out on the dusty street below. Fascinated, she watched a little whirlwind form, dip down, and then drift away. In the same way, she thought sadly, the earthly lives of their family of friends were slipping away. It seemed only natural that she and Vangie should be here together. She, being older, had taken care of Vangie in times of health, so why not in the sickness and death that they were fighting together in the settlement?

Downstairs, Joe would be conferring with Wilson as to how

the two of them could be of most help in trying to mend bodies or spirits. Maybe it would be both, she thought, remembering the haggard look of her brother-in-law's face as they entered the general store. And, in her sleep, Vangie—she thought tenderly—looked like a beautiful doll that some thoughtless child had tossed carelessly aside.

She checked her sister's forehead and was relieved to find that it was not feverish.

"You four are welcome to come 'n go as you can. Hope you don't mind sharin' Maggie's room?" Mrs. Solomon had offered.

Chris Beth was sure her surprise showed, for the woman continued, "She won't be comin' 'round. Run off with a stocking drummer—after all her pa and me's done for th' girl."

"I'm sorry."

Mrs. Solomon turned away, but not before Chris Beth saw the tears. "She'd made her bed. Let her lie in it!" she said brusquely.

When Vangie awakened, her first question was about True. Chris Beth assured her that all was well at home. Then the two of them talked about the epidemic. "It's bad—oh, it's bad." Vangie's lip quivered, but her chin was raised in determination. "The Smiths lost one of the twins and the other is very low. Oh, Chrissy, are you *sure* True's all right?"

"Right as rain," she smiled, "But are *you?*"

Vangie pushed back a curl and nodded. "But we need help. Wilson may not let you go inside, but if you can count out pills, take care of children, call on the ones who've had deaths in the family—"

"All of those. We're survivors, you and I. Haven't we proved that already?"

Vangie let two fat tears roll down her cheeks then, the way she always did as a little girl. "You always make me feel better. And we will survive. We have to. With God's help."

"With God's help," Chris Beth repeated. "We will lick this epidemic."

37
Why, Lord? Why?

❧

TIME LOST ALL MEANING. How long had they
been battling the epidemic, anyway? Two weeks? Or was it
months? Or years? Chris Beth hardly noticed whether it was
day or night. At Joe's urging, she ate. Under Wilson's watchful
eye, she scrubbed herself raw. And she must have talked.
People, whose faces she scarcely saw through her fatigue, kept
telling her what a comfort she was. But what had she said?
Even the pain and the fear she had felt when the scarlet fever
first broke out was softened by a merciful kind of numbness
around her heart.

Her only emotion was a gnawing sense of emptiness at
being unable to see little Mart. "Couldn't you do without me
just a few hours?" she begged.

"Actually, no," Wilson answered the question she had
directed to Joe. "But that's not the point. We can't risk
spreading this thing. So far we're holding our own."

"Maybe Mrs. Malone could at least get some word to me."

"Absolutely not!" And then his tone softened. "I'm sorry. I
understand, you know."

Of course, he did. But the ache would not go away.

330

"Are we winning?" she asked Wilson on another occasion.

"It's hard to tell. I'm beginning to think scarlet fever's not a disease but more a form of streptococci—sometimes it's the fever and sometimes in the same family it's a mild sore throat. Material for my next book—if we can just hang on here—"

The pink light of dawn crept in to touch Maggie's bed, where Chris Beth and Vangie had stretched out just two hours before. A shower of pebbles shattered the stillness. Still enveloped in a fog of sleep, Chris Beth dragged herself to the window. Joe stood motioning below. His waving was unnecessary. The toss of pebbles could only mean, "Another case. Another emergency. Come!"

Even as she turned to waken Vangie, Chris Beth saw the ancient carriage, its windows draped in black crepe. Its passing meant that Wilson had lost another patient. Another family circle broken. And nobody to mourn the passing except the grieving loved ones. Others looked out, white-faced through their windows, wondering, "Why, Lord, why?"

"Whose house?" Chris Beth asked woodenly.

"Two families occupy it," Joe explained as he helped her and Vangie from the buggy. "Boones, relatives of Orin and Susanah R-Robbins."

Joe stumbled over the name. Probably he had wanted to spare her any embarrassment. But didn't he know that she was feeling nothing these days? Nothing, that is, except for the driving urge to do what she could for the living. Go home. See the baby. Get on with life.

Wilson, having given up trying to protect even herself and Vangie, let alone himself and Joe, hurried inside the cabin. Wordlessly the rest of them followed. At the door, Joe stopped to tack up the dreaded sign: QUARANTINE, DO NOT ENTER! lettered in red. Numbly, Chris Beth adjusted her mask and murmured a little disjointed prayer: "Please, Lord, spare as many as You can—please, Lord." Then, squaring her shoulders, she moved through the door, wondering how soon the quarantine sign would be replaced with black crepe and which of the two families would be taken away in the funeral carriage.

After a quick, professional check of the others, Wilson moved to where Susanah lay motionless and still. A telltale frown creased his brow. "Susanah?" When there was no answer, Wilson began his quiet instructions, his tone diagnosing to the three who worked with him, "Scarlet fever." And his eyes communicated, "No hope."

All day the four of them worked with Susanah. "You'll have to help us," Wilson kept repeating to his weakening patient, but there was no response. She seemed not to move at all except for labored breathing.

Chris Beth left the bedside, where Vangie wiped the woman's fevered brow. Cold with apprehension, she tried to speak calmly to the children who kept trying to crowd into the small room. Death was inevitable for Susanah, and Chris Beth did not want the young ones on hand.

"Come and let me show you a finger game," Chris Beth told the children, "if you are very quiet, you can play it by yourselves."

When she was sure they were diverted, Chris Beth tiptoed silently back to where Wilson, Vangie, and Joe were leaning over the sickbed.

"Don't try to talk," Wilson said gently. "Go to sleep."

Susanah's face was wax-white and there was a faint blue tint to her lips, through which she was trying to whisper a message. Then, feebly, she motioned to Vangie.

"Forgive me—I didn't know—" She fought laboriously for breath. "I meant no harm—forgive me—her, too—"

Vangie dropped to her knees and, with tears streaming down her face, cradled the dying woman's head gently in her arms. "It's all right," she soothed, "oh, my darling, it's all right."

Vangie shouldn't be so close to Susanah—and her mask has slipped down, Chris Beth thought numbly. Foolishly, as if it would help, she reached out in an effort to adjust the shield. Inside, she knew that it was more than the disease from which she wished to protect Vangie and herself. Vangie looked helpless and frightened, but she shrugged off her sister's hand. Then a small sigh said Susanah was gone.

"Susanah!" The word was torn from Vangie's lips. And then she turned to Chris Beth for comfort. Both of them gave way to their grief as the men covered Susanah's now-peaceful face and spoke quiet words of consolation to Orin.

38

Hiyiu Cultus Seek!

❧

IN THE HOT, orange twilight, Wilson and Vangie hurried away on another call. Chris Beth remained behind with Joe to try to bring comfort to the home that death had touched.

Olivia Boone, looking little and frightened, asked haltingly, "What can I do?" And then she burst into tears. "I wish I were home. We never should have come. I'll catch the next wagon train—"

"Get a grip on yourself!" Chris Beth used her school-teaching voice in order to stem the other woman's hysteria. "You'll adjust here. We'll help you. And there's no way a wagon train will be allowed to pass until the quarantine's lifted. The streets are deserted." Then, adding more gently, she said, "Let's sit down."

With calm deliberation, she smoothed Olivia's brown hair from her pale face. And, working to control her own anxieties, Chris Beth tried to think and speak as Mrs. Malone would have—soothingly, calmly.

Did she know where Susanah's Sunday dress was hanging? The two of them must wash her face and fluff her hair. The men would prepare the grave . . . too far to take the body to Graveyard Creek Cemetery. Too dark. Too dangerous.

Couldn't they wait until tomorrow? Shouldn't there be a wake?

No, the burial must take place immediately. And no callers could come. The house was quarantined.

Move . . . move . . . don't think . . . just pray! Finally something resembling order came to the house, and then a kind of peace. Chris Beth realized with a strange kind of exhilaration that an onlooker would never suspect that she had not dealt directly with death before.

Chris Beth helped to put the children in bed before burial of the body took place. She and Olivia held lanterns for the men to see by. It was with a great sense of relief that she saw a flush of dawn in the eastern sky. Surely today would be better. *Anyway,* she thought, *the Lord has shown me that I can do what I have to do!*

But soon enough she was to wonder about that. First there was the muted sound of running footsteps and then an eerie scream. Out of nowhere came the swift-moving shadow of a near-nude figure. An Indian! But before the astonished group could grasp the situation, the man was speaking, "*Hiyiu cultus seek!* Come!"

Boston Buck! Remembering her one encounter with the young brave, Chris Beth felt fear vibrate up and down her spine. The sweating russet-brown body advanced. The intense, dark eyes sought hers desperately. "Come. *Seek!*" And he pointed to the forest in the general direction of the reservation.

Olivia's husband and Orin Robbins lifted their shovels. But Joe put up a restraining hand. "There's unrest already. Be careful!" Then, to Boston Buck, he said, "Sickness? Yes, I will go with you."

The young Indian crossed his arms and waited before speaking. Then, "*Bring Black Book* and squaw!" he said.

Joe must have sensed her apprehension. "Evil spirits," he

told her in a low tone when Boston Buck suddenly increased his speed to outdistance the riders.

Soundlessly, Boston Buck ran ahead of the horses. How fleet of foot he was! But why did he choose the more open woods or skirt the woods completely whenever possible and stare uneasily into the dark, thick forest stretches? Once Chris Beth had feared the young brave himself. Now she was more afraid of what *he* feared. Wild animals? Warriors from other tribes?

Then suddenly they were in an Indian village. But how strange! The huts were made of crude shakes cut from fir trees instead of animal skins as geography books had described them. And the buildings were stuck here and there beneath a bluff instead of being a part of the reservation just beyond. This could mean only one thing. Boston Buck must be the son of Chief Halo. Wilson had told her about the old Indian chief. He was shunned by other tribes because of his near-white skin and was called Halo (meaning poor) because he had few dogs or ponies, only one squaw, and only one son.

Chris Beth's fragmented thinking was interrupted by the sudden stop of the horses. Boston Buck blocked the way as he pointed with ill-concealed pride to his village. "*Splachta alla,*" he said.

"Home in a sheltered vale," Joe interpreted with a nod.

The young Indian then pointed to the reservation. "*Nika wake clatawa!*"

Joe hesitated, then asked haltingly, "I—will—not—go?"

This time it was the Indian who nodded. Then he *was* Halo's son!

Chris Beth's mind resumed its jumbled thinking. Better here than on the reservation—maybe. But if only Wilson were here—he understands. And, anyway, a doctor is needed. What can *we* do? Any action may endanger our lives. After all, Boston Buck's the chief now . . . and a chief's a chief—even if he's the son of a poor one! The fever will spread and—

There was no time to think further. Already Joe was helping her to the ground. Then, with Boston Buck in the lead, they entered the largest of the huts just as the sun touched its dry-moss roof.

Several women squatted around the central fire, stirring something that smelled of fish. It was hard to breathe. Chris Beth's lungs were filled with smoke. And surely she was going to be sick from the smell and drying skins. Fatigue gripped her body. Fear clutched her heart. The room and all its horrors reeled crazily.

"Steady," Joe whispered. "If it's too much—"

His words were interrupted by a low moan from a crude bench along a wall opposite the room's only door. Reflex action took her forward. When Joe would have followed, Boston Buck restrained him.

"Squaw stay! You come!"

Chris Beth did not know what she had expected. A small child, most likely. Critically ill of scarlet fever. Instead, the writhing body of a young Indian woman lay on the animal skin. And she was trying to give birth to a child! Automatically she waved Joe out with Boston Buck. At least she wouldn't have to contend with a witchdoctor. And the other women had been unable to deliver the baby. Small comfort! What could *she* do? But they trusted her.

"You'll have to help me this time, Lord!" she prayed aloud desperately. To the other women, she said, "*Pray!*" Their only response was to cringe back in fear. She tried again, reaching arms heavenward. "Great—White—Spirit," she said slowly. And, at that signal, the women began a strange chant, otherworldly in Chris Beth's ears but apparently soothing to her patient, who seemed to relax slightly.

"Hot water," she whispered to one of the younger girls, spreading her hands over the fire to communicate."

The girl understood. Hurriedly she brought a tightly woven basket filled with water and set it beside the fire. Then, with two sticks, she lifted hot rocks and dropped them one by one into the basket. There was a hiss of steam and then the water began to boil.

Hour after hour the two of them worked over the laboring

woman. Time and time again, Chris Beth thought they were
losing the battle. Then something of what Wilson had taught
her when they brought little True into the world came back.

"Push . . . relax . . . push . . ." she instructed, demon-
strating her meaning. "And you—" Turning to her helper, she
hesitated, wishing she knew her name.

To her surprise, the girl answered "White Arms" in a small
voice.

"You, White Arms, bathe her face like this. Then hold
her—"

"Boston Girl."

"Hold Boston Girl when I say—like this. Push . . .
relax . . . push . . . *hold her*—Oh, *Lord, help us!* . . .
Push . . . relax . . . push . . ."

Through the white maze into which her mind had blessedly
taken refuge, Chris Beth heard the unceasing chant of the
women's prayer, the occasional bark of a dog, the raucous call
of a jay, and Joe's voice. He seemed to be reading—but what?
She only knew that each time his voice, now hoarse, stopped,
Boston Buck commanded, "Read more. Heap more. Boston
Buck want *Talking Book*."

Talking Book! The Bible! "The Lord is my Shepherd . . ."
On and on Joe read. Then, as the evening sun dipped into the
Western sky, Chris Beth emerged from behind the skin
covering the door of the hut. "Come in and meet the new
chief!" she invited a beaming Boston Buck calmly. Then,
weeping, she collapsed into Joe's arms.

At the edge of the woods, the exhausted pair spotted a lone
rider. Chris Beth scarcely recognized the strained, white face
in the gathering twilight. But it was—it had to be—Wilson!
Fear clutched her heart. Where was Vangie? What was he
doing out here without the buggy?

"Vangie? Where's Vangie?" She cried out even as dust
choked back her words.

Wilson reined in beside her and Joe. "What are *you* doing
here?" His voice sounded angry. "Do you realize how danger-

ous this could have been, Joe? And you, you blessed idiot—"
He looked at Chris Beth.

If I didn't know him better, I'd think he was going to cry,
her tired mind thought. But what about Vangie?

"Vangie? *Wilson!*"

But Wilson turned to Joe. "Don't you realize—" he started
to ask again.

"How dangerous it was," Joe finished. "Yes, but don't *you*
realize how dangerous it would have been *not* to come? We
have to minister to them all. The Lord didn't specify which
color."

"I didn't mean that and you know it. I mean the hostility—
and now the spread of this epidemic."

"No epidemic," Joe said. "A baby."

"*Vangie!*" Chris Beth's patience had snapped.

"A baby yet. You delivered a *baby*? How convenient."

Without warning, Chris Beth's anger turned to quiet desperation. She simply dropped her head and let tears of exhaustion
roll down her face unchecked. It didn't matter. Something had
happened to Vangie.

For the first time, neither of the men seemed to notice.
They were engaged in a subject and she had missed part of it.

"You mean she's *there*? Is she going to be all right?"

"She wants to see Chris Beth."

Then, as if seeing her for the first time, both of them turned
to Chris Beth. "Vangie fainted and I took her in—"

"*Fainted*? Oh, Wilson, does she have the bad kind—I
mean—"

"No, the *good* kind. I'm so glad you're getting experience at
midwifery. Your little sister is going to have a baby!"

Even before she saw his ebony face, wreathed in welcoming
smiles, Chris Beth knew that the cabin the three of them
reached just had to be Ole Tobe's, the black man who had
brought the donkey to the Christmas program. "Coffee!"
Wilson sniffed with appreciation, Joe said, "Spice something
or other?" "Molasses cookies," Chris Beth replied. But neither

the wild beauty of the place nor the tantalizing odors held as much fascination for her as the mellow crooning coming from the cabin door. "Thet's the Sleepy Hollow tune, lika colohed mammy's croon to her sleepy lit-tle pick-an-ny on uh lazy aftahnoon . . ."

The voice! The slurring of the vowels and softening of the consonants, even the song itself! It had to be—it *had* to be—"Aunt Mandy." The wonderful mammy who had been more a mother to her than Mama!

Brushing past Ole Tobe, Chris Beth rushed into the room, where the ample-bosomed woman, her face partially hidden, leaned over Vangie's sleeping figure on the small cot. But her trained ear picked up the footsteps and, pushing a wisp of now-graying hair beneath the red bandanna, she turned the familiar, lovable face toward any intruder who dared wake her "baby."

A finger warned for silence. Then slowly it went down when the woman saw Chris Beth. The wonderful woman from a childhood past rushed forward. "Oh, praise de Lawd! He dun sent my Miss Chrissy back."

With a cry of delight, Chris Beth raced into the outstretched arms. "Oh, Aunt Mandy, Aunt Mandy—how? Oh, Aunt Mandy—"

"Don't you cry now, honey chile. Ain't ever gonna be no more tears fer you 'n me. Shh-h-h, y'all don wanna be wakin' yah baby sistah!"

Vangie slept through the reunion. Chris Beth was glad. So much needed asking and explaining. Why hadn't Aunt Mandy come to last year's Christmas program when Ole Tobe brought the sheep? *Us colohed folks ain't always welcome, chile.* Oh, things are different here—no need coming in back doors either! But how did this miracle happen?

Atlanta ain't de same since the burnin', dun drove us outta our homes. Me'n my man up 'n jumped de broom and comed West. Praise de Lawd!

39
Fire

❧

THE EPIDEMIC ENDED as abruptly as it began. Loss of life was "considerably light," city doctors told Wilson. The letter of congratulations was waiting at the general store when he, Chris Beth, and Joe returned to Centerville. What's more, the letter went on, if he wished to pursue his findings on "isolating the sick from the well," and continue his dissertation on "Streptococci, Species of," they could, under "certain circumstances," arrange a loan for him.

When Chris Beth and Joe would have interrupted with whoops of joy, Wilson put up his hand with a grin. "There's more! I received an advance royalty check on the botany book. And this is for you."

Joe accepted the envelope, then handed it to Chris Beth. Puzzled by the crude printing, she ripped the letter open. Inside was a vague note from Nate Goldsmith saying that the State of Oregon was helping out with schools, and would this be acceptable by her? *Acceptable!* A $100- warranty marked "For Services to Be Rendered"!

As if that weren't enough, Abe Solomon, (being "duly appointed by the actin' board o' deacons," he explained)

341

handed a mysterious-looking packet to Joe the day following.

"Money!" Joe gasped when several large bills spilled out.

"Cash money, no less!" Abe said proudly. "From us all. And don't go sayin' you cain't accept it and you're doin' the Lord's work. It's from our tithes and offerings. Then John Henry Dobbs sold his hawgs."

"How will I ever get it all written in my diary?" Vangie laughed when they went to pick her up two days later.

There was more. But now was not the time to share it, Chris Beth decided. While Joe and Wilson made final calls (and she was supposed to be resting?), she had slipped out the side door of the store and paid a visit to the office marked ASSAYER. Just how much, she wondered, would a pearl-and-sapphire brooch which she described be worth? The little man, wearing a dark sunshade and clamping a mouthful of gold teeth on a cigar which had long since gone out, looked at her cagily. Not much, most likely, he parried. As she was about to leave, he said, not to get too hasty. Could do a *little* better—if she would like to bring it in. Matter of fact, he hoped she *would* bring it. "And real soon, eh, lovely lady?"

Aunt Mandy wept when her "babies" left but smiled broadly when Vangie told her that she would be calling on her for help when the second baby came. Ole Tobe said he'd help buildin' on the school.

The buggy was packed. Dobbin was saddled. Good-byes were finished. Or so Chris Beth thought. She had forgotten Mrs. Solomon—or maybe she had supposed that thanking the woman who had been so kind was enough.

"Don't go bein' so hurried!" Bertie's voice was gruff in an effort to hide her tears. "Here's our tithes. Abe and me, we figured you'd be needin' some staples. They're sorta to thank you fer—fer bein' here and takin' the sting out o' Maggie's leavin'. Now take 'em and git!"

"Wolf" spotted the group and alerted the Malone-O'Higgin tribe. The geese sounded their alarm. And children descended upon Chris Beth, Vangie, Joe, and Wilson from all directions, all talking at once.

"School's beautiful . . . some of the men's gone workin' on the railroad . . . what'll we do 'bout a church if Miss Mollie and O'Higgin make Turn-Around Inn into a *real* inn? Yes, the stage is comin', too—Miss Mollie read me 'bout it in the Portland newspaper . . . Andy's got a pet crow . . . O'Higgin says it can talk if we'll let him split its tongue, but Miss Mollie says the only one in need of splittin's *his*!"

"Shoo! Ever' one of you, *shoo* this minute. I declare they'll talk a leg off'n a body."

But Mrs. Malone had handed an unbelievably bigger Mart, his face rosy with a recent nap, to Chris Beth. As she pressed her face against little Mart's fuzzy head, it wouldn't have mattered one bit how much the children talked or what they said. "My baby! My baby! Oh, thank You, Lord," she whispered over and over.

Through a maze of happiness, she managed a meal (never remembering what she ate), greeted young Wil when he and Elmer appeared on schedule, exchanged greetings with O'Higgin, and said good-bye. And then, blessedly, they were home.

An early frost turned the few remaining leaves scarlet and the wild apples along the fence rows to pure gold. There had been no rain to wash down the suspended smoke and dust particles. So the valley was wrapped in a gossamer shawl of Indian summer. The hollows echoed with the hammering of the woodpeckers and the chattering of the gray squirrels as they graveled the forest paths with the hulls of acorns and hazelnuts.

Out of the autumn haze, Elmer Goldsmith raced all over the settlement on the last Saturday in October. "Think you can squeeze into shoes next Monday?" Chris Beth teased the panting boy.

Elmer blushed. "I'll try, Miss Chrissy—and you'n ever'body else's supposed t' come to Turn-Around Inn tomorrow—

church 'n all, then dinner. More'n that, though, it's a Thanks-givin', you know, 'bout the sickness goin' away—and I'll be there, too."

"Not unless you slow down. Have some grape juice before you go."

The crowd gathered early. The Craigs and the Norths were there ahead of the others. There was so much talking to do. As it turned out, most of the words were left unsaid.

Mrs. Malone and O'Higgin were engaged in a heated discus-sion about the season—too pleasant, by far, to be interrupted.

"*Second summer*, I declare it to be," Mrs. Malone said.

"Sure'n a *squaw summer* to the likes o' ye!" O'Higgin's deep voice boomed back.

By then the crowd filled the house, with each person bringing another story as to how Indian summer came to be.

"Smoke came from Indian signals and hung in the heavens, proclaiming the last war, so I hear," Joe said with a smile.

"Not so," Wilson denied with a sober face. Then, imitating O'Higgin's Irish brogue as best he could, he added, "Be ye not knowin' now it came from Ireland, it did? Spread from the Emerald Isle to Canada—"

The others laughed. But something in the air bothered Chris Beth. Could be, she thought it was only the talk that made her imagine she smelled smoke. At first it was like the scent of drying apples. Then her nostril picked up what reminded her of the sweet-smoke smell that came from the controlled burning-off of the cured sugar cane just before it was cut for the mill . . . the time when Mama didn't worry if she cut through the woods. Hornets were at peace and chances were good that the snakes had crawled away to hibernate . . .

Her thinking was cut short. *Smoke!* She smelled real smoke.

Fire. The house was on fire! "Fire!" Chris Beth screamed the single-word warning and was sorry immediately. The result was mayhem. Panic-stricken, the worshipers rushed outside. Guided by emotion instead of reason, their instinct was to get home to protect their own homes. *They're leaving us* was all she could think. *In a burning house—*

The rest was like a horrible nightmare. "Giddyup!" Helplessly she watched one wagon after another rushed away. Teams, urged by overexcited drivers and the scent of smoke, snorted, pitched, and strained in the harness. Chris could only stand and stare in horrible fascination as one wagon went out of control, spilling its occupants to the ground, and then collided with another wagon.

Then her voice came. "Help!" she screamed. Why wasn't Joe at her side? Wilson—Vangie, where was Vangie? *The babies!* "Help!" she screamed again before rushing up the stairs to the upper room.

As she took the steps two at a time, somehow Chris Beth's reeling senses began to right themselves. Her first real focus of awareness was the odd yellowish glow of sun which, through the haze of smoke, tried to light the upstairs room of the inn. Then she saw Vangie.

"True and little Mart are all right," Vangie's voice spoke through the eerie light.

"Oh, thank God!" Chris Beth grabbed little Mart from Vangie's arms and the two of them descended the stairs hurriedly with the sleeping babies. Only then did Chris Beth realize that the fire was not inside the building. "Where then—"

She must have spoken, for Vangie was sobbing. "It—it's everywhere! The whole world's on fire! *Wilson!*"

"He's helpin' the needy ones close at hand," Mrs. Malone spoke from the bottom of the stairs. "Worst of the fire's to th' east. Problem bein' we've got an easterly wind risin'—you children come back here this minute!"

To the east, billows of black smoke belched from the mountains, Chris Beth saw from the front window. More frightening was the line of fire spreading through the trees, its hungry tongues licking at the dry forest floor and— unsatisfied—lapping at the lifeless meadows below. In the split second that Chris Beth watched numbly, the winds lifted sparks from the site and sent them spinning into adjoining groves. There was a booming explosion on contact and a firestorm roared through the treetops. And cabins! Cabins were burning . . . *lives were in danger* . . .

A new spiral of smoke caught her eye—closer. There was something they should be doing. She realized then that Mrs. Malone and Vangie had gone into the kitchen. She must follow. But as she turned, Chris Beth realized that she had seen a lone figure—or thought she had—standing motionless at the edge of the clearing. She looked to be sure, and what she saw brought her senses back completely.

"Joe!" She may have screamed the word, because suddenly Vangie and Mrs. Malone were at her side. "Joe!" Chris Beth heard her voice rise. "Something's wrong with Joe!"

"Joe's all right—" Mrs. Malone tried to soothe. "He's there—"

"He's *not* all right! Or he wouldn't just stand there! Take the baby—no don't! I want him with me—"

Aware that two pairs of arms were trying to restrain her, Chris Beth jerked free. "Try to be calm," Mrs. Malone begged. "Let me—"

"I can't be calm any longer! Flood—plague—epidemic—and now *this*!" Yes, *this* was the worst of all. She knew instinctively what was wrong with Joe. He was in a state of shock at the sight of fire—remembering, beyond all doubt, the inferno which had taken his childhood home, his mother, his father—and had shaken his faith in God and left him an emotional cripple at the very mention of the word.

"Chrissy, no!" But Chris Beth ignored her sister's warning cries and raced toward Joe, covering little Mart's face with her sunbonnet to protect him from the smoke as she ran.

Heat like the blast of a furnace rushed ahead of the main blaze. Above the roar of the fire, deafening explosions told of more and more firestorms. And then there was the unmistakable wail of a baby!

"Joe, Joe!" she tried to scream above the force of the rising wind. But her voice was sucked away. With a sob she reached

out to Joe to shake him, to arouse him, to alert him to danger.
She tugged at his arm, crying out words she never remembered . . . how much she loved him . . . needed him . . .
how much God needed him to save the baby . . .

"The *baby*!" Joe still stood as if paralyzed, but he had heard.
Oh, praise the Lord, he had *heard*!

"A baby, Joe" she sobbed, "a baby! A baby's in the cabin—
burning—a *baby*—"

"I have to go. I *h-have* t-to go-go." Joe spoke the words as
though he scarcely believed them. But he was breathing. He
was alive again. "I have to go, Darling." Suddenly as if alerted
to danger for the first time, Joe spoke to her. "Go back to
safety. I have to go."

Then, with his face protected only by his arms, Joe raced
through the smoke toward the cabin less than a hundred yards
away.

Chris Beth realized suddenly what she had done. She had
sent Joe into a burning building. She had asked him—*forced*
him—to risk his life. If anything happened, it would be her
fault. "Oh, dear God," she whispered, "what have I done?"

Smoke swirled around her, choking her, causing little Mart
to fret. She swayed dizzily on her feet. "Don't cry, Darling.
We'll go back soon, but we can't leave Daddy now." She stood
rooted, unable to move as, through the thickening smoke, she
saw Joe try the front door of the cabin. When it didn't yield, he
kicked it open.

"Joe—Joe—*don't*!"

But, like a swimmer preparing for a deep dive, Joe appeared
to take a deep breath and then plunged inside. No more than
seconds passed, Chris Beth knew later, but it seemed a
lifetime before his familiar face, blackened almost beyond
recognition, loomed out of the smoke. *He didn't even have
his face covered*, she thought numbly.

Then something inside her snapped. "Joe!" she screamed
his name again and again as she saw him stagger from the
cabin and then collapse. She must help him. She must take
the little blanket-covered figure from his arms. Chris Beth

raced toward his crumpled form. "Please, Lord, please let me be in time." But what held her back?

"Get back! Get back, you little idiot!" The voice was Wilson's. And the arms that held her were his. And she was being soundly shaken by capable hands that knew how to hold a baby and his mother together. "Snap out of it! This is not time for hysteria. Get to the inn so I can help Joe. Gather blankets—food—water—if we can save the place, it'll have to serve as emergency headquarters. Are you all right?"

She nodded. Yes, she was all right. And Joe would be, too. All right in every way. In control, she turned toward the inn and ran. Looking back, she saw O'Higgin join Wilson. The two of them disappeared in Joe's direction as the scene was swallowed in a wall of flame.

Vangie and Mrs. Malone met her halfway and the three of them ran across the fields to the temporary safety of Turn-Around Inn.

"Sniff this!" Mrs. Malone ordered, forcing an ammonia soaked cloth beneath Chris Beth's nose. "Th' Lord'll protect our menfolk."

Her head, if not her heart, cleared. Move . . . don't think . . . move . . . and pray! And, through it all, the wild feeling, "I've been through it before—too many times." Move . . . don't think . . . move . . . pray!

"Get the coffeepot boilin', girls. One of you slice the bread and spread it with butter—thick-like. Vangie, what medications do we need from the chest?"

Vangie stopped crying and was suddenly the nurse. "Bandages—you can roll them, Chrissy. Blankets for shock— all the blankets, quilts—even sheets—soap, hot water, turpentine—"

The three of them made every preparation they could. Maybe, just maybe it would work, providing the house stood. Mustn't think about that. Just draw water from the well. Fill every tub and basin. Wet down the roof as far as they could reach. Spread wet sacks over the doors and windows . . . and move . . . don't think . . . pray!

"I've had quite a talk with You, Lord," Chris Beth heard herself whisper over and over. "Save us. Bring the men back. Give me strength."

Wordlessly they worked on until, above the roar of the fast-approaching fire, there was a deafening explosion. It couldn't be. But it was! Thunder—and before there was time to absorb the suddenness of an approaching storm, there was a blinding flash of lightning that might well have heralded the end of the world. And then the rains came! In blinding sheets. By the bucket. By the barrel! And Vangie, so terrified of storms, didn't even whimper!

The three women danced wildly in a circle in the front room, stopping only long enough to embrace one another. "We prayed for this," Mrs. Malone said. "And the Lord answered in His own good time!"

40
Up from the Ashes

⁊

A GENTLE, FAMILIAR SQUEEZE of her hand awakened Chris Beth. Joe's face swam into focus. A shaft of sun touched his tousled hair with bronze. Did her husband or did he not wear a halo? Well, he deserved one—but what on earth were they doing on their knees? *Ouch!* She tried to pull herself up.

"Easy," he whispered. Only then did she realize that the two of them held hands over several sleeping children. "We've been here a long time."

She nodded and both of them smiled, remembering. "Right back where we started," she said. "It was here that you proposed during the flood—but, oh, Joe—the babies—our cabin—?"

"Safe. All safe. Saved by the rain and the grace of God! The fire took its toll—houses, livestock, timber—but no lives, and we have a lot of persons deserving praise. Including our junior deacon!"

How well she knew! Why, young Wil had been a modern-day Paul Revere. No amount of reasoning could have stopped the lad from doing his service to the Lord as he understood it.

Oh, how she loved him—as much as if he were her very own.

"He's growing remarkably," she said, making an effort to stand.

"Aren't we all?" Joe whispered softly. "You were wonderful last night."

Last night. It all came back in a flash. The fire . . . her fear, which dissolved into nothingness like a wisp of morning fog, in the face of Joe's greater fear . . . then his safe return . . . the look of victory on his face . . . and the night—so horrible and yet so wonderful—which brought them together closer to each other and to the Lord than they had ever been before.

"Wonderful?" Chris Beth smiled at her husband's compliment. "I guess we all were. I wonder how many people we tried to help. You mean they *all* will make it?"

Joe nodded. "A miracle. And, as to how many, I lost count. But together, Chrissy, we coped."

His eyes sought hers and her heart was too full to answer. It was enough that they understood each other. Yes, together they had coped.

"You two gonna talk all day or would you like t' partake of some vittles?" Mrs. Malone asked quietly from the door.

"Sourdough biscuits 'n honey ye be havin'!" O'Higgin promised. "Sure'n the coffee be a strong brew. Took Doc Wilson 'n Miss Vangie home, it did!"

Chris Beth tried unsuccessfully to smooth her hair, which had managed to come unbraided during the long dark night. Then, cautiously, she and Joe picked their way over sleeping bodies and followed O'Higgin and Mrs. Malone down the stairs.

"Th' good Lord only knows how many lives the four of you saved last night. Could've been a holocaust without Wilson and Vangie's doctorin' and comfortin' from the two o' you." Mrs. Malone poured coffee.

Chris took a bracing gulp. "We had help," she said, meaning it both ways.

Later, looking at the black, ghostlike statues of what only

hours before were beautiful green fir trees whose needles whispered a song, Chris Beth thought her heart would break. The trees were the beauty, the pride, the very livelihood of the settlement. But they were more than that to her. It was their song she remembered most—their soothing lullaby, the song that calmed her in time of crisis and whispered of eternity when earthly life tested her faith. Now the forest was silent. Maybe the gnarled, black branches could never sing again. "Oh, no!" she whispered.

"Now, now," Mrs. Malone said from behind her. "Nature has a way o' restorin' itself. You'll see." Then, shifting the subject, the practical woman said, "It's my drapes nature cain't restore. Just you come 'n look what that Irishman done with my drapes!"

Chris Beth looked, and what she saw hurt her almost as much as the sight of the dead forest. Mrs. Malone's green brocade drapes, her pride and joy, lay crumpled, watersoaked, and blood-stained on the floor of the front room. Obviously, having run out of blanket for wrapping those in shock or with their clothing burned off completely, O'Higgin had jerked down the draperies and put them to use.

"Oh, Mrs. Malone, I'm so sorry—" But Mrs. Malone turned and walked inside. Chris Beth knew the sign. It meant that the matter was closed. But for herself it was not. She and Vangie might have a plan . . .

November came with a bright-blue countenance. Little tributaries, fed by the autumn rains and laughing themselves right out of their banks, hurried to join the larger creeks and rivers. Thirst was quenched in the settlement—the old orchards to the south, the meadows to the north, and the tangled dogwood, laurel, manzanita, and firs which the fire had spared to the east and west. Why did so many people persist in calling autumn a season of sadness? Chris Beth wondered as she looked out the cabin window. "Even in its charred condition, the valley is filled with promise," she mused. "Nature's only sleeping . . . it's the seventh day of creation and God is resting."

"But not so with the rest of us!" Joe's voice startled her.

"I didn't know I spoke aloud."

"I'm glad. It gave your whereabouts away. And I've been wanting to talk with you—privately."

"Joe—" She would have pulled away, but his strong arms imprisoned her from behind. "Let go—there's so much to do. School will be opening in a month—you know that it's only because of the fire that they postponed the opening and—"

Joe laughed at her rushing words. *We know each other so well,* she thought dreamily. *He's aware that I talk too fast when I know what he's about to say. And I do know!*

"Do I have to act like a caveman? You know, grab you by the hair and drag you into a cave to teach you a lesson? Or do we start a family soon?"

"As soon as I learn how to knit."

"That will be forever," he moaned.

"Not on your life! Mrs. Malone's teaching me. Which reminds me, Joe—seriously, now—I need some yarn. Couldn't we go into Centerville tomorrow?"

"Oh, by all means! And with that promise, I will even release you—temporarily. That is, after a kiss?"

Chris Beth turned to give him a grateful hug. She did want to pick up some yarn. But she wanted to talk with the assayer too. . . .

Joe was right, Chris Beth realized, as the weeks passed. The settlers certainly were not resting. And, for that matter, neither was the Lord! He was greening up the meadows and opening the windows of heaven to let down exactly the right amount of rain—not enough to overflow the rivers, but just enough to furnish all the needs for next year's crops and to give O'Higgin just cause to predict (as he had earlier in the year) that sure to come was the most bountiful harvest ever. Even Brother Amos took to saying, "The lean times are past and fat times lie ahead if thou wilt but put thy trust in the Lord and thy hand to the plow!"

"Well, us folks're doin' both, wouldn't you say, Brother Joseph?" Nate Goldsmith asked at one of the roof-raisings where neighbors gathered to complete a new cabin.

"That I would," Joe agreed. "The school's coming along fine too, thanks to all the lumber donated by newcomers on the ledge. God surely must have intended their belt of timber to be spared."

"With equal thanks to them that hauled th' logs," Nate added significantly. "My team included. Y'knew the store-house was comin' along, too, what with Brother Amos supervisin' and all—say, best we be plannin' that thanksgivin' meetin' that the fires interrupted, huh? Guess I'll up 'n call a deacons' meetin' soon. This way we can give praise on the *real* Thanksgivin'!"

Thanksgiving Day dawned cobalt-blue—a day just right, the settlers agreed as they gathered in full force at Turn-Around Inn, for man and "all them over which he has dominion" to give praise to their Creator. Chris Beth had never been happier as she, Joe, Wilson, Vangie, and their combined families piled into the buggy and headed for the place so dear to their hearts: Turn-Around Inn, where miracles happened! And today would be no exception, she thought with a surge of joy. In fact, it well might be the day of the greatest miracle of all. Certainly she hugged the germ of one close to her heart. And she suspected that each member in the Craig-North party possessed one too. Never had she seen such secretiveness except at Christmastime.

The only touch of sadness she felt was the thought of Maggie Solomon. The news "Maggie's back" ran like wildfire over Centerville. "Yeah, stockin' drummer up 'n dumped 'er. Bitter pill fer Abe 'n Bertie t' swallow, sure enough." Chris Beth had walked away from such talk, but she wondered if the girl would have the courage to show up today.

"Are you all right?" Chris Beth realized guiltily that with

all the demands that other people had placed on her she had
had little time to devote to her sister. They had hardly had
time to discuss her good news.

Vangie laughed. "Never been better. You know pregnancy
always becomes me. Doubly so this time. I plan on twins, you
know—a dimpled, roly-poly frog-prince like little Mart and a
fairy princess like True!"

Turn-Around Inn, looking clean and inviting in its setting of
new-green meadows, loomed ahead. Young Wil whistled.
"Look at the crowd!" And then they were surrounded by their
loving family of friends.

O'Higgin's voice was in fine shape. The congregation,
following his strong lead, sang with more volume than ever.
And surely the tones were more mellow. "That's waken th'
dead forest," Mrs. Malone whispered to Chris Beth.

Chris Beth smiled and thought ahead to forming the choir
that O'Higgin had invited her to help lead. It would be good to
sing again—oh, so good. Aunt Mandy used to say in answer to
her questions as to why mockingbirds didn't sing in winter,
"They's busy storin' up love songs. But best remember, chile,
they's music in them silences between." Well, she had been
too busy herself this season to practice, too busy serving
others. Tomorrow's notes would be sweeter because of the
"rests."

"My message will be short," Joe said after the singing. "I
want to leave time for testimonials, sharing and real fellowship. Added to prayer, these are the basic ingredients for
preparing the heart for dining at the Lord's Table."

The testimonials were so warm and so obviously heartfelt
that Chris Beth was sure she cried throughout. The good
people praised Joe, Wilson, Vangie, and herself more than she
felt they deserved, but, oh, it was so wonderful to be loved and
appreciated!

Then came the sharing. "Mostly, folks it's a rehash of
what's been promised here afore—the buildin' stuff, man-
power, and offerin's that'll hold us together body 'n soul," Nate

summed up. "Still 'n all, it's pleasin' to us deacons that yer steadfast."

Well, now, there was a little more, the attitude of the crowd indicated. Newcomers came forward to rededicate their lives. A couple wanted to dedicate a child to the work of the Lord. And young Wil caused a few smiles and a lot of tears when he stood up tall, brushing at his cowlick, and declared. "I'd like to offer my tree fort to somebody who's been praying for one. I'm too big to use one anymore—and, besides, I've got the upper room here now. I'll even volunteer helpin' to tear it down."

At Vangie's signal, Chris Beth joined her, and the two of them walked toward the improvised altar at the fireplace. Chris Beth paused on the way to squeeze young Wil's hand and then helped her sister move the big package from its hiding place behind the sofa.

"Mrs. Malone!" Startled, Mrs. Malone went forward and, at their urging, opened the heavy wrapping paper from Mama's Christmas present. Velvet—beautiful blue velvet, yards and yards of it—fell into the woman's work-reddened hands.

"To replace your drapes," Vangie said softly. Then, for the first time, Chris Beth saw Mrs. Malone weep.

In the commotion of "oh's" and "ah's," the clearing of throats, and the chorus of blowing noses, Chris Beth was able to slip a large brown envelope onto the altar. Inside was a good sum of cash and a note written after she and Vangie had decided that the brooch had served its purpose—the breaking of one girl's heart and the mending of another. "My donation for roofing a new church," the note read, and there was no signature.

Joe spotted it soon afterward, opened it, and read it aloud. There was a great shout, much like that of the congregation when Joe had buried their worries at sea. And then something more! A little handful of men moved forward, and Chris Beth saw that they were Muslin City folk (only they had cabins now). The youngest man of the group turned to face the guests. "We're donating the piece of ground along the ledge for this new building," he said with clear diction. "And you can count on our lumber and our hands as well."

The second shout was greater than the first. When Chris Beth could hear above the hammering of her heart and force her eyes to focus, Chris Beth realized that yet another miracle was about to occur. Ordinarily, children of the settlement lining up to sing a little off-key song would be just a fitting finale to the worship service. But today the atmosphere was charged with excitement as Joe and then Wilson stepped out to meet the singing group.

> Jesus loves the little children,
> All the children of the world—

And there their voices stopped. There was pin-drop silence. And what the crowd saw next was unbelievable. As the children finished the little five-line song, Joe and Wilson pointed out a sight that their eyes had never seen before:

> Red and yellow, black and white,
> All are precious in His sight—
> Jesus loves the little children of the world!

Was that real *Indians* coming from between the blackened tree trunk? They asked each other. It had to be. That young buck looked familiar . . . maybe he was the one Wilson said had volunteered to help them through the winter—"them that could stomach wild sunflower-seed bread and camas-root cake." Yes, they had to be Indians—including a papoose!

Now, the "yellows," was understandable. Seeing as how they'd helped the Chinese and (*ahem!*), yes, the Chus *had* proved to be "above the average." But mercy sakes! Where *did* them "blacks" emerge from? Pretty brave of them, just standing there throughout, singing from that hill yonder. Good voices, too, mellow-like. All surprising—

And I'm the most surprised of all, Chris Beth marveled. *The vision's no longer a dream. It's happening here and now!*

Feeling Joe's gaze, Chris Beth let her eyes meet his. He gave her such a look of naked adoration that she felt her cheeks grown pink. *Oh, Joe,* her eyes signaled back, *I've let go of the past and put our future in the Lord's hands for safekeeping!*

Joe smiled, then stood as if for the benediction. "Thank You, Lord!" Chris Beth said fervently, not caring that her lips moved. "I asked for instant happiness, but You substituted lasting joy!"

Mrs. Malone tried to hurry into the kitchen, undoubtedly to make sure that her girls had laid the table out just right for the Thanksgiving Day feast. But Joe raised a hand to detain her.

"We've found wonderful ways of praising our Maker today, but there remains one more." Joe paused, seeming to make eye contact with every person in the large crowd. "It seems only fitting that we allow the time for opening our hearts and the doors of our church."

There were several *Amens.* Then Joe said slowly, "One d-day—" Chris Beth, noting his slight stammer, knew that he was about to take a giant step. The others seemed to sense it too. "One day," he continued, his voice gathering strength with each word, "*all* of God's children will be drawn together as He intended—red and yellow, black and white! Until then, let us draw closer to each other here. I invite anyone wishing to rededicate his life to come, or anyone wishing to make a profession of faith for the first time."

Olga Goldsmith's fingers moved softly over the keys of the old organ. "Just As I Am, Without One Plea—"

Then, except for the moving strains of the old hymn, there was a stunned silence. Surely all breathing had stopped at once. For, with eyes downcast and shoulders slumped forward as if in defeat, Maggie Solomon was slipping down the aisle—hoping, it seemed—to get past unnoticed.

There was a little stir as Joe welcomed the girl. Her voice was almost inaudible as she answered his gentle questions. Chris Beth, sitting so near to the front, was able to hear him tell Maggie that she no longer had anything to be ashamed of—that she could stand tall in her victory—and then he said, "I now offer you the right hand of Christian fellowship."

Maggie turned to face the congregation—or were they her enemies? The next few moments would tell. Chris Beth caught her breath as Vangie deliberately opened her eyes, stood her full height, and prepared to walk the short distance separating her from the other girl. Nobody else, she was certain, heard Vangie's whispered words. "This one's for *you*, Susanah," she said.

Maggie lifted her head almost in fear as Vangie approached. And then her eyes made contact with Vangie's. It wasn't much. Just a glance. And then a handclasp. But maybe it was enough to fan the little spark that had lain in the ashes of Maggie's troubled heart so long. Waiting. Just waiting for love to give it new life.

The crowd surged forward to shake hands with their newest member. Someone rang the great dinnerbell. Wolf gave out a tail-wagging kind of bark as somewhere a lark trilled. The very hills seemed to sing in their silence. And Chris Beth was sure that God in His heaven smiled as He saw His plan fulfilled.

"Bless this hoose!" O'Higgin boomed.

"House!" said Mrs. Mollie O'Higgin Malone.

Diary
of a
Loving Heart

Pioneer spirit—hale and hardy—
Ever seeing needs of others:
Though pioneer fingers gnarl with hardship,
Pioneer hands are helpful hands.
When a cabin's freshly wind-chinked,
Floored with puncheons, roofed with sky;
Ere the night falls, earnest effort
Will shingle out that patch of blue.
Coming with their bulging baskets,
Faces glowing in the hurry
Of the greetings and the work,
Happy children clapping, singing,
"London Bridge is Falling Down,"
Breezes blowing, wafting echoes
Of the ringing nails above;
Women talking food and quilting;
Girls—their eager thoughts of love.
Crimson sunset fades to darkness,
Sleepy cricket tunes his fiddle;
"Step up, gents, and choose your partners,
Form a ring and circle left!"

Contents

Preface

ONCE UPON A TIME, a hundred years ago, only Indian trails wound in and out of Oregon's mountain-ribbed valleys. Now, buses, automobiles, and logging trucks clog the beautifully-maintained highways. Most of the occupants of the automobiles are busy, progressive Oregonians or tourists who rest travel-weary eyes on the state's eternal green. But now and then, the descendants of those "in between" generations come back for ancient-recipe apple pie, venison roasts, or a start of sourdough. It is then that they listen and relive those lovely bygone days and, ever so briefly, hear the wail of distant fiddles mingled with laughter reduced to silence, above the whisper of the pines . . . gently, softly, weaving a magic spell. . . .

It is from those days that the series of pioneer-life stories in fertile valleys of the Oregon Country comes to lift your spirit, warm your heart, and renew your faith in the goodness of God who saw the first settlers through their strange and trying circumstances. *Diary of a Loving Heart*, a sequel to *Love is a Gentle Stranger* and *Love's Silent Song*, is a continuing saga of two vibrant and independent girls who came West to escape their pasts and seek new adventures. In their new home, they found the love of two fine men, a host of caring friends, and renewed their acquaintance with a caring God. But they found tragedy and conflict as well . . . until, in miraculous ways, they were able to resolve their problems and win against impossible odds. Those ways will surprise you!

Diary of a Loving Heart promises readers a new kind of courage, a new appreciation of beauty that celebrates life. With its reading, may you find a new appreciation of all that is lovely and a gentle reminder that the Almighty looks after His children!

June Masters Bacher

365

1

"Tempus Fugit"

⤳

MOCKINGLY, THE GRANDFATHER clock chimed as Chris Beth closed the bedroom door with a silent turn of the knob and stepped into the hall. She had grown to dread the clock's mellow song since Vangie had fallen ill. There had been a time when the two of them laughed like the carefree sisters they were at the 24-note tune the bells rang out just before striking the hour.

"What does it play, Wilson?" Vangie had asked her husband.

"*Tempus Fugit*," he said.

Vangie's voice, as golden as her hair, rose an octave higher as always when she was excited. "Speak English, Wilson!" she had demanded, and then to Chris Beth, "He loves teasing me with Latin!"

"Time Flies." Even then, five years ago, Wilson's voice had been sober. Being a doctor made him more aware, she supposed. Of time. Of life. And death. Now the translation tore at her heart, too.

Deliberately, Chris Beth waited until the great clock tolled its inevitable stroke of twelve, before walking into the living room of the North home. Noon. And somehow the old clock

367

knew. God had separated the darkness and light. But man had created an ingenious mechanism for marking equal periods of elapsing time and, in this case, housed the knowing instrument in a harmless-looking mahogany box. Frightened, she walked toward the front window to look out at the August rain.

"*Tempus Fugit!*" The grandfather clock ticked on. *Oh, Vangie . . . Wilson . . . Joe!*

Vangie would sleep only a short while even with the aid of the pain killer. When she awakened, she would be asking for Wilson. He would need a meal beforehand, just as he had needed the few short hours away from the confines of Vangie's room, her suffering, and the inevitable feel of death. All else was secondary—even his practice.

Hurriedly, Chris Beth set to work cutting thick slices from a loaf of graham bread. As she buttered it she tried to remember which of the three men preferred mustard to green tomato relish on their ham sandwiches. But even as her mind, numbed with loss of sleep, tried to concentrate on so small a matter, Young Wil's "Whoa!" said that he, Wilson, and Joe were back from Turn-Around Inn and lunch was not nearly ready.

Today it had taken Vangie longer than usual to doze. The medication did less and less good. Vangie had asked for her diary then, but unable to find strength to write, wanted to talk. Then, finding no strength for talking either, she cried. The crying hurt worst of all. Chris Beth's heart broke anew with each tear that coursed down the Dresden-china features of her sister's fragile, but nonetheless beautiful face. *Don't cry, Vangie . . . don't cry, darling. . . .* How many times had she, the older sister, whispered the words in their growing-up years? Vangie was afraid of storms. Vangie was afraid of the dark. Vangie was afraid of the wind . . . mice in the attic . . . the bears beneath her bed! Only this time, there was no way Chris Beth could bring reassurance. Death, the Grim Reaper, would not go away.

Busying her hands helped, Chris found. Purposefully, she set about peeling the last of the fall tomatoes. There would be no time for the fried potatoes Wilson, his always-hungry nephew, and her husband enjoyed. But coffee, strong coffee. They would need that.

"Horses are curried." How good to hear Young Wil's every-day comment. Chris Beth turned from the woodstove to look at the lanky youth. How like Wilson he looked, more like son than nephew—same dark eyes, broad shoulders, teasing man-ner. What concerned her was the 14-year-old's temperament, such a private person and yet so hard-loving. *What*, she asked herself as she asked God in her prayers over and over, *are these two men I love so much going to do without the woman they are going to lose? And what can Joe and I do to ease the pain?* Joe being a minister would help but—

Chris Beth was unaware that Young Wil had crossed the kitchen until he interrupted her thoughts with a wave of his hand in front of her eyes. "Yoo-hoo!"

"Sorry," she mumbled and moved into action again. "Want to set the table for me?"

"Anything to speed up production." Then, after a clatter of dishes, he asked, "How is she?"

Chris Beth concentrated on measuring coffee into the pot before asking softly, "Can't you bring yourself to call Vangie—well, something other than *she*?"

"Like what?" She didn't need to look up to know that the brown eyes had turned sullen and defiant.

"Try *Mother*. It would make her so happy—Aunt Vangie—even Vangie—"

"She's not my mother—or my real aunt—just my uncle's wife."

"I know, darling. But I am only your teacher, and the two of us have such a good understanding. I just wish—"

"*I* just wish *you'd* have married Uncle Wil!"

Chris Beth stared at him, stunned. She felt confused, her heart pumping wildly in her chest. Abruptly, he turned and stalked away.

When the boy mumbled something inaudible at the door, Chris Beth turned in hope of hearing his words. But to her amazement, Joe and Wilson were standing silently, watching the retreating figure. *How long had they been at the door? How much had they heard?*

"Oh, I didn't see you," she said too quickly. "Oh, the coffee!"

It was too late. The pot had boiled over. She grabbed at the handle, burning her fingers.

"Here, let me." Wilson took the sticky pot from her hand, poured out three cups, and set the granite vessel on the edge of the stove.

The brown liquid hissed on the hot stove, rolled into steaming droplets, and disappeared. But the odor of parched coffee filled the room. "I'm sorry," she murmured.

"No problem an open window can't handle," Joe said in the gentle manner she had come to expect of her husband. It won her heart and his congregation.

Returning to where Chris Beth stood, he smoothed the dark tendrils of her hair from her forehead and kissed her. "You are overtired, Chrissy. You must get some rest. You'll be needed even more later."

Joe's gentle words and the concerned look in his hazel eyes brought a semblance of order to her world. *I wish*, she thought fleetingly, *we were alone . . . that Joe would take me in his arms . . . that we were back to the way things used to be. I wish, oh! I wish, time did not fly. . . .*

But before the thought was so much as completed, the great clock chimed with warning and there was a small moan from Vangie's bedroom.

2
A Matter of Time

∽

MONDAY!

Only a week remained before Chris Beth would be returning to her teaching position. Vangie's illness had left no time for preparing her clothes, sorting through books, or talking with school board members about the possibility of adding another teacher. With all the newcomers, school enrollment had mushroomed. But clothes, books, and enrollment were not the main concern. Vangie had always kept Marty. . . .

"What," Chris Beth asked Joe over and over, "am I to do about the babies?"

And each time Joe laughed softly at her question. "They're hardly that any more—babies, that is."

Well, no. Hard as it was to believe, their Marty and Vangie and Wilson's Trumary were five years old. Marty had long since rebelled at their pet name of "Little Mart." With a jutting out of his round chin, which revealed the endearing dimple more than he knew, he declared himself a "big boy." The gesture hurt. He was growing too fast. And time was slipping away—without any more children. More than anything Chris Beth longed to bear Joe a child. But he has a son,

Mrs. Malone said. *No, a son of his very own—his "own seed,"
wasn't that what the Bible said?* Humph! Brother Joe wasn't
carin' none that his son was *grafted* onto the family tree. You
Craigs love Little Mart much as the parents he lost in the
flood. *Oh, that was true,* Chris Beth hastily agreed. *Still,* she
wondered, *why should Abraham's wife pray for a son and
God hear her prayers and not hear mine?*

"Not to worry!" the older woman assured her wisely. "Just
you wait'll you get to be Sarah's age!"

Chris Beth never talked about her barren condition with
Joe. He was so protective. So dear. So gentle. Joe was the kind
of husband who would feel the fault was within himself if he
sensed that Chris Beth were unhappy. Of course, she and
Vangie talked, but their conversations centered on Vangie's
despair, not her own. It seemed so unfair, Vangie lashed out,
when her only pregnancy by Wilson ended in miscarriage. Life
was unfair. Wilson was unfair for refusing to allow her to take
the risk of another pregnancy. Maybe even God was unfair! So
Chris Beth found herself reassuring her younger sister as her
dear friend Mollie Malone had reassured her. "Wait until
we're as old as Sarah!" Only Vangie wasn't amused. That
would be too late, Vangie said sadly with a sort of premonition
in her usually tinkling voice.

And how right she was. Even as the original pain of her loss
lessened, Vangie lamented the fact that Wilson was being
denied a man's "natural pride" in having a child of his "own
flesh and blood." Then, realizing what she had said, Vangie
clapped her hand over her mouth as she did in her childhood
when she had said something wrong. "Forgive me, Chrissy! At
least, True, is of *my* own body—oh, what *am* I saying? Those
words must make you feel worse."

Yes, considering the circumstances. But neither husband
seemed to care a fig! Wilson adored his fairy-princess daughter
and seemed to give no thought to her not being his own "flesh
and blood." And, of course, Joe idolized the orphaned Marty,
his "frog prince."

Maybe, Chris Beth found herself thinking, *it's better this way. There are going to be so many things we have to decide even now. And more children would only compound the problem for us all. . . .*

"You weren't going to cry today. You weren't going to *think*. Rest, that's what Wilson sent you home for," Joe said unexpectedly from the door.

Chris Beth walked gratefully into her husband's arms. "I know," she sobbed. "I know. It's just the sight of our cabin . . . the memories . . ."

Joe wiped a tear from the tip of her nose. ". . . And worrying about the future?"

At her nod, he ushered her toward the kitchen. "You're to sit down and look out the window. See? It's stopped raining. I'll heat you some bath water, take Marty with me and—"

I'll get in the tub for one mighty long bath. Some soap would be nice—the kind with heliotrope in it like the last batch I made for Vangie and myself. She would nap briefly for the very first time in months. Then maybe, just maybe, Marty would rest . . . and she and Joe could steal a few precious moments all to themselves . . . he would hold her tight, kiss her lightly, then harder. . . .

Between the line-dried, lavender-scented sheets, Chris Beth drifted into what should have been a blissful sleep. Instead, she dreamed wildly that she, Joe, Vangie, and Wilson were trying to synchronize their clocks. Through a dark layer of slumber, she heard Joe call across the creek to announce the time by the tiny, hand-carved cuckoo clock above their kitchen table. She ran into the bedroom to set the alarm clock at his count of, "One, two, three!" But, even as the cuckoo clock hiccupped the time, there came the mellow chime of the huge grandfather clock in the Norths' Big House playing its haunting 24-note tune ahead of the cabin clocks. Frantically, the two of them ran back and forth, adjusting the hand backward and forward—all the while knowing that the pendulum of the grandfather clock was swinging faster . . . faster . . . *faster!*

With a little cry, she awoke. Someone had rapped sharply at the door.

3
Like the Fragment
of a Dream

∼ᴥ

YOUNG WIL, white-faced and breathless from running, talked rapidly. "*Come* . . . come with me . . . please. *She*—I mean Vangie's worse—"

If the boy said more, Chris Beth failed to hear. With the kind of automatic responses born of fear, she dressed, followed Young Wil across the footlog, and entered the back door of the great, white farmhouse. Wilson, looking haggard and older than a man under thirty should, left Vangie's bedroom to meet them in the hall.

"I'm so tired," he said, swaying slightly on his feet. The way his hand crossed his face tore at Chris Beth's heart. The gesture meant to convey fatigue. But it conveyed more. The sensitive hand that had delivered babies, set limbs, and done delicate surgery, when more practiced physicians might have given up, conveyed grief—the kind of grief a strong man feels and dares not show.

I'm grieving with you, her heart cried out. *And yet neither of us can let go and comfort each other the way we should. We're afraid we will fall apart completely . . . be found out*

*by others . . . or, worse, by ourselves. Must we always be so
stoical because others think we are brave?*

But, with professional control, Wilson straightened. "Did
you get any rest?"

"A little," Chris Beth said. "Enough to talk with Vangie if
that's what she wants—and you think it's all right."

"Go on in. She wants to talk—alone," Wilson looked at
Young Wil meaningfully. A look of relief passed over the boy's
face. He hurried out the back door leaving Chris Beth and
Wilson alone.

For just a moment neither of them moved. It would be hard,
Chris Beth thought in some far-off corner of her mind, to
describe the minuteness of that moment. In a sense, it seemed
even less than the second between the *tick*-to-*tock* of the
grandfather clock in its shadowy corner. But, in a greater
sense, that moment's time was an eternity when soul and
body were one.

How did it happen? When did it begin—or end? Or did it
happen at all? Could it be the fragment of some dream that
neither of them could remember? The mind could not be
trusted and neither could the heart when the body was so
fatigued, the emotions so drained, and grief—so long denied—
swept down all defenses.

Wilson must have moved toward her, for when his arms
reached out she walked into them—without seeming to walk
at all. Like a puppet on a string. With no will of her own. No
voice. No feelings. And there they were—two heartbroken
figures drawn together and suspended by the magnet of grief
they were powerless to control, unable even to put feelings
into words that might have helped.

Then, just as quickly as her brother-in-law had embraced,
he let her go. The *tock* of the second had ended, but Chris Beth
knew that she had caught a rare glimpse of Wilson. He needed
comfort and reassurance just as much as the patients who
came to him. The sad difference was that Wilson refused all
balm, ointments, and poultices of concern. And nobody—

except for herself in this rare moment—realized that man and doctor were at points very far apart.

The clock ticked on as Wilson commented, "A pendulum's the most restless thing in the world. It no sooner gets to one side than it turns around and goes the other."

Chris Beth nodded mutely. *And all the springs, sprockets, weights, and chains reassemble themselves. Time flies. And life goes on. . . .*

"Try to get some rest, Wilson." With that, she turned and walked into her sister's room.

4

"It Is Finished!"

VANGIE'S GOLDEN HAIR lay spread out like an open fan on the rumpled lace-edged pillow slip. The flawless skin, which yesterday had looked like exquisite, blue-veined marble, no longer looked white. There was a tinge of yellow in the pallor today. And the kind of frightening serenity that said her suffering had ended. There was no movement except for one lone tear which had escaped the closed eyelids and slid slowly downward. *In the same way,* Chris Beth thought sadly, *my darling sister is slipping to the end.*

Sensing her presence, Vangie whispered weakly, "Don't let me be afraid, Chrissy."

Chris Beth knelt beside the bed and took the cold fingers in her hands. "There's no need to be frightened, darling."

It was true. Vangie had given her heart to the Lord long ago. A fierce, frightened child—victim of a "hell-fire and damnation" father—she had learned to love God in a new way here in the Oregon Country. How often she had said, "I'm not afraid of dying, Chrissy. It's *death* I hate!"

"Remember how I used to be so afraid—" Vangie paused to cough but resumed talking when the spasm passed. "—so

377

afraid of everything? Thunder, the devil, bad dreams—and *him*?"

Vangie's father. Chris Beth's stepfather. "I remember, Vangie." Chris Beth tried to keep her voice unemotional. "But you're not afraid now—"

The wide, violet eyes opened. "Except that there won't be time to talk."

"There will be time," Chris Beth said with a certainty she did not feel. Then, massaging the almost transparent fingers as if to sustain life, she added soothingly, "Just 'begin at the beginning and stop at the end,' like in *Alice in Wonderland*."

There was a flicker of a smile. "I was scared of childbirth, too."

"But you made it!"

"*We* made it—you, Wilson, and I. Remember?"

Chris Beth forced a small laugh. "I'm not likely to forget."

Vangie seemed to breathe for the first time. "That makes True part yours, Chrissy—you'll look after her—you and Wilson?"

"How could you ask, Vangie? True's a part of us all—and a part of Joe as well. Let's talk about what's troubling you."

It was important that Vangie conserve her energy. And, yes, it seemed important, too, that the conversation turn to something which had no connection with the circumstances of True's birth. This was no time to remember the painful past. She had long since forgiven her younger sister's folly. It no longer hurt that Vangie's precious little daughter belonged to Jonathan Blake, Chris Beth's one-time fiance.

"Vangie?" she prompted when the silence became prolonged.

Vangie opened her mouth to speak and was seized by another spasm of coughing. Each cough was like a knife in Chris Beth's heart.

"Some day—some day there will be a way to conquer this disease," Chris Beth whispered, as she tried to control the coughing by shielding her sister's fragile body with her own. "Wilson has promised!"

When Vangie spoke again, her voice was weaker. What she had to say must be said quickly. Panicky, Chris fought between calling Wilson and waiting to hear what Vangie needed to say privately.

Seeming to sense the thought, Vangie gripped Chris Beth's hands with all her strength. The grasp was like that of a baby bird which, knowing it is futile, clutches at the straw of a wind-rocked nest.

"*Stay*—I need you—not them—" she gasped.

There was no decision to make. Vangie's needs came first. "Relax, darling. I am here."

"It is finished!"

Vangie closed her eyes. Chris Beth waited. The fragile form under the light cover seemed motionless. But there was more to say! *Dear God, not yet. . . .*

"Vangie!"

"It is finished—the diary." The words were no more than a whisper.

Chris Beth inhaled gratefully. "Is *that* all?" She managed a light laugh which sounded as forced as it was.

The younger girl tried to lift her head then fell back weakly. "Is that *all*? Chrissy—it's everything—it's for you—you alone . . . read . . . do it . . . *for me*. . . ."

The weak breathing became labored. When Chris Beth asked if she should send for the others, there was no reply. Dropping the limp hands quickly, she fled in search of Wilson.

Vangie's words were forgotten in the wave of grief that spread over her. Overcome by near-hysteria, Chris Beth was unable to see the tall figure at the door. When strong hands grasped her arms, making her a prisoner, she tried to wrench away.

"Wilson! I have to find Wilson!"

"Get hold of yourself, Chris Beth!" Wilson's voice. Wilson's strong hands. But not Wilson the man . . . Vangie's husband . . . the best friend of her husband. Wilson the *doctor*!

As professionally as if he were calming a distraught child

who feared an iodine swab on a small cut, Wilson said, "You will be all right."

How dare he talk down to her! How *could* she have been attracted to this heartless, arrogant, domineering man before she met Joe—before Vangie followed her out West? Wildly, she searched for words that could wound as she was wounded. Her grief *must* find expression.

"I'll hate you all my life for this!"

"Probably," he said, dropping his hands from her arms and hurrying into Vangie's room. But Chris Beth was too buried in her suffering to catch the pain in his voice.

Slowly, the world righted itself. Somewhere a rooster crowed. That meant "company coming," Mrs. Malone said. And high above her own little world there was the unmistakable frost-remembered cry of wild geese. Canadian honkers seeking warmer climes. That meant winter. Then, from closer at hand, there came the carefree tinkle of childish laughter. Never mind the "signs" or the seasons. Life went on forever, like the creek the children loved, or the river that hugged the valley.

With a calm that surprised her, Chris Beth joined Wilson at Vangie's bedside. Wilson looked up. His face was stricken. But there was welcome in his brown eyes. The moment in the hall, like the one preceding it, would never be forgotten—completely—by either of them. But both encounters would be stored away, never to be shared, never to be reviewed or even understood. Raw emotions. Revealing. But past.

"She's gone, Chrissy."

"I know," Chris Beth said.

And then the others were all there. Later, she was to remember that Joe's arm was around her shoulder, that Marty clung tightly to her hand, and that Young Wil, with tears streaming down his face unchecked, went quietly to stand beside his uncle.

Wilson scooped True up and let her look directly into her mother's face. Like a tintype picture the family stood there, the silence unbroken.

"Does my mommy hurt worse, Daddy?" True whispered at last.

Wilson smoothed back the golden curls and kissed the tiny Vangie-in-miniature. "Not now, darling," he said softly. "Not ever again."

"Is she up in heaven with God?"

"She's there—or on her way." Chris Beth heard the catch in Wilson's voice and regretted with all her heart the harsh words she had spoken in her helplessness and pain.

"Did you see the angels, Daddy, when they came for Mommy?"

There was silence. *Why, he can't answer,* Chris Beth realized suddenly. *Not that he is unable to find the words but that he cannot find the voice.*

She knew the words, too. But dare she try to speak? The next moment would leave a lasting impression with the small children. She looked pleadingly at Joe, but he seemed unable to respond. But, of course! Her husband's slight stammer would return as always during stress. True's great violet eyes were on Wilson's face. And Chris Beth realized that Marty clung even harder to her hand. A slight whimper would open the floodgates. *Oh, dear God, for strength!*

"Very few people ever see angels, I guess. But I'll bet your daddy and Aunt Chrissy felt them hovering close." Young Wil spoke loudly and clearly.

"That we did, darling," Chris Beth agreed, finding her asked-for strength. "That we did."

She turned away then, no longer able to keep her strange emotions tethered. The months of her sister's illness had stratified her feelings, layering the first concern with shock, then overlaying the combination with pain, fatigue, and fear. Later came confusion, hysteria, bitterness, and anger, followed by today's sorrow which solidified all layers. And yet, it was Young Wil who found the strength for the greatest hour of need—a strength, which like the river, would sustain them all. Chris Beth felt pride, then a sad-sweet bud of acceptance.

"We will pray now," Joe said without the hint of a slur in

his speech. Silently, he knelt beside the bed. The others, as was their custom, joined hands and waited for his words.

"Lord," Joe spoke softly but audibly above the chiming of the great hall clock tolling out the fourth hour that memorable August afternoon. "Lord, there is no need to explain our pain to You. Each time we lose a loved one, we get a better idea of what it was like for You to lose Your Son. But we praise You for the hope that sacrifice cost. And we ask that, through that hope, our pain will ease. Keep Vangie close in spirit— living, laughing, and moving among us—until we are reunited. Don't let us lose our way! Amen."

Joe rose and placed a hand to Chris Beth's elbow, ushering her quietly out of the room. Marty hung back, wanting to remain with True, his constant companion. But Young Wil, who was following the Craigs, leaned down to take the small hand.

"We have lots of work to do, fellow! How would you like to ride over to Turn-Around Inn—and maybe into Centerville?"

Marty's eyes lit up and his mouth made a perfect "O." The older boy was barely able to close a silencing hand over the pursed lips in time to stop the squeal of glee. A horseback ride . . . a peppermint . . . life went on. . . .

Chris Beth hurried toward the stove. Neighbors would be coming. They would need coffee. And she needed the activity. Wilson would not prolong True's good-bye to her mother. Joe would help him then with what needed doing before the others came. *Don't think . . . move . . . hurry. . . .*

"Are you all right, honey?" Chris Beth jumped at the sudden sound. She had gone into action automatically as it seemed she had been compelled to do all her life. In that reflex, she had actually forgotten the existence of her husband and son.

"I'm fine—really, I am—oh, Joe! I appreciate you so much."

"And I appreciate you, God knows!" The words, torn from him, were almost a groan. "I was thinking in there—I—I don't know what I would do—"

When Joe stopped, Chris Beth supplied the words because they were hers, too. "Without me? I know. I feel the same."

Was it strange that the two of them should embrace in the house so recently visited by death's angel? Chris Beth did not find it so. She was feeling a kind of numbness. The pain would return and have to be dealt with. But for now, her great loss had served to remind her what a precious gift from God life was. Vangie had learned that through her suffering. That undoubtedly accounted for the painfully-scribbled diary she insisted be propped up in bed to write in until the last. Chris Beth would look for it—in time . . . but for now, she must leave her husband's loving arms and be ready for the hours ahead. She pulled away regretfully.

Chris Beth removed the pound cake from the cupboard. Still nice and moist. *Better,* she thought, *than any store-bought cake at the bakeries back home.* She sliced it, then remembered that she probably looked a mess. She and Vangie always made a point of "staying beautiful here on the frontier," as Vangie had phrased it. Certainly, today was to be no exception. Vangie would want all their practices to go on.

Laying down the knife, Chris Beth crossed the kitchen to look at herself in the mirror above the sideboard. But she was unable to see in the gathering darkness. Best light the lamps . . . *keep busy, keep busy* . . . and brush her hair.

The reflection she saw, in the glow of lamplight, was reassuring. Her dark, straight-browed countenance was no match for Vangie's golden fragility. But it stood up better under stress. There were no purple shadows to reveal her loss of sleep. Even her heavily-fringed eyelids carried no hint of pink to tell the world how many tears she had shed. *Brush, brush, brush . . . one hundred strokes makes the hair glossy. Braid, swirl upward, secure with a comb—maybe letting a tendril or so escape—*

Chris Beth was suddenly aware of a tug on her long skirt. It was such a gentle tug that she wondered how long it had gone unnoticed.

"Oh, True—darling," she murmured leaning down to kiss

her fair-haired niece. "Aunt Chrissy didn't know you were here."

"I didn't want you to know. I just wanted to watch. Your hair's so *be-U-tiful!* Why do you and Mommy look different?"

"Well, for one thing, we have different fathers," Chris Beth answered, being careful to use present tense as the child did.

True's golden head bobbed in understanding. "Like me and Marty."

"Sort of, yes."

True seemed about to say something then changed her mind. Instead, she drew a long, shuddering breath. Surely she would break into tears and that would be better. Wouldn't it? But there were no tears, just words.

"Do you want me to set the table? Mommy lets me help."

Chris Beth was uncertain whether to be relieved or disappointed. Maybe if they could have cried together . . . but she would go along with whatever True wanted. They would feel their way together.

"I *do* need help. There will be lots of people—coming for the wake. Do you know what a wake is?" Chris Beth asked gently.

Again the bobbing of the little head. "Daddy told me. It's lots of friends. To keep Mommy company. He's gonna let me light the candles. Are these the right cups, Aunt Chrissy?"

Holding back the tears, Chris Beth set out as many cups as she was able to find. Joe would need to add hers to the number as soon as he found time to make a trip to the cabin.

"Marty will be back soon—he's gone to tell the others—to ask them to come—" Chris Beth found herself stumbling for words for the first time with True. Wise for her age, the child would suspect. "You and he can play then, like always," she tried to sound more natural.

"No," True said soberly. "I can help you get Mommy ready. Daddy told me I could."

Something akin to anger flared in Chris Beth again. *How dare Wilson expose a five-year-old to this! Oh, there are so*

many things to be set straight! But this is not the time. I must
think of True only.

Outside, the air turned chill. Early autumn mists turned to
a drizzle and Chris Beth was grateful to see that Joe had laid
the first fire of the season in the fireplace.

"Shall we light it now, True?" she asked, noting that the
child's tiny face was pressed against the window, the little
button nose flattened comically against the cold pane.

True blew her breath against the glass and wiped it away
with her right forefinger. "You light it. I'm watching."

Watching for Young Wil and Marty, most likely. And they
should be back. She stooped to light the fire, then watched in
momentary fascination as the hot blue flames cooled to
yellow. *If only this were a normal evening—*

Resolutely, she put aside the thought. There was work to
be done, she reminded herself firmly. First, though, she had
to try to unveil little True's thoughts . . . break down the
barriers . . . become a new family. . . .

"Come and warm your hands, honey," she coaxed. "The
fire's so pretty. One of these nights soon we'll pop corn—"

True's finger traced a wide, wet circle on the glass before she
answered. "It won't be the same."

"No," Chris Beth said slowly, wondering what more to say.
One did not deal with this child with vague words intended to
divert her attention. Like Vangie in appearance, True was
more like Chris Beth in her behavioral patterns. They thought
alike and hurt alike, but there was a toughness of moral fiber
inside them that demanded the truth.

Suddenly, True's hand dropped to her side. Her back went
rigid as she strained forward to peer into the darkness.
"They're here," she whispered. "Oh, Aunt Chrissy, they've
come back!"

Chris Beth hurried to the window. The snort of a horse sent
a wave of relief over her being.

"Sure enough, they have!" she said with a little cry of joy.
"Oh, how good to have Marty and Young Wil home safely.
Let's go meet them."

She reached to take True's hand, but the child drew back. The great blue eyes were purple by the glow of the firelight— purple and filled with despair. An enormous tear rolled down the doll-like face.

"I wasn't waiting for *them*. I—I'm watching for the angels— to bring my mommy back."

"Oh, my darling," Chris Beth said softly, kneeling down beside the tiny figure. "I know you're hurting. I know— because I hurt, too."

"I don't hurt! I—I—" But the defiant little words were drowned out by convulsive sobs. "Oh, Aunt Chrissy—"

Chris Beth gathered her close. "Cry, darling. It's all right to cry—we'll cry together!"

5
The "Second Day" Dress

 ✎

NEIGHBORS CAME, bringing food and consolation. Chris Beth went through with it all in a white haze, aware of subdued voices, busy hands, and the sound of her own voice asking questions, answering them, even giving directions at times, yet knowing all the while that she was lying in the lap of a great pain—so great that it would blot out all detailed memory.

Faces she loved floated in and out . . . Joe, gentle and caring . . . Wilson, solemn and withdrawn . . . Young Wil, youthfully masterful . . . True, watchful, waiting . . . Marty, uncertain . . . and the countless settlers, supporting and loving, at their best in time of crisis.

Only a few incidents stood out before the funeral—Mrs. Malone's arrival, the "second day" dress, and little True's "getting Mommy ready."

Mollie O'Higgin Malone, the beloved friend who had taken her in as a stranger and welcomed Vangie—accepting her out-of-wedlock "condition" when others whispered unthinkable words—was her usual no-nonsense, efficient self.

"Let the horses browse, O'Higgin," Mrs. Malone said to her

husband. "I declare that Irishman gets more helpless with
ev'ry passing day!" she added good-naturedly, embracing
Chris Beth as she spoke.

Chris Beth felt herself smile through her tears. It was good
to be drawn close to the broad bosom, to be loved and treated
ever so briefly like a child herself, and to inhale the "gingerbread sweetness" of Mrs. Malone, who had mothered her from
the moment they met.

But the older woman did not prolong the greeting. "Now
then," she said with practicality, "the men'll take care of the
grave and all. Let's us women get Vangie ready."

True's little ears, from wherever she was standing, picked
up the words. "I'm going to help," she said, drawing herself up
to her five-year-old height as soon as she stood beside Chris
Beth.

"Well, let's see—" Mrs. Malone drummed on her chin with
three fingers and hesitated, her faded eyes seeking Chris
Beth's. At Chris Beth's nod, the older woman added, "I reckon
as how there's a-plenty you can do."

"I reckon so," the child said solemnly.

Looking back on the situation, Chris Beth wondered later if
she herself could have borne up as she did without the serenity
of the older woman and the courage of the little child.

"I'll wash your face, Mommy," True whispered to Vangie,
"but Aunt Chrissy'll do your hair. She knows how better
'cause she used to do it when you were little like me—"

As she worked gently, True kept humming a familiar tune.
Chris Beth tried to identify it. Remembering seemed important.

"Brahms' 'Lullaby'!" she said aloud in sudden recognition.

Little True smiled then for the first time. "Mommy sings it
to the bees. Remember?"

Present tense again! Chris Beth turned away to stem the
flow of fresh tears. *Memories . . . bittersweet to me, the
adult . . . but real, as yet, for her, the child.*

Even as she fussed with Vangie's flaxen tresses, fluffing soft
curls about the temples and forehead the way she liked, Chris

Beth found herself wondering: *How can I bring the two worlds together for her without letting them collide? How supportive will Wilson be in this—and, for that matter, with Young Wil? What's to become of him?*

Young Wil! Remembering his words, she stopped short: "I just wish *you'd* married Uncle Wil!" Ideas died hard with the boy.

True broke the silence in the room. "Are you stuck, Aunt Chrissy? It goes like this." And, taking the comb from Chris Beth's hand, she twisted a strand of her mother's hair around her small finger and pressed it close to the cheek—exactly where it should have been.

The two of them had been so engrossed that neither saw Mrs. Malone remove the top from a giant box and lay its contents at the foot of the bed. True, who was first to notice, gave a little gasp of delight.

"Oh, it's for Mommy, her right color, but—I wish she could've seen it—just once."

"She did, little darlin', she seen it just once. It was your mother's weddin' dress!"

Then, as they arranged the shimmering folds to cover the thinness of Vangie's wasted body, Mrs. Malone told True the beautiful story of the dress. It had belonged to herself, she said. 'Twas her "second day" dress, the custom of the time being that a bride must wear a new gown on the second day of her honeymoon. Vangie had borrowed it for her wedding trip. Why shouldn't she borrow it for this, the best trip of all? Wouldn't True agree? True would. Mrs. Malone told the whole story—except the part about the brooch. That part belonged to Chris Beth. Some day—maybe—it would belong to True also.

The story ended. Then, to the surprise of the two women, the golden head of the little child drooped wearily to her mother's bosom, nestling among the blue ruffles, where the flashing sapphire-and-pearl pin had nestled on her wedding day, and she slept.

The rest of the scenario, like that preceding it, went back into the white haze of Chris Beth's memory.

The black funeral carriage came from Centerville to bear Vangie's body to the newly staked out cemetery plot on the knoll east of the new church. There was rain—not heavy, just enough to gray the skies and dampen the dust so that it stuck to the wheels of the long line of wagons and buggies in the funeral procession.

For the first time, Chris Beth hated the rain. It seemed so wrong for a funeral, especially Vangie's. No, maybe it wasn't wrong at all. What kind of day *would* be right? Rain was too depressing. But sunshine would have been a mockery. . . .

Joe took complete charge of the service. Chris Beth marveled at his composure—not a hint of a stutter, not a quaver of the voice. She must tell Joe again, as she had so often in the past, what a comfort he was. And what a minister, husband, and father! It seemed only fitting that he should "stand up" with Wilson. After all, the two best friends had "stood up" together for the double wedding. Could there be such a thing as a "best man" at a funeral? she wondered foolishly through the colorless maze of her controlled grief.

Thoughtfully, the settlers turned away when the services ended, some going home and others returning to the North home to clear away any painful reminders and prepare the evening meal. Mrs. Malone and O'Higgin had to get back to Turn-Around Inn, thriving since dreams of the stagecoach link-up between California and Oregon had come to pass. But couldn't the "babies" go with them? Marty, always shy, clung to Chris Beth's skirt while True's violet eyes betrayed the feelings beneath the calm. *Any minute now*, the expressive eyes said, *the angels may come for another one of the people I love!*

"Another time," Chris Beth suggested significantly.

Mrs. Malone nodded with understanding. "But I'll be over. Meanwhile, keep a weather-eye cocked on Wilson. He's too tranquil-like."

"I don't know that I can do much for him, though," Chris Beth said.

Mrs. Malone turned to look directly into her face. "You're the only one who can."

When all had left but family, Wilson said to Joe, "Will you take the others home? I'd like to be left alone a little while."

Chris Beth hesitated, but Joe took her hand. "He must work his way through his grief. It will take time," he said softly.

When the children were in the buggy, Joe came to Chris Beth's side to help her step up. When she hesitated again, he said, "It's best this way. We must leave him, Chrissy."

Yes, it was best, she supposed, but she was unable to ride away without looking back over her shoulder. What she saw hurt her worse than any of the months, weeks, days, and hours leading up to the single moment. Wilson—the laughing, carefree, teasing Wilson of old—stood alone. A solitary figure . . . beside the new mound . . . braced defensively against the chilling rain. . . .

"Turn away, Chrissy," Joe begged softly so that the children would not hear. "We have to look forward."

In a moment, yes, she would look forward. But it was too soon. There had to be some hope back there. Chris Beth, her heart breaking inside her, forced her tear-filled eyes to travel up from the sod to where the spire of the new church pointed heavenward. Then she turned to look forward with Joe.

Mellow light flowed from every downstairs window of the Big House. *I will take comfort in the small things*, Chris Beth thought, *and all they symbolize. . . .*

When Wilson came home, she longed to rush to meet him and offer words of comfort. But there was an invisible wall between them—one that neither of them seemed able to understand. The loss should have brought them closer together. Time . . . it would take time, Joe said.

"Can I get you anything—food—?" Meaningless words.

"Nothing, Chrissy." Wilson turned toward her, an unreadable expression in his weary face. "Just look after True—and excuse me to the others."

With that, he walked to the door of Vangie's bedroom. For a moment, she supposed he would enter. Instead, he pulled the door closed gently but firmly and, shoulders erect, walked up the curving stairs.

It had been a good marriage, approaching the ideal in Chris Beth's mind—almost, she sometimes thought, enviable. To Vangie, the dreamer, it had been a storybook romance. Just what it was to Wilson was difficult to tell. He hovered over Vangie, caring for her as one cares for a precious possession that breaks easily, but there was a part of Wilson he seldom revealed—a part unknown to light-hearted Vangie.

What*ever* the marriage was to him, it was over. Finished. Like Vangie's diary. . . .

6
A Matter
of the Heart

❧

THE FUNERAL had occurred on Wednesday. On Thursday morning, long before dawn, Chris Beth sat at the kitchen table of the Big House alone, drinking coffee and making mental lists of all that must be done. Urgent. As soon as possible. And sometime. The "urgent" list meant school which was only four days away and topping it were the questions: *Who will care for Marty and True, and what about Young Wil who's ready for high school?*

Rain stomped against the roof. A branch from the giant fir tree scraped its thumbnails on an upstairs window. Chris Beth shivered and tried to shake off her depression. She had needed the privacy the early-rising promised, but she did not need the loneliness. And what was *that*? A whistle? At this time of day?

Sitting erect, she listened. The whistling grew more distinct, coming so close she was able to make out a tune. "My bonnie lies over the ocean," a great voice suddenly boomed.

O'Higgin! Chris Beth could imagine the crinkles of a smile around the merry blue eyes. Sometimes she wondered if everyone who lived in Ireland could be this cheerful and decided it was impossible.

Hurriedly, she unlocked the front door and, without lighting a lamp in the front room, motioned the ruddy-faced man
into the kitchen.

"The others are sleeping," Chris Beth cautioned after a
whispered greeting. Then, forcing a smile, she offered coffee.

"Sure'n 'twould be t'my likin', lass." The red-bearded face
wreathed in a twinkling smile, O'Higgin removed his plaid
jacket, shook off the droplets of rain, and sat down backward
on a kitchen chair with his massive arms along the back of it.
" 'Tis news I've brought—straught—?"

"*Straight,*" Chris Beth supplied as his "Mollie wife" would
have done. She felt her depression turning to curiosity.

"Aye! Straight from hisself, the president of our board."

"Nate Goldsmith? But at this hour—?"

"Emergency meetin' it was. And the coffee, be it hot?"

Murmuring an apology, Chris Beth poured her self-described
"gospel truth" friend a cup of his favorite brew. There could
be no doubt about the meeting, but what could have been so
important? Of course, one could expect anything in this
strange, but wonderful, settlement!

Chris Beth concentrated on the little puddle of water made
by O'Higgin's jacket he'd tossed carelessly on the floor. If Mrs.
Malone were here—

Deliberately, O'Higgin stirred his coffee, sampled it, and let
out an "Ah-h-h-h!" of satisfaction, before breaking the news.
Circumstances of the morning forgotten, Chris Beth felt a stir
of excitement.

"O'Higgin?" she prompted.

"Ah, yes, th' object of my call! Come Monday, ye be gettin'
the help y'er needin' at school."

Chris Beth set her Spode cup down with a clatter. "You
mean—you mean—" she said incredulously, "another
teacher?"

"Th' same lass. And now me Mollie Girl'll be wantin' a hand
at the inn. 'Tis best I be goin' before we waken th' family."

"A little late, old-timer," Wilson spoke from the door.

The two men shook hands. There was no mention of

Vangie's death or the funeral. Condolences were offered yesterday. And, while tears might be shed in secret, on the surface life in the valley went on.

"'Twas news I brought," the Irishman said.

"I heard." No more and no less. Wilson helped O'Higgin with his jacket, shook his hand again, and sat down in the chair he vacated. Chris Beth followed their guest to the entrance, thanked him warmly, and closed the door behind his retreating figure before realizing she'd forgotten to ask if the new teacher would be a man or a woman.

Wilson had poured two cups of coffee when she returned to the table.

"Join me," he said quietly.

"I've had more than my ration," Chris Beth began. Then, seeing the glaze of sleeplessness in his eyes, she sat down knowing that he wanted to talk to her alone.

"What is it, Wilson?" she asked, hoping they could have a few quick exchanges of words before the others came downstairs.

The tired brown eyes met hers with appreciation. "We have to decide about the future," he said simply.

Yes, heading her list was the future of the children. "Very true," she said slowly, stirring the coffee to which she'd forgotten to add sugar and cream. "I've been thinking about them—"

"Them? I mean *us.* Joe and me . . . you and me . . . the best of friends . . ."

Chris Beth felt a slow flush creep to her face. Her heart pumped against her ribs and it was difficult to breathe. The rain seemed to slow to a stop. Even the hiss of the black kettle softened to a sigh. The world was hushed around them. And for an impossible moment she and Wilson were back in the forest, young and carefree, crushing colored leaves beneath their feet . . . before they became family. . . .

Love was stronger than death. Vangie's absence couldn't erase that. Then, because she was frightened and surprised by her own doubts, her words came out harshly.

"*Friends!* Don't we mean more than that to you? We're a *family!*"

A look of surprise crossed Wilson's face, followed by hurt, then his eyes narrowed and he looked at her with something akin to mockery. At last he shook his head as if in disbelief.

"How is it that even under conditions like this," he asked in a flat, emotionless voice, "you manage to misinterpret every word I say?"

"I—I—" Chris Beth began in hot denial. Then, ashamed and embarrassed, she spread her hands out in despair. Wilson was right. She had always read more into his words than was there.

Whatever his next words would be she deserved them. Averting her eyes, she waited.

"Your coffee's cold," he said suddenly. When she would have risen from the table, he pushed her down gently. Then, he walked to the side table, rinsed her cup in the basin of water, poured it full of coffee, and refilled his own cup.

Situation normal. Everything under control. He was back to the Wilson of old. Vangie might never have existed in his life. And she, Chris Beth, was reverting right back with him. Almost quarreling . . . and over what?

But when he spoke again, he was the Wilson of this day—a young doctor, bewildered, widower, wondering how to pick up the pieces of his life.

"Will you and Joe move in with us?" he asked matter-of-factly, as if continuing a conversation.

Chris Beth measured sugar into a spoon, leveling it as if each grain counted. "I don't know," she answered, striving for his tone of voice. "I haven't talked it over with Joe."

"I talked it over with Vangie. She was going to write it all down for you—" His voice trailed off. Chris Beth waited for him to continue. Instead, he dropped his head into his hands with a slight moan.

Compassion washed over her. *Oh, Wilson! Forgive me*, her heart cried out. *I've let you down in your hour of need . . . let's start over. . . .*

Aloud she said, "It does seem practical. This is home to True and Young Wil. Home to Joe, Marty and me—and we all need each other—"

Wilson raised his head but did not meet her eyes. "Thank you, Chrissy," he said simply. "I'll make it as pleasant for you as I can. Even promise," he said, struggling for lightness, "not to bring in a new Ma!"

When Chris Beth gave a start, Wilson managed a little laugh. "Just an idea of Nate's—presented at yesterday's service."

"Oh, Wilson! How thoughtless of him! Just overlook it. Mr. Goldsmith's very—well, insensitive—"

Wilson met her eyes then. "Don't let what he or anyone else says upset you, Chrissy. He means well. We will do as we see fit."

The hall clock struck six. Picking up the cups, Chris Beth hurried away from the table. "Better stoke the fire. I thought they'd all be up sooner," she said over her shoulder.

"Exhausted—like we are." Wilson opened the firebox of the big iron range and adjusted the draft. Pausing then, he said almost to himself, "Vangie says this beast is always hungry. There's a new kind, you know, on legs you can sweep under—has a warming closet, a water reservoir—she wants—wanted—" His voice broke.

"Oh, Wilson!" Chris Beth cried out, her voice breaking along with his, "Keep it like that. Keep it in the present. Keep Vangie with us."

Then, without reservation, she grasped both his hands in a natural gesture. He clung to them tightly, fighting for control. The fire in the grate crackled with warning and Wilson let go of her hands to close the damper of the stove. Then he turned back to her.

"You see how impervious I am to such suggestions as Nate's?"

"Of course, I do! It will take time for all of us."

"More than time, Chrissy," he said softly. "Arrangements we can manage—you and Joe, the children—but marriage? Marriage is a matter of the heart."

7
Urgent,
As Soon As Possible,
And Sometime

URGENT! Maybe she'd said it aloud, Chris Beth thought in the half-light of Friday morning. She looked down at her husband, still bunched in sleep born of exhaustion, and tried to remember how much they'd been able to move from the cabin yesterday and what lay ahead today.

All in all, yesterday had gone well. Until the very last. *Maybe*, she thought, *moving possessions is easier than moving people.* There was very little left in the cabin—except a part of her heart.

Well, what had to be had to be. As quietly as possible, she eased out of bed, and—striving for her usual efficiency—began to dress for the new day. But, even as she hung the long nightgown on its peg, Chris Beth was aware of a musing frown. It all looked so easy. Just packing Joe's mother's china, rearranging it among Wilson and Vangie's . . . rolling up the bearskin rug . . . packing the family Bible, the research books, her school supplies. Nothing she, Joe, Wilson, and Young Wil (who was delighted) couldn't handle. *But how does one move a heart?* she had questioned at the last moment.

Seeming to sense her need, Joe had reached down from his

great height and kissed her gently on the forehead. "Would you like to stay a minute after the rest of us go?"

With a lump in her throat, she had nodded. And there in the museum-quiet of the empty cabin, she cried out the sorrow in her heart. It wasn't as if the Big House were new. After all, the four of them had shared the warmth of its sturdy, wooden arms on all the firelit evenings they spent planning the double wedding. And during the past five years it had been a second home . . . but the cabin—the cabin was a *first*. . . .

"Are you all right?" Joe asked out of the semi-darkness now.

Wonderful Joe! His voice came as no surprise. He always knew her moods. Even those, she was sure, that penetrated her sleep.

"I'm all right," she answered, realizing suddenly that she really was.

Marty, always adaptable, had taken the move in stride. Young Wil made no effort to hide his pleasure with the arrangements. And True's sober little face had softened with obvious relief at the news. So nothing remained but details the men could handle and adjusting which time would handle. "I'm fine," Chris Beth said with growing conviction.

"Good girl," Joe said, pulling himself up into a sitting position on the bed. "We can't always live by the old rules, can we?"

"No," Chris Beth said slowly. "We can't. So I guess we just have to invent new ones as life challenges us."

Joe set his feet experimentally on the floor. "It's safe," Chris Beth laughed, "but take this for good measure." She kicked the bearskin toward him and went into the side room to finish dressing.

Fumbling in the darkness of the small room, Chris Beth heard the scratch of a match and knew that Joe had lighted the kerosene lamp. She waited a moment and then called, "Are you decent yet?"

Even after five years of marriage, she was unable to resist teasing Joe a little. He was so serious, so earnest, so different from his lifelong friend. That is, the way Wilson was before Vangie's illness.

Joe never seemed to mind her teasing. Probably he was smiling. She could imagine him, his brown hair picking up bronze tones in the flood of lamplight. But Joe's voice sounded sober when he replied.

"Come on in. I need to know what new rules we're setting today."

Chris Beth crossed the room to sit down beside him on the bed. "No rules—just plans, priorities. There's so much to think about before Monday. Who can keep Marty and True now with—with Vangie gone?"

"Chrissy," Joe spoke slowly, "I've given this some thought and wondered—do you want to give up the idea of teaching this year?"

They had been all over this before. Joe should know they couldn't get by on what the church was able to pay, but how could she keep repeating the words without hurting him?

"I'm sure, Joe. I'm *very* sure. I love being with the children—and it's too late anyway. There's no time for finding another teacher."

Something clicked in her mind then. Her hand went to her throat with the sudden realization that she had forgotten to tell Joe about the new teacher!

"I can't believe this." The words were as much for herself as for her husband. "But somehow in all the turmoil of the past few days I didn't tell you about O'Higgin's news—"

"Wilson told me."

Did she imagine a touch of sadness in Joe's voice? No time to share with her husband. But time to share with another man? Nonsense! Joe knew better than that. Nevertheless, Chris Beth felt a need to reach up and pull his head to her shoulder. There had been so little *touching*—too little.

"I'm afraid I take you for granted, darling," she whispered.

Joe reached out with a suddenness that almost pushed her from the bed and drew her into such a tight embrace it was hard to breathe. "You just go on taking me for granted— always and always I'm yours!"

Joe's arms tightened, but Chris Beth pulled away. "Joe, the time! The children must be downstairs already—"

But the children were not downstairs! They were pounding on the door saying in one voice, " 'Open up! Or I'll huff and I'll puff and I'll blow your house down!' "

Joe grinned at Chris Beth, made an attempt at smoothing his hair, and opened the door. "Well, now," he said, "if it isn't 'The Three Little Pigs'!"

"Just two of 'em," Marty said excitedly. "Young Wil's with Uncle Wilson—and it's not about him, is it, True?"

"Not about him," True repeated soberly, but her eyes were dancing.

"Well then?" Chris Beth prompted.

True bit her bottom lip in mock concentration. Then, unable to hold back, she sang out, "Marty and I are going to start to school!"

Chris Beth felt her mouth fly open. Closing it quickly, she murmured, "We'll talk to Daddy about it, True."

"We talked it over already while you and Uncle Joe slept," she said.

"Then *Marty's* father has to think," Chris Beth said. "Five years old is awfully early—"

The two children, lined like twin soldiers, stared at her as if she had a lapse of memory. "We're smart," True said. "You said so!" Marty backed her up.

"Makes sense," Joe said slowly.

"Don't encourage this—yet," Chris Beth whispered to him. Then, smiling in spite of herself, she added, "You're as bad as they are!"

But, even as they all went downstairs together, Chris Beth knew that Item #1 on the "urgent" list had resolved itself. Item #2: Young Wil's education. Then today they must get to some of the "as soon as possible" items, going through Vangie's personal belongings, getting as much done as she could in advance of school's opening . . . oh, so much!

And some day, a long time from now, when the sharp pain of losing Vangie reduced itself to a dull ache, she would look for the diary. *But not now, Lord, not now. It would break my heart. . . .*

8
Storm Warning

~~

B Y   SATURDAY,   WITH   everybody's help, the Big
House took on a semblance of order. Chris Beth wondered if
the others—especially Wilson—found as many painful reminders as she did. Vangie's clothes, always carelessly tossed,
lay heaped in unexpected places. Then there was a lace-edged
handkerchief wadded into a little ball. She ironed it out with
her hand the way Vangie did when deep in thought and the
scent of violets was so real that Vangie might well have
entered the room. Photographs of the beautiful, fragile face
smiled hauntingly from bureau drawers. And, most painful of
all to Chris Beth, was finding the jar of sweet-smelling
ointment, lid screwed on but the contents deeply grooved
where Vangie's slender, impatient fingers had dug out a
pattern. Wilson shouldn't see this. It was too real. But
smoothing the surface seemed cruel. Quickly, she screwed the
lid back on and tucked the jar of ointment away.

A feathered fan Vangie had spread out grandly at her first
ball . . . a memory book, the signatures now faded . . .
Sunday school cards . . . and Mama's fur with tails. In a
single day Vangie, darling Vangie's life passed in review. *It has*

402

to be—it has to be! If Wilson and True can hold up, so can I. If I crumble, so will they. The unshed tears hurt so much more than those Chris Beth *had* shed. And yet, through it all, she clung to True's lovely wisdom. Vangie would be with them forever . . . if they thought of her in present tense.

When Mrs. Malone came in the afternoon, Chris Beth gave her a running report. "We're moved in by mutual agreement, and we—all of us—are carrying on. I'm especially proud of True—no nightmares, crying, or anything that signals danger."

Mrs. Malone pushed at a stray lock of graying hair, tucking it neatly into the tightly-twisted knot on top of her head. "Like you—so like you—" she mused. "But 'twasn't True who had me worried. It's Wilson."

Chris Beth bit her lip. "He's fine—remarkably so."

The older woman was unconvinced. "*Too* fine. Not like 'im a-tall. Keep an eye on Wilson. Acceptance on his part's a storm warning!"

9
The
New Schoolmaster

⤙⤚

WHAT IS IT that transforms this moment into a moment to remember? Chris Beth wondered as she watched little True standing silently beside Vangie's grave. Silence! That was it. The rains had stopped and on this bracing blue-ribbon Sunday one could almost hear the silence of the dried grasses and the bulbs settling themselves down for the winter season ahead.

But as much as she hated the thought of breaking the lovely spell, Chris Beth knew by the warning of the church bell that it was time the two of them went inside. "We have to go, darling," she said softly, trying to avoid looking at the lettering on the white cross marking the mound of earth which already looked as if it belonged there.

True was not to be rushed. "What does it say, Aunt Chrissy? Does 'Vangie' begin with an E?"

"Vangie was a short way of saying Evangeline, True. Mary Evangeline North."

"Was Mommy's name always the same as Daddy's and mine?"

The question caught Chris Beth off guard. Certainly, it was

not a subject that she wanted to go into now. One day, however, the matter would have to be dealt with. Right now, she would strive for a postponement.

"Your mother's name was once *Stein* just as yours is *North*. When you are married, you will have a new name, too."

True seemed satisfied, but something else troubled her. "Mommy's grave should have something on it—something pretty."

"It will in time," Chris Beth promised. "You and I will plant some violets for spring and chrysanthemums for autumn—"

"Mommy likes leaves better," True said. And before Chris Beth could restrain her, True ran to a nearby grove of vine maple and tugged at the lower branches until her small hands were filled with red-gold leaves.

Holding back tears, Chris Beth watched True scatter the leaves on the grave. Then, hand in hand, they walked quietly into the church. The singing was over and Joe had begun his message. Nobody would mind in this loving community where people helped in time of need but did not hover or condemn. How glad she was that this family could grow up in such a world—so different from the ritualistic services she and Vangie had been forced to endure in their childhood . . . where people had cared more about creeds and codes than faith.

Immediately after church Nate Goldsmith made his way to where Chris Beth stood in a group of women who had gathered to offer whatever help the family needed. It was obvious that the president of the school board was bursting with news.

Combing his sparse gray beard nervously with his right hand and gesturing with the other, Nate spoke confidentially. "He's here! Come to church the very first Sunday like'n the contract demands!"

Chris Beth knew, even before allowing her eyes to travel to the back of the big room where Nate pointed, that "he" referred to the new teacher. That she would be working with a man surprised and disappointed her. It would have been nice to have a woman, maybe somebody her own age. Not that a friend could replace Vangie, but—

"Seen 'im yet? The big feller with the strong right arm," Nate said with obvious pride.

It was easy to spot the newcomer, although *tall* would have been a more apt description than *big*. Some six feet eight or nine inches, a young man with incredibly blonde hair towered above the other men around him. *Strong arms? Maybe. They were certainly long enough, to make him look comically like Ichabod Crane.*

Repressing a smile, Chris Beth said, "I can't tell you how pleased I am that I will be having a helper."

Nate's pale eyes opened wide in surprise. "I'm obliged to tell yuh it's gonna be t'other ways around! It's only natural his bein' a man'n all that I've elevated Mr. Oberon to principal. So y'll be takin' orders from him."

Chris Beth drew herself up with a straightness matching the board member's. "He and I will have a lot to learn from each other," she said stiffly. "But as for my taking *orders*," she paused to suck her breath in, "that remains to be seen."

At that exact moment, the new teacher, who had been elbowing his way forward, paused beside Nate Goldsmith and extended a hand. Vigorously, it pumped Nate's smaller one and then dropped to dangle several inches below the sleeve of his shadow-check doublet-style jacket. But not before Chris Beth caught, with each pump, a glimpse of his bright-red waistcoat beneath the jacket. Had anybody dressed like that since the Renaissance? Surely no man in his right mind would wear such clothes to school!

Nate turned to Chris Beth. "Mr. Alexander Oberon!" he said with the pomp usually reserved for a formal ball.

"How do you do—and welcome, Mr. Oberon," Chris Beth said as warmly as she was able. "I'm Chris—" and then, unable to resist using the same formality Nate had used, "I'm Christen Elizabeth Craig."

Alexander Oberon accepted her outstretched hand and

pumped it as vigorously as he had pumped Nate's. "My pleasure, Miss Craig—"

"*Mrs.* Craig," Chris Beth corrected quickly.

With obvious disappointment in his pale blue eyes, the new teacher murmured an apology. But he continued to hold her hand.

Withdrawing it as unobtrusively as possible, Chris Beth wondered if she should straighten her tucked-velvet turban. The hat was six years old now and the wire frame bent easily. Surely her head had bobbed up and down during the handshake!

Regaining her dignity, she said politely, "You had no way of knowing. I am—"

But Nate interrupted. "Chris Beth here's the wife of Brother Joseph."

"I see," Mr. Oberon fingered his beaver derby. "Well, I look forward to a good year. I can foresee a lot of changes."

So can I, Chris Beth thought inwardly. Striving for a natural voice, she answered, "It should be a successful year. We're all so thankful for the larger school—the new books—"

Alexander Oberon didn't seem to hear. "I have a lot of new ideas from the *East.*" The way he emphasized the word sounded as if nobody west of the Mississippi had heard it before. "But I sense in you, Miss—Mrs.—Craig, a person of Eastern *bel esprit.*"

Chris Beth felt her face flush as the puzzling young man bowed and made his way toward the front door of the church.

When he was out of hearing distance, Nate turned to her in bewilderment. "What on earth was he talkin' about—the bell-*what?*"

"*Bel esprit?*" She smiled. "It looks even worse written down—meaning having wit and a fine mind—French, I think."

Nate shook his head doubtfully. "Well, I'll be sprinkled! Am I gonna haf to get the ole woman of mine to interpret ever' word fer 'im? Who'd a'thought havin' a French-German wife a blessin'?"

From the corner of her eye Chris Beth saw Brother Amos
and the other "disciples" gathering their families to leave the
worship service. Excusing herself from Nate, she hurried to
greet them. It was so good to have the Shaker group join in
with them here. But even as she spoke briefly with the rather
retiring women, her mind kept going back to the new schoolmaster.

It should be an interesting year—maybe amusing at times.
But, as much as she welcomed another teacher in the school,
Chris Beth felt a strange foreboding. Did it have to do with
school? She wasn't sure.

10
Unexpected Decision

◆

ON MONDAY MORNING Chris Beth was awak-
ened by a clatter of pots and pans, sounds she thought at first
were a part of her dream. At the cusp of dawn, she tried to
remember why this day was special even as she strained her
ears to identify the sounds from somewhere below. But
thinking was hard after working until midnight putting
together—*what was it? Oh, yes! School supplies!* She'd over-
slept on the first day!

Automatically, she reached for Joe, then finding his side of
the bed vacant and not even warm, she hurriedly backed out
of bed wishing hard for unstuck eyes, her toothbrush, and a
cup of coffee. As if some good fairy had heard her wishes, they
were—in part—granted. She couldn't be dreaming the smell
of coffee! Neither, she decided, slipping into the ruffled white
blouse and long black skirt carefully laid out the night before,
did she imagine the voices of Marty and True below.

"Tomorrow," Chris Beth had overheard True telling Marty
last night, "will be the most *extreee*-ordinary day we ever
lived!"

"*Extree*-ordinary," Marty mouthed. If True said so, it was true.

409

Probably neither of them slept a wink, Chris Beth thought, as with practiced hands she brushed, braided, and secured her heavy hair in a halo style. No time to button high-top shoes. Bedroom shoes for now.

Downstairs, to her surprise, breakfast was almost ready. Young Wil, fortunately, had supervised. He smiled a greeting, but the younger children hardly looked up.

"They're packing their lunch," Young Wil smiled.

Chris Beth squeezed his hand. "What would I do without you?"

"You couldn't get along," he said, "You know," he continued as if the idea were new, "maybe I should go along with you the first day. You haven't driven alone for awhile and these two," he nodded to Marty and True, "can be a handful—"

"Good idea," Chris Beth said, turning away. The real reason for his going along, she knew, was loneliness. She wondered anew what arrangements Wilson could make about the boy's education.

Probably, she thought as she flipped sourdough pancakes Young Wil had mixed, *it's all written down in Vangie's diary.* Had she given priority to the right items? Perhaps finding the key to the diary belonged under the heading of "urgent."

There was no further time for thinking. Morning chores finished outside, Joe and Wil came inside, bringing fresh milk to be strained, eggs to be stored, and appetites to be satisfied. True chose her favorite blue-plaid gingham dress for the first day then declared something was wrong with it . . . just as something was wrong with her bangs . . . Marty couldn't find his slate . . . and even Young Wil needed a button on the sleeve of his shirt.

Joe gathered up the breakfast dishes for her. "Can you manage?"

"I'll manage!" she said shortly. Regretting the tone, she turned to apologize but Young Wil beckoned Joe to help with hitching the horse to the buggy.

Wilson pushed his chair from the table. "Bring me the hairbrush," he said to True who was still fussing with her hair. "I'll help."

True handed the brush to Wilson obediently. Wiping crumbs from the table quickly, Chris Beth kept her eyes lowered. Hair needed a woman's touch and it hurt somehow to have Wilson offer to help. The gesture, like his closing the door to Vangie's bedroom, seemed so final.

"Ouch!" True's cry cut into Chris Beth's thoughts.

"Hold still or I'll use the brush where I think best!" Wilson's voice was teasing, but there was defeat in it—defeat and something else that was hard to define.

"Let me have it, Wilson," she said drying her hands as she crossed the room. "Your patients will be coming soon—"

"No patients."

Surprised, Chris Beth said, "But I thought you were opening the office again today—"

"No!" The single word cut across the silence with an emphasis that said more than additional talk. And yet she needed to hear more.

"Wilson—I—you—" Chris Beth fumbled for words that would say what she wanted them to.

"I'm tired of standing, Aunt Chrissy," True complained.

"I'm sorry, darling." Taking the brush from Wilson's hand, she fluffed True's bangs and curled the ends of the heavy braids. "Run and get the blue ribbons in the middle drawer of Mother's bureau."

When True hesitated, Chris Beth said, "It can be yours now."

"Mommy's and mine?"

"Mommy's and yours." Chris Beth managed to speak in spite of the enormous lump in her throat. Reassured, True skipped away like a small, golden butterfly.

"You see?" Wilson spread his hands out on the table, his right index finger tracing the intricate pattern of forget-me-knots Vangie had so daintily embroidered. "You see," he repeated softly, "why I must leave—"

"Leave!" The word was torn from Chris Beth's lips. "*Leave?*"

Wilson stopped tracing the embroidered design and clenched his fists. But he did not look up.

"There's no point in discussing it, Chrissy. I need away from the reminders—"

"We can put them away—I *promise*—"

Wilson's dark eyes raised to meet her own. There she read pain, despair, and a certain consuming fire she was unable to identify.

"You can't put *these* away."

Chris Beth studied the hand that touched the bosom of his shirt. Strong. Sinewy. Filled with nervous energy. Gifted. Capable of tying tendons, but not hair ribbons. Able to mend bodies but not his own heart. Unwilling, even, to let others help. She had to try again.

"Time. It takes time, Wilson, and we all need each other—nobody can handle life alone—Oh, Wilson, *stay!*" Her voice broke then and without realizing that she was going to move, Chris Beth found herself kneeling beside him, her face against the rough worsted wool of his trouser leg. If only she could reach that secret part again—

"Don't, Chrissy—don't," he whispered, touching the top of her head gently. "Time can heal—some things—but this—" He pulled her head roughly against him. "*Oh, dear God, help us!*" And he pushed her away gently, rising from the table and helping her to her feet.

Then, Wilson, the doctor, was in control. Taking a white handkerchief from his hip pocket, he shook it out and held it to her nose. "Blow!"

"I'm not a child!" she said, blowing furiously. Relieved to be back on familiar ground, even if it meant conflict, she smiled.

"That's better," Wilson said.

She turned away then, knowing that Wilson had left a lot unspoken. Maybe his decision was right for him. But what about the rest of the family? Wasn't it selfish of him to leave the rest of the decisions for them to resolve? Well, she had faced hardships before. She would face this one. And time, the gentle healer, would take care of everything somehow, no matter what Wilson said. . . .

11
Paradise Lost

T RUE WAS RIGHT, Chris Beth reflected, as the
wheels of the buggy rolled through the stretch of autumn
woods within minutes of the school. It certainly was an
extraordinary day—one which left no time for reassembling.
Already the events of early dawn seemed unreal. Maybe they
never happened. Looking back, she decided that her mind had
been seeing mirages instead of reality throughout Vangie's
illness. Fatigue would do that. Wilson wouldn't desert the
children at a time when they needed him most. And what
about his patients—the valley folks who depended on him to
mend their bodies as they depended on Joe to heal their
spirits? *No more thinking,* she admonished herself.

Not that there was an opportunity to think with both Marty
and True chattering away like magpies. Did Marty see the
orange pumpkins hiding behind the corn? Yes, and did True
see how the stalks were bent like teepees? Maybe, the two
agreed, Indians danced there at night.

Young Wil spoke above their excited voices. "Didn't Holmes
refer to 'chill September'? How could anybody write that on
such a day?"

"It was Holmes," Chris Beth smiled, her spirits lifting some. "And it was Lowell who claimed the rarity of June days. I guess neither of them saw Oregon in September!"

Surely, she thought looking around, *God is showing me something on this full-of-leaves day. Maybe it's new horizons of faith, greater hills of strength—or maybe He's testing the bedrock of my purpose—*

"Whoa, Dobbin!" At Young Wil's quiet signal, the aging horse stopped at the edge of the schoolyard and immediately the buggy was surrounded by children of all sizes.

Chris Beth inhaled deeply. The sky was clear and clean. The air was crisp without being chill, the wind free of dust. Young faces were filled with anticipation. And the nation's flag, bearing 33 stars, proudly striped the autumn sky above the newly-enlarged school building. Her sense of belonging, of reality, and of foreverness returned. Oh! It was good to be back.

Handing Marty and True over to the Malone children, Chris Beth turned to Wong Chu. "My goodness, Wong! You've grown another foot. So now you have three," she teased.

Wong's almond-shaped eyes crinkled with humor. "Which gives me a better *understanding*," he jested in return, his English precise and perfect. What a miracle! Five years ago the Chinese lad was little more than able to mouth a simple "Yes" or "No" other than in his native tongue.

"Come with me and I'll put the balls out—" she began.

A look of fear crossed the boy's face. "Wait! Miss Chrissy, there's a man inside, a stranger, who says, 'No admittance' each time I knock."

Chris Beth forced a tight smile. "The strange man is a new teacher, Wong. You can spread the word for me. And, Wong, will you explain to the other students that we must make him feel welcome?"

"I'll try," he promised. "And now the balls, please?"

"I'll get them," Chris said firmly. It might take some doing, but this man, schoolmaster, principal, whatever title he chose, had better brace himself for some compromises. She opened the door and went in.

"Good morning!" she called brightly, once the door closed behind her. Alexander Oberon stood at the front of what used to be the building's only room and would now serve as a gathering place when there were to be assemblies as well as housing the upper grades during the regular school day.

The new teacher turned quickly but took time to consult his vest pocket-watch before responding. "Good morning, Mrs. Craig," a frown in his voice matched the one on his face. "What time are you accustomed to arriving?"

"Earlier than this," she admitted, striving to keep irritation from her voice. "It was a trying morning," she added, hating herself for feeling that it was necessary to explain. Who did he think he was anyway?

"May I suggest that you arrive at least an hour before we begin classes?"

Well, things might as well be set straight. "You may suggest anything you wish, Mr. Oberon, but I shall come and go as my schedule dictates."

A look of shock crossed the man's face. "I—I—" he sputtered.

But, realizing she'd seized an advantage, Chris Beth said quickly, "I'll set the playground equipment out for the children, then we'll need to do some planning."

Shouts of glee rose from the children when Chris Beth opened the door and placed the box of assorted balls, gloves, and bats on the step. *Hooray!* the shouts said. *Our teacher won!* Oh dear! She hadn't meant to divide loyalties. *I'll have to be more careful,* she thought.

"It was nice of you to hoist the new flag," Chris Beth said once she had covered the distance between them. Determined to make an effort at cooperation, she went on, "And that's a nice bulletin board! Usually, I get over here several days in advance of opening day, but there's been a death in the family."

The tall frame beside her seemed to relax a bit. "I understand. And, of course, the first day's hardest. Now, shall we divide the two groups according to age or gender?"

"You mean," she said incredulously, "separate the boys and girls?"

"Precisely." Chris Beth saw then that Mr. Oberon wore a full, flowing tie, but at least he'd chosen ordinary trousers and a less formal coat.

"Does Mr. Goldsmith know about this division?" she asked.

"His idea, ma'am."

Well, there was no fighting the two of them. "Given a choice, then, I suppose it's best that I take the smaller children."

Something resembling a smile crossed the man's thin face. At least, she'd said *something* right. "Very wise." And the way he said the words, he might as well have rubbed his hands together in delight.

"By the way," Chris Beth said, as she helped him sort the books and put them into separate stacks for the children to carry, "I plan to start my son and my late sister's daughter in a beginner's class. They'll be younger than the others, but—"

Mr. Oberon blew dust off his pile of books. "I foresee no problem" he said, fanning at the dust he'd blown into the air. "I plan to start an upper-grade class as well. There are at least six students registered now who are ready for a higher education."

Chris Beth straightened. "You mean—" Her heart beating so heavily against her ribs that it was hard to go on. "*Ninth grade?*"

"Ninth grade." Mr. Oberon's head bobbed up and down as he spoke, his Adam's apple bouncing like his head. "There's tentative approval from Salem, Mr. Goldsmith tells me— although I must say that change comes slowly here in the backwoods. Still," he granted, glancing at Chris Beth as if really seeing her for the first time, "they *did* hire a married woman, which is, to say the least, progressive. And generous."

Chris Beth opened her mouth then closed it. *Backwoods?*

Mr. Goldsmith would straighten that one out before the year was finished. And, as to her employment—she shrugged. What did it matter what this newcomer thought? He'd learn. Beginning today! Anyway, there was little he could say or do that would destroy her elation over the addition of a ninth grade. What wonderful news for Young Wil!

She realized suddenly that Mr. Oberon was speaking and that she had missed the first part. "—so if you can sing in tune and will follow along?"

Dismissing the idea of telling this pompous man that she was a soloist, Chris Beth said with false modesty, "I can sing in tune."

"Good! Then I shall lead while accompanying with my mandolin."

Well, that should be some feat, she thought, turning away with a smile. Her irritation was rapidly giving way to amusement. Why, she wondered suddenly, didn't his obvious disdain of women hurt her as she'd been hurt by Wilson's needling about her "Southern-belle helplessness" when she first came to the settlement?

Resolutely, she opened the turquoise- and rose-enameled case of her pendant watch then snapped it shut and secured it back into the ruffles of her blouse with the gold chatelaine. To compare Alexander Oberon with Wilson North was ridiculous—especially in terms of feelings. Wilson had aroused her ire because she *cared* what he thought. While Joe—well, Joe, gentle, loving Joe, was different from either of the other two men. *My husband,* she thought with a warm surge of affection, *does not search out my Achilles' heel. He loves me as I am* . . . Chris Beth brought herself back to the classroom with a start.

"We should be calling the children. Should I ring the bell?"

"*I* will!" Mr. Oberon drew himself up full-height and marched to the door as if who rang the bell were a matter of great importance.

It took awhile to line the boys and girls up to his satisfaction. Filled with the very exuberance of living, they found much to talk about and giggle about. Obviously curious about the new teacher, they were even noisier than usual. It had taken Chris Beth five years to gain their full confidence and respect. Mr. Oberon expected to accomplish the same relationship immediately with rigid discipline. Well, she wished him lots of luck. He'd made it clear that her services were unwelcome so she would make no effort to intervene.

"Chins up, chests out, and straight forward! One word or one twitter will bring three raps of the ruler across the palm!" he said sharply.

Brown eyes, blue eyes, gray, green, and all the shades between looked startled and then sought her face. Chris Beth tried hard to hide her distaste. Surely a smile would do no harm. She was wrong.

"And no smirking!" Mr. Oberon ordered when the children returned her smile.

Once inside and seated, the children were pin-drop quiet. "*Attention!* Class, rise—all together—and we will salute our nation's flag."

Young Wil's hand went up. "One of them leads," he suggested.

The way he said "one of them" told Chris Beth that Young Wil, as yet, did not know that he was among the group. Oh, she hoped that the new teacher did not alienate himself from this one. Like his uncle, Young Wil was a "still water" person.

Mr. Oberon eyed the boy. "*Used* to lead!" he corrected.

When Young Wil turned palms up in surrender, she breathed a sigh of relief. The others, watching the example, turned palms up beneath their scarred desktops then stood and, hands on their hearts, saluted in singsong.

"We read the Bible next," one of the boys up front whispered.

"No speaking without permission, young man! And *I* read a passage after group singing."

Taking a pitch pipe from his vest pocket, Mr. Oberon put the instrument to his lips and blew. The result was something akin to a nasal snort—a relationship not lost on the children.

They burst into laughter. When the teacher responded with harsh words and threats of removing one recess, maybe all recesses of the day, Chris Beth realized that the matter was out of hand. Knowing that her actions would lead to displeasure, she rose from where she was seated at the back the room and went quietly to stand beside Mr. Oberon. Immediately, the laughter stopped.

To her surprise, he handled the situation well. "Thank you for joining me, Mrs. Craig. We're ready for group singing."

Reaching behind him, he lifted a black, morocco leather case from the floor, unlatched it, and removed a beautiful mandolin from its flannel-lined resting place. There were "oh's" and "ah's" from all the children which Mr. Oberon chose to ignore, picking up a tortoiseshell pick instead, strumming a few bars and, to her dismay, sang out in a series of notes in the diatonic scale. "Do-do re-re fa so la!"

At the first sounds of laughter, Chris Beth put a warning finger to her lips. If Mr. Oberon saw, he gave no indication. "All of you will learn to sing like that!" he promised.

There was no enthusiasm. Neither did the children seem inclined to sing.

Chris Beth wished fervently that they could get on with classes, but there was more to come even after Mr. Oberon ignored the requests for the Twenty-third Psalm and read an obscure passage from Job.

"I sometimes read at the close of the day. Today, however, since we are assembled, I shall read from John Milton's *Paradise Lost*."

The smaller children began to fidget. The older ones looked perplexed. Both signs were lost on the reader who seemed to enjoy the sound of his own voice.

When at last the reading was finished, Mr. Oberon raised his long-fingered hand for attention. "Chart class through fifth grade will follow Mrs. Craig through yonder door," he said. He paused significantly before adding, "Sixth through ninth remain."

"*Ninth!*" At least, Chris Beth saw no irritation when the

whoop came from the several boys and girls who had come back nostalgically for one last look at the building and their friends before terminating their education. Mr. Oberon looked pleased at the enthusiasm.

She gave Young Wil's hand a squeeze in passing. He squeezed back appreciatively.

Once inside her own room, Chris Beth engaged the children in a game which allowed small legs to exercise. Then she told them in simple language the story behind *Paradise Lost*."

"What's a paradise?" Jimmy John, youngest of the Malones, asked.

"The Garden of Eden, huh, Aunt Chrissy?" True spoke out as she was accustomed to doing at home.

"The Garden of Eden," Marty repeated.

"Then how could anybody lose it?" Jimmy John asked reasonably.

"Let's get to our ABCs now," Chris Beth said, closing the matter. They were too young to understand about losing *sight* of the Garden.

The rest of the day went well in both rooms. Chris Beth's little charges were eager to learn and Young Wil, once he heard the good news of the added grade, handled his new teacher with tact.

"He'll learn!" Young Wil laughed as Dobbin jogged lazily along at the close of the day. "And wait till I tell Uncle Wil about ninth grade! That should do away with his ideas of—of taking me with him—"

"You knew?" Chris Beth asked.

"I suspected, so I asked. I guess it's for the best—feeling the way he does." Young Wil urged the horse forward with a cluck then said slowly, "He hurts a lot and besides he wants to study some more about diseases—pathology?"

Chris Beth nodded and then asked, "Because of Vangie's illness?"

"Partly—then I think he just wants away—maybe from us all. Oh, Chrissy! You won't let him take True?"

The idea hadn't occurred to Chris Beth. Now fear clutched

her heart. Oh, she mustn't let that happen! There had to be another way. Of course, if Wilson had his mind set . . . oh, not *another* conflict!

"I'll talk with him," she murmured.

There was no opportunity during the evening. No opportunity even for Young Wil to say much regarding the news. True and Marty monopolized the conversation. "And we heard about *Paradise Lost!*" True said as she kissed Wilson good night. "And Aunt Chrissy understands."

"*Paradise Lost,*" he said slowly. "I wish I understood, too."

12
Promise
of a Rainbow

❧

TWO WEEKS AFTER school opened Wilson prepared to leave for Portland. They had been busy for weeks and Chris Beth was glad. Busy minds did not brood. Brooding would not bring Vangie back anymore than it would stop Wilson from leaving, she thought bitterly. Joe could be right. Maybe she did expect too much of a recently-bereaved man. But wasn't Wilson expecting too much, too, she asked herself between listening to the guttural noises of children trying to master phonetic sounds of *McGuffey's Readers* at school and holding mornings and evenings together at home. Wilson wasn't free. After all, he had a family to think about . . . and what about his practice? Then, resolutely, *I won't think about it.*

The late September rain moved out after clearing the summer haze from the sky and October came with a burst of glory. Bright leaves, bringing back memories of other autumns to Chris Beth, dropped one by one until the vine maples stood in deep pools of their own glory. Goldenrod flamed and milkweed offered bolts of silk to every teasing breeze. Chris Beth looked at the beautiful valley and felt that yesterday lay all around her. Gone was the growth of spring, the maturity of summer, and September's ripeness.

"It's evening of the year," she said sadly to Joe on one of their rare moments alone.

Joe took her hand. "But evening means stars, then dawn of another day."

Chris Beth tried to take comfort in his words, but a part of her reached out. Beyond the realm of too-busy days, the too-sad past, and the too-uncertain tomorrow. She needed something more reassuring—something perhaps she could find if there were a margin of time in her day to see October through the eyes of the forest . . . listen to the trees' soft whisperings . . . watch squirrels at their hoarding . . . letting her mind and muscles relax and just *be*.

"If I could escape and feel the world about me and see it, I could understand and become a part of its big rhythm instead of all the little humdrums of my day!" Over and over she said the words, knowing how futile they were. They would only bring her back full-circle to the realization that she belonged here, she *wanted* to be here . . . why, then, the sense of longing? Did other women feel this way? Probably not . . . but maybe they didn't listen to the wild geese calling at night . . . or try to convince a man like Wilson that he should stay here when, deep down, she might be wishing she were going away, too. . . .

Yes, it was good that she was busy! Nature's pace might slow in autumn. But for valley folk it was not yet time for leisure. There were fences to mend, fields to tidy, and gardens to bed down for the winter. And for Chris Beth there were inquisitive minds to satisfy at school and a family to hold together at home. *So*, she told herself firmly, *stop acting like a schoolgirl!*

And, blessedly, school was going well. Mr. Oberon, once he had "laid down the law," laid down the stick as well. Even Nate Goldsmith who was a firm believer in "lick 'em and larn 'em," ventured to say that the "Yankee gent was maybe goin' a piece too fur." But, "One o' these days you'll show 'im that he'll be catchin' a site more flies with sugar than vinegar!"

Well, it was stretching a point to say that she was responsible, Chris Beth knew. But, whatever accounted for the change, she was grateful. Now *home*—home, she thought a little hopelessly sometimes, was another matter. . . .

"Will Daddy be home for Thanksgiving?" True wondered. *Better ask Daddy. Aunt Chrissy doesn't know.*

"Who'll be taking over Uncle Wil's practice—till he comes back? He *is* coming back, isn't he?" *Better ask Uncle Wil. . . .*

Chris Beth did know, however, that Joe had spent many long hours with Wilson and was sure that, as close as the two of them were, Wilson had told him a great deal more than she knew. Joe told her only that Wilson was arranging for a Dr. Mallory to see his patients.

"Here?" she had asked, hoping not. This house needed no more commotion than it had already.

"Oh, no," Joe reassured her. "He has an office in Centerville now. I'm not sure about house calls though."

And maybe even more important was the fact that settlers would have to drive for miles for a doctor's services, she'd said. But not forever, Joe had answered. *No, not forever . . . nothing was forever. . . .*

More storing, packing, rearranging. Another bedroom door closed. And another member of the family circle about to leave. Only "temporarily," of course. With all her heart, Chris Beth wished neither Joe nor Wilson would use that phrase again. Life was too precious to spend doing *anything* temporarily. One must live every moment as if it were the last. Indeed! It might be. Time was no longer friendly.

"Well," Wilson said, rising from a squatting position where he had been sorting out enough emergency instruments to fill his doctor's kit, "that does it, I guess."

"Would you like a box lunch to take with you on the stage?" Chris Beth asked. "I've fried chicken—"

"Sounds wonderful, but you know our Miss Mollie. The

stage leaves from there at twelve and she'll insist on feeding us a square meal before we board."

"You'll write?" Chris Beth asked.

"And send me a picture of the big hotel?" True broke in.

"Yes, Chrissy. And, yes, True."

Joe and Young Wil finished loading in Wilson's box of books and his one trunk. Coming inside, they joined Wilson, Chris Beth, and the two younger children. There was so much to say. Yet, there was nothing at all. The six of them stood awkwardly in the front room which had grown suddenly dark.

"It's going to rain," Joe said in surprise when there was a sudden clap of thunder. "I saw the little clouds earlier—"

Then without additional overture, there was a sprinkle of rain. Not much. Just enough to give the world a good-earth smell. And, then, astonishingly, there was sunlight.

"What do you know?" Wilson exclaimed. "Our Oregon storm is over!"

"There ought to be a rainbow!" True ran to the window with Marty at her heels. "Look, Daddy! It sucked up the colors from Mommy's zinnia bed."

Wilson turned toward Vangie's daughter but not before Chris Beth saw him wince in pain. But his voice, when he spoke, was steady.

"Look at that," he said in wonder. "They say rainbows have one foot planted in the garden and the other planted in heaven."

What a lovely thought! Chris Beth had never heard it before. The words were unlike Wilson, but he was filled with surprises.

"Is there really 'n truly a pot of gold at the end, Uncle Wil?" Marty wanted to know.

Wilson smiled. "O'Higgin says there is. Where's my spade?"

True giggled. "He's teasing, Marty. But, Daddy, isn't the rainbow God's promise?"

"It is," he said gently. "He promises never to destroy the world with a flood again."

"I like it when you talk like that," the little girl said, then tugging at his hand, "can't we go out and stand in it? Maybe God will promise *us* something special."

"We'll try it," Wilson said, picking up his kit. "Another thing O'Higgin says is that it's the 'luck o' th' Irish' to stand at the rainbow's end."

Wilson lead True and Marty to the flower bed in the front yard. Chris Beth felt such a lump in her throat that she didn't want to risk crying. She stayed behind the others, watching through the thin, white curtains. A tear spilled down her cheek and then, unexpectedly, she felt the warmth of Joe's arms from behind her. Depend on Joe to be at her side. And, yet, as she watched the others through a maze of color, Chris Beth had a strange feeling that she and Joe should have joined them. It was a wonderful way to say good-bye—beneath the promise of a rainbow. . . .

13
The Diary

⌒

WILSON LEFT TWO MESSAGES. Not notes. Just reminders. But Chris Beth saw neither of them until several days later. She was too busy watching for signs of heartbreak that True might show. Losing her mother and then her father surely were too much for the young mind.

"Something has to give," she said worriedly to Joe.

"Not necessarily," he said. "Did she tell you about the rainbow?"

When Chris Beth said no, Joe went on. "She's convinced that the Lord made them a promise out there in the yard—a promise that Wilson will be back. Oh, for the faith of a little child!"

Chris Beth bit her lip in concentration. "I'm not so sure," she said uncertainly. "She could be very hurt by this. At this formative stage of her faith—"

Chris Beth paused, uncertain as to where one drew the line. "Just pray for his safe return," Joe said gently.

And Joe was right. Praying did help. It seemed like a sign her prayers were heard when Chris Beth saw Wilson's first message that he would be coming back to resume practice. At least, she took it as such.

Sweeping off the front porch on Saturday morning, Chris Beth raised the broom over her head and brushed it across the front door in search of cobwebs. It was then that she noticed Wilson's plaque still mounted to the left of the door. WILSON K. NORTH, M.D., the chiseled inscription read, as if his office were open for business.

"Joe, look!" she called excitedly to her husband who was sorting apples beneath the gnarled old tree where the children were picking the fruit for cider.

Joe selected two tree-ripened apples from the basket, polished them on his overall bib, and came to where she stood. Handing her one, he bit into his before answering. " 'Delicious' is the right name for these!" Then, smiling, he added, "I knew about the plaque."

Chris Beth bit into her apple. "Um-m-m," she said with appreciation. "This means that he really *is* planning to come back to stay—Oh, Joe, I hope he didn't just forget to take it down."

"He didn't forget, Chrissy," Joe said reassuringly. Then, when she did not reply, he added half-teasingly, "Come on now, 'oh, ye of little faith'!"

"It's not that exactly—Oh, I don't know how to explain."

How *could* she explain this feeling she had that the four of them who had become two now were only three after Vangie's untimely death? That the remnant of the family would never be reunited? Trying to shake off the sense of strange foreboding, she said, "How about some apple dumplings for supper?"

"Like I said, 'Delicious,' " Joe said, squeezing her arm.

"Not the Delicious apples," she said absently. "We'll need some Pound apples from the cellar."

Then, when Joe would have moved away, she detained him with a question. "Did Wilson discuss the children? I never did ask exactly how they came to stay—or what we should do in case—well, anything happened."

"Nothing's going to happen, Chrissy. But, to answer your

questions, yes, we talked. He loves that nephew and step-daughter as if they were his own—which they are!"

Chris Beth nodded and he went on, "He would have taken them, however, if he'd had any permanent plans."

"I couldn't have stood that!"

"All the more reason to pray." Joe smiled and went for the apples.

That evening Chris Beth found Wilson's second message. Vangie's diary! The thick, velveteen-covered book lay beside her best set of hairbrushes on top of the high chiffonier. And on top of her silver-scrolled hand mirror lay the small gold key that would open the book and reveal the messages meant for herself alone. Longing to open the diary and skim through the pages, and yet fearing to at the same time, Chris Beth tucked it beneath the linen sheets in the bottom drawer. She would open it tomorrow. No, tonight. No—*right now!*

Turning back the counterpane, Chris Beth sat down on the edge of the bed and fitted the small key into the lock of the diary. Almost reverently, she opened the first page and read the name, *Mary Evangeline Stein.* Vangie's maiden name! Then her sister had started putting down her thoughts long before her illness. Carefully, she turned the page to read the date in Vangie's delicate, spidery handwriting. The first entry was dated five years ago—almost to the day! Why, that would have been just before Vangie left their Southern home and came to the Pacific Northwest. With a shaking hand, she turned to the next page—at first tempted to skim the page, Chris Beth forced herself to read the words, so deeply emotional for both of them, one by one. And one by one, the words tore at her heart.

Dear Diary:

It is with a pained but loving heart that I write these words. Actually, the words are not for you—or me—as much as for Others, two others. God, because the words confess my sins. And my beloved sister, whom I have wronged. . . .

Gently, Chris Beth laid the diary on the bed beside her, facedown, to stare dry-eyed out the window at the last glow in the western horizon where the autumn sun had gone down. Evening meant stars, Joe had said, and after that the dawn. She wasn't sure. She wasn't sure about anything these days—even life itself, considering how Vangie's fragile breath, like a tiny candle, had fluttered and failed.

"I don't think I should read this," she said softly in the gathering dusk. "The words aren't meant for me."

Only, she new better, of course. Vangie's last words had been a request that she read the diary—abide by it. . . .

With an aching heart, Chris Beth picked up the book and tried to read it again, each word squeezing her heart a little drier.

Word has reached me of Jonathan's accident and his death. I do not know what I shall do without Chris Beth and she is so far away—by miles and because of my folly. How can I ask her forgiveness? How can I tell her that the child I carry is Jonathan's, knowing that she and Jonathan were to have been married? And how—Oh, Dear Diary, how—can I make my mother and father understand? They will never believe that I loved Jonathan—my sister—them—or God. Maybe it would be better if I simply ended my life. . . .

With a cry of pain, Chris Beth laid the diary aside and gave way to a flood of tears. For the first time she realized what might have happened if she had followed her human inclinations and refused to accept her younger sister when their mother and her stepfather disowned Vangie and drove her from the family home. Some day she would read the rest of the heartbreaking diary. Some day. But not now. Now, she must say a long prayer of thanksgiving to the Lord who had arranged circumstances so that His will ruled over the human inclinations which would have ended in tragedy . . . and seek strength to go on.

14
Rebellion

❧

CHRIS BETH HAD HOPED that the hands of the clock would slow down once she had completed the tasks listed under "urgent." Instead, they seemed to pick up momentum as the October days sped past. Corn was in the cribs; stalks cut for fodder; apples were in the bins; all the canned fruit labeled and lined up neatly for winter. The hills filled up with wood smoke and other people seemed to find a bit of leisure. The slowing of their own time clocks pushed Chris Beth's ahead.

Added to the already overcrowded schedule was a growing sense of insecurity among the settlers. Folks needed a doctor closer 'n better'n them new ones in town. Old Doc Mallory had come to Centerville to retire, so they heard. Easy to tell he was a-mind to . . . had no memory a-tall and couldn't see his shadow without them spectacles he pinched on his nose. Shucks, he couldn't be up on the new way of doctoring. 'Course the other extreme was the likes of the "feisty feller" calling himself Dr. Spreckles. Too young to be a real doctor, he was. Too cocky, too. Mr. Oberon had never heard tell of such a school as he made claims of attending . . . probably one of

431

them mail-order credentials. Nate Goldsmith granted that there just might be a few pint-size things even Alexander Oberon didn't know. He paused to look significantly at Chris Beth following a Sunday service and then continued, "But I wager he made a *D* when it comes to fixin' up liver ailments!"

Listening, Chris Beth supposed that she would have laughed behind her fan at such talk when she, Mama, and Vangie attended church back home. Or, more recently, perhaps she and Vangie would have looked at each other in amused tolerance under lowered lashes. But now—well, now their murmurings were disturbing.

Chris Beth expressed her concerns to Joe. He listened and then said, "Yes, I see it too. And besides—" he hesitated, lowering his voice, "I don't want the children to know, but there's a lot of friction between the Basque people and those living below."

"What kind of trouble, Joe?" Chris Beth was immediately alert. There had been an undeclared war between the sheep raisers and the cattlemen for years.

"Just unrest. One of these days things will explode. I'm going to have to spend more time calling on people—seeing if I can help mediate."

"Oh, Joe, we spend far too little time together as it is! I keep hoping things will slow down—"

"They will, Chrissy. You're doing a fine job and I often feel I neglect you in order to take care of the people's needs—"

"You are taking care of *God's* needs, Joe," she said loyally.

Joe had taken her hand that evening and pressed the palm to his lips. "It will all go better when Wilson finishes his courses in pathology and comes home."

If he ever came, she thought bitterly. She found herself half-wishing the courses Wilson planned to take would not be available or that something else would intervene so that he would return to help carry on here. So many people depended on him and Joe was so overworked.

"Joe," Chris Beth asked, suddenly remembering, "are you going to operate the mill alone?"

"Not alone. I'll have Young Wil."

Then came Wilson's telegram! The telegraph office was new in Centerville and whenever a "wireless" came through, the two "runners" continued to bring the exciting yellow envelopes to the recipients.

Back home, telegrams had meant bad news to Mama. Shivering, Chris Beth watched Joe open the envelope, her memory going back to little-girl days when she stood wide-eyed watching her mother read the words and, more often than not, burst into tears without sharing the contents with Chris Beth. But, of course, one of those telegrams did bring the shattering news of her own father's death. . . .

Breathlessly, she waited for Joe to read the telegram and then share its message. Instead, he read aloud: CLASSES ARRANGED—STOP—WILL STAY AWHILE—STOP—MAY SEND FOR WIL—STOP—RAINBOWS TO TRUE—STOP—LOVE—WILSON.

"That's good news," Joe said in a sincere voice. "Isn't it?"

Chris Beth could not bring herself to answer. "We'd better call the children," she said instead.

The two smaller children jumped up and down. "The *rainbows* means our promise!" True said over and over, dancing around the living room. Marty danced with her, probably not caring why.

But Young Wil stood aside, making no comment. "Of course, we'd better not plan on your going right away," Joe said to the boy. "Your uncle and I talked about this—the possibility of your joining him there. You'll be ready for tenth grade next year and—"

"I've *been* in school there before. Remember?" he said and stalked out.

"Well!" Joe looked at Chris Beth in surprise. "That's news."

"Not to me. Young Wil has unpleasant memories of Portland—his mother's leaving his father for another man."

"It's a subject Wilson seldom mentions to me. He's still hurt by it, too. He told you that she sent for Young Wil after Wilson took care of him but he was unhappy and came back?"

Yes, he'd told her. Chris Beth remembered with a smile her confusing the names and, sure that they were father and son, summoning Wilson to school. That the boy was Wilson's nephew, his sister's son, surprised her. But remembering the rest of Young Wil's history erased the smile from Chris Beth's face . . . his dislike of the big city school . . . his striving for recognition and acceptance in the little one-room school where she'd struggled that first year as his teacher . . . and the final breakthrough when she'd won him over. . . .

"You and Wilson are the only ones who can really get to him—I mean, the part he holds back like Wilson," Joe said.

And Wilson was not here. So it was her job. Fine, but how? *How* was she to smooth out his security blanket with Wilson tugging at its corners? Well, she would do the best she could. But she was unable to resist saying, "It's Wilson's responsibility."

Maybe nothing would come of it. Maybe Young Wil would adjust to the idea . . . no, Chris Beth admitted to herself, she didn't want that! He was too dear to her. Maybe Wilson would come home and no decision would have to be made. *Time would heal.* Her own words.

But time ran out. The day following arrival of Wilson's telegram Mr. Oberon asked if he might see her after school.

Chris Beth smiled at his formality. "You need not make an appointment," she teased.

"I would not wish to infringe upon your privacy," he said stiffly, "except in matters of extreme importance."

Alas! Alexander Oberon had taken her declaration of rights too seriously. Well, at least, they had achieved a workable relationship if not a total understanding.

What time did he wish to see her? *Immediately after school.* If it concerned one of the students, should she bring records? *No.* The man's reluctance to give an inkling of what the "matter of extreme importance" was about puzzled her.

Once the students had cleared the building, Chris Beth invented a task for Young Wil and asked him to keep an eye on True and Marty, promising not to be long.

Mr. Oberon came right to the point. "Something happened to Wil Ames today which greatly disturbs me. You're his guardian, I understand."

"That's close enough," Chris Beth answered, then asked anxiously, "what happened?"

"This," the teacher said. He spread a paper on his desk and smoothed it with quick, nervous fingers. The handwriting was unmistakably Young Wil's.

"The lad seems in possession of a fine mind, has asked provocative questions, and, *ahem!*, until today conducted himself like a gentleman."

Chris Beth picked up the paper with trembling fingers. "Will you explain this to me? I'm not sure I understand."

"An examination over what I thought he had mastered. And look at this!" Mr. Oberon's voice rose as it was prone to do when he was agitated. " 'Parse a noun,' the assignment was."

Chris Beth looked at the writing and was torn between amusement and concern. "*Dog* is a noun with his tail sticking up and his feet hanging down."

While the answer might be funny, the problem behind it was not. Chris Beth had been through this before. There was the *"naked* old Nakomis" phrase the boy had misquoted purposely from *Hiawatha*. She'd know then, as she knew now, that Young Wil was clowning because he was troubled. But he must learn not to be impertinent.

Quickly, she skimmed the remainder of the tedious examination. The idea that any student would miss every problem in any subject, even geometry which she struggled with herself, seemed pretty unlikely. But it was downright preposterous to think that *this* one would write "Don't know" beneath the science questions when he knew the genus and specie of every living thing, as far as she could determine. And grammar!

Chris Beth laid down the paper in despair. "He knows the parts of speech backward and forward," she said. "This is—"

"Most distressing, most distressing!" Mr. Oberon broke in.

"This is," Chris Beth began again, "a sure sign that the boy's troubled about his uncle's leaving. I'll speak with him."

How many times—how MANY times—I've said that lately, she whispered to herself as she hurried to where the children waited in the buggy. The problem came under "urgent" all right, but then there would need to be a right time.

The right time came as the buggy rolled almost silently over the needled trail that led through the strip of woods near the North house. Marty was chattering away like a nut-gathering squirrel when True interrupted with a silencing finger to her lips.

"Quiet," she whispered. "We're close to Starvation Rock."

Marty's eyes widened, obviously pleasing True who loved to grab his attention with her sometimes hair-raising tales. "Did the Indians *really* jump down—" Marty began.

"Down, down, down! Into the canyon. Because they were starving to death, huh, Wil?"

Young Wil smiled. "Yep, I guess they did. So say those more resourceful than we."

"Than *us*," Chris Beth corrected automatically. "Object of the preposition."

"Beg pardon, Teacher," the boy said teasingly. "*Than's* not a preposition the way I used it. It's a connective of the understood subject—*So say those more resourceful than we are resourceful!*"

Chris Beth looked at him in amazement. "So it is. Then how on earth did you come to miss every single answer on today's test?"

Young Wil dropped his head. At that precise moment the buggy rolled into the clearing. A shaft of late-afternoon sun touched the pale, straw-colored head, but it brought no light to his eyes. There was a momentary sadness which turned to defiance as his chin went up determinedly. "I've lost interest in school. I want to be a monk!"

Chris Beth burst out laughing in spite of herself. "And you think *they* don't study?"

Marty joined the laughter. "I wanna be a monkey, too!"

Little True sat upright. "It's not monkey, silly! It's *monk*. Monks live—oh, never mind." Dismissing the matter, she turned to Chris Beth. "Wil's mad because Daddy wants him to come to Portland. And I'm mad, too. If he wanted anybody, it oughta be me—he's *my* daddy—" An unexpected sob interrupted her words.

And before the buggy came to a safe halt, True jumped over the wheel and ran inside the front door. Marty followed, wailing in sympathy.

"Oh, Chrissy! I'm sorry," Young Wil murmured in remorse.

"I'm sorry, too, darling," Chris Beth answered through tight lips, "about *everything*."

15
"He Loves Me—
He Loves Me Not!"

❧

THERE WAS NO MENTION of the incident during the evening meal. When Joe drew Chris Beth close in bed that night he said, "Want to tell me about it?"

Needing the warmth of his nearness, she snuggled close—grateful as always for his strength.

Joe's arms tightened around her. "Something *is* troubling you."

"Just one of the students," she murmured against his chest. "Nothing to worry about in a wonderful moment like this."

Things went normally at breakfast, too. Maybe the children were a little less talkative—or maybe Chris Beth only imagined they were. There was no further word from Wilson, but the telegram served to answer questions neighbors asked at church. Debating whether to open the matter again with Young Wil, Chris Beth decided against it. That's how relationships fold, she knew—a wrong word or a right word but at the wrong time. It would be best to stay in close contact with Mr. Oberon. It would be best, too, to see this thing through alone—not push her suffering off onto others . . . Joe . . . the smaller children . . . or her friends.

438

"How is Wil responding these days?" Chris Beth asked Mr. Oberon when she felt sufficient time had elapsed.

Mr. Oberon fingered the stickpin in his necktie. "Satisfactorily, but," he paused to motion ups-and-downs with both hands, "the lad's seesawing. And he wears a 'You-figure-it-out' expression."

Yes, she knew the expression very well. For the first time, Chris Beth felt a sort of sympathy for the teacher. And, she admitted inwardly, a certain respect. Alexander Oberon was trying in his own way to understand a complex situation she hardly understood herself.

Days ran into weeks and suddenly it was November. It was a cold fall. There was a misty rain that made everything sticky to handle. The sky was always dark, giving the look of perpetual late afternoon. Joe, who made frequent calls on congregation members, settlers in the Basque section, and the cattle ranchers who were non-church goers, stopped for mail at the general store at every opportunity. Marty, who could outdistance True only when his watchful eyes spotted Joe's horse, always rushed forward to give Joe a welcoming hug. True always waited her turn with questioning eyes. *A letter from Daddy!*

"Not today, sweetheart." Each report made Chris Beth sadder.

On one such evening in mid-November, True asked, "Uncle Joe, my daddy'll be home for Thanksgiving, won't he—for sure?"

"We hope so. But," he said evasively, "Portland's a long way."

Sensing the child's sadness, Joe said, "If the weather permits, let's all burn leaves tomorrow. Would you like that?"

An autumn bonfire! It was a seasonal ritual the children loved. Raking. Burning. Watching the colored smoke and trying to guess which color leaves were making the crimson-orange blazes.

Chris Beth was as excited as Young Wil, Marty, and True when the first pile was heaped high. There was always a sense of adventure when Joe bent to light the pile from under-neath—even a little quiver of danger. Everybody gathered close to watch as a blinding flare of heat and fragrance filled the chill air. "Victory!" they all sang out and went to gather more leaves.

Chris Beth left the group to prepare hot chocolate. Joe joined her soon, saying he'd best skip the chocolate and go to his study. "It seems that I get around to other things and not my priorities," he said.

"Amen, Brother Joseph," Chris Beth smiled. "Goes for me, too."

When the bonfire died down somewhat Young Wil came in for his hot chocolate. "Shall I pour?" he asked.

"Yes, do. I'll sit down with you as soon as I take these mugs to our fireflies out there."

Chris Beth started across the kitchen, carrying a mug in each hand. Then, hearing a noise that sounded more like a scream than a whoop, she hurried across the living room. There she stopped in astonishment.

Marty, holding a long stick, was poking the base of the leaves to send an explosion of sparks and rekindled flame into the air. And, as the blazes leaped high, True was attempting to leap over the burning bonfire—her long skirt billowing out as if to dare the tongues of flame.

Sloshing the hot chocolate over her hands and onto the cabbage-rose design of the carpet in her hurry to set the mugs down, Chris Beth rushed out the door to stop the dangerous game. But not before she heard True screaming wildly, "He loves me—He loves me not!"

"True, darling—no!" Chris Beth cried, running forward to grab the tiny figure. "That's dangerous!"

To her surprise, True collapsed into her arms, burying her soot-covered face against her breast. "I know," she sobbed. "I know and I don't care. He's not coming for Thanksgiving—my daddy's not coming—"

16
A Beautiful
Hope

❧

CHRIS BETH COULD not withold True's unhappiness as she had Young Wil's. Joe overheard and helped soothe the child who obviously had been grieving more than they knew until today. Now that the children's feelings were out in the open, she hoped Joe would sit down and talk to her.

Still shaken, she said, "Join me for chocolate—"

But, before the sentence was finished, Joe answered. "I need to work on my sermon. And then," he said thoughtfully, "I guess I'd better make a trip to the general store—supplies for the mill—" His voice trailed off as the door of his study closed behind him.

Disappointed and hurt, Chris Beth went back into the kitchen. Young Wil was gone. And the chocolate was cold. In a sudden need for release of pent-up emotions, she seized the mugs and hurled them into the dishpan of soapy water left from the breakfast dishes. With a heavy thud, the mugs struck their target, splashing water onto the window above, their flight leaving a trail of syrupy brown. There, that should make her feel better. But it didn't.

Joe had built a fire beneath the wash pot in the backyard.

The first pot of laundry should be boiling. But there was the floor to scrub . . . pressing and mending to do . . . the ironing would have to go, much as she detested spending evenings at the ironing board . . . and what about baking, lesson plans. . . .

Tears of despair filled her eyes as she mopped up the chocolate trail from the kitchen floor. That was her own fault, but what about the remaining work? There always seemed to be something she could or should be doing to make the lives of her family happier and more content, something more important than her own needs. The routine things to keep them clothed and fed. And the not-so-routine ones, but nevertheless important, like burning leaves and being together. Didn't that "clothe and feed" them in another way?

"Then why, Lord," Chris whispered as she wrung out the mop, "do I feel guilty? Why do I feel as if I am cradling the people I love in my womb—trying to insulate them from hurt, pain, *reality*?"

She paused to look out the window, inhaling deeply the arid-sweetness of the smoke mingled with overripe apples which had clung to the trees too long. Swallowing hard, Chris Beth let her taste buds follow the bonfire's luminous haze down to the musky odor of foliage in the damp woodlands down along the creek banks. If only, if *only*, she could get away . . . have a moment to herself . . . but the thought made her feel guiltier yet.

"Forgive me, Lord," she continued her almost inaudible prayer. "I need to get away. I need—oh, You know what my needs are—"

Chris Beth's lips stopped moving when there was the sound of quiet footsteps behind her. Before she could turn around, Joe spoke.

"I've been thinking, Chrissy—things have been very hard here—" He paused and in a strong voice asked suddenly, "Would you like to go to Portland?"

"Portland!" *Portland?*

She turned to all but crumple in Joe's arms. He laughed

softly and held her close. "There's a great need for the children to see Wilson—for all of us to have a planning session. It's been long enough now since—since our loss. But, Chrissy," he paused to lift her face, push back the tendrils of hair from her forehead and plant a kiss at her hairline, "Most of all, I want the trip for *you*."

"Oh, Joe, I know we can't afford it, but yes, *yes*, I want to go—Oh, it's a wonderful idea—wonderful, *wonderful*!"

To ride on the stagecoach again . . . stay in a hotel . . . see a big city . . . after five years. Outside, the sky had turned leaden again. It would probably rain. The family wash might never dry. It did not matter. Let the gray clouds come. There was a cobalt sky beyond. A beautiful new hope filled her heart.

17
Anticipation

CHRIS BETH WATCHED her golden niece standing at the mirror, her back arched as she tiptoed to see her reflection. As True swept her pale hair up off her slender neck, Chris Beth fastened it with a silver barette, and then let it fall loose in a cascade below her shoulders. Her big, violet eyes with heavy blonde lashes—so like Vangie's—like her little-girl body, were never still. Her life would be filled with romance, if only it were not cut short like her mother's.

Watching her, Chris Beth felt a deep-down ache of sadness. But the sadness was overlaid now with the new-found happiness the family had found. Anticipation was mounting. The air was charged. "We're goin' to Portland. We're goin' to Portland!" Marty sang over and over as he hopped from one foot to the other. But True was too busy at the mirror to join his "silliness." She was suddenly a young lady, making elaborate plans for winning the heart of her father who was already head over heels in love with her, Chris Beth knew—even before his letters came.

When Joe made the planned trip to the general store, he found Wilson's letters which somehow had bunched up in the

444

mail. Thoughtfully, he had written a letter to Young Wil, True, and Marty and, of course, a separate one to Chris Beth and Joe.

Young Wil, white-faced, opened the envelope and then fumbled with the single sheet of writing it contained. It was easy to see that he dreaded to read the lines. He now talked openly about not wanting to go to the city again. But if the letter said come—

True, who was learning to read at an uncanny pace, ripped her letter open and read the words aloud stumbling very little. Daddy loved her. Daddy had found just the right gift . . . Daddy had seen another rainbow . . . it would bring him home . . . someday.

Marty, by far less mature than True, handed True the letter to read aloud to him. But he kept the envelope! Receiving a letter addressed especially to him was of much more importance than what the letter said.

Wilson wrote in much greater detail to Chris Beth and Joe, of course. The courses he was taking were difficult, his schedule heavy—which was good leaving "no time to think." There was no other reference to loneliness or grief.

"That's a good sign," Joe said when he finished reading the letter. "He's working his way through it." Then, picking up the letter again, "There's a postscript on the back," he said. "Did you see it?"

When Chris Beth shook her head, Joe read it aloud: "There's so little time. Had hoped for Thanksgiving with you but will have only the one day. And Christmas seems so far away!"

"He won't have to wait!" True said happily and went back to experimenting with her hair.

Joe looked at Chris Beth in amusement and then lowered his voice. "Have you mentioned our plans to your principal?"

"Mr. Oberon loves that title," she smiled. "If I could use it somehow in making the request—and, to answer your question, no, I haven't. I guess I'm afraid to—like Young Wil was about opening the letter. By the way, what *did* it say?"

"I don't know, but nothing earthshaking, I guess. He seems fine."

Chris Beth hoped that she would feel fine—after tomorrow. Yes, tomorrow for sure she must approach her "principal."

When she approached Mr. Oberon the following day after school, Chris Beth was surprised how willingly he listened to her request for a short leave and the reasons behind it. He kept nodding in encouragement and before she realized it, Chris Beth found herself confiding some of her misgivings—things she had kept carefully to herself.

"I understand completely," he said when she finished. "And I concur. Of course, as your principal, I may find it necessary to speak with the president of the board before reaching a decision. You understand?"

Chris Beth understood. But how did Mr. Oberon feel?

Mr. Oberon had taken charge of larger bodies of children than this before. Mr. Oberon could manage. As a matter of fact, Mr. Oberon said, with a squaring of his thin shoulders, that he had been thinking—just thinking, mind you—that it might be wise if one of them attended the Teacher's Institute held in Portland on Thanksgiving weekend. *Thanksgiving weekend!*

"Oh, Mr. Oberon, that would give us two whole days with our brother-in-law—put the family together—"

"It can be managed!" he said as if the matter were settled. "I am glad to help you out in time of trouble. Remember that, Mrs. Craig."

With a sudden rush of warmth, Chris Beth said, "Oh please, when we are out of the presence of the children, can't you call me by my first name?"

Mr. Oberon's pale eyes met hers. They seemed to have lost the glint of cool arrogance that she felt was designed to provoke her.

"Thank you," he said as if acknowledging a first compliment.

Carried away on the wings of excitement, Chris Beth said daringly, "Then I think I shall call you Alexander—no, Alex. Has anyone called you that before?"

Alexander Oberon looked flustered. "No. *Alex*," he licked his upper lip as if sampling the word. "I like that. Yes, I like it very much!"

Chris Beth left him standing, still stunned, in the middle of the larger classroom and hurried out to tell the children the good news. Then the four of them urged Dobbin ahead so they could tell Joe.

"Well, it's all settled—except for the biggest part of all. Getting tickets on the stage and warning Wilson we're coming!" he smiled. "I'll ride over to Turn-Around Inn tomorrow, check schedules—"

"Oh, Joe!" Chris Beth interrupted, feeling reckless. "I have so much to do, but I haven't seen Mrs. Malone for ages and—"

When she looked questioningly at Joe, he said, "We'll get it all done. Come along that far."

But Mrs. Malone had other ideas. The air in her kitchen was heavy with peeled fruit and boiling vegetables in preparation for the evening meal. On top of the stove she was boiling a smoked ham. So dinner at the inn was under control, she said.

"Just gimme a minute t'leave a note for O'Higgin and I'll be comin' along."

The suggestion caught Chris Beth by surprise. "That would be nice," she murmured, "but I hadn't planned—"

"'Course you hadn't," she said, wiping her hands on her apron, "but then you hadn't planned on goin'—and *that* calls for a brand spankin' new dress!"

"No—no, really—I mean, we can't afford more than the tickets."

"Amelia!" Mrs. Malone called up the stairs to one of her stepdaughters. "Bring down my winter felt." Mrs. Malone turned to look into the mirror above the hall tree as she smoothed back the strands of graying hair and tucked them into the practical bun at the nape of her neck. "You know, maybe you won't have t'scrounge around as much as you might think money-wise. Trustees pay *your* board 'n keep so that's one less ticket. We'll invest in some taffeta. You seen th' new dress shops?"

Chris Beth had not. Well, they sure beat the catalog-ordered one all to pieces. Custom-made? Oh! That would cost too much. Now, who was talkin' 'bout hirin' it done? Why, Mrs.

Malone could take "one gander" at them shop windows and copy that French lady's work. . . .

While Joe went to the ticket office to arrange transportation and send a wireless to Wilson, Chris Beth and Mrs. Malone went into the general store to look for the right fabric for *The Dress*.

Mrs. Solomon, looking little changed from the raw-boned, somewhat domineering proprietress Chris Beth had met five years ago, stepped from behind the coffee grinder. "We grind for customers nowadays," she explained. "So what can I be doing for you ladies?"

While Mrs. Malone explained their mission, Chris Beth looked around, surprised at the changes. Fewer picks and shovels. More laces, buttons, and ribbons on the newly-oiled counters. The store, looking large since the three windows were added, still smelled of camphor; but it was less overwhelming since installation of the line of colognes marked: ESPECIALLY FOR MILADY'S TOILETTE!

"This calico would be practical for traveling," Mrs. Solomon said as she and Mrs. Malone joined Chris Beth.

"Not this time, Bertie," Mrs. Malone said. "Show us something in taffeta—less'n you'd rather we shopped around—"

"This way!" Bertie Solomon's words tumbled over each other as she swished through the bolts of dry goods.

Chris Beth's heart beat rapidly with excitement as she fingered the luxury of the waterfalls of taffeta in brilliant autumn colors. They were *all* so tempting—until she saw the indescribably beautiful color that seemed to come alive in her hands.

"Oh, this is it, Mrs. Malone! This is it!"

Mrs. Solomon cleared her throat. "The latest," she said with a quick eye for business. "Still and all, it's expensive— but worth every penny, wouldn't you say, to have the very newest? 'Ashes of Roses' it's called."

"'Ashes of Roses' it's gonna be, Bertie. But put down them scissors till I've done a bit o' lookin' in Madam Francois's window. Then I'll not be needin' a pattern!"

Once Mrs. Malone was out the front door, Bertie Solomon

turned to Chris Beth. "So you're going to see Wilson. Surprises folks around these parts he's not been home looking after his practice."

In spite of herself, Chris Beth felt a liquid trail of anger flood her chest. Bertie was Bertie, Mrs. Malone said—"comin' through in time of trouble but prone to meddle." How true!

"Wilson is in school, Mrs. Solomon—studying pathology." Try as she would, the words were defensive.

Mrs. Solomon swung the scissors to and fro by the string suspending them around and below her neck. "While people hereabouts could be dyin' off like flies," she clucked her tongue. "Not proper he should be alone there in Portland either—too eligible—and all the temptations of the big city—"

"I'm sure Wilson can handle himself," Chris Beth said stiffly.

"All the same it's good you'll be checking. Our Maggie reports that he's well, but it's best you, well, look in on 'im."

The front door swung open to let Mrs. Malone enter, giving Chris Beth a chance to turn away before Bertie Solomon could read the shock in her eyes. Maggie? Maggie was in Portland? She had seen Wilson? Would Mrs. Solomon never give up trying to match her daughter up with Wilson North? How obvious could she get?

Surprise gave way to anger—as if the fire in her heart had never died out where Maggie was concerned. Maggie, the woman who had tried so hard to hurt Vangie with her back-biting ways, would always fan a furious flame in Chris Beth's heart. *Wilson was too busy to see his family. Wilson was too involved in his studies to resume his practice. Wilson's heart needed mending . . . but he was not too busy, involved, or broken-hearted to see Maggie Solomon, this "changed woman" who went back to her old ways. . . .*

A little of the autumn glory went out of the day. A bit of the anticipation went out of Chris Beth's heart. But she determined not to let it show. They would go to Portland as planned. And there she would have a very long, very private talk with her brother-in-law.

18

A First Snowflake— A Growing Fear

❧

IT WAS BEST, Chris Beth decided, to make no issue of the petty incident at the store. Why add a twist of lemon to Joe's plans? She and Mrs. Malone could discuss the ambitious mother and her 'When-I-would-do-good-evil-is-nigh' daughter (Mrs. Malone's apt description) when an opportunity presented itself. But when the older woman brought the partially-finished dress to the Big House for a fitting, Chris Beth felt that it would be a shame to spoil the moment with unpleasantries. Mrs. Malone was obviously excited. And when she lifted the "Ashes of Roses" dress from the faded newspaper wrapping, it was easy to see why!

"Oh, it's beautiful, *beautiful!*" Chris said again and again, holding the dress against her body.

Mrs. Malone's eyes glowed with pleasure; but there was a look of fatigue in their gray depths. Suddenly Chris Beth felt selfish. How could she have let this woman with a husband, six children, and keeper of an inn, always overflowing with guests in need of beds, baths, and meals, take on another project? As a matter of fact, she didn't have to have a new

450

dress just because her own trip came as an unexpected stipend. The old guilt was back. . . .

"Tell me now, how long you plannin' to sit there moon-eyed instead of modelin' my first 'French creation'?" Mrs. Malone asked.

"I'm sorry," Chris Beth said quickly. "It's just that you have so much to do—"

"Th' good Lord gives me a hand. Now, get this dress on!"

Obediently, Chris Beth allowed Mrs. Malone's capable hands to slip the whispering folds of taffeta over her head, letting the soft luxuriousness caress her skin. Mrs. Malone had refused to reveal the secret of *The Dress's* style and Chris Beth found it difficult to stand still during the pinning session. What would it look like?

"Can't I look now—just a little peek?" Chris Beth begged.

"Y'er worse'n my Lola Ann, Amelia, 'n Harmony added up," Mrs. Malone complained, her words muffled by the mouthful of pins. "Lucky us folks today don't have t' keep others standin' while we stick a garment in place. Turn a bit to th' right."

Chris Beth turned. "'Most finished," Mrs. Malone said. "Times was, y' know when we had no pins. Turn!" Waiting for Chris Beth to turn, Mrs. Malone talked on, "Had only one needle here in the settlement when Ma sewed my clothes. Used to share with folks around us. Us kids took the needle for patchin' from one homestead to th' other. Our Ma's threaded th' precious piece of steel with red yarn and stuck it in the eye of an Irish potato—once we lost it—like I lost my listenin' audience, it's plain t' see. All right, go ahead, child, and have yourself a look!"

Chris Beth ran to the full-length mirror above the lowboy in the adjoining room. There she stopped in absolute awe at the reflection she saw.

The demurely-high, lace-edged stock collar offset by daringly-short, three-quarter length sleeves . . . the bolero effect made by Valenciennes lace and insertion stitched onto the bodice . . . the high-style tucks nipping in the waistline . . . the exciting skirt made with front panel and wide, wide fullness at the sides. Chris Beth whirled around as if dancing to silent music, causing her cheeks to take on a rosy glow—the exact shade of the beautiful gown.

In a burst of excitement, Chris Beth cried out, "Oh, Mrs. Malone! I'm beautiful—"

Then, embarrassed, she stopped short. But Mrs. Malone picked up the conversation matter-of-factly. " 'Course you are, but th' dress didn't create it—just let it show."

Then, picking up a spool of thread and three fallen pins, Mrs. Malone put them into her pin cushion, tucked it in her paisley bag, and said, "Let me help y' out of the garment. O'Higgin's probably chompin' at the bits of loneliness—or scarin' the young'uns stiff with them Spook Hollow tales brought over from Ireland," she said affectionately.

At the door, Chris Beth paused before saying good-bye. "Mrs. Malone, you *do* think it's proper for me to be going to Portland?"

"To see Wilson? Well, of course!"

"No—I mean, on a pleasure trip—so soon after—"

Mrs. Malone sighed. "Chris Beth, it's been almost three months since our Vangie left us. Life goes on. Or could it be," Mrs. Malone asked suddenly, "that what you're really wonderin' is if you oughta be wearin' black?"

"Well," Chris Beth admitted, "I did wonder if the color was too bright."

"Humph! Think Wilson won't be needin' that? Me, I never was one for long faces and shrouds! I plumb refused a black shawl for my head when I lost my Mr. Malone, rest his soul. Wore me a green bonnet instead. And you know what? O'Higgin spotted it that very day—and in due time, well, you know the rest. We just never know what the Lord has in His pocket, but 'tis always better'n we expected."

Chris reached out and embraced Mrs. Malone, wondering what she would do without her. For a moment, they held each other in the kind of silence between women that says more than words. Then, Mrs. Malone opened the door to let in a gust of late-November air which had grown suddenly chill. And how had the sky darkened without their noticing?

Mrs. Malone climbed into the buggy then called, "Well, what do you know? A first snowflake—pretty early, I'd say. Best I hurry!"

Waving goodbye, Chris Beth closed the door quickly, wincing as the cold air it fanned poured over her, seeming to seep to her bones.

Usually, she welcomed the snow along with the children. But not today. If it stuck . . . well, she mustn't think like that. All the same, she could not resist going to the window to peer through the drapes. Maybe the lonely little flake was all. But no! Big, soft flakes were melting against the glass. Any minute now, if the temperature dropped, they would stick.

Chris Beth turned from the window, her sense of elation gone. Somehow she knew that she would never wear *The Dress*—the beautiful "Ashes of Roses" dress.

19
Emergency!

❧

WITH AN ENTHUSIASM she did not feel, Chris Beth called upstairs to where Young Wil was tutoring Marty and True in their vowel sounds, "Dismiss your class, and come see the snow!"

"We saw it a'ready," Marty called back morosely.

When the trio came down, there was no spring to their steps, no excitement in their voices. They loved snow, but it could close the roads.

Still trying to dispel the gloom, Chris Beth said to True, "My mother, your grandmother, used to say when it snowed that Mother Goose was picking her goslings for stuffing pillows."

True eyed her gloomily. "My mummy said the feathers came from angel wings. I like that better. *She's* an angel now—my mummy is—huh, Aunt Chrissy?"

Chris Beth hesitated. "I don't know a lot about angels, darling," she said slowly. "I believe they're especially created—"

The child shook her head slowly from side to side. "My mummy's an angel. She's my angel-mother. These feathers could be hers—"

454

An enormous lump formed in Chris Beth's throat. It was with great relief she heard the door of Joe's study open. But before she could welcome him into the group, there was a knock at the front door.

"Brother Joseph! Brother Joseph!" a man's frightened voice called without waiting for an answer to his knock.

Darkness had settled over the valley. But a different kind of darkness settled over Chris Beth's heart. A strange premonition—worse than any she had ever before experienced—gripped her entire being, paralyzing her so that she was unable to move. It was Joe who had to hurry across the big living room and open the door.

Ruben Beltran, one of the Basque sheep raisers, stood shivering in the darkness. His hair was disheveled. He wore no coat. And there was the unmistakable stain of blood oozing from his left shoulder. Blood!

Oh, dear Lord! Chris Beth's numbed mind could pray no further. As if in another world, she heard Mr. Beltran's incoherent words. Shooting . . . cattlemen first . . . then vigilantes taking "law and order" in their own hands had joined the masked men . . . crosses burned in yards . . . burned Ole Tobe's house . . . determined to get "black blood" out of the settlement . . . slaughtered his sheep. . . .

"Inside before you freeze, Mr. Beltran," Joe urged gently as he ushered the man in and closed the door. "Is Tobe all right?"

"Not killed, but left with a wandering mind after losing his Mandy short while back. Oh, Brother Joseph, come—come *now*. It's my Liza. She's shot!"

Little Liza! Chris Beth felt a wave of nausea sweep over her. Liza, the beautiful little 8-year-old cripple who was unable to travel the long distance to school daily but visited sometimes and was a member of Chris Beth's Sunday school class.

"They wanted a '*human* sacrifice,' they said," Mr. Beltran sobbed. "Called her my 'sacrificial lamb'—my Liza—"

Chris Beth forced her leaden feet to move, forced her limp hands to reach for the sheep raiser's work-calloused ones. "I'm so sorry—so sorry," she whispered through frozen lips.

Sympathy she would offer. Hot coffee . . . and she would bind up his wounds with the gauze and disinfectant Wilson had left for emergencies . . . then tomorrow she would visit. . . .

But even as the thoughts crowded through her mind with confusion, Chris Beth knew what would happen. She would turn around to see Joe donning his heavy coat, buckling his boots, picking up his Bible.

"No!" The word forced its way from her lips. "Joe!" She ran to her husband, clutching at his arms to keep them from pushing into the wool windbreaker. "Don't go—not tonight—don't get involved—"

When Joe pushed her hands from his arms gently, her panic turned to hysteria. "You *can't* go! Don't get mixed up in their quarrels. Let them settle it. You—you're a minister—not a doctor or sheriff—or a judge! A *minister!*"

"Which is why I have to go, my darling. I won't be long, I promise. Lock the doors and try not to worry. We'll be together soon, I promise." He kissed her tenderly and was gone.

As if in a trance, Chris Beth watched the two men mount horses and ride away in the gloom. The snow was beginning to stick, her dazed mind noted. Joe was gone—gone as he's never left before—gone to settle a shooting. Gone without a last word of love from her . . . and she hadn't even offered to bind Mr. Beltran's wound. What good were their years here anyway? The valley was more troubled than before she, Joe, Vangie, and Wilson had dedicated their lives to it.

Suddenly, she was on her knees. "O Lord," she cried out in the words of David. "How long will thou be angry against the prayer of my people . . ." Her prayer dissolved into dry sobs of despair.

20
A Distant Prayer

❧

CHRIS BETH ROSE from her knees at length, but the peace she had hoped for had not come. Uneasily, she peered into the darkness again. It was still snowing and the flakes were smaller. That meant the snow would stick. As she replenished the wood in the fireplace, she wondered where Young Wil could have taken Marty and True. She remembered vaguely that Joe had cautioned the older boy to look after the family while he was gone. Wasn't that unusual—for such a short trip?

Forcing her mind another direction, Chris Beth prepared tomato soup and cornbread. At the sound of feet on the back porch, she opened the door to find Young Wil standing with milk pails in his hands. The two younger children, carefully muffled in their snow clothes, walked behind him—each swinging a lighted lantern.

Surprised, she stooped to kiss them both and give Young Wil a look of appreciation. "Come in," she said quickly. "Get your mittens off and we'll have supper in front of the fire."

They ate in near-silence, each buried in private thoughts. There was no need to force small talk none of them wanted,

457

Chris Beth knew. Somehow she managed to hear their prayers, mostly pleas that the snow would stop, then she and Young Wil went downstairs to keep watch. Their concerns went deeper than disappointment. Joe's safety was at stake and they both knew it.

For a few minutes neither of them spoke. In the silence, Chris Beth heard the scrape of a branch against the west window. That meant the wind was rising. Snow would drift over the roads, hiding them . . . and somewhere out there her husband was fighting to save lives . . . maybe his own. The fire crackled again and she tried to concentrate on the comforting warmth of the flames. But something happened to her vision. Her eyes went out of focus. The flames blurred. And in their place she saw a field of snow, drifted in waves sculpted by angry wind, piled high against the trees—*melting in pools of blood!*

Raising a hand to her mouth, Chris was barely able to stifle the cry of horror that began in her throat. Then, mercifully, Young Wil spoke.

"I never did tell you what was in Uncle Wil's letter."

"No," she managed, her voice trembling, "you never did."

Reaching into the breast pocket of his plaid shirt, he drew out a crumpled sheet of paper. "It's a prayer. My Uncle Wil wrote it. He's a writer, you know."

Yes, she knew. And even with the terror she was feeling, Chris Beth was able to detect the pride in Young Wil's voice.

"I'll read it if you want me to—it's good."

She nodded mutely.

Loving Father, open my eyes and my heart that I may see this fair earth which You have created. Open my heart that I may feel this beauty pulsate through my soul. Let me see, let me feel, the warm joy in Your sunshine, the quietness of Your forests, the strength of Your everlasting hills. Through these, let me know that I am safely held in Your strong hands and be sustained by Your love. And, in time of storms, Lord, remind me that I am near nature's heart. Still my restless spirit. Remind me that the frozen brook, though silent, is running underneath and that the sleeping bulbs will awaken one day to become lilies of the field. And, for these storms, make my life better, stronger, more worthy—more aware that the Eye watching over the sparrow is watching over me.

Young Wil read the words clearly and beautifully. When he finished, Chris Beth was too overcome to speak.

"Did you like it?" he asked folding it carefully, and returning it to his pocket.

"I think it's one of the most beautiful prayers I ever heard," she said truthfully.

"Did it help? I mean—it always makes me feel better."

Yes, it made her feel better, Chris Beth told him. But she did not say how. It brought no peace—not the kind she needed. But the prayer Wilson had written added a new dimension to him. *Surely,* she thought, *a man who writes like that to a boy must have more understanding than I've allowed. Still, why isn't he here where he belongs? Why does he pray at a distance?*

"The man who brings peace to th' settlement can't be no outsider," Mrs. Malone had said when Joe was weighing his ability to minister here. "He has to be one of us who understands folks' ways and sets a good example even when Sunday's finished!"

That was well and good. But wasn't Wilson one of them, too?

21
All-Night Vigil

❧

THE FIRE WAS nearly out. The logs hissed in the grate
and a pencil line of smoke trailed up the chimney. The room
felt suddenly colder and Chris Beth wrapped her arms around
her chest and held onto her elbows. "You'd better try and get
some sleep," she said to Young Wil. "I—I think I'll read
awhile."

When the boy's long legs disappeared around the bend of the
stairway, Chris Beth put another log in the fireplace and paced
the floor restlessly. Outside the wind shrieked. It was easy to
imagine such force blowing snow in horizontal sheets past the
windows. She must do something—*anything*—to get herself
under control. It was then that she remembered Vangie's
diary. She would read through it until Joe came home.

Skimming what she had read before, Chris began anew:

Today I told Mama about the child I am carrying. She will
tell Father Stein and I am terrified of his wrath. Oh, if only I
had Chrissy with me . . . my sister would forgive my every
transgression . . . together we would talk to the Lord and I
would be forgiven by them both. . . .

460

Misty eyed, Chris Beth read on, stopping at points to stare into the corners of the big room where shadows tangled against the massive furniture as the logs in the fireplace shifted restlessly. Each time it was harder to return to Vangie's spiraled handwriting and read the broken-hearted messages which clutched at her own heart and squeezed it dry. But she forced herself to read on.

Vangie's father knew . . . pushed her from the house, calling her a "woman of the night" and saying that God would punish the baby . . . her lonely trip west after Jonathan's accidental death . . . and being reunited with "my beloved sister to whom I dedicate this book."

But how can Chris Beth love me? I deliberately came between her and Jonathan—only then I did fall in love with him, deceiver though he was . . . I always envied my older sister, but I never meant to hurt her. How could I have been so fickle, so vain? But I have paid—oh, how I have paid! There are times, even now, when I take a good look at myself in the mirror and ask what would have happened had I not come here? Would love have bloomed between Wilson and Chris Beth . . . did I make the same mistake all over again? But enough rambling, I must set new day-to-day goals and look forward to the wonderful, long, *long* life which lies ahead for the four of us. . . .

Softly at first then in a swelling of volume the grandfather clock chimed the mellow notes of "*Tempus Fugit*," a plaintive reminder that life for the four of them did *not* go on for a long, long time. Vangie, dear little Vangie, lay beneath the first blanket of snow. Startled by a new thought, Chris Beth sat erect to count the strokes of the clock's gong. *Maybe Joe was buried in this snowstorm, too . . . and Wilson was far away. . . .*

Three o'clock! Reason told Chris Beth that she should be in bed, but she was unable to leave the spot where Joe had left her. Reason told her that he would be all right. It would be foolish to ride back in the storm. He would stay with the Beltrans . . . but a force stronger than reason told her this wasn't so. Joe would be home as soon as possible. He had promised. Nothing would hold him back . . . unless . . . yes, something had happened . . . *something*.

To curb her wild imaginings, Chris Beth picked up Vangie's diary again. Once past the emotional prologue, Vangie wrote on a day-to-day basis concerning her arrival . . . her enchantment with the beautiful Oregon Country and her love for its warm, gentle people.

After awhile, Chris Beth forgot that she was reading from the pen of her departed sister and it became a sad-sweet pleasure to taste again with her the excitement of their early days here. The pages filled up with their move into Joe's cabin—a doll's house, Vangie called it—the evenings around the fireplace where she sat now . . . only it was the four of them then, planning their weddings, spinning dreams like dew-pearled cobwebs that lasted but a single night . . . Wilson's acceptance of the baby . . . his claiming it for his own.

Some of the writing was too personal. It belonged to Wilson. Chris Beth wondered anew why her sister had insisted that it was she who should read it and follow whatever instructions lay somewhere within the pages. It was important that she read on, but she was so tired.

She leaned back wearily and dropped into a strange, restless world of sleep. In her dreams, Chris Beth was in a cramped room—airless, with sooty curtains hanging motionless over crooked window frames. Out! She wanted out! Wildly, she fumbled for a door which seemed nonexistent. Until suddenly it appeared right in the center of the dream and opened for her by an unseen hand. And there before her lay a beautiful garden, sun-splashed and green-carpeted, with purple waterfalls of wisteria cascading over the high stone walls. There were no faces, but she knew the voices! Joe, Vangie, Wilson calling for her to join them. The door was open. Why then was she unable to pass? Instead, she crashed into an invisible wall.

Damp with perspiration, Chris Beth came slowly out of the dream. Burnt orange flames were crackling around three newly-stacked logs before her. A long arm reached out with poker in hand to adjust them.

"Joe!"

"He's not here yet, Chrissy," Young Wil said softly.

She tried to sit up. "What time is it?"

"Six thirty. The milking's finished and I have coffee for us."

"Oh, darling, you're wonderful," Chris Beth said, licking her dry lips and trying to remember clearly events of the preceding night.

Stiffly, she drew herself up, sensing immediately that something in the room was different. There was a peculiar, glaring quality to the faint rays of dawn—a certain brightness that she knew could not be artificial. And yet it couldn't be the beginning of sunrise either.

Pulling her woolen robe around her, she went back to the east window. And, with sinking heart, she saw a world gagged by snow.

Young Wil joined her at the window. "I'll saddle Dobbin right after breakfast. Don't you think I should ride over to the inn?"

"I don't know—I just don't know. I'm so worried," she confessed, "but I don't want you taking chances. Look!"

She pointed a shaking finger at three figures, apparently wearing snowshoes, moving slowly toward them in the dim light. It was strange, she was to think long, long afterward, how neither she nor Young Wil rushed to meet the men. Somehow, they knew something was wrong.

22

*"We Be Comin'
To Tell You . . ."*

❧

THREE MEN WITH grim faces. O'Higgin, Nate Goldsmith, and Alexander Oberon stood hesitantly at the front door.

O'Higgin, his usually ruddy face pale even against the
whiteness of the snow, was first to speak. "We be comin' to
tell you—"

The booming voice broke. He was unable to go on. The
other two men stood statue-still, silent in sorrow.

"It's Joe, isn't it?" Chris Beth was unable to recognize the
voice that must be hers.

O'Higgin nodded and shook his head to indicate that he was
unable to speak more than the single word, "Accident."

He didn't need to. Chris Beth knew. She had known all
along.

"*Accident?*" The voice of Young Wil, who had come to
stand behind her, was no more than a horrified whisper.
"What kind of accident?"

None of the men answered. They simply stood like actors in
a pointless play who had forgotten their lines. And she, the
main character in this tragedy, would have to prompt them.

"Joe's dead," she said woodenly.

464

They spoke then, the three of them at once. It was a mistake . . . a terrible mistake. It was easy to make mistakes in horrible mixups like there had been . . . they—nobody would even know whether it was a drunken cattle-man, sheep rancher, or vigilante—fired wildly. But Joe wasn't hit, ma'am . . . 'twas his horse . . . and when the animal fell. . . .

Joe was pinned beneath. Yes, she knew. Somehow she knew. And she had been unable to reach him through the invisible glass door of her dream. But the men wouldn't understand how she had failed Joe. She had allowed him to go. And she had known. All the while, she had known. But these men hadn't known—and they were offering help.

They'd take care of everything—less'n she had requests?

Yes, the grave should be beside Vangie—there was room. And on the south side, closer to the church.

Joe's personal effects? Yes, she'd take them. Thank you.

No way you can cross the snow—maybe in a day or two. They'd get the new reverend in Centerville weather permit-tin'. If not, would she be opposed to Brother Amos sayin' the final words?

Brother Amos would be fine. Joe loved the "disciples." Yes, plenty of food . . . no, she wasn't afraid to stay here . . . not with Young Wil and Esau . . . the old dog was old but still a good barker. . . .

Best they be goin' then. Lots to do.

"Shouldn't they get word to Uncle Wil?" his nephew prompted from behind.

Oh, they had a'ready. And the missuses were bakin'—only problem bein' how soon roads would be passable. But they understood. . . .

"Y'll be needin' some time fer—things," Nate Goldsmith said. "Now, jest you take them days off you was plannin'."

"Thank you. You've all been very kind," Chris Beth said from the stage of unreality on which she stood. "There's no way I can repay you."

"Mrs. Craig—Chris Beth—" Alexander Oberon said softly, "there are no words—"

"I know."

"If you need my assistance, you will let me help? It would give me much pleasure—I mean, considering the circumstances—"

"I know," Chris Beth said again. "But for now, I need to be alone. Just let me be alone." He bowed and the three men left.

Young Wil would warm up some coffee for them before the little ones got up, he said. He would take care of her. He had promised—

Chris Beth allowed herself to be led across the living room and helped onto a couch. Thoughtfully, the boy drew a quilt over her while pain tried to dip below the surface of her unfeeling heart.

Dispassionately, she remembered that once upon a time— many, many years ago, six, wasn't it now?—she had thought *jilted* was the ugliest word in the English language. *Death* was better, she had said then. Well, maybe it was—if it happened to the right person. Right now, she would welcome it. Here she was, alone again—widowed now—with a family of children to look after. In a strange, detached sort of way, it was good that the weather had made her a prisoner. Good not to be going to the funeral and hear words she no longer believed about God's mercy, His goodness, and love. If God cared, where was He now? Like Wilson, He had forgotten her.

Did she doze? Or was the dream real, after all? Chris Beth was back in the airless little room—no, she was looking into it. She was in the garden this time but still alone. Joe, Vangie, and Wilson were in the smaller room judging from their distant voices—only she was unable to break down the barrier between them. And behind her were mocking voices, "We be comin' to tell you . . . they are gone, all gone . . . Wilson's gone, too . . . we be comin' to tell you . . . you are alone, alone, *alone!*"

The reverie ended when Young Wil touched her shoulder

lightly. "The coffee's ready," he said gently. He was alive. This world was real.

She touched his hand in appreciation and drank the scalding liquid gratefully. Telling Alex that she wished to be alone did not preclude this Young Wil. She'd meant she needed time— time to sort things out when she could think. And, yes, she'd meant something more. She didn't need other people, outsiders, in her life. And certainly not another man. Look what men had done to her life. They had taken her heart to an early grave. . . .

23
The Days
Thereafter

❧

THE DAYS THEREAFTER were white—utterly devoid of color, just layer upon layer of white drifting in, blotting things out, barricading Chris Beth against the world. She felt nothing, nothing at all. Years later, old-timers were to speak of the "Year of the Big Snow" and she would not remember what they were talking about. The snow made her world soft, dreamy. It insulated her against the punishing voices—for a time.

Days were dark. The skies were sullen with sackcloth clouds sifting down their angry ashes to drift higher and higher, up to the windows and almost to the roof of the Big House. Not a trace of civilization remained above the snow. On the first night, the winds grieved over the roof, and then a final layer of ice shut out its cries. The silence thickened. Ticking of the clocks was deafening.

"Are we all right, Mommie?" Marty whimpered. "And why's my daddy not home?" Chris Beth bit her lip and poured coffee for herself.

"He's with my angel-mother," True answered his question.

Chris Beth knew then that Young Wil had tried to explain to her.

Marty's eyes sought Chris Beth's in a dazed, vacant stare. "But why didn't he say good-bye like Aunt Vangie—why?"

Chris Beth set her coffee cup down hard, the noise pleasing her somehow in the silent house. "People say good-bye in different ways," she improvised in an effort to explain a matter she did not understand herself. "Maybe it's easier for some to go."

Marty looked at her suspiciously. Then his lower lip quivered, a sure sign that he was about to burst into tears. And how could she help? She couldn't even cry—let alone find words. She had nothing to give. Nothing at all. Her insides were empty and there was rock where her heart used to be.

"Come here, fellow," Young Wil spoke up masterfully. "You know how it is with people. Some stand at the door with hats in their hands and talk for an hour, letting the cat out and the wind in."

Chris Beth saw a flicker of a smile cross the child's face. "And others—well, they just grab their hats and run. Like you and I are going to do as soon as this blizzard's finished. Tell me, have you ever ridden a bobsled?"

Marty's eyes lighted up. "Could we ride one to Portland?"

"Part way, I promise!"

I should be thankful for him, Chris Beth thought numbly. But she could no longer praise the Lord for anything.

Three days passed, each taking on a sameness of numb routine. Vaguely she was aware that somewhere ahead lay an enormous black sea of time that she had to cross—sometime. It was hopeless. She could never make it by wading. She had to swim. But she was too tired . . . still, she would realize even in her trance, she had to keep moving her limbs. Otherwise, she would drown . . . and, even in her depression, she wasn't sure she wanted to drown. There were the children, three of them, who depended on her. . . .

Impersonally, Chris Beth picked up the effects O'Higgin had brought. Joe's gold watch—his father's initials on back. His

Bible, marked in a million places. And the simple gold band that said once she had had a husband. Carefully, she put them away near Vangie's diary. One day the pain would come. One day she would find an outlet, and yes, then the pain would claw its way inside, twisting, writhing, living there forever. But for now, she preferred this dark Garden of Gethsemane— where there was no remembrance of former things. . . .

24
The Thirteenth Day

ON THE THIRTEENTH DAY of the "Big Snow" Chris Beth awoke. She knew she was awake when terror gripped her heart. There was a sudden clarity of what she was doing to herself. Unless there was a change, a drastic one, she would vanish into nothingness. Not like Vangie and Joe who had no control over the final chapters of their lives. But, heaven help her, because she willed it so.

Somehow, she must cross that great, dark lake. Not that she would feel the waters rushing past. She was beyond feeling anything except the hard core of bitterness inside. It was a unique kind of bitterness. Not one that demanded retaliation or prosecution of that faceless person who had snuffed out Joe's life. That would do no good. It couldn't bring her husband back. Rather, the bitterness was directed at the place she heretofore had loved. The Oregon Country with all its magnificence, its challenges, adventure, and mystery, had betrayed her. Where was law and order? Where was justice? Where was God?

In the cold silence of the dawn of awakening, Chris Beth closed her eyes for a fleeting second before rising to go about reentering the world of reality—bitter, but no longer wrapped in a gauze of deep, pervasive depression. Behind her eyelids there paraded an endless procession of indifferent, unfeeling, uncaring people. The drunken ones—on alcohol, power, or unrestrained emotion—went on with their quarreling, persecuting, *killing*! The others sat in the wings watching the parade pass . . . helpless children . . . grieving widows . . . old people, robbed of family, friends, and life's few possessions, but too weak of muscle or spirit to fight. She would have to get away—get away and take the children—before they, too, became victims of what might have been. Where didn't matter. Just away. And nobody cared now.

With that purpose in mind, it was easier to swing back into the morning routine. Almost pleasant to imagine the look of surprise and excitement lighting the faces of Young Wil, True, and Marty when their noses picked up the trail of browning sage sausage, buckwheat cakes, and fragrant coffee.

They did not disappoint her. With whoops and bounds, as if it were Christmas morning, they bounded down the stairs. Poor little tykes! They must wonder where she had been.

True and Marty gave her a wet kiss on both cheeks and with many an "Ooooooh" and Ahhhhhh" sat down at the table with small hands folded for prayer. Young Wil squeezed her hand, surveyed the table, and said, "Don't you think it's a little early to milk?"

"Much too early," Chris Beth answered, forcing a smile. Then, in a voice she hoped wasn't too false, "True would you like to say grace?"

All heads went down and True rushed through with: "God is great, God is good; and we thank Him for this food!"

Chris Beth busied herself at the stove. One good thing about pancakes. Frying them keeps the cook busy.

Finally, pouring herself a cup of coffee, she sat down beside Young Wil. "I've been thinking," she said carefully, "we are going to have to find a way out as soon as possible—" She paused wondering just what she meant herself. Out for help?

Or away? *Both*, probably, but she did not intend to mention the longer-range plan. Not yet.

Young Wil folded his napkin neatly and placed it beside his plate. "I've thought of several things," he said. "Some of them wild. Like hitching Esau to a sled—no, I guess that's crazy. And I don't think Dobbin could make it—*Dobbin!* Did they—did anything—?"

"I don't know," she said tightly. "That's one of the things we have to find out. And how Liza is—as well as—" She found herself unable to go on.

"I could try making snowshoes like O'Higgin and the others."

"No!" The word came out sharper than intended, but Chris Beth saw again the mocking vision of blood in the snow and Young Wil's body pitifully injured, motionless—*dead*. The vision passed and she softened her voice. "I can't have anything happening to you—we'll just have to wait."

The wait was not long. In her state of merciful unconsciousness, Chris Beth had been unaware that the wind had subsided. And, while the skies remained threatening, the best she could tell from the little patch of sky she could see, the snow had stopped. The children, busy with a homework game in ciphering Young Wil had improvised, had stopped talking about the snow.

It was with great surprise then that, shortly after sunrise time, there was a thundering rumble on the housetop followed by a soft thud. The snow was melting from the roof! Somebody would get through to them. Even in her bitterness, Chris Beth knew that this was a place where miracles not only happened, but they happened all the time. The warm-hearted settlers were not in the procession of unfeeling people. They were the victims!

And with that realization came her first wave of compassion. The settlers had lost first Vangie, their trusted nurse . . . then Wilson, their life-or-death doctor . . . and now, Joe, the spiritual leader who held the flock together. If she could bring herself to pray, it would be for them.

25
Familiar Arms

⤚

To HER AMAZEMENT, Chris Beth saw blue sky through the upstairs window the next morning. Just a patch, but it offered promise. Then in the afternoon, the sun came out. The children talked excitedly. A rooster crowed. Esau stretched his legs stiffly and sampled the outdoor air. But Young Wil frowned in concentration.

"Chrissy," he said uneasily, "there's a Chinook wind starting."

"Surely not this time of year. It's usually February or so—"

It occurred to her then to wonder just what day it was and, checking the calendar, she saw all days crossed off except November 30. That was today—the last day of the month! Thanksgiving had come and gone and she had done nothing about it. There was so much she had to make up to her family for. She determined anew that her own bitterness would not twist their souls as it had twisted hers.

Chris Beth realized with a start that Young Wil was talking. "—and with a snowpack like this, the warm, east wind can cause flooding."

With a shudder, she recalled the devastation of the one flood in the valley. Oh, she hoped that would never happen again. Well, so much for Wilson and his rainbows! Let him go on chasing them forever. It didn't matter any longer. Her need for him and his promises was gone.

Chris Beth had thought that she and Young Wil were alone until True spoke up suddenly. "Well, I know what! We'll all pray that the wind blows just enough to make a road to our house—like God caused the east wind to part the Dead Sea."

"*Red* Sea," Young Wil corrected.

"Red Sea, Dead Sea—whadda *I* see?" Marty singsonged from upstairs. But before Chris Beth could reprimand him, Marty's young voice went on excitedly, "it's somebody coming! We're having company!"

Chris Beth ran up the stairs two at a time. And, sure enough, she spotted the distant outline of what had to be a human being! Without conversation, both she and Young Wil hurried downstairs and to the back door where the shovels stood. And without bothering to don heavy, outdoor clothing they began to shovel furiously, pushing the snow from the front door to make a passageway. While Young Wil continued to scoop a path, she went back to replenish the fire sending a plume of smoke into the air. No wayfaring stranger must miss their signal!

Then she returned to help Young Wil, digging frantically until her back ached. It felt good to be so involved, so deliciously tired, and so excited.

When she raised her head, she realized that the traveler—though moving slowly on heavy snowshoes—was almost close enough for recognition. Already, she could tell that the caller was a man. A peddler maybe, judging from the bulky pack on his back. She went back to tunneling. And the two smaller children, released from prison and away from the watchful eye of adults, went back to their snowball throwing. *Scoop, shovel, dig . . .* nothing else seemed important.

Chris Beth became aware suddenly that her heart was pounding strangely in her ears and that the white world around her swirled strangely like the frosting on a giant, wedding cake. Almost without warning, the world tilted crazily and she sank into the snow.

Someone bent over her, then someone she knew, she believed. "What are you trying to do—give yourself pneumonia?" The voice was brusque, but the arms which picked her up were gentle, warm, and familiar. . . .

26
A Velvet Rose

❧

CHRIS BETH'S FIRST AWARENESS was one of color. Ribbons of light wound in and out behind her closed eyelids like the winding of a May pole. Squeezing tightly. Inflicting pain.

Experimentally, she opened one eye and then the other. The lids drooped heavily, causing objects around her to emerge only in fuzzy outlines. She tried again and something above her moved. A kitten? *We don't own a kitten,* she thought, *so where am I?*

Weakly, she tried to rise on an elbow but sank back in bed with a little moan. The throbbing pain in her head was unbearable and her chest felt as if a heavy weight lay across it. And why was it so hard to breathe?

Above the roaring in her ears, Chris Beth heard the faint ticking of a clock. And something else, eyes closed against the light in the room, she strained to listen—not moving. The sound was rhythmic, soft, and velvety. The kitten was purring! Again, she struggled to open her eyes, this time making out the outline more clearly. It was her own chiffonier with a gray kitten with incredibly green eyes perched on top. Then

477

she was in her own room? And a window must be open. It was cold, so cold. With an effort, she turned her head ever so slightly to the right. There, framed by the open window, was the outline of a man—tall, lean, and clad in a heavy sweater to ward off the cold.

"Joe—oh *Joe!*" The words were torn from her lips.

He turned then and his face was fully illuminated for the first time. "Wilson," she whispered, trying in vain to put the fragments of her thinking together. A weight on her chest. A weight in her heart.

Wilson bent over her. "You have been ill, Chrissy—very ill. And still are—"

"I'm so c-cold," she said through chattering teeth.

Wilson tucked the quilts high up around her neck and reached beneath the covers to feel her feet. "I think we can heat some rocks to warm you up now. Fever's been too high until now—you *did* contract pneumonia."

Pneumonia! The dread disease. The killer. She had *pneumonia! And there was no cure.* Well, she had wanted to die, she remembered as the past weeks began to take shape in her mind. No, that was before she'd determined to swim her way out . . . maybe she wanted to live.

"Am I going to die?" Chris Beth knew that her voice was stronger now. A million questions sometime, but the truth now.

Did she imagine it or did Wilson hesitate a moment? "Of course not!" he said professionally. "My patients live forever." But his attempt at the old caustic manner failed. It was too soon. The transition was too great.

"C-close the window," she begged, wondering if the ice in the marrow of her bones was from the low temperature or her aching heart.

Wilson sat down on the edge of the bed, tucked at the covers again, and then leaned his body over hers as if to shield her against the cold. She could feel his warmth against her cheek. The feel of it comforted her. Here was life—where there had been so much death.

"I can't risk closing the window—not now when I believe the new method's working," he said softly. "We used to think keeping the patient warm was the solution—rooms over-heated, stuffy, stale, nothing to breathe. Now we're experi-menting—" Wilson paused as if regretting his use of the word. "Breathe deeply, Chrissy. Inhale . . . one, two, three . . . that's it . . . exhale . . . one, two, three . . ."

Chris Beth relaxed against him, grateful for the occasional brush of his warm, woolly sweater against her face. It seemed so good, so natural to have him here. There were questions to ask, but her mind could not formulate them . . . some of the past seemed missing. But in her numbed state, she could ask only, "Who's *he*?"

Her tongue was thick, but Wilson understood. "*She*," he said with a smile in his voice. "The kitten's a gift to Marty—and her name's 'Emerald' because of her eyes." Now that made sense. And it was about the only thing that did.

Wilson's arms tightened around her cocooned body protec-tively. Drowsiness flowed through every limb and she slept.

The fever came back. For days, Chris Beth hardly knew anyone. Dimly, she was aware of the children's voices, but they came no closer than her bedroom door. Neighbors came and went . . . murmuring in the halls . . . lighting lamps, sitting with Wilson, waiting for the "crisis." When it came, she lapsed into unconsciousness.

All the while, even when she hovered between life and death, Chris Beth was aware of Wilson's presence—soothing her as one would soothe a child, then speaking words of warmth and encouragement she would never remember. Willing her to live.

The next time, consciousness came with an explosion of awareness. Wilson's high-cheekboned face bent over her own. The dark deep-set eyes burned into hers. His mobile mouth, which could be sensitive and tender, even smiling at times, was tight with concern.

"Drink this!" he commanded.

She tried to raise her head, but it doddled foolishly. Supporting her forehead with one hand, Wilson held a cup of odd-scented brew to her lips.

Weak as she was, Chris Beth sniffed suspiciously. "What's in it?"

"Hot tea, honey, lemon juice, with a little brandy."

"I won't drink it."

"You will if I have to force it down you! You've passed through the crisis, Chrissy. You must have a stimulant and this is all I have in my kit."

When she would have turned her head, he pushed the cup between her teeth. "Drink! Or do I have to drench you like we do the new calves?"

Frowning darkly, she sipped, tried to swallow, and went into a spasm of coughing. When it passed, the hateful cup was still at her lips. Nostrils flanged, she gulped down the remains and sank weakly back onto the pillow.

"Bully!" she muttered.

"Patient's going to live," Wilson said with a caustic grin. Then, sitting down beside her, he leaned his head back against the armchair, closed his eyes, and dozed. It was probably the first brief rest period he had taken since coming home she realized in sudden pity. She had put him through a lot. A shame for she certainly did not want to be in his debt. Wilson didn't need sympathy and understanding. He had made that clear. And she was going to protect herself this time—harden her heart. The tired circles beneath his eyes probably came from the pace he and Maggie kept in Portland! He had chosen that life even when she needed him most.

Wilson, his eyes still closed, spoke suddenly. "Stop staring at me and get some rest."

"I'm tired of resting—and I'm hungry. I want some sausage with fried potatoes, sourdough biscuits—"

"You'll get broth."

When he brought her the broth on a tray, Wilson sat beside her and drank a cup of coffee. "I'm sorry I was cross," he said. "The strain of it all, I guess."

Chris Beth laid down her spoon. Wilson picked it up and murmured, "Sorry. Should have known you're too weak to handle this." And carefully, he spooned the hot, bracing broth into her mouth.

"Thank you," Chris Beth said meekly. "And thank you for everything. You saved my life, I guess."

"Spare your gratitude," he said gruffly. "Except for me, you wouldn't have contracted pneumonia. That was a fool-thing to do, incidentally—shoveling like that in the freezing wind with that thin thing on you call a dress."

Chris Beth's breath caught in her throat. "Where is that 'thin thing'—my dress? *You* didn't—"

"I did. Name me ten other people who were on hand to thaw a frozen woman. Oh, my goodness!" His voice took on a teasing falsetto. "What will people say?"

Chris Beth felt her cheeks flame. It was good to be angry. It was good to feel *anything*. But what right did he have—

The moment was saved by a small knock on the door. "You're about to have company," Wilson said with a grin. "Feel up to the 'Children's Hour'?"

Before she could answer, the three of them rushed in, smothering her with kisses, drowning out her weak protests with words of their own. "Uncle Wil brought me a kitten—all my own—and he won't ever sing for anybody else in this world!" That was Marty.

"He's a *girl*, Emerald. And my daddy brought me—oh, wait till you see!" True brought a bisque doll head from behind her. "Aunt Chrissy, it has real moving eyes—"

Marty interrupted her to say that his Emerald had moving eyes, too, and a *body!*

"Aunt Chrissy'll put a body on Minerva, won't you?"

"Whoa, now, you two!" Wilson put a restraining hand on each shoulder. "Give her air and some peace. The sewing will have to wait."

Young Wil stepped shyly up to the bed. "I wanted to show you this." And he handed her a white Bible with a name stamped in gold on the front cover—WILSON NORTH, JR.

North? His name was Ames. "It's beautiful," she said, but her eyes sought Wilson's questioningly.

He returned her gaze steadily but waited for the boy to speak. "It's arranged," Young Wil said. "My name's North—like it should be. Uncle Wil had it done in court."

As long as I live, I'll never figure this man out, Chris Beth thought tiredly. *Which is the real man anyway?*

When her eyes drooped, Wilson shooed the children out of the room then walked out quietly himself, leaving the door ajar. Almost immediately she dozed. There were no dreams, but when she awoke there was a soft velvet rose in her hand.

27
Another Parting

⤙⤚

NEITHER CHRIS BETH nor Wilson made mention of the rose. In fact, they seldom had time alone. The Chinook winds, so feared by the settlers, subsided before melting snow in the higher elevations. Temperatures dropped but not sharply, just enough to allay fears of flooding and bring bright blue days to the valley. Wilson and Young Wil, with the smaller children trailing at their heels, sawed the damaged trees on the North homestead into firewood and put the rest of the place in order. Soon now, Wilson assured Chris Beth, the damaged roads would be repaired enough for use. They would need supplies from the general store at which time Chris Beth would contact Nate Goldsmith to check on the date set for resuming classes. Right? Right, she told Wilson. But neither of them mentioned what was closest to Chris Beth's heart. They must go to the cemetery. Only then would she believe that Joe was gone.

In the few times that there was an opportunity for conversation between them, Chris Beth asked Wilson how he came to know about—and she was unable to put the rest into words.

"Telegram," he said, "and I would have come immediately except for the blizzard. You know that, don't you?"

Deep down, yes, she supposed she knew. No need to tell him of her hurt, her resentment, her need. He either understood or he didn't.

She wanted to know more about the accident but not now. It just wasn't real that it had taken Joe's life. Not possible at all.

"Do you know the extent of the storm damages?" she asked instead as they sat by the fire when finally Wilson would allow her to be downstairs.

"Bad, as I understood from the neighbors. Probably killed the young orchards. Lots of livestock lost. Lots of illness, too. Some day we'll talk about the pneumonia cases—" Wilson looked pensively into the flames that hissed and sputtered around the snow-dampened logs. "There's so much to learn about this thing—so much I can do for others. It was worth my going, you know, but I am undecided what to do—pursue what I know needs research or—"

Chris Beth caught her breath sharply. "You aren't considering leaving your practice—not coming back?"

Wilson's eyes left the fire to study the pattern in the rug. "I don't know." Suddenly, his head jerked alert. "There's something more important I need to discuss with you."

Chris Beth met his gaze, wondering what could be more important than such a decision. Or, for that matter, how he could consider it a decision. It ought to be clear to him where his responsibility lay.

"Chris Beth?"

"Sorry," she murmured and waited for him to go on.

"I wanted you to know that I've appointed you as guardian for Young Wil and True—just a precaution for their protection."

"From what?" she asked, feeling a tightening in her chest. Wilson shrugged. "Probably nothing. It just seemed the thing to do—in case—well, things do happen, you know."

When she caught her breath with a little involuntary moan,

Wilson looked at her with concern. "I'm sorry. We both know, don't we?" he said miserably. And, then, after a moment, "Is it all right?"

"My being guardian?" *Was* it all right? Chris Beth wasn't sure.

"Is there something wrong, Chrissy? I mean, something I don't know."

"I didn't want to talk about this now," she said slowly, "But I—I may not be available. Not always. It's too soon to think things through when I can't realize—" Her voice broke. When Wilson did not speak, she tried again, "I haven't even discussed this possibility with the children—like I said, it's too soon—oh, Wilson, I'm lonely, confused, in need of . . . I can't cope alone . . ."

She turned toward her brother-in-law wanting to say more, needing to pour her heart out. And in that flickering moment she could have. But Wilson's face was closed. And when he spoke his voice was cold.

"I hope you will serve as guardian at least until I can make other arrangements."

"But I'd want to take the children—"

"You will not take the children!" Chris Beth had seen Wilson in what she thought were all his moods, but nothing matched this one. His face was twisted in fury. At what? And at whom?

A sudden exhaustion closed in. "I want to go to bed," she said.

Coming down the stairs, she had leaned on Wilson's arm to steady her legs. But now he scooped her up, tucking a blanket around her legs, and carried her up the stairs as if she were as light as True's bisque doll's head without the body. He deposited her onto her bed then turned on his heel and left the room without saying good night.

Dry-eyed, she lay awake listening to the ticking of the clock. Why was it that every time they were close to talking, having the kind of understanding she coveted and believed him capable of giving, that Wilson had to become another person? On guard. Suspicious. Wary. It couldn't be her fault. Not this time. He hadn't even given her a chance to say that she no longer felt like coping here on the frontier. That she wanted to get away, take the children, and try to start a new life. Wearily, she closed her eyes wishing she could cry, pray—*feel*.

As she lay in what she'd come to think of as the state of the living-dead, Chris Beth was sure she heard footsteps at the door. She listened, but there was no further sound except for the crowing of a rooster announcing the dawn.

The next morning, after chores were done, Wilson announced that he and Chris Beth would be going to the general store. "If you feel up to it?"

"Yes," she said, knowing that the trip would entail more.

"Us too?" True said hopefully.

"Not this time, sweetheart," Wilson said gently. "Aunt Chrissy and I have to talk. You stay here with Wil and we'll bring you some horehound sticks."

True accepted the decision, leading Chris Beth to know that Wilson had talked with the children. She was grateful and would have said as much, but the barrier was between them and she lacked the strength to tear it down. What lay ahead was enough for one day.

As she dressed, Chris Beth wondered what people at the general store would say about her clothes. Maybe she should be wearing black, but the only black dress she had was silk, and she needed something warmer. The six-year-old suit she'd worn on the stagecoach coming to Oregon would have to do. Longingly, she looked at the soft pink of the velvet rose. It would look so beautiful pinned on the lapel of her navy blue jacket. Wearing it was out of the question, of course. It was too frivolous. And she admitted to herself, it would make her uncomfortable to wear the rose in Wilson's presence. She wasn't sure why.

After telling the children good-bye and reaffirming that they would bring back the promised candy, Chris Beth waited on the front porch for Wilson. To her surprise, Wilson had hitched Charlie Horse to the single-seat buggy. He had no trouble convincing the children that they were to stay home. Why, then, the larger vehicle? But, of *course!*

Involuntarily, Chris Beth's hand went to her mouth. Dobbin had been killed. Biting her lip for control, she lowered her hand and busied herself with her gloves. There could be no tears for a draft animal when she was unable to weep for her husband. Stoically, she walked to the waiting buggy and allowed herself to be helped up into the seat.

The trip passed almost without conversation. Ordinarily, Wilson would have talked. He wasn't given to Joe's companionable silences. But today there were no words and Chris Beth was glad. It was good to look about the countryside, to see anew silvered mountains brushing their peaks against a near-cloudless sky, to feel the wind in her face, and just to *be*. Thoughts would be unwelcome intruders.

To Chris Beth's relief, Mrs. Solomon was not in the store. Abe did not attempt to engage her in conversation, talking directly with Wilson instead, and she was able to complete her shopping quickly.

As they were about to leave, Abe Solomon thanked her for the business and reached timidly for her hand. "And if there's anything we can be doin'—"

"I know, Mr. Solomon, but—no, on second thought, there is something you can do for me. Could you find out when school commences now that the storm's over."

Mr. Solomon looked apologetic. "I thought you'd been notified by Nate. He likes to tend to business—it's Monday. But if you're not up to par—"

"I'll be fine," Chris Beth said. "And Mr. Solomon—tell me, what happened to Liza? Will she be all right?"

With breath sucked in, she waited.

"Flesh wound," Abe assured her. "Now, you be takin' care."

Chris Beth thanked him, picked up the horehound sack and a few lighter parcels, and walked out the door. Abe would help Wilson load the heavier bundles.

At the door, she dropped the horehound sack. As she bent to pick it up, she overheard Mr. Solomon's words—obviously not intended for her ears. "And we're pleased to hear you've been lookin' after our Maggie. She sounds so happy."

"She's very happy," Wilson said. "And so am I. She has made the right decision."

So I was right! Chris Beth thought angrily. *He is keeping company with another woman—an archenemy of Vangie's. How could he? How could he? And everybody knows what she is—that—that—*

Squaring her shoulders, Chris Beth hurried to the buggy. Little did she care *what* Wilson North did!

If Wilson noticed her silence, he gave no indication. At his urging the old horse cantered along the deserted road to the turnoff. There Wilson pulled the left rein and the buggy turned toward the churchyard.

It was easy to locate the graves. Even after the snow, they looked raw and new. Before Wilson had tethered the horse, Chris Beth leaped unassisted from the buggy and walked toward the graves. Then, overcome by an emotion she hadn't felt since Vangie's death, she began to run, forgetting in her haste to lift the long skirt of her suit. Her foot must have caught on a stone, else how could she have become hopelessly entangled in the skirt's lining and the heavy petticoats beneath? With a little cry, she fell to the ground, her left ankle turning painfully beneath her.

"Oh, Chrissy, Chrissy," Wilson said softly. "Can't you ever let me help?" Gently, almost tenderly, he lifted her and carried her the short distance to the new mounds.

When he put her down, Chris Beth felt pain in the ankle but more in her heart. She burst into uncontrolled sobs and sank to her knees on Joe's grave. "Oh, Joe, Joe—Why, *why*, WHY?"

"Don't Chrissy, don't Chrissy, darling. He wouldn't want it this way." But as Wilson wiped her tears away with a large white handkerchief, Chris Beth saw through her own tears that his cheeks were wet too.

It seemed the most natural thing in the world that she

should be in Wilson's arms. He held her until the sobbing turned to little exhausted gasps.

At last Wilson spoke. "It's the way he'd have chosen, Chrissy. Joe died for God's work."

Something welled up inside Chris Beth then—something ugly, cruel, and devilish. Like a demon, she turned on Wilson, beating him on the chest with all her strength. "Who are you to tell me what's right? To justify his death? To dare speak to me of God's will at such a time? I don't believe in a god any more—do you understand?"

Wilson took her hands and held them imprisoned. "I hear," he said softly. "I hear and I understand. And so does He . . ."

Two days later Wilson left for Portland. Another parting. Chris Beth bade him good-bye woodenly. Life would go on and she would handle it alone—the way she always had.

28
The Greatest Plague

⤔

WITHOUT REALIZING THAT she was calling
upon a Source of Strength greater than herself, Chris Beth
drew herself erect and walked tall as she entered the schoolhouse door early Monday morning. Her personal tribulations
were stored away carefully like Vangie's diary and the velvet
rose—items to be lifted from the folds of time one day,
examined and kept or discarded. But for now she was The
Teacher, the only remaining member of the Fearless Foursome as she, Joe, Vangie, and Wilson had called themselves
once upon a happier time.

The darkly-attractive young woman, wearing the typical
attire of the schoolmistress, smoothed her long blue skirt and
shifted the weight of the books she carried. The severity of the
heavy braided hair was broken by the soft ripple of the white
ruffles of her simple blouse, framing the ivory face. Chris Beth
felt keenly aware of her surroundings: the needs of the
children in her charge, every detail. But of herself she was
totally *un*aware. How could she know that the planes of her
face, deepened by time's mixture of joys and sorrows, added to
her ageless beauty? That her skin, though weathered by the

490

sometimes cruel weather, still cried out to be touched? And
that her dark eyes had distilled a certain mystery from her
suffering? And, most of all, how could she know—for certainly she would reject the idea—that an aura of sanctity
surrounded her? Unaware, she passed from girlhood to woman-
hood—a pioneer.

But Alex Oberon was very much aware apparently. At the
sound of Chris Beth's footsteps, Alex hurried to close the door
behind her and relieve her arms of the high pile of books,
admiration in his glance.

Once he had deposited the books on her desk, Alex turned
to her, adjusted his plum-colored ascot nervously, and said, "I
have come to think of you as a very dear friend, Chris Beth."

"And I have come to think of you in the same way, Alex,"
she said, realizing that she meant it.

"You have?" Alex seemed surprised. He reached to touch
her hand and looked down at her intently. "I have prayed for
you and your family daily. Sometimes it seems my prayers are
of no use." Letting go of her hand, Alex allowed his pale eyes
to travel over her face. "Still I keep praying . . . but you
aren't looking strong—so pale and much too thin . . ."

Chris Beth turned away. "I'm in excellent health. I've been
under the care of a doctor, you know," she said, forcing a
smile. "But you look very tired yourself," she added. "Have
you been ill?"

"Not ill—no," he said slowly, "but Mrs. Bynum's boarding
house was a casualty of the storm. Did you hear of its demise?"

"The house? You mean—"

Alex looked at her solemnly. "Collapsed completely. I have
been staying temporarily with Mr. Goldsmith's family—an
unsatisfactory arrangement." He cleared his throat. "Most
unsatisfactory."

The beginnings of a laugh stirred somewhere deep down
inside Chris Beth—so foreign in these recent months that she
hardly recognized it. But the thought of the carefully-proper
schoolmaster being in the household with Nate Goldsmith,
his innocent-looking bird-like wife who could get her message

across when it was necessary with a burst of German sprinkled with French . . . their countless children . . . the baying hounds and the half-wild chickens that squawked and took to the air at the slightest sound. . . .

Tucking in the corners of her mouth to keep from smiling, Chris Beth began, "There's Turn-Around Inn—"

"Too crowded these days—which is good. Too expensive for my modest income, I am afraid, even were board and keep available for me."

Chris Beth was wondering how she would survive herself. Nate and the other members of the school board he had appointed had raised her salary from the beginning 50 dollars a month to 60, "most generously," the president of the board pointed out. It was all the settlers could afford to pay, she was sure, considering that there were two teachers now. But without aid of a second income . . . and the cost of such necessities as children's shoes soaring from 69¢ to 98¢ . . . not to mention *clothes* . . .

Alex interrupted her thoughts. "You look worried. Now, you must not concern yourself for me and my abode—or, for that matter, my safety—"

"Safety?" Chris was surprised. Of late, she had caught her mind wandering into the private realm of her own thoughts instead of listening to others when they were speaking. "Do you mean—" But she was unable to formulate the question. The thought was too frightening.

Alex looked at her worriedly. "I must go back to my Eastern manner of keeping my eyes and ears open and my mouth shut concerning such matters—and certainly it must be a painful subject for you now—"

"*Vigilantes?*" The word was no more than a whisper that caught in Chris Beth's throat.

Casting a furtive eye toward the windows, Alex lowered his voice for the benefit of small ears, she supposed. "Vigilantes, yes—and others posing as the militants. And the battle continues between the sheep men and the cattle raisers—"

Chris Beth turned away when she felt her chin quiver. *How*

long . . . how long, oh, Lord . . . the thought died away as quickly as it came. What good was prayer anyway? Even Alex Oberon realized its futility.

"It is possible, too," Alex began again, "though bear in mind that I should not be giving voice to this, that thieves and murderers have infiltrated the ranks of the groups. But then, you have been here longer than I and would know more of such matters."

When he looked questioningly at her, Chris Beth answered slowly. "I'm not sure I can justify any of the groups' 'conversion by the sword,' so to speak. The Basque people are quiet, hard-working—but the ranchers claim the Basque let their sheep trample the good range lands, so the fight goes on. It's only recently that it got out of control—and as for the vigilantes—" A wave of bitterness swept over Chris Beth and she was unable to continue.

Alex ran a nervous finger around the rim of his stiffly-starched collar. "I do abhor violence, all forms of it," he said with a shudder.

At one time Chris Beth would have said that the settlers— all of the groups—needed what Mrs. Malone called a "good old-fashioned dose of religion." But now she said instead, "There's no hope until we get some law and order in here. People aren't able to live without rules no matter what we idealists would like to think!"

"Ah, yes," Alex Oberon said, seeming relieved to be back on comfortably-familiar ground, "our society must have rules. 'Man cannot live by bread alone.'"

Chris Beth opened her mouth then closed it. The meaning of the passage in Matthew that Alex quoted should be corrected . . . or should it? Maybe rules *were* the answer. Love hadn't worked.

"The U.S. Marshal comes through on occasion—more to check on the Indian welfare than crime and what lies behind it, I think. There's talk of getting a sheriff. We can hope."

"Oh, indeed we can hope!" Alex said more cheerfully. He paused to open the case of his vest pocket-watch and looked at

Chris Beth significantly, but when she would have moved to attend to last-minute details before the children came in, Alex spoke again. "But I want you to know that in spite of all the threats and dangers we know exist here, I have come to love this strange and wonderful land of yours. It is entirely possible that I shall therefore consider settling down here and becoming one of you permanently.

"We can hope that, too!"

Too late, Chris Beth realized that Alex Oberon mistook her warm response personally. His pale eyes lighted with an unmistakable spark of interest making him, she thought fleetingly, almost handsome in a rugged way. She turned away quickly lest he read in her eyes that she had seen him for the first time as a man rather than a somewhat staid and proper, sometimes comical, fellow teacher.

Mr. Oberon lined the children up at the door and then looked at Chris Beth questioningly. *Where are the students?* his eyes asked.

Could it be that only a few parents knew that school had reopened? Hardly. News traveled fast in the valley in spite of the distance between homesteads. With a sinking heart, Chris realized that most likely it was fear. Parents had kept their children home because they no longer felt safe. They'd seen what mobs could do. They could slaughter each other's animals, burn crosses, destroy houses—no, *homes!* It was one thing to destroy a family's shelter . . . but a building was nothing compared to the loving members inside. One child shot . . . a man murdered . . . leaving behind a widow . . . three orphaned children. Who could blame them for being afraid? The violence would go on, gathering strength as hysteria blotted out reason. The horror of it all closed in around Chris Beth with long, bony fingers of apprehension and despair. If Joe's death did not restore sanity—Joe, their beloved "Brother Joseph"—nothing would. *This would be a good time for a miracle,* she thought bitterly. *Why don't those who believe ask?*

Fighting back panic which threatened to overwhelm her,

Chris Beth walked ahead of her class and into her room with outward calm. Mentally, she checked the roll. *Beltrans*, missing. Understandable, since they were among the Basque. *Chus*—their absence was understandable, too, in view of the racial violence. Sighing, Chris Beth accepted that it would be easier to check the names of the children who were present rather than those absent. *Malones*, all present. *Goldsmiths*, present. Conspicuously absent were children of the cattlemen and the sheep raisers. But what about the others?

"Does anybody know why the Smith children aren't here today?" she asked the class.

Randolph, the youngest Goldsmith, raised a chubby hand. "Their daddy works fer the railroad 'n some people're mad 'bout them rails comin' through th' fields."

That too? Was there no end to this? Where would it all lead? Chris Beth wondered as the day wore on.

Charlie Horse, in spite of his years, made remarkable time going home. Unaccustomed to the confines of the school-ground, he was more than anxious to graze in the North's wide pasture. Chris Beth concentrated on the rhythmic clop-clop of the horses' hooves and the greening meadow. She had never become accustomed to Oregon's turned-around seasons. Back home the grassland would be bare and cold until spring. Here, with the first mists of autumn, the grasses flourished. Maybe if she concentrated hard enough, ugly thoughts of the day would go away.

But it was no use. Marty interrupted her efforts by saying to Young Wil, "We didn't have many in our class and we're scared."

"*I'm* not," True said brightly. "I don't think it's true that the mean men will try and burn our school, do you, Aunt Chrissy?"

"Where did you hear that?" Chris Beth asked, striving to sound calm in spite of the lurch her heart gave.

The child shrugged. "Around," she said vaguely.

Over her head, Young Wil nodded silently. So Chris Beth's suspicions were true. The situation was going to get worse, not better. A great sadness welled up inside her heart. *Oh, Joe, she nodded inwardly, I grieve not as much at your dying—as for your dying in vain.*

At bedtime, Young Wil locked all doors as usual. Then, after covering the live coals remaining in the fireplace with ashes to preserve them for the morning's fire, he rechecked each door and window, drew the drapes, and opened the front-hall closet.

Chris Beth, busy with laying out Marty and True's school clothes for the next day, did not look up until she heard him setting something beside the front door. When her eyes caught sight of the object, partially hidden by the brocade drape, she let out a gasp of horror.

"A *gun*! Put it away—put it away this minute!" she whispered fiercely. "Oh, what have they done to you—" A sob drowned her voice.

"Chrissy—Chrissy—*listen* to me! Be reasonable. You know what happened to—to someone we love—and you know what can happen to the rest of us. Uncle Wil's afraid for us—"

"If he's so afraid, what is he doing in Portland?" Chris Beth realized that her voice had risen, but she was unable to stop. "He doesn't care—" Then, at the stricken look in Young Wil's eyes, she stopped. "Where did you get that gun?" she asked instead.

"Uncle Wil gave it to me—told me to look after you. It's—it belonged to Joe. He used it riding shotgun on the stagecoach—"

"I remember," Chris Beth said tonelessly. "Forgive me for being sharp. It's just that there's so much."

"I feel that way, too," Young Wil said, his voice suddenly more that of a little boy than a brave young man. *Maybe,* she thought desperately, *this is the worst of it all—what the hatred is doing to the little ones.* None of Brother Amos's past prophesies, all of which had occurred—flood, famine, fire and the invasion by hordes of destructive grasshoppers—were as deadly as the plague of fear that gripped the hearts of every settler now.

29
A House Divided

CHRIS BETH COULD FEEL the tension growing. School attendance grew smaller instead of increasing as she had hoped when people "forgot." The problem was that they did not forget. They remembered—some moving away; some fighting back in retaliation which added salt to the wounds; and some barricading themselves inside their houses. The tension was present in each tone of voice, the touch of each hand, and the way eyes of the settlers scanned each stretch of woods, outlines in the darkness, and the face of every new-comer. Out of respect to Joe, they said, church services were discontinued temporarily. When "temporarily" stretched into weeks, worship services did not resume. "Don't seem t' be a called man hereabouts," Nate explained it, but nobody thought that was the true reason.

Once-happy hearts were in mourning. Chris Beth felt as if she herself wore a shroud of dark grief. She grieved for Vangie, for Joe, and the settlers. She grieved for what used to be and what could have been . . . but, most of all, she grieved for the three children within her care. They were too young to understand adult behavior. Not understanding, they vented their wrath on one another—particularly Marty and True. Once inseparable, they now busied themselves looking for small incidents to quarrel over, little aggravating ways of tormenting one another. And Young Wil, who had been Chris Beth's right arm, seemed to be less open, drawing back into his former defensive ways.

"The clocks have turned backward," she whispered to nobody in particular one December evening when she should have been thinking of how to brighten the forthcoming holidays somehow. "And in their backward flight, the time-keepers have taken away all that's beautiful from me and from this once-wonderful land." She wished that she had not lost the power of prayer. But time had taken that, too . . . dividing her heart as it had divided her house.

Maybe the change in the children came gradually. Chris Beth was so buried in her own concerns that at first she hardly noticed. The conflict burst out in animosity a week before Christmas. Marty came running into the room where Chris Beth was trying to juggle figures around to justify the purchase of a few gifts.

"She called me dumb. Said I didn't know *nothing*!"

"*Something*!" True said with devilish delight.

Chris Beth turned from her work. It was a bad moment. "*Anything*," she corrected gently. "So, you see, you were both wrong. Do you mean this is what started the trouble?"

True looked at her with big piteous eyes then lowered her gaze. Momentarily, she was subdued by the correction of them both. Then she stiffened with anger again. "He *is* dumb! He won't let me pet Emerald—and she's part mine!"

Marty's eyes were bright with unshed tears, but his chin was jutted out aggressively. "She rubs the cat's fur wrong and makes it pop and Emerald don't—doesn't—like it. And besides it's not either part her cat. Uncle Wil brought Emerald to me."

"He's *my* daddy. So take your dumb old cat. You don't *have* a daddy!"

Marty's eyes widened in anguish. And then he went into a

rage. "I hate you . . . I hate you . . ." he screamed repeatedly as huge tears spilled down his face. "Me and my mommy are going to run away . . ." He stopped in mid-sentence as Chris Beth sat frozen to the chair in a horror that would not let her move. "That's right, *my* mommy! You don't have a mommy! She's like your dumb old doll without a body!"

"Stop it! Stop it, both of you!" With a cry, Chris Beth sprang between the two children who were trying to tear at each other's hair. "That's enough—no more or I'll send you both to your rooms!"

They stopped in mid-scream—mouths open wide and eyes so large they took up half the little faces. Chris Beth could feel no anger at Marty and True, just a deep pity, and a helplessness such as she'd never known. The children's angry words had stopped, but they were sobbing and hiccupping in a way that broke her heart. Kneeling between them, Chris Beth put her arms around them both, but she knew that there would be other such incidents. They'd both lost people they loved and the loss was bringing out the worst in their grief-twisted hearts. *Wilson ought to be here,* she thought with a surge of anger. But the anger gave way to an even stronger emotion, her own sense of total inadequacy. She who had always been so in control so remarkably self-sufficient, had reached the end of her resources. And that, of all the fears that assailed her, was the greatest fear yet.

Suddenly, Chris Beth realized that Marty and True had stopped crying completely. Releasing her hold on them, she said as quietly as she was able, "It's only natural that people who love each other quarrel sometimes, but we don't have to fight like Esau and Emerald, you know—"

"Or the cattlemen and sheep herders." Chris Beth had not realized that Young Wil had joined them until she heard his voice from the top of the stairs. Eyes averted, he descended.

The color drained from Marty's face. He appeared to be thinking and then he spoke to Young Wil who had come to stand in the doorway.

"Did one of the mean men shoot my daddy?"

Oh, this must stop! But before Chris Beth could find her voice Young Wil was saying calmly, "Not exactly, but quarreling is responsible. That's what our mother means."

Marty's eyes sought Chris Beth's—large and haunted. "Mommy, will I ever get a new daddy?" he asked in a small voice.

The question was startling. It hung there in the silence of the study waiting to be answered. "I—I don't know, darling—" she began.

"And, Aunt Chrissy, will I ever get another mommy?" True's blue eyes turned to Chris Beth.

"That's up to Daddy," she answered, turning helpless eyes to Young Wil. But the look he returned was unreadable. Somewhere she's seen that look before. *Of course!* she thought suddenly, *Wilson's eyes.*

Unable to sleep once the children were in bed, Chris Beth lighted the lamp and read for hours in Vangie's carefully-detailed diary. She read and re-read the beautiful account of the sisters' double wedding in the enormous front room of Turn-Around Inn, surprised that she was able to treat the reading like the tender memory it was instead of experiencing only the agony of losing her sister and her husband. Nobody could have made her believe that she could remember Vangie's golden-haired beauty and Joe's wonderful gentle face with any emotion other than bitterness. She must remember to tell . . . then with a great pang of loneliness, she realized that there was nobody to tell.

Misty-eyed, Chris Beth turned down the wick of the lamp and extinguished the blaze with a quick puff of breath. Pulling the covers beneath her chin, she tried to put the events of the day behind so she could sleep. But the last line she had read in the diary remained behind her eyelids. "We are a family now, all four of us—Chrissy and Joe, Wilson and me—learning to share our differences as well as our love . . ." Only, they weren't family now . . . something was wrong.

30
A Heart-to-Heart
Talk

❦

CHRIS BETH WAS HUNGRY for a heart-to-heart talk with Mrs. Malone. There was so much comfort to be had when the two of them talked. But it was unwise to attempt a ride to Turn-Around Inn. The valley was unsafe. And maybe that was a permanent condition, too. *I have to talk to somebody,* she thought desperately. But who would want to listen?

The solution came unexpectedly. It was time the two of them made some kind of plans for a Christmas activity at school, Mr. Oberon said. The man had been extremely gracious to her in recent weeks and Chris Beth realized that his consideration could not have come at a better time. Not that she wished to be consulted on every detail as he seemed to do, but she needed his friendship. And she had come to think of him as a dear friend indeed.

They decided on a small Christmas tree and afternoon program inviting parents. But, admittedly, they expected very few to come. The students could decorate. Mr. Oberon would accompany their singing of Christmas carols. Had she noticed that they had come to appreciate his mandolin? Yes, she had noticed. She appreciated his efforts to bring "Eastern culture" to the children she loved.

"I'll bake gingerbread boys for the tree and we might consider making popcorn balls," Chris suggested boldly.

"*Here?*" But Alex recovered quickly. "Yes," he said thoughtfully, "we just might. Or, I might be persuaded to come and help at your house. I have wanted to see some botanical collections Wil had mentioned."

"You are welcome any time, Alex. But let's do the popcorn here."

Chris Beth collected her notes and prepared to leave. Alex usually rose when he saw she was about to do so, but today he said, "If you don't mind, could we—could we just talk?"

It was during the talk that Chris Beth learned he had been unable to find lodging and was sleeping in a tent in the stretch of woods where the old Graveyard Shack had stood until the flood waters carried it away. Any day now the light rains could turn into downpours. It was one thing to manage in a tent during intermittent showers, quite another to remain in one. But where could she send Alex to inquire?

While she was still wondering, there was a sudden turn in the conversation. "I wanted you to know how well the boy is doing," Alex said.

"Young Wil?" The report was surprising. In view of his behavior at home, she had feared he would neglect his schoolwork.

Alex raised a quizzical eyebrow. "Is there a problem?"

Chris Beth had not intended to, but before she realized it, she was telling how the two younger children goaded one another, her struggle to end the animosity between them, and her frustration at being unable to help.

"Then there's Young Wil—" Chris Beth stopped a minute, afraid she was going to cry.

Alex was silent for so long she didn't think he had heard. When he spoke, she was sure it would be to tell her to use a strong hand—probably quoting, "Spare the rod and spoil the child." But, to her surprise, Alex said quietly, "Are you sure

it's as serious as you think? We're all under such tension . . .
I for one find myself enlarging minute happenings . . . and,
of course, Marty and True are confused by two bereave-
ments—and in need of a man in the house."

Alex looked at her shrewdly. She knew then that he had
figured out that she had revealed some of her own sorrow and
loneliness as well as the children's. Still, it was good to have
talked with an adult, be listened to and answered. So before
she left, Chris Beth invited him to dinner on Sunday.

31
Dark Christmas

༚

LOOKING AT YOUNG Wil's leaf collection on Sunday, Alex said with surprise, "Did you say this was myrtlewood? I am led to believe the tree grows only in the Holy Land."

"*And* on the Oregon coast," Young Wil said proudly, "My uncle transplanted one tree and it reseeded itself."

Alex asked to see the little grove of rare evergreen trees and the two of them walked toward the cabin. Chris Beth washed and rinsed the dinner dishes and True dried them in silence. When the job was completed, True tossed the towel onto its rack and looked angrily at Chris Beth.

"I don't like him!" she said in a tone of final judgment.

Before Chris Beth could answer, she heard Alex and Young Wil at the door. Alex carried several of the pointed, glossy leaves, but his mind seemed to be elsewhere.

When he and Chris Beth were alone, Alex praised the "satisfying" dinner and said he must be going. But he lingered, fingering the leaves a moment, and then asked suddenly, "do you think it would be proper for me to ask you to consider if I might rent the cabin across the creek? It's unoccupied—and—" He seemed to find words difficult.

DIARY OF A LOVING HEART

Chris Beth, completely taken aback, murmured that she would have to think it over. Something told her not to discuss the possibility with the children. It was obvious that none of them liked the man and there were some choices that she felt belonged to her. While it would be painful to have another person occupy the only real home she and Joe had shared— the only thing she owned actually except for half-interest in the mill—it sounded practical. It seemed heartless to deny Alex Oberon a shelter over his head and certainly she could use the added income. Seeing another couple move in would have been too painful a reminder, but this man's presence could stir no memories.

On Monday morning she told Alex her decision. "It's only temporary, of course," she explained. "When Wilson returns, I will need the cabin—unless I decide to leave—" When he looked at her quizzically, she rushed on, "and there are some extra pieces of furniture—"

Alex's eyes lit up with pleasure. That night he moved in.

The trio of children said nothing concerning the arrangement. They simply looked at Chris Beth with accusing eyes. She would sit down and have a long talk with them as soon as the program was over. She kept hoping that something would bring the community back together. It could be as simple as a Christmas gathering. So she devoted every waking hour to preparations, putting all else aside for later.

On Wednesday before the Friday afternoon program was scheduled, Chris Beth heard Charlie Horse neigh, his way of announcing arrival of another animal. She left the children seated on the floor stringing popcorn and looked out the window. Nate Goldsmith was tethering his horse near the buggy. Something was wrong, she knew immediately. He was cautious about venturing out in broad daylight, except to accompany his children part of the way to and from school. He advanced with a purposeful stride, but even at a distance his face appeared gray. Waving to him, Chris Beth opened a window. Nate nodded, looked cautiously over his shoulder, and ran to where she stood.

"They's been trouble," he whispered hoarsely. "One of th' Beltran children took a shortcut through Judson Smith's winter squash patch he ain't harvested 'n Jud claimed damage—with Beltrans raisin th' woolly critters, 'twas sure to bring trouble and did—"

Nate's breath gave out, but even as he paused, Chris Beth found it difficult to find a voice of her own. "You'd better come inside," she whispered.

Mr. Oberon was explaining "ablative mood" to a roomful of concentrating students and did not look up as Nate entered and passed hurriedly into Chris Beth's room. She motioned him to the back of the room and they continued the conversation in guarded whispers.

The masked men had gone to the Beltrans again, Nate reported breathlessly, set fire to his barn and killed an unknown number of his sheep. Threatening the entire Basque settlement. Going to kill animals and owners "sayin' ain't a heap of difference." Then fighting broke out in the general store. Bad. Real bad. A "knifin'" where Barney Ruggles was holding an auction. But that wasn't the worst of it.

With a pounding heart, Chris Beth waited what seemed an eternity for Nate to tell her anything that could be worse than his previous news. Was there no end to this? No hope?

"And it's gonna git worse. Lots worse!" Nate seemed to be answering her unspoken question. "Both sides joinin' enemy camps, less'n our plan works out—"

Nate's last words did not register at the moment. Her mind was still on what had happened already. "But the fire—and casualties?"

"Put the fire out afore it destroyed th' other out-buildin's—some bad burns resultin'—speakin' of which is the worst part of all. Sure you want t'hear this?"

She didn't want to. She *had* to.

A look of terror crossed the man's face. "Three men bled to death—"

"But the doctors—couldn't the new doctors—" She bit her lip until she could control the hysteria that rose within her.

"That's the worst," he whispered hoarsely. "They've threatened lynchin' both of 'em. That feisty new pup, Spreckles, who calls hisself a doctor tucked tail 'n run—not that y' could blame 'im—but ole Doc Mallory sayin' he ain't got long, he refused t' be bullied—"

"What happened to Dr. Mallory?" she asked, dreading the answer.

Did she remember John Robert Mullins? Chris Beth nodded, recalling an image of a plushy man with sagging muscles who was forever in to see Wilson, complaining of dropsy and catarrh and "complications." When reassurance failed to convince him differently, Wilson had gone along with the patient's diagnosis. That made him happy so he came in daily to report to Wilson on his "progress."

"Pore John Robert," Nate said, "he was in fer a checkup when the hoodlums come in to deliver the ultimatum. Doc refused t' be intimidated-like 'n they taken John Robert hostage—"

Through a haze of unreality, Chris Beth heard Nate's plan . . . a Citizens' Council formed . . . trying to get help from the governor . . . hoped to get troops in before the entire town of Centerville was burned to the ground . . . and there was more senseless killing. Would she pass the word to the principal? First meeting tonight . . . at the church, safer there . . . no lights, just come in quietly . . . and she was to have Mr. Oberon hold the children at the school until parents came for them this afternoon . . . safer.

Nate Goldsmith glanced nervously out the window. When he had reached the door between the two classrooms he turned quickly to hold up a packet of mail. Then, tossing it on a desk for her to pick up, he left her room on tiptoe. Chris Beth listened, but there was no sound from the other room.

Chris Beth did not look forward to breaking the news of the uprisings to Alex. *Maybe,* she thought, *he will see this as putting him in a secondary position.* He wouldn't relish that. However, when she told him about Nate's visit during the children's afternoon recess, he seemed more concerned about the situation than how she had come to know about it. Which was as it should be. Or was it? Ashamed of the feeling though she was, Chris Beth felt a gnawing suspicion that the principal's concern was for his own safety. Was that why Nate came to *her*?

Forcing the idea out of her mind, "We must keep the children here until parents come for them," she said.

"Yes, yes," Alex agreed, glancing nervously out at a knot of children who appeared to be looking at something in a nearby grove of trees. "But, tell me, does Mr. Goldsmith expect me to attend this meeting of Citizens' Council?"

Chris Beth thought back. "He didn't say, as I recall. I just supposed—"

At his obvious look of relief, Chris Beth did not say what she had intended. That his attendance would be welcome, she was sure.

Once the children were collected and safely on their way home, riding—she noted with a shudder—close to fathers who were all armed, she prepared to leave the building. "You'll be riding with us," she said gratefully as Alex locked the schoolhouse door.

He turned and, to her surprise, reached for her hand and said in low tones, "You have extended the invitation I had hoped for. I shall do all within my power to see that you and your family remain safe during these perilous times."

Chris Beth watched him, an upright figure pocketing the key with a certain importance, and tried to think of him in terms of a masculine strength upon which she could lean. The image would not come. He was a kind friend. Nothing more. With some relief, she put the idea out of her mind. She would go home. Prepare supper. Act normal.

The children were her concern. How much should she tell them? Nothing, she was to find out. They knew. "You'll teach me how to shoot, won't you?" Marty asked Young Wil at the supper table.

"Don't even say such things!" Chris Beth said a little more

sharply than she had intended. How quickly ideas of violence spread!

"Will my daddy come home now?" True asked in a small voice. "Will he come back and take care of us?"

"I don't know—oh, that reminds me!" Quickly, she got up and went for the packet of mail. Six letters. All from Wilson. Momentarily, in the excitement of opening and sharing, the crisis in the valley was forgotten.

Chris Beth only half-listened to the children's chatter as she was busy trying to absorb all Wilson had written in the one letter to her. The writing was detached and businesslike for the most part. Inquiries about Young Wil, Marty, and True. Admonitions for her to take care of her health. Chris Beth read with interest that royalties were coming from his second book while the first book went into its second edition, and would she believe that his research had been mentioned in a medical journal? Unaware that she was doing it, Chris Beth found herself searching for something Wilson had left unsaid, uncertain herself just what. He was enclosing a money order, mostly to help on household expenses as he would be bringing the gifts. *Bringing?* Stifling an impulse to let out a little cry of excitement, Chris Beth realized that such a reaction was premature. She must go back calmly and read what Wilson had written.

> You see, I plan to be there by Christmas Eve . . . traveling by the new Oregon Stagecoach Line which connects at Turn-around Inn . . . slower and not as dependable, some say, but it must be since Wells-Fargo transports via OSL . . .
>
> Why not keep my plans between you and me so we can surprise the children? . . . . . .There will be plenty of time for talking, but I'll say in advance there is something important I will be asking you. . . .

In spite of herself, Chris Beth's heart gave a sudden lurch. *Why, I'm blushing like a schoolgirl,* she thought. But it had been so long since a man had said anything personal to her.

Then, quickly, she had herself under control. Wilson probably meant nothing personal at all. *And if he does,* she thought primly, *most likely it will be of no interest to me.* Why then did her fingers tremble as she read on?

There was only one line remaining. Chris Beth read it and her elation died immediately. "Don't worry about me. I'm in good hands. Maggie will be travelling on the same stage."

She flung the letter from her then hastily picked it up again. Wilson had asked that she keep his arrival a secret. She would indeed! It would be her pleasure to hold back anything to do with Wilson North and Maggie Solomon . . . there was soon to be a crisis here she must deal with.

As routinely as possible, Chris Beth saw that the children were bedded down for the night. Then, in an effort to calm her raw nerves, she picked up Vangie's diary. Alex Oberon was living nearby now, so there was really nothing to fear. Removing the purple velvet bookmark from the diary, Chris began to read.

I hope my sister will remember the real binding significance of our evenings around the fireplace, popping corn, dreaming in a way that can never be undone. I think God meant for us to be one body, the four of us, and I doubt if He cared how we arranged it. He just sent a band of angels down and wrapped us together with the cords of love . . . strange, looking back on it. I doubt if any of us knew who would marry whom! We just knew we'd be together . . . I guess I never knew for sure how it would all turn out until that bright Christmas Day at Turn-Around Inn, the exchange of gifts—no, the exchange of *love* with the O'Higgin-Malones . . . then the wonder and the glory of what happened afterward. *Oh, please, God, don't let my loved ones forget that You married us all that night!* I think the four of us said, "I do!" when Wilson placed his mother's ring on my finger and Joe fastened the safety hook of his mother's lavalier around Chris Beth's throat. In a strange sort of way, I feel that maybe it's best I won't be here when it's time to explain to our mutual family about their backgrounds. I

would have become confused. But Chris Beth will know
what to say, just how much to tell True that makes her
understand that she is not without a father and need feel
no remorse at her out-of-wedlock conception. She has an
earthly father who loves her so deeply that she need not be
bone-of-his bone, flesh-of-his flesh. And she has a Heavenly
Father Who loves her even more!

Vangie's writing seemed to quiver along the lines of the
diary then and there were several stains which all but obscured the words. Undoubtedly, she had wept as she wrote.
And no wonder. Chris Beth realized that she was weeping
herself. Touched by the words. Touched by the memories. But
touched even more deeply by something more. *I just never
thought of things the way Vangie expresses them*, she thought.
*I just never realized she was consumed by so much unselfish
love.* And, yet, within some small corner of her mind, Chris
Beth was puzzled by what her sister could be leading up to
saying. Not given to deep thinking, Vangie had never been the
one to cast new insights.

Curious, she resumed reading. But Vangie continued the
subject of the children rather than the adult relationships . . .
Chris Beth would be able to explain to True just as she
explained Marty's background to him—at the level of their
understanding. How Marty's mother died in childbirth on the
same night his father was swept away by the currents of the
river the night of the terrible flood . . . and then there was
Young Wil. "She'll know how to handle Wilson's nephew,
Lord. You won't have to worry about that. He loves her so
deeply that it shuts me out. But I don't mind. I am glad . . .
she knows about all kinds of love—my sister does."

With a little sob, Chris Beth closed the diary. *Oh Vangie,
don't put wings on me, darling. You make me sound so
strong—so noble. And here I am at the end of my resources,
not able to cope with life here any more, and no heart left
within me! You wrote this diary for God and me—and we're
no longer partners. I can't reach Him or Wilson. . . .*

She turned the wick of the lamp low, laid the diary aside, and eased from Joe's rocker. Wondering at her own caution, she walked silently to the window to peer out through a corner of the pane. Something or someone was out there. Chris Beth felt it rather than actually seeing a movement. Suddenly, a light gleamed in the woods and was shielded quickly. Extinguishing her own light, she stole to the door and listened. Sure enough, there was the sound of hoofbeats. The best she could tell there was only one animal.

She was right, she knew, when a single rider emerged from the darkness of the woods. Chris Beth's thoughts raced. Who was the man? And what could he want? Frightened, fascinated, and unable to move, she watched him dismount and stride toward the door. Should she scream for help? No, no matter what was to happen, she would handle this alone. For a fraction of a second, her eyes went to the gun propped where Young Wil had placed it conveniently beside the door. She dismissed the thought. Weapons, even as a bluff, were out of the question.

Chris Beth didn't know what she expected. Maybe the dreaded white hood of the vigilantes, maybe somebody injured, bleeding, or, by miracle, one of the settlers. Least of all would there have been any idea of a soldier—a member of the cavalry and an officer. Even in the dim light the lantern cast, it was easy to see that the young man wore a dark blue, single-breasted short jacket with braided shoulder straps denoting an officer's rank.

The presence of a soldier would be reassuring, Chris Beth tried to reason. But, accustomed to the all-gray uniforms of the back-home Confederate soldiers, she felt no reassurance. Nevertheless, the man had to be dealt with. So, pulling her robe closely about her, she opened the door cautiously rather than have the night visitor knock so as to awaken Young Wil and the two younger children. Laying aside embarrassment at appearing before a man in her night garments, Chris Beth stepped onto the porch, leaving the door ajar for a hasty retreat. Painfully aware of the soldier's eyes on her, Chris Beth realized that she was standing in the glow of the lamplight.

Before she could decide on the safety of stepping aside, the man spoke. "Captain Ellery St. John at your service, ma'am. You are Mrs. Craig, I believe?"

"I am."

The young man was every inch an officer—cool and direct—not a man to be turned aside, dismissed, or deceived. "I should like a word with your brother-in-law."

Wilson? Chris Beth was too surprised to speak for a moment. "Dr. North is not here. He is in Portland. If you could tell me the nature of this call—"

"But you expect him?" Chris Beth could feel his eyes penetrating her very being.

"Why do you ask?" she evaded.

The captain hesitated. "Because I know that he will be coming and because it will be better," he said in a voice no longer friendly, "for him, yourself, and all others if you tell me when."

Chris Beth met his gaze directly, forcing her stare to be blank. "I'm sure I don't know what you are talking about."

"I am talking about his possible involvement in the illegal practices going on in this settlement. It is difficult at this point to determine Dr. North's affiliations. But I can see that I am wasting my time. You do not deem it necessary to cooperate with the law officials."

"You are hardly the law."

Captain St. John gave her a tight smile. "The cavalry serves where there is a need—" he drew himself up proudly, "and certainly there is a need tonight. I don't suppose you would care to tell me where this meeting is to be held in secret?"

Again Chris Beth evaded the question. "Am I supposed to know about that, too?" She forced her brows to knit.

"Never mind, Mrs. Craig. Just remember that perhaps you could have spared some bloodshed. The Citizens' Council, if discovered, very well may be acting in a similar capacity to the vigilantes—and going over the head of the Army is unwise. If your brother-in-law is the individual who went directly to the governor—"

Fighting down a tidal wave of fear that threatened to sweep her away, Chris Beth said in a calm voice, "What is it you are saying exactly? You sound as if you are threatening us!"

"Threatening, my dear Mrs. Craig? I need not do that. You know already what violence can do—"

"And yet you would resort to it?"

"If need be. But that is different. I am under orders to protect at any cost. And what am I saying? That it will be a dark Christmas—a dark Christmas indeed."

Captain Ellery St. John lifted a finger to his hat in mock salute. Chris Beth watched him ride away, the gold braid of the uniform reflecting menacingly from the lantern. And then she moved stiffly inside the door, closed it softly, and sank down slowly on the window seat, drawing her hands over her weary eyes.

The officer's call alarmed and confused her. How had he known about Wilson's expected arrival? The meeting to be held in the church? And why was the Army opposed to any contact with the governor's office? She had heard some frightening stories when she lived in the South about the soldiers who were on the "wrong side" going to almost any means to protect their braid. But she had dismissed such stories—until now. But what puzzled her was Wilson's possible involvement. And in what? No, that wasn't what puzzled her most of all, Chris Beth admitted suddenly. What bothered her was why she had been reluctant to give the Captain the information he had asked for. *Time.* She needed more time to think. But time was running out. Christmas could be dark indeed. . . .

32
Discovery
at the Church

❧

CAUTION MADE CHRIS BETH say nothing of Wednesday night's alarming encounter. Alex Oberon did not seem to notice anything unusual about her behavior Thursday. He was preoccupied with tomorrow's program and the day's even poorer attendance—notably the Goldsmith children. When Elmer Goldsmith, the neighborhood "runner," appeared out of nowhere Chris Beth steered him into her room before Mr. Oberon, his teacher, saw him and declared him "truant." Something was wrong. She knew this part of the world better than Alex and sensed such things.

Pale-faced and shaken, the boy handed Chris Beth a note from his father. She read the hastily-scribbled words with surprise and apprehension. Nate was "holed up" at the church. Would she come immediately after school? The matter was urgent.

It took some arranging, but Chris Beth managed. She needed to see Mrs. Malone, Chris Beth told Alex. That was true and she hoped very much that she would be able to manage a moment with her dear friend.

"I must ask a favor, Alex. If I could borrow Portia—she's a

gentle mare—then you could drive the children home. Would you?"

When he hesitated, she assured him airily that she would be all right. "I could come along—" Alex said uncertainly. But Chris Beth shook her head and said that she was in need of "woman talk." The thought seemed to frighten Alex more than her previous suggestions.

Then, gathering Young Wil, Marty, and True around, she explained her plans matter-of-factly and won them over quickly by saying that Young Wil could get the Christmas tree decorations from the attic. "You might even make some red and green paper chains." She handed them the scraps she had saved for making the school festive for the program. There would be no program. No need for canceling it or even discussing it. Both teachers knew and the handful of children had given up planning. Probably there would be no school at all tomorrow.

Somewhat amazed at her courage, Chris Beth urged the sure-footed mare across a shortcut to the church. On the way she passed the steep canyon atop of which stood Starvation Rock. One wondered how the earthen walls of the canyon supported the massive rock and kept it from plunging into the swirling river below. Boston Buck, one of the local Indians, had told her that the Indians never went there anymore. Spirits of their ancestors who chose leaping to their death rather than starve roamed the area. Superstition, of course. But Chris Beth did find herself wondering if the Indians she had grown to love lived in quiet desperation, too proud to admit to the Army of Indian Welfare that they were hungry. In a sense, they still stood on Starvation Rock, supported only by the earth bank. A tiny weakness anywhere could send them plunging to a watery grave. Chris Beth shuddered at the image of bronzed bodies struggling against the relentless currents, clawing at the air, as they were carried out to sea. Like the settlement, she thought sadly. Like home. Like her life. . . .

Although it was early afternoon, heavy fog was closing in. The church spire rose suddenly—somber and solitary—as if reaching for a ray of sun. Chris Beth dismounted, not taking time to tether Portia. The animal would not wander far away. Realizing then that she was only steps away from the cemetery, she looked sadly at the silent tombstones, loneliness deeper than she had ever known before overwhelming her. A woman alone. *Here!* Here, where peace had once abounded and now danger lurked. For the first time, a sense of uneasiness began at the nape of her neck, traveled down her spine, and weakened her knees so that they could scarcely support her. Maybe this was a trick.

Quietly, she eased the door open, slipping in, and closed it behind her. Inside it was dark and silent. The chill in the air caused her to pull her cloth coat closely about her. "Mr. Goldsmith?" Her whisper echoed against the walls, seeming to bounce back into her own ears.

Fighting against panic, she moved down the aisle, pausing just before she reached the pulpit. Her eyes were adjusting to the darkness, but the movement of the white cloth covering the rough top of the pulpit was so slight she wondered if it could be her imagination. The cloth moved again. There was no draft, Chris Beth knew. The movement had to be a signal. Quickly, she stepped forward.

And there she found the huddled form of Nate Goldsmith. Without intending to, Chris Beth let out a low cry. Nate was injured.

Kneeling beside him, Chris Beth saw that his face was bruised and battered almost beyond recognition. "Oh, what happened?" she whispered in horror. "You must have a doctor—"

"No doctor," Nate whispered painfully. "Ole woman will take care of me. But had to warn you—we was wrong in thinkin' we'd be safe—they come to th' church." His voice gave out.

"Who? *Who!* Vigilantes—surely not the sheep or cattle raisers—"

Nate tried to lift a protesting hand but winced in pain. "None o' them. Soldiers—"

"Soldiers! Are you sure?" But inside she knew the answer. If the Army would do this, where was their help to come from? "But why—*why* would they be brutal? And what happened to the others?"

"I was here first, thank th' good Lord. Th' others seen the horses and never got close—never knew I was trapped." Nate inhaled deeply. "They was lookin'—th' soldiers was—fer Wilson. I had t'warn you—"

Chris Beth bent her head low to be sure she would hear the answer to her question. "What has he done?"

"He's been workin' secretly fer a long time—one reason fer the long stretches he ain't home—they's more'n local trouble hereabout." Nate gave a long, shuddering sigh and looked up at her. "Wilson's been workin' on investigatin' money intended fer the redskins—*Indians*—as well as tryin' t' git a carin' sheriff. Somehow the barbarians knew. Now, help me up. You gotta be gittin' back—findin' jest when Wilson's stage's due. My guess is you're carin'?"

"Of course, I care!" Chris Beth said quickly. Then before she could give pause to how or why, she saw that Nate was attempting to pull himself up. Quickly, she slipped a helping hand beneath his blood-matted hair and helped him to rise on unsteady legs.

"Now, if y'll bring my horse around—"

"You can't make it, Mr. Goldsmith. Let me go for help!"

"You go fer home! That's what this meetin' was 'bout."

Knowing that there was no need to argue, Chris Beth brought Nate's horse to the front door and helped him to mount. Hunched forward as he was, Chris Beth was sure that it would be impossible for him to stay astride until he reached home and have Olga examine his wounds. She would detour by way of Turn-Around Inn, check out the Oregon State Line schedule and have O'Higgin catch up with Nate—

In the gathering darkness, Nate cautioned in a hoarse whisper. "We must keep this between th' two of us. We don't know fer sure enemies from friends," he whispered.

Heartsick, Chris Beth realized that the man was right. She

watched him ride away, slouched forward with pain, then rode home through the dark woods, letting her tears flow unchecked. There was not room for fear in a heart as crumpled in anguish as hers, she thought as Portia galloped silently over the shortcut which was heavily padded with dry pine needles. It was during that ride that Chris Beth realized with a jolt that the heart within her had come alive with emotion. So it wasn't dead, after all . . . it had only been sleeping. Only it had been awakened by the wrong emotions—not at all like the gentle call of love that had turned her life around when she came to live in the Oregon Country.

33
Proposal—
and Decision

~

HOW MUCH SHOULD SHE TELL the children?
Nothing, Chris Beth decided, reining Portia toward the back
of the cabin Alex now occupied. She longed to share the awful
story of Nate's brutal beating with Alex but remained true to
her promise to Nate. The president of the school board had
reasons of his own for not having alerted Alex instead of Chris
Beth in the first place.

"Hello out there," Alex interrupted her thinking with a
cautious call from behind the drape at the Dutch door in the
back of the cabin. "Oh, it's you, Chris Beth," he said with
obvious relief. "I was worried—most concerned. It is unwise
that a lady be out alone."

"I know," she agreed. "But I was quite all right, thanks to
your Portia."

"A wonderful steed, one I should like to keep." Chris Beth
wondered at the tone of regret in his voice but felt that this
was no time for small talk.

"I must get home," she said.

Alex Oberon stepped from the back door into the darkness
of the back yard. "Not without a light, surely!"

520

"I could cross the footlog between the two places with my eyes closed," she assured him, remembering with a pang the countless back-and-forth crossings the four of them had made during the previous five wonderful years.

"Then I shall accompany you partway. I want—there is something I wish to discuss," Alex said determinedly.

"Very well," Chris Beth agreed wearily, her eyes looking for and finding reassuring lights on in the Big House.

Alex cleared his throat in the darkness. "I—uh—am drafting a letter of resignation. The board may wish to accept now if enrollment continues to decrease."

"Oh, Alex," Chris Beth protested in her surprise, "The children will be back. This—this crisis will pass. Just ride it out—"

"No," he said firmly as they walked along. "My mind is made up even if this violence which I so abhor passes. If my services are needed, I will complete the year, but I am not of a strong enough constitution to stomach the perils of the frontier."

"But you will be," she insisted. "We all feel that way at the beginning—" Chris Beth stopped in mid-sentence, realizing that she was trying to convince the other teacher to remain when she so recently had made herself a promise to leave. What was the matter with her?

Chris Beth realized that Alex had reached out and was fumbling for her hand. In the darkness, she accepted his proffered hand supposing that he meant to help her over the path which must seem a threat to someone unaccustomed to it. But when he spoke, the words were so unexpected that she was totally unprepared.

"Come with me, Chris Beth. Let us go back to the more civilized East, be married, and start life anew." Alex raised her hand to his lips in the darkness. After a moment, she gently removed her hand.

"Thank you, Alex. You have paid me the highest compliment a man can pay a woman. But I must remain here—no matter what happens."

Standing on tiptoe, she brushed the side of his cheek with her lips and hurried across the footlog. Alex, she knew, stood watching her until darkness hid her from his view. He loved her, she knew, and her heart ached that she was unable to return his love—even respond to it. Ahead of her lay a future of uncertainty and fear—maybe offering little happiness . . . or the love of another man . . . but she belonged here. She quickened her footsteps toward the lights of home.

34
Secrets
of the Night

෯

CHRIS BETH DREADED facing the children. She simply wasn't up to acting as mediator in the quarrels which had become habitual. Even more, she did not look forward to Young Wil's direct questions and shrewd glances if she gave evasive answers. But the pungent smell of evergreen as she opened the back door was reassuring even before the excited chatter of young voices reached her ears.

Marty and True ran to greet her when they heard the back door close. "Come see! Come see!" they shouted. There she saw such a touching domestic scene that for a moment she shed the dark shroud of the day's awful happenings: a crackling fire beneath a bough-decked mantel, red stockings strung along the banisters of the staircase, and mountains of pine cones, ribbons, and colored yarn in which Emerald was tumbling in wild glee. The only thing lacking was the real spirit of Christmas within her heart, but somehow she managed the right words and escaped to the kitchen to prepare supper. The evening passed quickly.

Chris Beth did everything she knew to force herself to relax . . . a tepid sponge bath, a leisurely brushing of her long dark hair, and her softest flannel nightgown. Then, a glass of warm milk in her hand, she propped pillows beneath her head and stretched out her full length on the feather mattress. When sleep would not come, she turned up the wick of the lamp and picked up Vangie's diary.

At first, it was hard to concentrate and then she became deeply engrossed in Vangie's frightfully realistic account of little True's birth. "Only Wilson, Chris Beth, and God could have pulled me through," she wrote. "But it was worth it, every second of the agony and I am more than ready for my twins!"

Vangie wrote on and on how she was determined to bear the babies for Wilson, recording every detail. They would be named for two grandfathers "which makes everything just about perfect, since Wilson's middle name is *Kearby* like his father's . . ."

Chris Beth had known that, but what about the other grandfather? Surely, she thought, Vangie would never have considered naming a child for her own father—not with the fear she had of the man and her memory of being thrown into the streets. Quickly, she read on, each word becoming a bit more painfully-sweet.

I have come to think of Joe's father, whom I never knew, as a godfather—even a surrogate grandfather—and I love the name of *Jerome* . . .

Jerome—Joe's middle name. The gesture was so touching that she allowed herself to relax with tears. And then she slept.

Her light sleep was interrupted by the faint clink of a pebble against the window pane. Startled, Chris Beth sat upright in the dark room. When the sound repeated, she crept out of bed and peered into the heavy mists below. Someone was waving a lantern frantically.

Raising the window cautiously, Chris Beth called softly, "Who's there?"

The swinging of the lantern stopped. There was dead silence and then a familiar voice said brokenly, "It's me— Maggie, Chris Beth—"

Maggie? But that was impossible. She was in Portland and what would that girl be doing here anyway? How dare her!

Forcing back angry words, Chris Beth asked quietly, "What do you want?"

"It's Wilson," Maggie whispered. "He's calling for you— you must come quickly. There's no time to lose!"

Stifling a cry of panic, Chris Beth whispered back, "Where— how—and how did you—"

Maggie shielded the glow of the lantern with her shawl and looked uneasily over her shoulder. "Please—*please* there's no time for questions now. They're all over the woods—Indians! Attacked the stage and Wilson's wounded badly—oh, *hurry!* Even now they may have discovered him in the old barn. There was a trail of blood."

Horrified, Chris Beth grabbed a wool coat, taking no time to sort out the dreadful events. Only one thing was paramount in her mind. Wilson at one time had been her husband's best friend, her sister's husband, and he was now the only father her niece knew. In addition, he had pulled her back when she was about a breath away from death's door. No matter what the risks, he could not be left bleeding and dying in somebody's barn. A million questions later. . . .

Lighting a candle, she fumbled for a piece of paper and scribbled a note for Young Wil, not knowing how long the mission would take. She would prop it on her nightstand against the diary . . . what could she be thinking of? Vangie's diary was sacred, intended for her eyes only. Propping the note against the kerosene lamp instead, she unconsciously tucked the diary into one of the pockets of her coat. Quickly extinguishing the candle, she opened the door of her bedroom and was about to leave when she paused.

Chris Beth did not know why she acted as she did. There were some things which could not be explained, she had learned. But turning, she opened a drawer of the nightstand

and felt for her small Bible, dropped it into the other pocket, and went to join Maggie in the yard below.

"Will your horse ride double?" Chris Beth asked.

"I have no horse," Maggie said quickly. "Walked—rather, *ran*—the two miles. The attackers killed the horses. It's safer we go by foot anyway."

"But how can we move Wilson? We can't risk leaving him there."

At the snap of a twig, both women jumped. But it was Young Wil who spoke. "I've saddled Charlie Horse already— heard most of the talk. You two ride. Let me have the lantern, Maggie, and I'll run ahead."

Before Chris Beth could protest, the boy was hurrying forward toward the woods. There was nothing left to do but climb quickly into the saddle and reach a helping hand to Maggie who settled behind her in the saddle. *Some day*, Chris Beth told herself silently, *I will figure this tragic melodrama out—if we survive*. But for now she concentrated on watching the lantern's glow ahead.

Chris ventured a whispered question to the girl who sat behind her. "The others?"

"Killed—all four of them—and the strongbox carrying payroll taken."

"Then it was robbery?"

"It was an ambush—men with painted faces," Maggie gulped. "I'll see them the rest of my life," she shuddered.

It made no sense. Indians no longer painted their faces except with marks to identify their tribes. It was like the jigsaw puzzle she, Joe, Wilson and Vangie had tried so desperately to put together their last Christmas together. She tried to put the pieces together now to reconstruct the most horrifying tragedy yet to strike the once peaceful settlement.

"How did you and Wilson escape?" Chris Beth whispered.

Maggie drew a shuddering breath. "He made me run and he—he—they left him for dead—and he may be—" Her voice trailed away in a sob.

The two miles had seemed to reach into infinity. But at last, a ramshackle building loomed out of the darkness. To her relief, she saw Young Wil pause and heard Maggie's whisper in her ear. "Rein in."

The second they were dismounted, Chris Beth would have rushed inside. But Maggie laid a restraining hand on her shoulder and searched the area with quick eyes. Another ambush? Once her heart would have choked her, made it impossible for her to move, but tonight Chris Beth gave no thought to fear or her own safety. *Wilson!* She had to see Wilson and help save him if she could.

When Maggie seemed satisfied that no Indians lurked in the shadows, she motioned Young Wil ahead with his lantern. Wilson lay in a corner of the old barn, his body covered by straw. Chris Beth sprang ahead of the other two and dropped on her knees at his side. At first, she thought he must be dead. There seemed to be no motion beneath the straw to indicate breathing. And Wilson's face was ashen, what little of it she could see from beneath the blood-stained bandages. She wondered who had bandaged the wounds so professionally. A wave of relief swept over her when she felt his warm breath, even though the breathing was labored. Alive then—but deeply unconscious.

Maggie stooped beside her and reached a hand beneath the hay, brushing it aside, to feel for a heartbeat. "Steadier than when I left him," she said with an air of certainty that Chris Beth found puzzling. "I removed the bullet."

"You *what*?" Chris Beth gasped.

It was Maggie's turn to look puzzled. "Nurses sometimes have to fill in when there's no doctor in the house. I thought you would have known that from Vangie."

Nurse? Maggie was a nurse! So, that explained her being in Portland. Vangie knew there was a nursing school there. But never would it have occurred to Chris Beth that Maggie Solomon knew about the school or cared about people.

"People do change," Maggie said as she checked the bandages. "I would think a preacher's wife would know that!"

The words stung like an adder. But Maggie was right. And

she herself had been wrong about a good many things. Well, she would make them right, if the Lord would just see them all through this.

"I'm sorry, Maggie. I really am. But your mother—"

Maggie smiled a little bitterly. "My mother probably gave the impression that I was up to mischief in the big city! And that Wilson did more than lend me a helping hand on the medical terms—I can see by the look on your face that I was right. Give me a hand, will you two?" Maggie raised her eyes to Young Wil's face. He had come to join them and had stood looking silently at his wounded uncle.

"What're we going to do with Uncle Wil?" he asked.

"It's risky to move him, but there's no choice. We've got to try and get him to Turn-Around Inn—closer than your home. Besides, I'm not sure he'd be safe there after what he's told me?"

At the question in Maggie's voice, Chris Beth shook her head. Then to her surprise Young Wil, easing a hand beneath Wilson's feet, said, "No, don't let's take him home—not yet. The Army's blaming him for going over their heads."

In a state of shock, Chris Beth shook her head in an effort to clear her mind. So the boy had known all along? He and Wilson had been writing and she could have had a confidant with whom to share but for her own over-protectiveness—of the children and of herself. The revelation came with a jolt. Well, there were things she could do—things she *was* doing right now as she slipped her arms beneath Wilson's limp shoulders and followed Maggie's orders. Then there were greater things ahead if only—if only—*Dear Lord,* Chris Beth moved her lips in quiet prayer, *get us through this a step at a time.* And that, she knew, with a strange feeling of elation, was the miracle of God's love. His children might forget Him, but He never forgot *them.*

And a step at a time is how the strange quartet reached Turn-Around Inn—an unconscious man lying across the back of a horse, two women—one with hands, face, and hair caked with dried blood; the other in her woolen coat supporting the limp figure on either side—and a determinedly courageous youth leading the animal with one hand and holding a low-burning lantern in the other.

At the door, Young Wil turned to Chris Beth. "Can you manage from here? O'Higgin will help and I should be back when Marty and True wake up."

Chris Beth met his gaze gratefully. "Oh, darling, words can't tell you how much I appreciate you!" she said warmly.

"They just did," he said softly and somehow she knew that, by tonight's miracles, they were back together again.

Young Wil turned to go, but she felt a need to say something more. "You'll be all right? We couldn't stand having anything happen to you—and you will pray for Uncle Wil?"

"I will be all right. I promise. And of course I'll pray! Don't preachers always? I am going to be one, you know."

The young voice which had deepened into man-tones only recently faded into the night. And Chris Beth wondered as she pulled the latch string at the door of the inn just how many more secrets this strange night held. A light blinked on upstairs and she heard O'Higgin's soft but distinct merry whistle as he came out to meet them.

35
The Long Watch

⤴

UNUTTERABLY WEARY, Chris Beth was only too happy to allow O'Higgin and Mrs. Malone to carry the still-unconscious Wilson. Quietly, a step at a time, the two reached the top of the stairs and put him into the large bed in the Upper Room. The other rooms were occupied and the patient would stand less chance of being detected here, too, where the door was locked except for a large gathering. Gatherings, of course, had been discontinued in view of the fear and unrest which plagued the once peaceful valley.

Once Wilson was in bed, Chris Beth and Mrs. Malone bathed the pale face while Maggie prepared to put on clean bandages. O'Higgin drew the drapes as a precaution and asked Maggie to give an account of the ambush. Chris Beth hardly heard because Maggie's busy fingers had unwound the blood-stained bandages on Wilson's head and Chris Beth's heart was churning in dismay at the sight of the ugly gash so danger-ously near the temple.

Seeing Chris Beth's face, Maggie stopped her story. "He'll not give up. Men with his guts don't die easily!" Then in softer tones, she added, "The wound will heal. See—the

530

blue's gone from around it already where I removed the bullet."

O'Higgin started toward the stairs then stopped. Turning slowly, he said in hushed tones. "Did ye be sayin' the strongbox was packed away by the ambushers?"

"Yes, they took it," Maggie replied, securing the bandage.

O'Higgin shook his tousled red head. "Indians don't be needin' gold—trinkets maybe—scalps once upon a time. But gold? Now, that's a white man's god!"

The three women stared at him in astonishment. It was then that something else clicked in Chris Beth's mind. "Maggie," she whispered, "that was a bullet you removed—not an arrow or a tomahawk—a *bullet*!"

The Irishman came back to stand in the midst of the women. "It's been known t' happen elsewhere—white men disguised as Indians. It's careful we must be 'til aid comes t' separate the sheep from the goats." The women stared at him in dismay.

A finger of light probed at the darkness warning of dawn. Maggie would go home after having coffee, she said. Chris Beth refused coffee and Mrs. Malone's offer to spread out the feather bed for her alongside Wilson. Instead, she pulled the chair to his bedside, waited until the three others were outside the door, and dropped on her knees.

She prayed then for Wilson, pouring out her heart, in a way she hadn't done for months: asking forgiveness for having hardened her heart; praising God for the time He had allowed her with Vangie; thanking Him for the new meaning He had given her of love through her marriage with Joe; and expressing her joy at His leading Young Wil to follow the same ministry "leaving a part of Joe—Your vibrant Spirit—with me forever through this choice."

She prayed then for Wilson, begging God to spare his life, and asking another chance to hold together the remnant of the four lives He had molded into one. "Until death do us part, oh Lord, if only it is Wilson's desire—and Your will."

Hardly aware of her actions, Chris Beth shrugged off her

coat and, forgetting that she was clad only in her nightgown, she lay her head on Wilson's chest and sobbed. There was nothing more to be done but wait . . . to pray . . . to wonder if the Lord would see fit to answer her prayers. For yes, Chris Beth acknowledged, she loved Wilson. Loved him with all her heart. She'd always loved him—in a special way that needed no explaining even to herself. Love, she thought wearily, is like a violin. The music may stop now and then, but the strings remain attached forever.

36
Grim Warning

❧

A FAINT BUT disturbing noise outside awoke Chris
Beth. The light had changed little so she must have been
asleep no more than minutes. Instinctively, she knew that the
muffled sound on the fallen leaves beneath the window came
from soft leather of Indian moccasins. Quickly she glanced at
Wilson. When he made no movement, she whispered his
name. But there was no response. Without taking time to put
on her coat, Chris Beth tiptoed down the hall and descended
the stairs, praying that none of them would creak under her
weight.

Without taking her safety into account, she opened the
door, pausing to listen when it gave a small squeak in protest.
When there was no sound to indicate that anyone had heard,
she stepped into the chilly dawn and waited.

The wait wasn't long. A tall, muscular figure emerged
cautiously a few steps then stopped. Although the man was
partially obscured by the dripping branches of a great fir tree,
his features were recognizable to Chris Beth. *Boston Buck!*

Outwardly, she was calm. Inwardly, her stomach churned
with fear—not of Boston Buck, but of his mission. Remem-

bering his new rank, Chris Beth greeted him formally. "Good morning, chief! What may I do for you?"

Boston Buck, clearly apprehensive, wasted no time. "See friend!"

With all her heart, Chris Beth wished that Wilson were able to talk with the Indian. Wilson knew their ways, a bit of their language, and most of all, the Indians trusted him.

She shook her head sadly and was about to say that Wilson was injured but caught herself in time. "Your friend is sleeping," she said in low, guarded tones. "May I help?"

Boston Buck's dark, fathomless eyes appraised her. "You squaw," he said doubtfully.

"I delivered your son," Chris Beth reminded him. "Your next chief."

The Indian nodded with a grunt. "Buck not do. Evil of white man."

The ambush! Then they were right in suspecting that somebody else had robbed and murdered. "Who? Tell me, Boston Buck, *who*?"

The Indian looked sullen. "Friend sleep. Not tell squaw." Then with a finger pointed to the east, Boston Buck circled the sky to stop the arc at the western horizon. *Sunrise to sunset*, he must mean. Then, stooping, he picked up two small rocks and laid them beneath the tree. *Two days* . . . but until what? Attack? Arrival of militia—or would the Indian know that?

But there was no time to ask. The bronze figure was gone. Without warning, he seemed to vanish—leaving Chris Beth to ponder whether the signs Boston Buck had made were a promise or a threat. She hurried upstairs.

At the top of the stairs, she let out a little cry of dismay. There in the shadows stood Wilson, hardly recognizable in the swath of bandages and rumpled clothing. "Wilson—oh, darling! You mustn't be on your feet—" She hurried to him, seeing him sway on his feet.

"I heard and I know," he said in a clear voice. Then, reaching for her hand, he kissed the palm almost reverently.

"They're coming—" But the words faded away. His face blanched of all color. She tried desperately to support him, but it was no use. Wilson crumbled into a heap at her feet.

In the two days that followed, Chris Beth refused to leave the injured man's bedside more than minutes at a time—even when Maggie came to relieve her. Maggie assured her that fever was a good sign that Wilson's body was fighting the infection caused by the bullet. "But praying won't worsen the cause!" she said.

So, drawn together by a common cause, the two of them often knelt on either side of the bed. Never praying aloud. Just praying. Each in her own way.

Between Maggie's faithful calls, Chris Beth was vaguely aware that Young Wil brought fresh clothes for her, that Mrs. Malone helped her freshen up and change, and that Elmer Goldsmith, against his father's orders, slipped out to say that Nate had improved. School was dismissed . . . and Mr. Oberon had been persuaded "to stay for a spell." Words . . . meaningless words . . . except for the safety of the children! With a start, she realized that anything could have happened. She must send for them immediately, she told Mrs. Malone.

"Now, child, just you relax. Young Wil's looking after 'em as good as you and me could do. Then they've got Mr. Oberon—did I tell you he made Maggie's acquaintance here and unless I miss my guess, the two hit it off like a team o' mules! She's been lookin' in on Marty and True—Alex, too, I suspect. And, besides," Mrs. Malone added wisely, "the family's safer there—now that Wilson's *here*. Ain't able to determine how like, but seems news is a-travel faster'n on foot!"

Chris Beth had heard little the older woman said—other than the word *safer*. Was anybody safe anywhere? With a shudder, she realized that the sun was traveling rapidly toward the western horizon to end "the second day." She knelt by Wilson's bedside and prayed anew.

37
The Impossible
Is Possible

❧

WHILE SHE WAS still deep in her prayer, Chris Beth felt a gentle touch. At first she thought she must be dreaming. Surely Wilson had not reached out to lay his hand on her head! Slowly, fearing that the feeling was but an illusion that would fade, she lifted her eyes to meet Wilson's gaze. The dark eyes were tired but not fever-glazed. Wilson awake! Wilson was conscious . . . he was going to live!

Chris Beth could only drop her head into its former position and murmur, "Amen, Lord, amen!" in completion of her prayer.

Then, without reservation, she grasped both Wilson's hands in her own, letting the tears flow unashamedly. "Oh, Wilson! I've been so worried—so heartsick—so—so—but you know how I feel. Just don't try to talk. Don't do *anything* that will keep you from getting well!"

"Just one question—" Wilson began weakly.

But the question hung in mid-air. Maggie rapped softly and entered. "Well, the patient's going to live in spite of us, Chris Beth," she said airily, giving her first hint of a smile since the terrible night that brought them all together. "Let me check him—and, no, not a word from you doctor!" she ordered, feeling first his forehead and then finding his pulse, counting silently to herself.

"No fever. Pulse, normal. But I'm not going to dress the wound just now—or even order broth for you," Maggie said slowly. "I know you shouldn't see anyone, but this is urgent—"

Wilson tried to rise only to be pushed back firmly. "I'll prop you up. Nothing more. And we'll cut this visit short. No need to tell you who's waiting below—not that it's a response you hoped for."

Chris Beth stood up uncertainly. Shouldn't she excuse herself? She had no idea what this was about . . . but from the windows she caught sight of a big gray horse and its rider cantering toward the inn. The man was dressed in a dark suit with a frock-tail coat. The hightop hat and drift of dark beard gave Chris Beth a distinct sense of de ja vu. The likeness of Abraham Lincoln was amazing . . . but the approaching stranger was obviously a dignitary. By the time Maggie, who followed her gaze, joined Chris Beth at the window, a long line of military men in full dress seemed to appear from all directions.

Maggie caught at Chris Beth's sleeve. "I must alert Mrs. Malone and her brood. She'll never believe this—the governor himself!"

"I'll go with you—and help," Chris Beth said in hope of escaping.

"You will stay here and help me greet the party properly— just as you greeted President Hayes," Wilson said in a surprisingly strong voice which carried a command. "Your duty, you know, as my future wife."

In spite of herself, Chris Beth felt color rushing to her face. Hoping that the other woman would not notice, she turned away. But Maggie agreed without any show of emotion, "And they'll need to speak with me, too, I'll be right back." With that, the door closed behind her and Chris Beth was left alone with Wilson. There were only minutes to wash her face and try somehow to sweep back the bedraggled hair . . . not a

second to waste. But something of the old spirit was back—
the spirit that would not call a challenge to Wilson North's
presumptuous announcement a "second wasted."

"Wilson North, you are an impossible egotist!" she said
angrily as she snatched a towel from the bar on the washstand
and splashed cold water on her face furiously. "You're domineering, you're—" She sucked water into her mouth, choked,
and coughed, "determined to have your own way—pompous—
unpredictable—" then, overcome by a fit of coughing, she was
unable to go on.

When the spasm passed, Chris Beth pressed the towel to her
hot face longer than was necessary. There was no sound, so
she parted the folds enough to see a look of total amusement
on Wilson's face.

"All of those," he admitted with pride. "I am also very
much in love with Christen Elizabeth Craig and plan to make
her my wife. Why shouldn't the world know?"

Chris Beth swept damp hands hopelessly at the strands of
hair at the nape of her neck. "It would be nice if I knew first!"
she said hotly. "And anyway—I—I—"

"—love you very much, Wilson North," he finished for her.

Then suddenly, hopelessly, she began to laugh. "Oh, Wilson, you are impossible!" She ran to his bedside, stooped
down to plant a hard kiss on his waiting mouth, and said with
emotion, "And I love you very much, Wilson North!"

The investigation lasted only a short while. The governor, a
mild mannered, soft-spoken man, was far from pretentious.
Removing his hat and coat informally, he sat down at Chris
Beth's invitation and spoke earnestly for a few minutes with
Wilson. He had spoken with numerous others, he said, and
Wilson's written reports had been "both comprehensive and
enlightening." A voucher would reach him shortly as a small
token of appreciation and his service would be needed as a
permanent resident of the settlement. Meantime, he would be
leaving an undetermined number of soldiers whom Wilson

was to use according to his own judgment. There would need
to be a full report, of course. . . .

As Chris Beth listened, the missing parts of the puzzle fell
into place. The governor himself questioned Wilson and
Maggie about the massacre. They explained that the attack
took the driver and man who rode shotgun beside him, as well
as the passenger, by complete surprise. One moment, silence.
The next, the air was full of shots, curses, and cries for help.

"Wilson forced me to leave him and I had to stumble over
bodies as I escaped from the fighting, struggling men. Hid
myself in the bushes . . . searched for Dr. North after the
slaughter . . . we checked, but there were no other survivors . . ." Maggie related. Her voice broke and the governor
patted her hand in praise, then turned to Wilson and waited
for him to speak.

"They were after the gold—did you recover it?" When the
governor nodded, Wilson continued, "Of course, I was the
prime target and you know why. Somehow they knew of my
involvement with the state government." He paused. "There
were no Indians, of course. No local men either—at least, that
I recognized."

The governor shook his head sadly. "Soldiers, regretfully.
And, while it is a great embarrassment to the upright regi-
ments here who have done a commendable job heretofore,
some of the vigilantes were hired soldiers, too."

Again the two men talked in general terms about the
uprisings on the reservation . . . how the funds intended for
the people had been stolen and how peace could be restored.
The differences between the cattle and sheep men could be
mediated more easily, they both thought, now that outsiders
were eliminated . . . but there would be a marshal to help
maintain order when well-meaning folks got carried away and
deserted the principles of justice. "And," the governor smiled
for the first time, "it is my prayer that worship services can be
resumed once fear dies down. A lot of folks have been misled,
you know, by misuse of the Bible. Disgusted with due process
of the law, emotionally they take matters into their own

hands and exact their own 'eye for an eye' sort of vengeance."

Chris Beth saw Maggie's look of surprise when the governor turned to where she stood. "Your turn, Mrs. Craig—just a few simple questions in order for us to nail down some of the officers who do not deserve to serve their country, let alone wear distinguished braid."

Kindly, he instructed Chris Beth to answer with a simple *Yes* or *No*. At first, she was ill at ease. Then the feeling passed.

Did a certain Captain Ellery St. John call on her? *Yes*.

Did he ask the whereabouts of Dr. Wilson North? *Yes*.

Did he indicate an awareness of the meeting of Citizens' Council? *Yes*.

Did she divulge any information? *No*.

Was Captain St. John abusive? *No*.

Was his behavior threatening in a manner unbecoming to an officer? *Yes*.

And finally, "Now, Mrs. Craig, it was dark and there was rain, I understand. This is very important. Could you identify the man?"

"Yes, sir, I could," she answered.

The governor pushed back his chair, stood and shook hands with the three of them warmly. Then, with a smile, he thrust long arms into the frock coat which Chris Beth had taken from the hall tree to hold for him. "I do believe," he said with appreciation, "that I smell freshly-brewed coffee. If ever I can be of further service—but then you and I will be in touch, Dr. North. Or is there something more I can do for you now?"

Wilson grinned wickedly. "You could fetch me a morsel of food if you can get past these lady guards. Rest assured that your congenial hosts have prepared enough food for the entire cavalry, including the horses!"

After the guest had gone downstairs, Maggie brought broth, said that she would be going home "for keeps" now, and asked Chris Beth to see that he stayed in bed for several days. Chris Beth gave her a warm embrace of gratitude at the door, then turned to spoon the hot broth between Wilson's protesting lips. He was asleep almost immediately, exhaustion coupled with a look of peace written on every line of his face. She bent down and kissed him softly on the cheek.

Mrs. Malone tiptoed in to whisper, "Miracles, miracles, I do declare! And," she added, looking wisely from Chris Beth to the sleeping Wilson, "most of 'em originatin' right here in the Upper Room!"

Yes, Chris Beth thought sleepily after Mrs. Malone left as quietly as she came, *miracles*! She let her head droop wearily onto Wilson's chest where she could hear the steady rhythm of his heart. *The Upper Room where the impossible was possible, after all. . . .*

38
The Schemers

❧

WILSON SEEMED TO GAIN GROUND hour by hour. The stress and loss of blood had weakened him and he slept a good deal of the time. Chris Beth spoke of going home to check on the children and prepare for their return together. But Wilson would not hear of her leaving. Almost desperately, he clung to her hand and, in his stronger moments, made all sorts of threats about escaping to die of starvation and unrequited love. Inwardly, Chris Beth took a certain satisfaction. So it was possible, after all, for the powerful Wilson North to bend if not fold!

She read aloud to him daily from her Bible. Then, after he'd drifted off to sleep, she managed a few short visits with Mrs. Malone: The older woman was more awed by the governor's mission than the fact that he had dined at her table. "Always was a dream them two boys had, Wilson 'n Joe, t'keep this piece o' the world peaceful-like. Real sons o' the soil," she kept repeating. And on one occasion, she added, "Th' outcome's like Joe was back, but then he never left us, did he? Not so long as we've got Wilson, you'n th' children. . . ."

O'Higgin looked up from the hearth where he was cracking

hazel nuts for his wife's fruitcakes. Holding the hammer in mid-air he said softly, " 'Tis rememberin' I am how in Joe's eyes God lavished a special abundance of lovin' gifts 'long this river and surroundin' wilderness. Used to say, our Joe, 'Now, ye be havin' th' power to destroy it, but only th' Almighty can create ye a new one'!"

Well, Mrs. Malone agreed, it was true. God had spared this blessed corner because of "a handful of the faithful." Best take no more chances. Time to rally 'round, draw closer, love one another more.

During one of the brief chats, Mrs. Malone, claiming to have misplaced her thimble, swung open the slatted door of the front-room closet. An odd way of searching for a missing item, Chris Beth thought as she watched the older woman step aside, drop to her knees, and began feeling around blindly. And then her eyes came to rest on *The Dress!* The beautiful "Ashes of Roses" dress she was to have worn to Portland with Joe! At her little cry, Mrs. Malone said matter-of-factly, "Yes, 'tis that lovely and a shame t' be hangin'—a real shame."

It was a sin to waste, Mrs. Malone went on subtly, still crawling around on her hands and knees—looking and sounding so foolish Chris Beth was tempted to laugh. 'Course a dress so special should be saved for an extraordinary time. Like maybe a *wedding!*

Before Chris could have answered, Mrs. Malone switched tactics. Speaking of weddings, there was going to be one of sorts, she said. Love of a good man was hard to find. O'Higgin, bless him, had proved himself. Good man, O'Higgin. Good provider—contrary-like, but a man of moderation. And how could she have managed, a woman left with her late husband's seven young ones, if the Lord hadn't had something up His sleeve?

O'Higgin?

The same. Mrs. Malone blew her nose and smiled mistily, "So 'tis time I take *his* name. Young'uns are growin' up mighty fast. Thought we'd repeat our vows come New Year's Day. Th' deacons tell me they've rounded up a preacher t' fill

in till we can get goin' again . . . and one o' these days Young
Wil'll take th' pulpit. Mark my word!"

Chris Beth smiled gratefully at her friend. It was all wonderful, wonderful! But it was simply too much to grasp at one
sitting. There had been so much grief, so much heartache, so
many fears, tears . . . loneliness . . . misunderstandings. She
would have to find her way back gradually.

"I'm happy for you and O'Higgin. You have such a good
marriage—" She hesitated, then said slowly, "I suppose there
were those who said it was a marriage of convenience—"

Mrs. Malone laid down her tatting needle to stare out the
window. Almost to herself, she said, "Folks thought they
knew exactly the reason for our teamin' up. O'Higgin a lonely
bachelor. Me a widow with a hungry brood. But," she said, her
eyes leaving the window to meet Chris Beth's significantly,
"they was wrong! Oh, 'twas handy all right, but, confidentially, when the good Lord brought us together, we couldn't
stay apart! You understand?"

Chris Beth felt herself flush under the old woman's steady
gaze. "I think I do," she said softly. "I—I would have to feel
the same way." Then without realizing she was going to say
it, the words burst out, "But I feel so guilty wanting a
romantic love."

"Guilty? Oh, my child, don't ever feel guilty about love.
Feel grateful!"

She's talking about me—about Wilson and me, Chris Beth
thought. But, admittedly, *she'd* been talking about the two of
them, too. *We've both loved before,* her thoughts went on,
*and we know how much more wonderful life can be now
because of it. . . .*

Tears filled her eyes and she turned away quickly, rising in
preparation of making a hasty exit. But Mrs. Malone had seen
her tears. She knew what they were about. Tatting away, she
spoke to Chris Beth's retreating back.

"Time goes so fast. You know, Chrissy, you'll be needin' to
think on the "Ashes of Roses" dress. Think I'll fashion a hat

for it. There's enough matchin' material for coverin' your summer leghorn picture hat."

Unbidden, there came a vision of herself to Chris Beth . . . *The Dress* . . . matching hat . . . Wilson's velvet rose atop her white Bible. Almost angrily, she shook her head to clear it. New Year's Day would be a perfect time for Mrs. Malone and O'Higgin to renew their vows. And, of course, she thought primly, she and Wilson would stand up with them, providing he was able. So thinking, she hurried up the stairs.

At the door of Wilson's room, she stopped at the sound of voices. Young Wil's? But how and when had the boy made his way upstairs undetected? He must have come in by way of the back entrance and passed through the one end of the front room while she and Mrs. Malone talked. Probably heard every word and interpreted it his way!

She would have entered immediately except that her ears picked up the mention of *guns*. Oh, not again! But the words Young Wil spoke left her speechless, unable to move or let them know of her presence.

"So, Uncle Wil, you've got yourself a real surprise. Well, not a real surprise since I spilled the beans. But I couldn't wait to tell you. They wanted to bring them, a whole wagonload, before you got back. Said laying down the weapons would be your Christmas present. Then, they're all coming back Christmas Eve bringing food and stuff—both sides, cattle and sheep men—you *will* be home?"

Chris Beth couldn't hear Wilson's answer, but she formulated a mental one of her own. They would have to be home for such a joyous time! What greater gift than *peace* at this blessed season?

She was tempted to run back down the stairs and share the news with O'Higgin and Mrs. Malone. Then she remembered that it was supposed to be a secret. They would know soon enough. The day after tomorrow was Christmas Eve. And with a pang of regret, she realized that she had done nothing to prepare. But Young Wil's next words made her realize that she had no cause of concern.

"Chrissy let Marty, True, and me decorate. I even put up a big, big tree—so tall I had to cut the top off. But it won't show. I covered it with a star. Oh, I forgot something! One of the soldiers brought your packages, the gifts from Portland and they're under the tree. Maggie wrapped them while Mr. Oberon was nailing up a WELCOME HOME sign above your name plaque. She put that up, too, Maggie did. You know what? I have a feeling she's planning on marrying that fancy pants! He needs a strong wife!"

Chris Beth heard Wilson's chuckle. "He's got himself one!"

"Is she going to be your nurse?"

"You ask a lot of questions," Wilson said good-naturedly. "I want to talk it over with Chrissy—but, yes, I had given it some thought."

"Well, then," the boy said smugly. "I guess they'll have to live in the cabin and there'll be no room for Chrissy over there—so you two will have to get married. You know how people talk."

"I know how *you* talk! Now, how are the children?"

"They're making taffy."

Chris Beth shuddered. But then he went on, "Under Maggie's directions. She and Mr. Oberon are going to pull it and make candy canes. You know," he said slowly, "It's odd how Marty and True are not fighting anymore. They stopped all the clocks—"

"Why, may I ask?"

"So time would stand still, they said, and you couldn't go away again. That way we'll be family—and True can be co-owner of Emerald, as soon as she learns to stroke the cat's fur the right direction."

Wilson spoke in a conspiratory tone, "If you want to surprise us, you'd better make a getaway before Chrissy returns. She thinks I'm still asleep."

At the sound of hasty footsteps, Chris Beth stepped back into the shadow. At the door, Young Wil paused, "You aren't going away, are you? We need you so much—"

"I am not going away. Not ever again. And I probably need all of you far more than you need me," Wilson said huskily.

Chris Beth inhaled deeply, trying to make herself very flat against the wall. Without a glance, Young Wil passed her by and tiptoed down the stairs.

Schemers, that's what they were. *Schemers.* But, then, so was she, Chris Beth acknowledged. If only, if only, she could set a few matters straight. . . .

39
Legacy of Love

ᴇ

CHRISTMAS EVE! Without looking out the window
of the Upper Room, Chris Beth knew there would be a light
dusting of snow and that the sky would be sparkling clear.
The bracing smell of coffee and rising sourdough biscuits
climbed the stairs and crept tantalizingly through the partially-
open door. Chris Beth pulled her robe about her and securing
it with the corded and tasseled belt, she crossed the room to
part the curtains partitioning Wilson's bed from the rest of the
area. He was still asleep so she left quietly and went downstairs to join O'Higgin and Mrs. Malone. The Irishman's voice
reached her halfway up the stairs.

"So the wagon be ready for haulin' Wilson home. Otherwise, it's apt he'll be insistin' on ridin' a horse afore he's ready.
Doctors 'ave a way o' pronouncin' theirselves well."

"Speakin' of which, what happened to the doctors? Are they
safe? I keep forgettin' to ask," Mrs. Malone answered.

"Well, now, the young'un up and hightailed it. Never was
cut out for the good life, he wasn't. And Ole Doc Mallory
never much be wantin' to' practice anyhow. So the commo-

548

tion done him in—the cavalry rode in, the good men not the scalawags, and rescued pore ole John Robert away from danger. He be itchin' t' see Wilson fer seein' how damagin' th' strain was on his dropsy and catarrah!"

Chris Beth was about to clear her throat to make her presence known when she heard Mrs. Malone say softly, "I up and approached Chrissy 'bout the weddin's and all—just kinda hinted there might be more 'n one . . . Olga tells me we're surprisin' 'em tonight. . . ."

Chris Beth cleared her throat and called with a note of exclamation in her voice, "It's Christmas Eve!"

After a hearty breakfast, Chris Beth prepared a tray for Wilson, allowing Mrs. Malone to load it to her heart's content for the first time. He ate ravenously and insisted on getting up. "Rest," she begged. "Please do—we've a big day ahead, a busy evening—"

"And the merriest Christmas ever!" Wilson reached to take her hand and hold it firmly in his own.

Then New Year's Day! Well, who knows what it may bring! But aloud, Chris Beth said, "So rest just a little while—then we'll go home!"

"*Home*," he murmured. "Oh, wonderful word . . ." His voice trailed off and when his grip released on her hand, Chris Beth sat down and picked up the diary.

The little book was drawing to a close now. She had progressed to the point of Vangie's terminal illness. After reading a page or two of the carefully-documented details, she decided to share the particular section with Wilson later. It would be invaluable in his study of Vangie's puzzling disease and determination to find a cure. Chris was about to move onto the closing section of the diary when mention of Joe's name caught her eye. Quickly, she thumbed back a page in order to make the proper connection. Right away it was evident that her sister was writing about her disappointment at being unable to bear another child after True's birth—"a child of Wilson's genes."

I can understand Chrissy's disappointment because of my own. Now, I wonder if I should have told her that the fault did not lie within herself, but with her husband. Wilson and I agonized over this—wondering which would hurt more, the truth or our concealing it, a dilemma all doctors face, I guess. But it would have explained so many things . . . including the fire and Joe's unnatural fear of it. Maybe he should have known that the surgery performed to repair the injury sustained when he tried to rescue his parents, rendered him sterile . . .

Stunned, Chris Beth read and re-read the page. Joe sterile? The thought had never occurred to her and consequently she had borne a burden of guilt about her own infertility. But better that, she decided, than for Joe to have known that the fault lay within himself. Joe had taken pleasure in assuring her that it made no difference. She was first a *wife*. Second, the Lord willing, a *mother*. And, besides, they had Marty whom they loved as their own. But it made a difference now. Vangie had known it would. Realizing that this was one of the more revealing sections, Chris Beth read on:

It is therefore my hope—*my prayer, Lord!*—that should there come a time in the unforeseeable future when by cruel circumstance Chrissy is left alone, she and Wilson will remember that we are God's "chosen people" here on the Oregon frontier—not to wander the wilderness but to live out His plan for our lives—*together!* Whatever remnants remain must be woven in accordance with His will— whether the remnants be the three beloved adults I leave behind, two of them, or our children. *And may there be children, Lord, the twins I coveted for You and Wilson . . . give them to my sister. . . .*

Chris Beth felt the salty taste of tears. Then she sobbed in silence, trying hard not to awaken Wilson. Laying the diary facedown, she went to stand looking out the east window at the eternal hills, purple in the distance, that hugged the

verdant valley so protectively. In due time she drew strength
from their agelessness—God's reassurance that life and love
were stronger than death. Returning, she picked up the little
book and read the final words, written she remembered only
hours before Vangie's death.

> God bless you one and all, my wonderful family. Know
> that I will remain with you always. I will blossom with
> the dogwood in the springtime and hum with my bees in the
> summer sun. I will sparkle with the snowflakes and in the
> ribbons of each rainbow. I will laugh when you laugh. Cry
> when you cry. So long as you are together! For I leave with
> you my legacy of love.
>
> Your Vangie

Chris Beth closed her eyes and sat silent as each scene of the
lovely days and years together here in the Oregon Country
came back in sad-sweet remembrance. Yes, Vangie would be
with them forever—like her wonderful, gentle Joe. As she saw
Vangie in the miracle of nature, she would see Joe in the
miracles of the people he had served so faithfully in the
beautiful valley. And it was up to her and Wilson, the
"remnants," to carry on through their children and their
children's children.

When Chris Beth opened her eyes, Wilson was looking at
her, his dark eyes no longer unreadable. The diary lay open in
her lap, an everlasting tie between them. Neither of them
spoke. There was no need. He simply opened his arms and she
walked into them—silently, "paradise regained."